THE GRAMMAR BIBLE

EVERYTHING YOU ALWAYS WANTED TO KNOW ABOUT
GRAMMAR BUT DIDN'T KNOW ~~WHO~~ TO ASK!
WHOM

THE GRAMMAR BIBLE

BY MICHAEL STRUMPF
CREATOR OF THE NATIONAL GRAMMAR HOT LINE
AND AURIEL DOUGLAS

KNOWLEDGEOPOLIS
Los Angeles

KNOWLEDGEOPOLIS™
1902 Westwood Blvd. Suite 201
Los Angeles, CA 90025-4614

Book design by Carson Elder (on a Macintosh®)
File cabinet illustration by Wil Lin

Publisher's Cataloging-in-Publication
(Provided by Quality Books, Inc.)

Strumpf, Michael.
      The grammar bible : everything you always wanted to know about grammar but didn't know whom to ask / by Michael Strumpf & Auriel Douglas. — 1st ed.
      p. cm.
      Includes bibliographical references and index.
      Preassigned LCCN: 98-65662
      ISBN: 1-891968-00-9

      1. English language—Grammar. I. Douglas, Auriel. II. Title.

PE1112.S78 1998   428.2
                                    QBI98-420

Manufactured in the United States of America

07 06 05 04 03 02 01 00 99 98   10 9 8 7 6 5 4 3 2 1

First Edition

For Carol Strumpf

—Michael Strumpf

For Heather and Russell Douglas, and Dariel Walsh

—Auriel Douglas

Acknowledgments

The writing of this book has truly been a team effort. The publisher wishes to acknowledge the tireless efforts of Eric Ericson, editor-in-chief, whose sharp eye and insightful commentary have helped to make this book the thorough and accessible volume that it is; Ke Zou, Ph.D., whose scholarly consultation has held this tome to the highest standards of accuracy and clarity; and Carson Elder, whose graphic design and organizational talents are impeccable. Additional thanks also go to Gretchen Ericson for her invaluable Latin consultation and to Candice Chen for her editorial contributions.

Finally, we must thank the many callers to The National Grammar Hotline. Inasmuch as their questions and comments appear in this volume, we not only give them due credit, but, additionally, thank them for providing such thoughtful queries and scholarly observations.

Contents

Acknowledgments   vii

Preface   xiv

Part I   *The Parts of Speech*   1

Chapter 1: Nouns   3
Types of Nouns   5
Properties of Nouns   8
    Gender   8
    Number   9
    Person   24
    Case   26
Some Other Things You Should Know About Nouns   31
Test Your Knowledge   36

Chapter 2: Verbs   39
Action Verbs and Linking Verbs   40
Verb Phrases   40
Characteristics of Verbs   42
    Number   42
    Person   42
    Voice   43
    Mood   45
    Tense   48
Subject-Verb Agreement   53
Conjugation   56
Objects and Complements of Verbs   76
Some Other Things You Should Know About Verbs   83
Test Your Knowledge   95

Chapter 3: Adjectives   97
Types of adjectives   97
Degrees of Comparison   100
Positioning the Adjective   110

Some Other Things to Remember About Adjectives   112
Determiners   115
Test Your Knowledge   122

Chapter 4: Adverbs   125
Categories of Adverbs   129
Degrees of Comparison   130
Positioning the Adverb   134
The Truth About Adverbs and Adjectives   137
Some Other Things to Remember About Adverbs   143
Test Your Knowledge   149

Chapter 5: Verbals   151
Participles   152
Gerunds   164
Infinitives   169
Perfect Forms: A Last Point About Verbals   176
Test Your Knowledge   178

Chapter 6: Pronouns   181
Types of Pronouns   182
    Personal Pronouns   182
    Possessive Pronouns   189
    Reciprocal Pronouns   191
    Reflexive Pronouns   191
    Demonstrative Pronouns   194
    Interrogative Pronouns   195
    Relative Pronouns   197
    Indefinite Pronouns   203
Agreement Between Pronouns and Antecedents   206
Some Other Things You Should Know About Pronouns   217
Test Your Knowledge   224

Chapter 7: Prepositions   227
Partners of Prepositions   229
Prepositional Phrases   230
Some Things You Should Know About Prepositions   236
Test Your Knowledge   258

Chapter 8: Conjunctions 261
Coordinate and Subordinate Conjunctions 262
Some Other Things to Remember About Conjunctions 267
Test Your Knowledge 273

Chapter 9: Interjections 275
Punctuation of Interjections 277
Test Your Knowledge 278

Part II   *Dissecting the Sentence*   281

Chapter 10: Subjects & Predicates 283
Subjects and Predicates Defined 284
Diagramming: The Lost Art 288
Test Your Knowledge 292

Chapter 11: Sentence Types & Structures 295
Sentences Types 295
Word Order 298
Declarative Word Orders 298
Interrogative Word Orders 301
Imperative Word Orders 302
Exclamatory Word Orders 303
Diagrams and Basic Sentence Structures 304
Some Other Things to Remember
About Sentence Structures 309
Test Your Knowledge 312

Chapter 12: More Diagramming 315
Prepositional Phrases 315
Contractions 318
Verbals 319
Appositives 326
Test Your Knowledge 327

Chapter 13: Compound & Complex Sentences 333
Simple Sentences 333
Introduction to Clauses 334
Compound Sentences 335

Complex Sentences   341
   Relative Clauses   342
   Adverbial Clauses   351
   Nominal Clauses   355
Some Other Things You Should Know
   About Compound & Complex Sentences   367
Test Your Knowledge   378

Part III   *Spelling, Vocabulary, & Punctuation*   381

Chapter 14: Spelling   383
Spelling Rules   385
Heteronyms, Homonyms, Homophones, and Homographs   392
Other Confusing Word Pairs   412
Reading   417
Test Your Knowledge   428

Chapter 15: Vocabulary   431
Definition Distinctions   433
Q&A: Roots, Prefixes, and Suffixes   457
One Thousand Words You Should Know   461
Word Origins   474
Q&A: Synonyms for **Said**   482
Misused Vocabulary   484
Q&A: Phobias   487
Peculiar Words and Phrase   488
Some Other Things You Should Know About Vocabulary   490
Test Your Knowledge   495

Chapter 16: Punctuation   497
History of Punctuation   498
Rules of Punctuation   499
   The Period   500
   The Comma   513
   The Colon   526
   The Semicolon   528
   The Apostrophe   529
   The Question Mark   535
   The Exclamation Mark   536

Parentheses 537
Brackets 538
The Hyphen 538
The Dash 541
Quotation Marks 543
Some Other Things You Should Know About Punctuation 548
Test Your Knowledge 551

Glossary 553

Bibliography 571

Index 573

Preface

Communication is the essence of the human experience. Despite the ease with which the average person thinks, speaks, and writes complicated ideas on a daily basis, the process of communication is extraordinarily complex, and the distinctly human ability to weave sounds, gestures, and expressions into meaningful units that communicate our thoughts and feelings to our fellow humans is at least worthy of note, if not awe and admiration.

Why then, if the process is so complex, are humans able to communicate so easily and effortlessly? The complete answer to that question is quite beyond the scope of this book and even beyond the limits of modern science. A topic that is within our grasp and the one that this book will tackle is the regular system of rules that we use to weave sounds into the meaningful units with which we express our thoughts and ideas, creating language. We call this system **grammar**.

In a simple sense, grammar is the study of words and the ways words work together. It is a sort of invisible hand that guides us as we put words together into sentences. Any person who is able to communicate using a particular language has knowledge of the grammar of that language, even if his or her knowledge is unconscious. Grammar is pervasive.

We study grammar so that we may speak and write in a clearer and more effective manner. The unconscious knowledge of grammar that every communicator possesses may be sufficient for simple language use, but those who wish to communicate artfully and well will seek the greater depth of understanding and proficiency that the study of grammar provides.

For the past twenty five years, Moorpark College in Moorpark, California, has sponsored The National Grammar Hot Line to aid students of English grammar in their quest for knowledge. The service is free. During the Hot Line's existence, thousands of callers have telephoned with questions about the English language and its use. For a quarter of a century, I, Michael Strumpf, an English teacher at Moorpark College, have fielded questions from congressmen, governors, ambassadors, editors, writers, teachers, attorneys, students, copywriters, journalists, housewives, secretaries, and vice presidents (even calls from the White House are not unheard of). People from just about any occupation and walk of life have called to ask a question that has puzzled or stumped them:

"Where do I put this comma?"

"What case should this pronoun be in?"

"How do I form the possessive of 'Dickens'?"

This book combines the most insightful and revealing of the calls to The National Grammar Hot Line with a scholarly discussion of grammar. We begin with the parts of speech in the first third of the book, move on to the creation of sentences in the second third, and end with a discussion of spelling, vocabulary, and punctuation in the final third. In each chapter, you will find a discussion of a particular topic in grammar, interspersed with Hot Line questions and answers that I feel will strengthen your understanding of the topic. Though the book is a reference book, it has, I hope, been written with a sense of style and a sense of humor. Grammar should be a topic that you enjoy as well as one that you understand.

As I mentioned before, communication (and, by extension, grammar) is an exceedingly complex process. The authors and editors of this book have done their best to explain each grammatical issue in a clear and concise manner, but even the most careful writers cannot answer every question or clear up every troublesome matter. If the text doesn't answer your question or, after careful reading, a topic is still perplexing, please contact The National Grammar Hot Line:

Professor Michael Strumpf
Moorpark College
7075 Campus Road
Moorpark, CA 93021

TEL: (805) 378-1494
FAX: (805) 378-1499

Happy Learning

If I had my choice of weapons with you, sir, I'd choose *grammar*!

—Lady For A Day (1933)

I know you believe you understand what you think I said, but I am not sure you realize that what you heard is not what I meant.

—Anonymous

Part I

The Parts of Speech

1.

Nouns

> **Nouns** are naming words. They give titles to people, places, things, and ideas.

Imagine a world without names. Imagine, for a moment, the horror and absurdity of ordering a simple meal without naming words. "I'll take one of those things with the two soft, round things on the outside and one of those brown mushy things on the inside, and it's got some red stuff and some yellow stuff and some round, green things on it." Oh, you must mean a hamburger! You see, I couldn't even get through this ridiculous scenario without using a couple of generic naming words, such as **stuff** or **things**. What's in a name? Sometimes, a name is everything.

The word **noun** comes from the Latin word **nomen**, meaning "name." Nouns are names of people, places, things, and ideas. Anything we can imagine has a name. If someone discovers a person, place, thing, or idea without a name, you can be sure that steps will be taken to remedy that situation.

Any nutritious sentence is chock full of nouns. In the examples below, each of the bold words is a noun.

My **friend**, **Buddy**, has a **Ph.D.** in **physics**.

The **squirrel** stole **nuts** from the **chipmunk**.

My **dog** watches **television** in the **evenings**.

The **purpose** of this **exam** is to scare the **life** out of you.

The **weight** of **gold** is measured in **karats**.

A TEST TO DETERMINE WHETHER A WORD IS A NOUN

Q. "Is there a litmus test to determine whether a word is a noun?"

A. While there is no sure-fire way to determine whether a word is a noun in every situation, some people find it helpful to apply the following technique in puzzling it out. This procedure works for all nouns **except** names of specific people, places, or things, also known as proper nouns.

There are three words in the English language called articles: **a**, **an**, and **the**. If in doubt about whether a word is a noun, just place an article before it. If the combination makes sense on its own, the word is a noun. Test the word **joy**: the joy. **Joy** is a noun. Test **pride**: the pride. **Pride** is a noun. Try **exultation**: an exultation. **Exultation** is a noun. See, it works. All three of these article-noun combinations sound correct.

Conversely, the test differentiates other parts of speech from nouns. What happens when we apply the test to the adjective **beautiful**: a beautiful. The combination does not make sense, so we know that **beautiful** is not a noun. **The rambunctious** doesn't make sense either, so **rambunctious** can't be a noun. Apply the test to the verb **eat**: an eat. The test verifies that **eat** is not a noun.

Beware of those sentences in which the noun is described by adjectives. For example, in the sentence "The large, round apple lay on the table," the article **the** comes before the word **large**. The sentence makes perfect sense although **large** is still an adjective. Even though the article may not directly precede a noun, its presence in a sentence indicates that there is a noun nearby. To find the noun, we test the words that follow the article. First, test **large**: the large. The combination does not make sense. Next, test **round**: the round. This combination doesn't make sense either. Then, test **apple**: the apple. Eureka! We've found the noun.

TYPES OF NOUNS

In English there are different types of nouns. First, nouns can either be **common** or **proper**.

1. **Common nouns** are general nouns: magnet, gargoyle, angel, orchid, subway, persimmon, petticoat. Common nouns do not begin with capital letters unless they start sentences.

2. **Proper nouns** are nouns that refer to specific people, places, or things: Dmitri, Sisley, Scarlet O'Hara, Little Orphan Annie, Rutherford B. Hayes, Marlon Brando, Ichabod Crane, Zaire, Denmark, Alcatraz. Proper nouns always begin with **capital letters**.

Nouns can also be **concrete** or **abstract**.

1. **Concrete nouns** are nouns that can be touched or held: house, taxicab, typewriter, computer, shoe, stove, refrigerator.

2. **Abstract nouns** are nouns that cannot be touched or held: love, fear, honesty, hostility, truth, intrigue, regrets. They exist only in our minds as ideas or feelings.

All nouns will fall into two categories, one from each set, simultaneously. **Toyota** is proper as well as concrete. **Love** is common as well as abstract.

ABSTRACT AND CONCRETE NOUNS

Q. A weatherman at one of the TV stations asked, "What kind of a noun is the word **smog**? A case could be made for it as a concrete noun, and a case could be made for it as an abstract noun."

A. Since it contains particulate material which can be measured by sophisticated meteorological instruments, The National Grammar Hot Line votes for "concrete."

CAPITALIZING PROPER NOUNS

If you are unsure whether or not a noun is proper and should be capitalized, check these rules. Always capitalize

- names of specific people: Clark Gable, Emily Dickinson, Napoleon.

- names of specific places or regions: Yosemite, Los Angeles, France, Jupiter, the Milky Way, Wrigley Field, Chicago.

- names of specific agencies, organizations, or bodies: Supreme Court, Red Cross, Greenpeace, National Science Foundation, Bureau of Public Works, Daughters of the American Revolution.

- names of historical events, periods, and documents: the Middle Ages, D-Day, the Magna Carta.

- names of days, months, holidays, and special days of observance: Monday, January, Thanksgiving, Mother's Day.

- titles of rank or respect before a name: Lord Nelson, President Truman, Mrs. Robinson.

- the principal words in titles of books, magazines, articles, plays, movies, songs, or pieces of art: *The Last Supper*, A *Tale of Two Cities*, *The New Yorker*, *The Foreigner*. Articles (a, an, the), conjunctions, and prepositions are not typically capitalized unless they begin the title.

- words which show family relationship when they are used as names and when they are used with names: Grandma, Mother, Aunt, Uncle Jon, Cousin Mark.

- words referring to deities or holy books: Krishna, God, Allah, the Koran, the Talmud, the Bible.

BOARD CHAIRMAN VS. CHAIRMAN OF THE BOARD

Q. A gentleman who sounded distinguished by his tone and choice of words was sending out a business letter. He asked, "How do I sign the letter? Should it be 'Board Chairman,' 'Chairman,' or 'Chairman of the Board'?"

A. The Hot Line asked who the recipients were. Were they casual acquaintances, or were they well acquainted with him? He said that some were and some were not. He was advised to write "Chairman of the Board." If the recipients had been all intimates, then "Chairman" would have been fine. Some might feel that this was more of an etiquette question than a grammatical one.

SYNONYMS FOR *LOVE*

Q. "What noun has the most synonyms?" asked a journalism teacher in Montana.

A. That is a difficult question to answer. Synonyms are words with similar meanings. To find the winner, one would have to compare all nouns. However, a case could be made for the word **love**. Here's the list:

admiration	emotion	le grande passion
adoration	enamor(ment)	liking
affair d'amour	endearment	merriment
affair de coeur	enjoyment	passion
affection	entertainment	piety
amorousness	enthusiasm	pleasure
amour	Eros	preference
appreciation	exultation	rapture
ardor	fancy	raptus
attachment	feeling	regard
attraction	felicity	relish
benevolence	fervor	satisfaction
charity	flame	sensuality
charm	flavor	sentiment
comfort	fondness	stellification
Cupid	friendship	sweetheart
darling	gladness	tang
dear	gratification	tenderness
delectation	gusto	transport
delight	happiness	worship
desire	indulgence	zeal
devotedness	jocularity	zest
devotion	joy	
ecstasy	la belle passion	

These seventy words are listed in *Sisson's Synonyms, An Unabridged Synonym and Related-term Locator* by A. F. Sisson. Sisson lists only fifty-three synonyms for **hate**. Maybe that's a good sign.

FROM MY FILES: HIDE-AND-SEEK

Many of my callers have asked what the nouns which are shouted at the conclusion of "Hide-and-Seek" mean. They sound like "Ollie, ollie oxen free." Could this have been Paul Bunyan calling for Babe to return from the pasture? Not at all. It does mean "All thee, all thee outs in free." Players can come home "free" without being tagged "out."

PROPERTIES OF NOUNS

Nouns are characterized by four properties: **gender**, **number**, **person**, and **case**.

GENDER

Gender refers to the classification of nouns according to sex. Many languages assign this sex or gender to their nouns rather arbitrarily. In the Romance languages, for instance, all nouns are either masculine or feminine. In French **la ville** (the city) and **la lune** (the moon) are both feminine, but **le village** (the village) and **le soleil** (the sun) are masculine. **Le crayon** (the pencil) is masculine, but **la plume** (the pen) is feminine. There is no logic to this system.

Latin and German add a third gender to this mess, the neuter gender. The German word for **sun** (die sonne) is feminine, and the word for **moon** (der mond) is masculine; but the German words for **girl** (das madchen) and **woman** (das weib) are illogically neuter! Such distinctions impose the additional task of incorporating the genders of nouns into the articles, prepositions, adjectives, and verbs that function alongside them.

English smartly negates these confusions by employing a natural gender. Nouns that refer to males are of the masculine gender: **man, boy**. Nouns that refer to females are of the feminine gender: **woman, girl**. Nouns that could refer to males or females are of the common gender: **animal, child**. Nouns that refer to sexless objects are of the neuter gender: **toy, apple**. The meaning and usage of the noun should reveal its gender. This system makes sense. Most nouns are of the neuter or common genders. The issue of gender will become more important when we reach the chapter on pronouns (Chapter 6).

It is a simple matter to identify the genders of words that are specifically either masculine or feminine. In most cases, the gender is inherent in the meaning of the word. The noun **hen** refers to females, so it is always feminine. The noun **rooster** refers to males, so it is always masculine. We also differentiate between men and women, boys and girls, fathers and mothers, monks and nuns, lords and ladies, and rams and ewes, among many others.

Other words add one of the suffixes **-or, -ess, -ine**, or **-trix** to distinguish the feminine forms from the masculine forms. We differentiate between actors and actresses, heros and heroines, dukes and duchesses, and executors and executrixes, among others.

Such gender distinctions are fading as society becomes more equality-minded. No one with any sensibility has spoken of an executrix since Nixon was in office. The bottom line with most gender-specific nouns is that sex is irrelevant, and many words once masculine now refer to both males and females. Discriminate according to merit. Leave sex out of it!

NUMBER

The **number** of a noun indicates how many people or objects it refers to. Nouns that refer to just one of anything are **singular**, and nouns that refer to more than one of anything are **plural**. In their simplest forms, nouns are singular. Pluralization requires changes. Let's allow some callers to demonstrate the rules for pluralizing nouns.

A GENERAL PLURALIZING RULE

Q. "Is there a general rule for making nouns plural?" asked a menu writer.

A. Yes, of course, there is. For most nouns, add **-s** or **-es** to their singular forms. If a noun ends with a sound that melds smoothly with **s**, then simply add **-s**.

kite → kites	cake → cakes	waiter → waiters
bib → bibs	field → fields	hunter → hunters
flag → flags	trip → trips	birthday → birthdays

If a noun ends in a sound that does not meld smoothly with **s**, then add **-es**. These sounds, **/ch/, /sh/, /s/, /x/,** and **/z/,** are called the **sibilant sounds**.

wish → wishes	arch → arches	church → churches
quiz → quizzes	fox → foxes	lunch → lunches
mess → messes	fish → fishes	waltz → waltzes
class → classes	dish → dishes	box → boxes

Please note that you must double the final consonant **z** before adding **-es**.

PLURALS OF NOUNS ENDING IN Y

Q. "I'm always confused about nouns ending in **y**. How do I make these words plural? Why didn't they teach all these things in elementary school?"

A. Perhaps they did, and the caller has just forgotten. But, if they didn't, let's straighten out the issue now. When a noun ends in **y** preceded by a consonant, change the **y** to **i** and then add **-es**. In many cases, the **y** will make a long **/e/** sound (long **e** says its own name).

lady → ladies	cherry → cherries	Mounty → Mounties
fly → flies	candy → candies	county → counties
city → cities	berry → berries	enemy → enemies

When a noun ends in **quy** (again, the **y** makes a long **/e/** sound), change the **y** to **i** and then add **-es**.

soliloquy → soliloquies	colloquy → colloquies

When a noun ends in **y** preceded by a vowel, just add **-s**. These words use the vowel and the **y** in combination to make a single vowel sound. Changing the **y** to **i** would destroy their partnership.

boy → boys	tray → trays	chimney → chimneys
play → plays	ploy → ploys	valley → valleys
clay → clays	toy → toys	alley → alleys

PLURALS OF NOUNS ENDING IN F OR FE

Q. A ranger in the high Sierras was creating posters warning tourists of predators. He asked, "What do I do to make **wolf** plural?"

A. As a general rule, make words ending in **f** or **fe** plural by changing the **f** or **fe** to **v** and adding **-es**.

calf → calves	leaf → leaves	shelf → shelves
elf → elves	life → lives	thief → thieves
half → halves	loaf → loaves	wife → wives
knife → knives	self → selves	wolf → wolves

However, this rule is subject to exception. For some nouns ending in **f**, simply add **-s**.

belief → beliefs	roof → roofs	dwarf → dwarfs
chief → chiefs	safe → safes	

Other nouns ending in **f** can take either of the above forms. You can change the **f** to **v** and add **-es**, or you can just add **-s**.

beef → beeves *or* beefs	scarf → scarves *or* scarfs
hoof → hooves *or* hoofs	wharf → wharves *or* wharfs

If in doubt, consult your dictionary.

Please be careful not to let this rule lead you to confuse the plural noun **beliefs** with the singular verb **believes**.

I respect the **beliefs** of my astrologer.

My astrologer **believes** in the signs of the zodiac.

PLURALS OF NOUNS ENDING IN *O*

Q. "How do you spell the plural of **piccolo**? I'm a musician, and I often write articles about music for the local newspaper. I have been criticized in the past for spelling the plurals of instruments incorrectly."

A. In general, for nouns ending in an **o** preceded by a vowel, simply add **-s**.

cameo → cameos	rodeo → rodeos	folio → folios
stereo → stereos	Oreo → Oreos	tattoo → tattoos

For nouns ending in an **o** preceded by a consonant, add **-es**.

echo → echoes	tomato → tomatoes
potato → potatoes	torpedo → torpedoes

This rule, too, is full of exceptions. For musical terms, many of which end in an **o** preceded by a consonant, just add **-s** to form the plural.

alto → altos	piano → pianos	contralto → contraltos
piccolo → piccolos	cello → cellos	soprano → sopranos

For other words that end in an **o** preceded by a consonant, also add **-s** to form the plural.

zero → zeros	halo → halos	albino → albinos

As for these others with the consonant plus **o** ending, add **-s** or **-es**.

cargo → cargos *or* cargoes	tornado → tornados *or* tornadoes
hero → heros *or* heroes	volcano → volcanos *or* volcanoes

When in doubt, look it up.

IRREGULAR PLURALS

Q. "I'm having a heck of a time figuring out how to make some words plural. Some are easy because they have a nice rule to tell you what to do. Then, there are some others that just change, as **mouse** changes to **mice**. Is there anything that I can do to learn these sorts of plurals?"

A. My sad answer has to be no. There are some nouns that form irregular plurals. They make changes specific to their own cases. These we simply must memorize. However, most changes are changes of vowels. Consonants are, for the most part, left alone.

foot → feet	mouse → mice	woman → women
goose → geese	tooth → teeth	man → men

There are even some nouns that do not change at all between their singular and plural forms.

deer → deer	sheep → sheep	moose → moose
fish → fish[†]	trout → trout	species → species

For a very small number of words, add **-en** to their singular forms to make them plural.

child → children	ox → oxen

The best way to verify that the plural form of a noun is correct is to look it up in the dictionary.

[†] The plural form of **fish** can be **fish** or **fishes**. Use **fish** when referring to a collective of individual fish. *The fish are jumping.* Use **fishes** when referring to multiple species or kinds of fishes. *We caught several kinds of fishes on our canoeing trip.*

IRREGULAR PLURALS: PEOPLE/PERSON

Q. Heard by many of our callers on a national radio broadcast, a physician, who had recently arrived in America, was expressing concern about the lack of blood at his hospital. "If we have more than one people requiring blood . . . ." They asked about the use of the word **people**.

A. Obviously, **people** should be **person**. The doctor has mistakenly used the irregular plural of the noun **person**. The word he used implies one group of people rather than one individual, a **person**.

PLURALS OF FOREIGN ORIGIN: LATIN

Q. "Is Latin really dead?" lamented an executive. "When I used the word **memoranda** in my office, my secretary criticized me."

A. Latin is certainly not dead. It is alive in English, and we use it in many of our words. **Memoranda** is the Latin plural while **memorandums** is the English plural, but both are acceptable. Similarly, the singular noun **referendum** can be made plural in the Latin way, **referenda**, or the American way, **referendums**.

American English has co-opted many foreign words to its own devices while other words still keep only their foreign plurals. The singular noun **basis** becomes **bases** in its plural form. The singular noun **nemesis** becomes **nemeses** in its plural form. These Latin words just keep the Latin plurals.

Latin is not the sole language from which modern English words have originated, and there are many other methods of pluralization from across the globe that you can find in English. If in doubt of the plural form, consult your dictionary.

PLURALS OF FOREIGN ORIGIN: MORE LATIN

Q. The headmistress of a girls' preparatory school asked, "How do you spell the plural form of the word **alumna** on the commencement announcement?"

A. A singular female graduate is an alumna; plural female graduates are alumnae. A singular male graduate is an alumnus; plural male graduates are alumni. These are English words that have retained their Latin plural forms. The pronunciations of the masculine and feminine plurals are the same. Both end with a long /i/ sound (long **i** sounds like **eye** or the **i** in **ride**).

PLURALS OF COMPOUND WORDS

Q. Several writers called on a conference line. "We're still not confident that we're correctly pluralizing compound words and words linked by hyphens," they said. The writers were dealing with material widely disseminated to the public through newspapers, and all owned many style guides plus a half dozen handbooks.

A. Creating the plurals of simple compound words, such as **steamboat** or **hatbox**, is easy. Simply apply the appropriate rule to the second half of the compound word; thus, **steamboat** becomes **steamboats**, and **hatbox** becomes **hatboxes**.

inchworm → inchworms	afterthought → afterthoughts
chophouse → chophouses	lightsaber → lightsabers
housewife → housewives	werewolf → werewolves

Pluralizing other compound words whose pieces are connected by hyphens, such as **mother-in-law,** or whose separate words are regarded as a unit, such as **court martial**, is almost as simple. Just make the most important word plural. **Mother-in-law** becomes **mothers-in-law**, and **court martial** becomes **courts martial**. This most-important-word will always be a word that can be described or modified, a noun.

Chief of Staff → Chiefs of Staff	brigadier general → brigadier generals
son-in-law → sons-in-law	attorney general → attorneys general
looker-on → lookers-on	daughter-in-law → daughters-in-law
runner-up → runners-up	deputy sheriff → deputy sheriffs

One of the writers then asked, "What if none of the pieces of the compound word are nouns? Like **drive-in**. Neither **drive** nor **in** is a noun, so we can't really tell which one is the main word." The answer is to pluralize the last word of the compound. **Drive-in** becomes **drive-ins**. The plural of **play-off** is **play-offs**, and the plural of **has-been** becomes **has-beens**. While neither of the pieces of each of these compound words is a noun on its own, they work to become a noun together.

PLURALS OF NUMBERS, LETTERS, AND ABBREVIATIONS

Q. "How do I pluralize numbers? Everyone's telling me a different way. Help! I want to be correct."

A. These are the rules for pluralizing numerals, letters, and abbreviations:

- To form the plurals of numbers written as numerals, just add **-s**.

  My parents loved the **1950s**.

  I feel safest flying on **747s**.

- To form the plurals of single letters, add apostrophe **s** ('s).

  Elementary school taught me the three **R's**.

  Watch your **p's** and **q's**.

  Don't forget to cross your **t's** and dot your **i's**.

- To form the plurals of strings of multiple letters, add **-s** without an apostrophe (').

  I gave her three **IOUs**.

  My daughter learned her **ABCs**.

- To form the plurals of abbreviations with internal periods, add apostrophe **s** ('s).

  C.P.A.'s, D.D.S.'s, M.D.'s

  My brother has two **Ph.D.'s**.

- To form the plurals of abbreviations that end with periods but that have no internal periods, add **-s** before the terminal period.

  eds., Nos., chs., figs.

  There are ten **vols.** in the complete set.

- To form the plurals of abbreviations without periods, just add **-s**.

  APPRs, MIRVs, kWs, kgs

  The tunnel was twenty **kms** in length.

PLURALS OF WORDS NOT NORMALLY PLURALIZED

Q. Another caller asked, "How do I make the plural of a word that doesn't really have a plural, like **if**, **and**, and **but** in the phrase 'ifs, ands, or buts'?"

A. Here is yet another confusing plural issue. To create the plural forms of words that do not have true plural forms, simply add **-s**. As you can see in the written version of the caller's spoken question, the plurals of **if**, **and**, and **but** are **ifs**, **ands**, and **buts**. Here are two more examples:

> Lenny will teach you the **dos** and **don'ts** of small engine repair.

> How many **totallys** does the average teenager utter each minute?

Notice that I did not change the **y** to **i** and add **-es** in **totally**. The word is an adverb and cannot have a true plural form. The plurality of **totally** involves multiple occurrences of the word **totally** in a teenager's utterances. The meaning of the sentence is clearer if the **y** is left alone.

PLURAL OF *Ms.*

Q. "How do you form the plural of **Ms.**?" asked an editor at a women's magazine.

A. **Ms.** is a title of respect attached to a woman's name that does not imply a particular marital status. Since **Ms.** lacks internal periods, add **-s** to form the plural, **Mss.** Take heed, however. Without the capital, **mss.** is an abbreviation for **manuscripts**.

It is also this scholar's opinion that since men do not have to identify their marital status, it is difficult to understand why women do. This is an inequality which should be rectified, and is by the use of **Ms.** instead of **Miss** or **Mrs.**

PLURALS OF NOUNS CONTAINING APOSTROPHES

Q. "How do you make a plural out of a noun containing an apostrophe?" asked a representative of Weinstock's Department Stores.

A. That's easy! Your noun does not require any changes. Just say, "There are two Weinstock's in St. Paul." Pluralizing other nouns with internal apostrophes is not always so easy, but that discussion must wait until we reach the possessive case.

FROM MY FILES: PLURALIZING PROPER NAMES

At Christmas and Hanukkah time, hundreds of grammar-con-scious citizens call, asking how to spell the plurals of proper names on holiday cards. Many of the calls come from the stationery stores that print the cards. Here are a few rules that will help the curious pluralize proper names. Please note that, in every case, the spellings of the proper names should not change except for the addition of **-s** or **-es**.

With proper names ending in a sound that blends well with **s**, simply add **-s**.

Brown → the Browns	Lindberg → the Lindbergs
Ericson → the Ericsons	Shaw → the Shaws
Hogan → the Hogans	Whitlock → the Whitlocks

With proper nouns ending in sounds that don't blend well with **s**, the sibilant sounds, add **-es**.

Cox → the Coxes	Jones → the Joneses
Douglas → the Douglases	Martinez → the Martinezes
Firch → the Firches	Nemetz → the Nemetzes

Do not forget that other than the addition of **-s** or **-es**, the spelling of a pluralized proper name does not change. With names that end in **y**, you do not change that **y** to **i**. With names that end in **f** or **fe**, do not change that **f** or **fe** to **v**. The name remains the same.

Cory → the Corys	Montgomery → the Montgomerys
Handy → the Handys	

NUMBER ISSUES

Number, on the surface, appears to be a simple matter. A noun is singular, or it is plural. End of story. Oh, but you must not forget that there are exceptions to every rule and complications to any simple situation. If you take one thing away from this book, it should be the lesson that any language worth its salt has more twists and variations than any one person can explore in a lifetime. English is certainly one of these.

SEEMINGLY SINGULAR PLURALS

Some nouns that appear to be plural in form are treated singularly: news, politics, physics, mathematics, measles, mumps, etc.

> **Politics** is a bloodthirsty business.

> The **news** these days is never illuminating.

These nouns, though plural in appearance because they end in **s**, are generally treated as singular. Popular usage has changed their natures so that we usually regard each of them as a single object or idea.

STRICTLY PLURALS

Other nouns are only used in their plural forms.

billiards	nuptials	remains	suds
clothes	pants	riches	tongs
forceps	pincers	scissors	trousers
gallows	pliers	shears	

> Hand me that pair of **pliers**.

> My **trousers** are missing!

> The garden **shears** sliced through the branches.

In singular forms, these nouns do not have any meaning as nouns. Imagine each of them without the plural ending. **Riches** becomes an adjective, **rich**. **Remains** becomes a verb, **remain**. Others are not even real words without the pluralizing **s** (trouser? sud?). These nouns are plural through and through.

COLLECTIVE NOUNS

There is yet another class of nouns for which number can be problematic, the **collective nouns**. Collective nouns, though singular in number, name a group of people or objects.

army	band	clergy	company
audience	class	committee	congregation

corps	family	mob	team
crowd	flock	multitude	
faculty	herd	number	

Collectives are troublesome because they can be treated as singular or plural depending on usage. If we regard the members of the group that the collective noun names as a unit, then the noun is singular.

The **crowd** shouted its approval to the mayoral candidate.

The **team** of mules pulls the plow through the field day after day.

The **company** is declaring bankruptcy.

The members of these groups are a unit, so the nouns that name them are singular.

If we regard the members of the group as separate entities, then the noun is plural.

The **class** turned in their research papers last Friday.

The **congregation** are faith personified.

My **family** took our vacation early this year.

Here, the members of each group act on their own and not as a unit, so the collective noun is plural. However, we rarely use collective nouns in a plural manner.

ANIMALS AND COLLECTIVE NOUNS

Q. "When our family went whale watching, one of the crew members pointed at two of the beasts and said, 'Look at the gam of whales.' He explained that a gam is a group of two or more whales. Are there similar words to describe other groups of animals?"

A. Yes, there are. Here's a list. There are some wonderful words in it, such as *a shrewdness of apes, an exaltation of larks*, and *a murmuration of starlings*.

Ant *colony*	Bee *swarm*	Duck *plump*
Ape *shrewdness*	Bird *flock*	Elk *gang*
Ass *pace*	Buffalo *gang*	Finch *charm*
Badger *cete*	Cattle *herd*	Fox *skulk*
Bear *sloth*	Coot *covert*	Frog *knot*

Geese *gaggle*	Peacock *muster*	Teal *spring*
Hog *drift*	Pheasant *nide*	Vermin *skulk*
Kitten *kindle*	Quail *bevy* or *covey*	Walrus *pod*
Lark *exaltation*	Seal *trip* or *pod*	Whale *gam* or *pod*
Lion *pride*	Sheep *flock*	Wildcat *clowder*
Mallard *sord*	Snipe *wisp*	Wild fowl *skein*
Meadowlark *pod*	Sparrow *host*	Wild hog *sounder*
Nightingale *watch*	Starling *murmuration*	Woodcock *fall*

Many of these are infrequently used, but shrewd word watchers will know about some of their curious origins. With popular use, they evolved into dictionary-defined words. If you have an interesting one you have made up, please share it with The National Grammar Hot Line. Spreading the word is how American English grows.

TROUBLESOME PLURALS

The plural forms of many nouns are often misused. The following list has been excerpted from the context of questions called in over the past twenty-five years. Each caller had used a plural incorrectly.

SINGULAR	BRITISH PLURAL	AMERICAN PLURAL
abacus	abaci	abacuses, abaci
agendum	agenda	agendums, agendas, agenda
alumna (fem.)	alumnae	alumnae
alumnus (masc.)	alumni	alumni
apparatus	apparati	apparatuses, apparatus
attorney general	attorneys general	attorneys general
bacillus	bacilli	bacilli
beau	beaux	beaus, beaux
brontosaurus	brontosauri	brontosauruses, brontosauri
cactus	cacti	cacti, cactuses, cactus
campus	campi	campuses
caucus	cauci	caucuses
chief-of-staff	chiefs-of-staff	chiefs-of-staff
circus	circi	circuses
court martial	courts martial	courts martial
crisis	crises	crises
criterion	criteria	criteria, criterions

SINGULAR	BRITISH PLURAL	AMERICAN PLURAL
curriculum	curricula (preferred)	curriculums, curricula
domino	dominos, dominoes	dominoes
esophagus	esophagi	esophagi
eucalyptus	eucalypti	eucalyptuses, eucalypti
father-in-law	fathers-in-law	fathers-in-law
fetus	feti	fetuses
focus	foci	focuses, foci
genius	genii	geniuses, genii
gladiolus	gladioli	gladioluses, gladiolus, gladioli
genus	genera	genera, genuses
hippopotamus	hippopotami	hippopotamuses, hippopotami
medium	media	media, mediums
mongoose	mongooses	mongooses
octopus	octopi	octopuses, octopi
PDR	PDRs	PDRs
phallus	phalli	phalluses, phalli
podium	podia	podiums, podia
potato	potatoes	potatoes
rebus	rebi	rebuses
radius	radii	radiuses, radii
sarcophagus	sarcophagi	sarcophaguses, sarcophagi
spoonful	spoonfuls	spoonfuls
stratus	strati	strati
stylus	styli	styluses, styli
syllabus	syllabi	syllabuses, syllabi
taurus	tauri	tauri
thesis	theses	theses
virus	viri	viruses
zero	zeroes	zeroes, zeros

PLURAL OF *MONGOOSE*

Q. "Could you tell me what the plural of **mongoose** is? I think I know, but I want to verify my decision. I'm not asking for any reason in particular, other than to satisfy my curiosity."

A. Let's start with what the plural is not. It is not **mongeese**. Please use **mongooses**, instead. I know it sounds weird, but it's right. This is one of those special situations where the standard rule does not apply.

What on earth are you doing with more than one mongoose? Have you heard about the man who had too many snakes in his backyard? He knew that a neighborhood pet shop had several mongooses in its care and decided to order one to get rid of the slithery pests. He wrote a letter saying, "Please send me a mongoose." Realizing that his job probably required more than one, he changed **mongoose** to **mongeese**. Looking at **mongeese**, he decided it was incorrect. He changed the word to **mongooses**, but this did not look right either. Frustrated, he wrote another sentence. "On second thought, send me another one."

AFTER HOURS PLURALS

Q. A bartender was utterly confused about filling an order. Many of his customers enjoy a gin and tonic before a hearty meal. At dinner one of them asked the waiter for "three gins and tonic, please." The bartender dialed the Hot Line after hours, wondering if he should have sent over three gins and one bottle of tonic.

A. The bartender made the right move, sending over three individually mixed drinks of gin and tonic. He was right, though, to question the customer's use of the plural. Since the man ordered three of the potions, he could have said, "Three gins in tonics, please." Each of the gins would then be accompanied by a tonic. But, if they are heavy drinkers, then they really might want three gins and just one tonic. The key is to make each noun in the name of the drink plural. Each is equally important to the final cocktail.

How would a diner ask for more than one Scotch and soda? Would he ask for "three Scotch and sodas"? No. The correct order would be for "three Scotches and sodas."

AFTER AFTER HOURS PLURALS

Q. The same bartender called several weeks later with a question about his appetizers. He was serving scrumptious shrimp canapés to his customers and wanted them to sound as good as they looked. The bartender knew that one appetizer would be an hors d'oeuvre, but was unsure of what form the plural of this French word would take.

A. One *hors d'oeuvre* becomes many *hors d'oeuvres*. One *canapé* becomes many *canapés*. Both French words are pluralized in the English manner.

Time—Singular or Plural

Q. "Is the word **time** singular or plural?" asked an executive from an educational publishing house. "The sentence in question is 'Rather than continue wasting both our time, we need to set matters straight.' "

A. This same question has been asked in different forms numerous times during the last twenty-five years of the Grammar Hot Line's existence. If the time in the sentence is actually two separate blocks of time, one belonging to each party, then use the plural.

> Rather than continue wasting both our **times**, we need to set matters straight.

If you both share a single block of time, then use the singular form.

> Rather than continue wasting both our **time**, we need to set matters straight.

In other words, it's a judgment call. My personal preference is for the plural form, **times**. Since the word **both** is used in the sentence ". . . both our times . . .", I see two separate blocks of time. This is but one humble opinion.

The Hot Line actually advised the executive to take a more direct approach by eliminating the word **both** and using the singular form of the noun.

> Rather than continue wasting our **time**, we need to set matters straight.

This is a sentence that anyone can utter, free from grammatical doubt or worry.

FROM MY FILES: GRAMMAR CRISES

Some mistakes deserve forgiveness. When your Average Joe makes a grammatical slip, we can understand. Our world is quite lacking in equality, and not everyone gets the same opportunities to study and learn. What I find almost unforgivable is an educated person who makes similar mistakes. Even more aggravating is a recognized and well-educated civic leader who is gauche enough to commit these offenses. Such an individual was once granted a radio interview. She sputtered, "I know that you could have one crisis, but in your particular situation, you claim to have many financial crisises." No. No. No. Review your plurals. One **crisis** becomes many **crises**.

PERSON

The grammatical term **person** describes the relationship of a noun to the speaker. The person of a noun indicates whether it names the person or persons speaking, spoken to, or spoken of. There are three persons: **first**, **second**, and **third**.

The **forms of nouns** do not change because of the change of person. A noun such as **mouse** will take the same form whether it is in the first, second, or third person. Clues as to what person a noun is in come from the context in which it is used. Pay close attention to the verb in the sentence and any pronouns that refer to the noun. Why these features are so important will become clear when you complete the subsequent chapters on pronouns (Chapter 6) and on verbs (Chapter 2).

FIRST PERSON

A noun in the first person names the person or persons speaking. Always use one of the pronouns **I** or **we** to refer to the first person. The first person **I** or **we** may have a standard noun as an appositive. We will deal with appositives shortly.

I, **Eric**, will meet you there.

We, the **people**, seek to form a more perfect union.

In the first example, the proper noun **Eric** is in the first person since it is some person named **Eric** who utters or writes the sentence. In the second example, the noun **people** is in the first person because there are some people who utter this sentence to express their desire for a more perfect union.

SECOND PERSON

A noun in the second person names the person or persons spoken to.

> **John**, please pass the salt.

> Hurry up, **children**!

In the first example, the proper noun **John** is in the second person since it names the fellow toward whom the speaker directs his or her request to pass the salt. In the second example, the noun **children** is in the second person because it names the individuals to whom the speaker issues the command to hurry.

THIRD PERSON

A noun in the third person names the person or persons spoken of.

> The **knight** defeated the **dragon**.

> The **princess** escaped from the evil **wizard's clutches**.

> The **king** was joyful at her safe **return**.

In the first example, the nouns **knight** and **dragon** are both in the third person. In the second example, the nouns **princess**, **wizard's**, and **clutches** are all in the third person. In the third example, the nouns **king** and **return** are in the third person. Every third person noun names an individual or thing spoken of. None of them name the person(s) or thing(s) speaking or spoken to.

CASE

In grammar **case** describes the syntactical relationship of a noun or pronoun to the other words in the sentence. Both nouns and pronouns possess this property, but we will limit our current discussion of case to nouns. There are three cases: **nominative**, **possessive**, and **objective**.

NOMINATIVE CASE

Nouns in the nominative case name the words that statements are made about. Nouns in the nominative case may be subjects of sentences, or they may be **subject complements** (also called predicate nominatives), nouns which follow a linking verb and describe the subject of the sentence. The subject complement and subject must always agree in case, person, number, and gender because they refer to the same individual.

> The **catcher** missed the ball.
>
> **Elvis** is a car **salesman** in Beauford, Oklahoma.
>
> The **guitarist** broke his G string.

In the first example, the noun **catcher** is in the nominative case. It names the person who missed the ball, the subject. In the second example, the nouns **Elvis** and **salesman** are both in the nominative case. The former is the subject of the sentence. The latter is a subject complement following a linking verb, **is**, and renames the subject. In the third example, the noun **guitarist** is in the nominative case, since it names the subject of the sentence, the person who broke the guitar string.

OBJECTIVE CASE

Nouns in the objective case are 1) **direct objects**, the targets of the actions of verbs, 2) **indirect objects**, the objects that are recipients of the actions of verbs and that precede the direct objects in sentences, or 3) words that are connected to other words in sentences, such as **objects of prepositions** (see Chapter 7, p. 230) or **objects of verbals** (see Chapter 5, pp. 156, 166, 171).

> My dog buried her **bone**.
>
> Peter gave **Jill** a **gift**.

Bill's excuses for his **behavior** are irrelevant.

Giving my **cat** a **bath** is an unpleasant task.

In the first example, the noun **bone** is in the objective case because it is the target of the dog's action, the thing that was buried. **Bone** is a direct object.

In the second example, both **Jill** and **gift** are in the objective case. **Gift** is a direct object, the target of Peter's action because it is the thing that was given. **Jill** is an indirect object, since she is the recipient of the direct object **gift**. Please see Chapter 2 on verbs (p. 76) for a clear distinction between direct and indirect objects.

In the third example, the noun **behavior** is in the objective case. It is the object of the preposition **for**. Objects, as you might expect, are always in the objective case.

In the final example, both the nouns **cat** and **bath** are in the objective case. **Bath** is a direct object, the target of the gerund **giving**, while **cat** is an indirect object, the recipient of the action of giving. Both are objects, so both are in the objective case (see Chapter 5, p. 164 for information on gerunds).

There are no differences in form between nouns in the nominative and objective cases. Understanding the differences between the two, however, will enhance your own speech and writing and help you to use more precise English. Look for context clues to determine which case a noun is in.

This section has introduced several new grammatical concepts without providing solid, in-depth definitions. Direct objects, indirect objects, prepositions, verbals, and gerunds are not parts of our current grammar vocabulary. For now, suffice it to say that they do exist and that a more detailed discussion has been postponed for later chapters.

POSSESSIVE CASE

Nouns in the possessive case show ownership. They are words which own. Nouns in the possessive case do differ in form from nouns in the nominative and objective cases.

The **pirate's** treasure was lost at sea.

The **children's** toys littered the playroom floor.

The **treasurer's** note has made me a little nervous.

In these three examples, the words **pirate's**, **children's**, and **treasurer's** are all in the possessive case. The treasure belongs to the pirate, the toys belong to the children, and the note belongs to the treasurer.

The rules used to put a noun in the possessive case are simple. For all singular and plural nouns that do not end in **s**, add apostrophe **s** ('s).

SINGULAR	PLURAL
boy → boy's	mice → mice's
baker → baker's	children → children's
judge → judge's	brethren → brethren's

Grammarians disagree over how to punctuate the possessive forms of singular nouns that end in **s**. It is the Hot Line's opinion that one should add apostrophe **s** ('s). Stick to the general rule when possible.

boss → boss's	Jones → Jones's	bus → bus's
Charles → Charles's	lass → lass's	Dickens → Dickens's

Please see Chapter 16 on punctuation (p. 529) for a few notable exceptions to this rule.

For plural nouns that end in **s**, just add an apostrophe (').

sailors → sailors'	girls → girls'	scientists → scientists'
dogs → dogs'	friends → friends'	soldiers → soldiers'

Many of you may remember those writers who called to ask about the plurals of compound nouns. You are wondering about how to make the possessive case forms of these words.

Fortunately, this answer is simple. If the compound noun, whether it is singular or plural, does not end in **s**, add apostrophe **s** ('s).

> sister-in-law → sister-in-law's
>
> Chiefs of Staff → Chiefs of Staff's
>
> editor-in-chief → editor-in-chief's

If the compound noun is plural and ends in **s**, just add an apostrophe (').

> has-beens → has-beens'
>
> brigadier generals → brigadier generals'
>
> deputy sheriffs → deputy sheriffs'

The same set of rules applies to names of organizations, companies, or political bodies that consist of more than one word.

> Supreme Court → Supreme Court's
>
> Planned Parenthood → Planned Parenthood's
>
> Johnson & Johnson → Johnson & Johnson's

Sometimes possession is shared by several nouns. In these cases, just make the last word in the series possessive.

> **America and Canada's** timber resources are dwindling.
>
> **Thomas and French's** discovery shocked the world.
>
> **Leslie and Eric's** lasagna is to die for.

These sentences all contain nouns that show joint ownership. In the first sentence, the resources belong to America and Canada. In the second sentence, the discovery belongs to both Thomas and French. In the third sentence, the lasagna belongs to both Eric and Leslie.

To show individual ownership, apply the possessive sign to each item in the series.

> **America's and Canada's** timber resources are dwindling.
>
> **Thomas's and French's** discoveries shocked the world.
>
> **Leslie's and Eric's** lasagnas are to die for.

In these examples, each noun has individual ownership of resources, of a discovery, or of a lasagna. These things are not shared.

Many English teachers advise against applying the possessive case to inanimate objects. Possession is a privilege limited to living things. It does not make sense for a car or a house or a bicycle to own anything in the way that the possessive case expresses ownership. The type of possession allowed inanimate objects is typically expressed by a phrase beginning with **of**.

the roof of the house *not* the house's roof

the hood of the car *not* the car's hood

the tire of the bike *not* the bike's tire

Like many grammar issues, however, this one requires a judgment call. Through popular usage, some nouns that name inanimate objects have acquired the rights to their possessive case forms.

my mind's eye	a moment's delay	a week's vacation
two week's notice	the sun's rays	the Season's Greetings

At times creative license may grant you the right to make use of an inanimate object in a possessive form. Think hard. Work carefully. You will make the right decision.

A POSSESSIVE ERROR

Q. "Announcing the Opening of Ventura Counties Largest Bookstore." This pathetic announcement was sent to most of the residents in the general Ventura area. Several callers wondered about the grammatical correctness of this advertisement.

A. There is only one Ventura County. If there were more, then one would spell them "Ventura Counties." However, in this single Ventura County, a bookstore, presumably the area's largest, belongs to the county. The noun **county** needs to take its possessive case form. The advertisement should read, "Announcing the Opening of Ventura County's Largest Bookstore."

USES OF NOUNS

Q. "Can nouns be used in different ways?" asked a curious caller.

A. Certainly, they can. Nouns can be subjects, appositives, direct objects, indirect objects, subject complements, objects of prepositions, objects of infinitives, objects of gerunds, or objects of participles. We even see nouns masquerading as other parts of speech, but no matter how they are used, they are still nouns.

These issues will all be discussed in full detail in subsequent chapters. Please be patient!

SOME OTHER THINGS YOU SHOULD KNOW ABOUT NOUNS

We have looked at the major classifications and properties of nouns, but there are a few more things to note before this discussion of nouns ends.

PERSONIFICATION

Personification is the act of treating an inanimate object or an idea as if it had human qualities. Accordingly, personification allows nouns that name inanimate objects to take animate characteristics such as masculine or feminine gender.

> I heard **Death's** knock at my door and then felt his icy hand on my shoulder.

> The **sea** was unkind today, refusing to share her treasures.

In the first example, the noun **Death's** is proper. It is a particular name of a particular individual and is capitalized as proper nouns should be. This noun is possessive, a property that would be denied to a normal inanimate noun. Personification of death also gives the word an active intelligence, making Death an individual who knocks at doors. The pronoun **his** provides Death with a masculine gender. Personified, death becomes Death, an animated, willful character.

In the second example, the *sea* is personified. It gains the distinctly human abilities to be unkind and to refuse to share. The feminine pronoun **her** gives the usually neuter **sea** a feminine gender. The sea has taken on the characteristics of a selfish woman.

HETERONYMS AND HOMONYMS

Q. "Is there a name for words which have identical spellings but different pronunciations and meanings?"

A. Yes, these words are called heteronyms. I assume you're talking about **row** (means "a line" and rhymes with **slow**) and **row** (means "a fight" and rhymes with **wow**) or **lead** (means "to conduct" and rhymes with **weed**) and **lead** (means "a metallic element" and rhymes with **red**). There are many, many others, but these should suffice to explain.

Homonyms, of course, are words which have the same sound and spelling but different meanings. Some homonyms are: **Catholic** (means "of or pertaining to the Catholic church") and **catholic** (means "universal") or **Pacific** (means "of or pertaining to the Pacific Ocean") and pacific (means "peaceful"). See Chapter 14, p. 392 for a comprehensive list of heteronyms and homonyms.

SUBSTANTIVES

Q. A caller asked, "What is a substantive? I've gone back to teaching after a hiatus and was bemused to find that my students were unfamiliar with the term."

A. Although the term **substantive** is somewhat dated, the Hot Line continues to receive inquiries as to its meaning. The updated term for substantive is **nominal**, and it applies to any noun or pronoun or any word, phrase, or clause that performs the same function as a noun.

> **There** is an olive in each martini glass.
>
> I knew **that she did not like meatloaf**.

In the first example, the substantive or nominal **there** displaces the subject **olive**. More specifically, **there** is a *dummy element*, a word that fills the place of the subject and introduces the sentence. In the second example, the substantive or nominal clause **that she did not like meatloaf** functions as a single noun. It is the direct object in the sentence, naming the thing that I knew.

NOUN PHRASES

Q. "Could you tell me what a noun phrase is? I'm in school preparing to become an English teacher. I went into teaching because my mom spent most of her adult life in the teaching profession. She always used the term **noun phrase** when she was explaining sentence construction."

A. A noun phrase is a group of words that is composed of a noun and a number of optional modifiers and that lacks subject or predicate. Phrases do not have subjects and predicates.

Clauses do. Put those issues on hold for now, however, and take a look at these sentences:

My shopping cart hit **that expensive Mercedes**.

My poor kitty has a cold.

Pigs are filthy.

In the first example, **that expensive Mercedes** is a noun phrase that serves as a direct object. It names the target of the action of the verb. In the second example, **my poor kitty** is a noun phrase. It serves as the subject of the sentence and names the animal that has a cold. In the third example, the single, unmodified noun **pigs** is a noun phrase that serves as the subject of the sentence and names the animals that are filthy. Even though it is composed of only one word, we still consider it a noun phrase. Noun phrases, since they do the work of nouns, are nominals or substantives.

APPOSITIVES

The word **appositive** comes from two Latin words, **ad**, meaning "near," and **ponere**, meaning "to place." An appositive is a word, phrase, or clause that is placed beside another word to re-name, explain, or enhance it. The appositive is a substantive or nominal set off by commas from the word which it identifies. We say that the appositive is used *in apposition* with the other word.

The king, my **brother**, has been murdered.

We spotted Tom Hanks, the movie **star**, at the cafe yesterday.

In the first example, the noun **brother** is used in apposition with the subject **king**. The appositive renames or describes the subject **king** by specifying which king the sentence is about.

In the second example, the noun **star** is used in apposition with the proper noun **Tom Hanks**, a direct object. The appositive clarifies the proper name, telling us which Tom Hanks was seen. For all we know, the writer could have a cousin named Tom Hanks. Remember that the appositive and the noun to which it refers always share the same four properties—gender, number, person, and case—since they both name the same entity.

The Value of Appositives

Q. "I'm a businessman," the caller stated. "I find that my letters are very boring to read. Is there any way I can improve them? Let me give you an example of my sentences: 'I am the president of a large corporation. The name of the corporation is the XYZ Corporation.' " (Names have been changed to protect the innocent.)

A. The caller had never been taught about appositives. One of the greatest strengths of the appositive is its ability to combine separate ideas into a single, clear sentence. With the knowledge of appositives, the caller could have written, "I am the president of a large corporation, XYZ." **XYZ** is an appositive, renaming **corporation**.

Restrictive and Nonrestrictive Information

When we write sentences, it sometimes becomes necessary to add pieces of information, as we just saw in our discussion of appositives. Some of this information is essential to the complete meaning of the sentence. Other pieces which are not essential are present in addition to the complete meaning of the sentence and may be removed without any significant change in meaning. The essential information is **restrictive**, while the nonessential information is **nonrestrictive**.

For example, a friend of mine from a large family uttered this sentence: "My brother Peter sent me the chess service." The sentence contains a piece of added information, the proper noun **Peter**. It is an appositive, renaming the subject of the sentence, **brother**. Whether the proper noun is restrictive or nonrestrictive depends upon the nature of the family.

If my friend has just one brother, then the information is nonrestrictive. When my friend said that his brother had given him the present, we knew whom he was talking about since he has only one brother. The meaning is complete without the added information.

If, on the other hand, my friend has several brothers in addition to Peter, the information is restrictive. It indicates precisely which brother gave my friend the present. Without this information, we could not know which brother my friend was talking about. The proper noun is then essential to the complete meaning of the sentence.

We punctuate sentences differently to distinguish between restrictive and nonrestrictive information. Nonrestrictive information is always set off from the rest of the sentence by commas.

My brother, **Peter,** sent me the chess service.

Restrictive information is never punctuated.

My brother **Peter** sent me the chess service.

As our knowledge of grammar grows, we will see more examples of restrictive and nonrestrictive information in clauses and phrases.

?

TEST YOUR KNOWLEDGE

¿

QUESTIONS

1. What is a simple way of determining that a word is a noun?

2. What are the four categories that nouns can fall into?

3. What types of nouns are **sand** and **friendship**?

4. What kind of gender system does English use?

5. What does it mean to personify a noun? Write an example illustrating the personification of the noun **winter**.

6. Give the plurals of the following words: wolf, piccolo, carriage, candy, father-in-law.

7. Are collective nouns singular or plural?

8. Who or what does a noun in the third person name?

9. What roles can nouns in the nominative case play in sentences?

10. Why must an appositive agree with the noun it refers to in gender, number, person, and case?

(SEE ANSWERS ON FOLLOWING PAGE)

ANSWERS

1. Place **a**, **an**, or **the** in front of the word.

2. Nouns can be common, proper, abstract, or concrete.

3. **Sand** is a common concrete noun. **Friendship** is a common abstract noun.

4. English uses the natural gender.

5. To personify an inanimate noun is to give it the characteristics of a living creature.

6. The plurals, in order, are: wolves, piccolos, carriages, candies, fathers-in-law.

7. Collective nouns can be singular or plural depending on how we view the members of the group that the collective names.

8. A noun in the third person names the person or thing spoken about.

9. Nouns in the nominative case can be subjects or subject complements.

10. The appositive and the noun it refers to must agree because they both name the same person(s) or thing(s).

2.

Verbs

> **Verbs** are words which express action, existence, or condition.

Verbs are the life of language. Because of them, our words take action and we are able to express who we are and how we feel. Without verbs, speech and writing would be reduced to trivial naming and static description. Verbs are beyond compare.

Some verbs express **action**:

> We **danced** till three in the morning.

> The rock band **appreciated** its drummer's unshakable sense of time.

Other verbs indicate a **condition**.

> Bobby **is** miserable after losing his dog.

> This new car **looks** beautiful.

Still others speak of the **existence** of some person or thing.

> Some of the buried workers **are** still alive.

> This old car **is** on its last legs.

ACTION VERBS AND LINKING VERBS

We can divide verbs into two general categories: **action verbs** and **linking verbs**. The action verb, as its name suggests, expresses action.

> The boy **ran** home from school.

> The lemmings **leapt** into the sea.

The words **ran** and **leapt** both express an action that some person or thing takes.

The linking verb, sometimes known as a copulative verb, joins the subject of the sentence to some word or words in the predicate. Perhaps the most common linking verb is **be**.

> I **am** happy.

The word **am**, a form of the verb **be**, links the subject **I** to the subject complement **happy**. It indicates the subject's condition or existence.

A few verbs can be either action or linking verbs, depending on how they are used: feel, grow, keep, look, prove, remain, smell, sound, stay, taste. If these verbs serve a linking purpose, they are linking verbs. If they express action, they are action verbs.

ACTION	We **taste** the fine wines.
LINKING	The wine **tastes** fine.
ACTION	We **stay** in the penthouse suite.
LINKING	The crowd **stays** silent.
ACTION	I **feel** some pain from the injury.
LINKING	The comforter **feels** soft.

If you are unsure, substitute the appropriate form of the verb **be**. Does it fit? If the answer is "yes," the verb is a linking verb.

VERB PHRASES

Verb phrases are composed of more than one verb.

> The mayor **has remained** in office for three consecutive terms.

In this sentence, **has remained** is a verb phrase because it is composed of two verbs.

PRINCIPAL OR MAIN VERBS

In a verb phrase, the **principal verb**, known as the **main verb** in modern grammar, is the meat of the phrase. By itself, it can express complete action, existence, or condition. In the verb phrase mentioned previously, **remained** is the principal or main verb. It tells us what action the mayor has taken. The principal or main verb is always positioned at the end of the verb phrase.

AUXILIARY VERBS

Auxiliary or **helping verbs** are the verbs in the verb phrase that precede the principal or main verb. A verb phrase may contain as many as four auxiliary verbs. These verbs can specify characteristics of the principal or main verb but cannot stand alone as complete verbs. The verb **has** is an auxiliary verb in the example given above. Other auxiliary verbs are **be**, **have**, **do**, **can**, **may**, **will**, **shall**, and **must**.

In a verb phrase, it is the first auxiliary verb that indicates the tense of the phrase (please stay tuned for an in-depth discussion of tense).

I **was** shopping for a new pair of shoes.

John **is** boarding the plane as we speak.

I **will** arrive shortly.

In the first example, the auxiliary verb **was** in the verb phrase **was shopping** tells us that the phrase is in the past tense. In the second example, the auxiliary verb **is** in the verb phrase **is boarding** indicates that the phrase is in the present tense. In the third example, the auxiliary verb **will** in the verb phrase **will arrive** indicates that the phrase is in the future tense.

FROM MY FILES: READING AND WRITING CAREFULLY

Many years ago, I wrote to President Gamal Abdel Nasser, former president of Egypt, asking him to share his wisdom and overwhelming optimism with my junior high school students. To my delight, he responded. Of great interest to me was the postscript to his letter. It read, "Michael, what do you think about my sentence structure? I read the *New York Times* every day."

President Nasser's writing was impeccable. I picked up my copy of the *Times* and scanned the syntax of several articles. They were identical in structure to those of President Nasser's. Here was another invaluable, albeit unintentional, lesson from a great man: the person who reads is a person who writes, and the individual who reads carefully is one who writes carefully.

CHARACTERISTICS OF VERBS

Verbs are associated with five primary characteristics: **number**, **person**, **voice**, **mood**, and **tense**. These determine what form a verb takes and how it is used in a sentence. We will look at each characteristic in turn.

NUMBER

The number of the verb indicates how many people, creatures, or things a verb refers to. Number comes in just two flavors: **singular** and **plural**. A singular verb refers to only one person or thing, while a plural verb may refer to many.

SINGULAR	PLURAL
He **runs**.	They **run**.
She **is** winning.	They **are** winning.
I **swim**.	We **swim**.

PERSON

We use the category of person to describe the perspective from which the speaker makes his or her statements or observations. Is he or she the person speaking or spoken to, or is he or she the person or object spoken of? There are three different persons or perspectives that the verb can take: **first person**, **second person**, and **third person**.

FIRST PERSON

In the **first person**, the speaker includes himself or herself as one who takes the action or whose condition is described. This person is appropriate to situations where the speaker wants to describe what he or she is doing, seeing, or feeling. The first person employs the pronouns **I** and **we**, and the first person verbs take the forms appropriate to these pronouns.

I **laugh** at danger.

We **were** not pleased.

SECOND PERSON

In the **second person**, the speaker addresses the person or people around him or her. This category of person employs the pronoun **you**, both the singular form (you, the individual) and the plural form (you, a group). Again, the second person verbs must take forms appropriate to these pronouns.

You **are** not **going** to be happy when your father gets home.

All of you **drove** here from Phoenix in that tiny car?

THIRD PERSON

To speak in the **third person** is to speak or write about those around you. The third person perspective might be that of a normal human observing his or her environment. It could also be that of an omniscient observer, looking at the world from on high, able to see and hear everything that is going on. The third person employs the pronouns **he, she, it,** and **they** or any third person noun. The third person verbs must take forms appropriate to these pronouns or nouns.

She **thinks** of him fondly.

They **caught** the last train to Clarksville.

My old car **may be** ugly, but it **runs** well.

VOICE

The voice of a verb indicates the strength of the subject in a sentence. It tells us whether that subject takes action or receives action. There are two possible voices: **active** and **passive**. In the active voice, the stronger form, the subject of the sentence takes the action of the verb.

Our army **won** the battle.

The subject **army** is strong since it takes action. This sentence uses the active voice. In the passive voice, the weaker form, the subject is acted upon.

The battle **was won** by our army.

In this sentence, the subject **battle** is weak because it receives the action of the army. It takes no action of its own—a battle cannot win itself—and so the sentence uses the passive voice.

Computer grammar checkers put a great emphasis on flagging and discouraging the passive voice. The passive voice, according to these programs, is unnecessary in most cases and can weaken your content. It is wordier than the active voice because it requires a verb phrase, vaguer than the active voice, and, at its worst, deliberately deceptive. However, some fields, notably the sciences, require the passive voice for description of a process. You and your grammar checker should choose the voice appropriate for your audience.

But why depend upon grammar checkers when it is so easy to spot the difference between active and passive voices on your own? The best way to find the passive voice is to look for the preposition **by**. The action of verbs in the passive voice is usually done *by* one party to another.

The party was given **by** my best friend.

If the word **by** isn't present, is it possible to insert a phrase beginning with the word **by** that indicates who performed the action?

The boxing match was thrown.

or   The match was thrown **by** the crooked fighter.

If you can, you have found a sentence in the passive voice.

Voice Lessons

Q. A supervisor at Pacific Gas & Electric asked about a sentence he had written. He said, " 'It fell to me to write the report.' Is that a correct sentence?"

A. In general, grammarians prefer the active over the passive voice. It is usually better to speak of action taken than of action received. The supervisor's statement was in the passive voice. The "falling" of the report was received by him, the supervisor.

Before we pass judgment on this man's grammar, however, we must acknowledge that the passive voice exists for a reason. One cannot always express an idea deftly in the active voice, and, in such situations, the passive voice is entirely appropriate. The supervisor has written that he was the only person with the ability or inclination to write the report. Any attempt to alter the verb to the active voice will result in a less concise sentence or in a sentence with a different meaning. The supervisor has used the grammar that his situation demands.

ANOTHER VOICE LESSON

Q. A teacher of report writing at a police academy needed to know if his sentence was correct. It read, "What you need is not mentioned in any of the pamphlets that are requested."

A. Please change the passive voice to the active. "None of the pamphlets mentions what you need."

MOOD

In grammar the mood of a verb does not describe its emotional state—as if a verb, a word, could feel joy or rage. Instead, mood is a form of the verb that indicates a speaker's attitude toward his or her use of that verb. Like an emotion, a grammatical mood is a state of mind. To be more precise, it is the speaker's mental conception of the verb he or she is using. And, as opposed to the hundreds of emotions we can feel, there are just three grammatical moods: **indicative**, **imperative**, and **subjunctive**.

INDICATIVE MOOD

To use the indicative mood is to make a statement or ask a question. It is the most commonly used of the three moods. Take a look at some examples that contain verbs in the indicative mood.

The pavement **shimmered** in the hot afternoon sun.

Did you **see** that light in the sky?

In the first example, the verb **shimmered** indicates what the pavement did. Here, the speaker is stating the fact that "the pavement shimmered." The indicative mood always involves statements, questions, or exclamatory sentences.

In the second example, the verb phrase **did see**, broken by the pronoun **you** since the sentence is in the form of a question, indicates what was seen in the sky. This sentence questions a fact.

IMPERATIVE MOOD

Verbs in the imperative mood give commands or make requests. Any time someone is told or asked to do something, the verb used is in the imperative mood.

> **Wipe** that grin off your face!

> **Set** the VCR to begin recording at 9:30.

> Please **fetch** me my slippers.

The first two examples are commands. The final example is a request. The verbs **wipe**, **set**, and **fetch** are all in the imperative mood.

Verbs in the imperative mood are, by necessity, in the second person. A request or command is always spoken directly to another person or other persons. The second person pronoun **you** is often left out but can be put back if the speaker so desires.

SUBJUNCTIVE MOOD

Subjunctive mood verbs express wishes or make statements contrary to fact. They express hypothetical or imaginary situations.

> I wish I **were** with you.

> If I **had been** there, none of this would have happened.

> If we **lived** in San Francisco, we'd be much happier.

> Unless we **go** now, we'll be late.

The conjunction **if** is frequently used with the subjunctive mood, but the conjunctions **though**, **lest**, **unless**, **that**, and **till** may be used as well.

> **If** I were thinner, I'd eat more chocolate.

The verb **were** is in the subjunctive mood. It expresses a condition contrary to fact. Sadly, I am not as thin as I would like to be, so I must limit my chocolate consumption.

These constructions normally come in two parts. One starts with a conjunction, such as **if**: if I were thinner. This part contains the subjunctive verb and is called a subordinate clause (see Chapter 13, p. 334). It has a subject and a predicate but cannot stand alone and make sense. The other shows the result of the hypothetical situation: I'd eat more chocolate. This part can stand alone.

As mentioned before, the subjunctive mood can also express a wish. I wish that I **were** in the Bahamas. Oh, that I only were. In spite of some very realistic day-dreaming, my body still resides in Southern California.

The subjunctive mood is also used to make commands.

I is necessary that he **be told** immediately.

The verb phrase **be told** is in the subjunctive mood. It is part of a subordinate clause beginning with the conjunction **that**.

Other verbs are put in the subjunctive mood to express a parliamentary motion.

I move that Mr. Bugle **be permitted** to keep chickens in his yard.

Be permitted is a subjunctive verb, part of a subordinate clause beginning with the conjunction **that**.

A SUBJUNCTIVE QUESTION

Q. A Frenchman living in the United States asked if these sentences expressed the same idea. "I'm not sure which one says what I really mean: 'I wish I were there' or 'I wish that I had been there.'"

A. The meanings of the sentences are similar but not identical. The difference involves the forms of the verbs. Both sentences are perfect grammatically. They express wishes, so their verbs are in the subjunctive mood, the mood of choice when verbs express conditions contrary to fact. They differ as to when the wish could come true. Using the first, the Frenchman would wish that he were present at some event in the present.

I wish I were with you now.

Using the second, he would wish that he had been present at some event already concluded.

I wish that I had been there three days ago.

The meanings are similar. The time frames are different.

TENSE

Every verb has a place in time. The action or state of being may be immediate, in the here and now. It may have happened some time ago. Or it may not have happened yet. We talk of the placement of a verb in time, its tense, as being in the **past**, **present**, or **future**.

PRESENT TENSE

In the present, you are reading this very sentence. The verb phrase **are reading** is in the present tense. The present tense includes only those actions or states of being that exist in the immediate moment. Perhaps you are also considering a trip to the kitchen, thinking, "I am hungry." The verb **am** is in the present tense.

PAST TENSE

In the not too distant past, you read a sentence that starts several lines above this one. The verb **read**, pronounced with a short e, is in the past tense. In the more distant past, you wisely purchased this book from the local bookstore. The verb **purchased** is also in the past tense. The past tense includes any action or state of being that we could find between the dawn of time and a split second before the present.

FUTURE TENSE

In the near future, you will finish this page. The verb phrase **will finish** is in the future tense. In the more distant future you will finish this book and will recommend it to all of your friends. The verb phrases **will finish** and **will recommend** are also in the future tense. The future tense encompasses all actions or states of being we might encounter between the briefest of moments after the present and the end of time.

A verb in the future tense is, by necessity, in the form of a verb phrase. Because there are no future tense forms for single verbs, grammar demands that we use one of the auxiliaries **shall** or **will** with a principal or main verb in a verb phrase to create the future tense.

Our armies **will vanquish** our enemies.

I **shall return**.

The verb phrases **will vanquish** and **shall return** are both in the future tense.

A MATTER OF STYLE

Q. A deejay asked if the sentence "James Taylor still got his friends" was correct.

A. **Got** is the past tense of **get**. If James got his friends, then he acquired them in the past. Whoever made that statement meant to say that James Taylor still retains his friends. He should have said, "James Taylor still has his friends."

Of course, the deejay was playing off the song *You've Got a Friend*. Most critics and listeners believe that the grammatically incorrect version may be a better choice of style. The power of music is due to the personal connection it makes with listeners. Music that speaks to us speaks a common language, a language that does not always respect the conventions of grammar. While song writers do not need to show a blanket disregard for these conventions, they may write around them with poetic license.

WHICH TENSE?

Q. "Does this sentence need a present or past tense verb?" asked an attorney. "She, the deceased, is/was a cousin of Mrs. Jones."

A. **Was** is correct because the deceased no longer exists on the material plane. If the words were reversed, "Mrs. Jones, among the living, is a cousin of the deceased," then **is** would be correct because Mrs. Jones is still here.

PAST TENSE VERBS IN THE PAST, PRESENT, OR FUTURE

Q. "Do all past tense verbs have to take place in the past?" an editorial advisor asked. Her question caused the Hot Line to do some serious thinking.

A. The answer wasn't as obvious as it first seemed. By using the subjunctive mood to express something that might or could happen but has not happened, a condition contrary to fact, the action, expressed by the past tense verb, could take place in the past, present, or future.

If I **lost** it all tomorrow, I simply would not care.

Lost is in the past tense, but its action occurs in the future. This was a bright question from a very intelligent caller.

SIMPLE, PERFECT, AND PROGRESSIVE FORMS OF VERBS

In the discussion of tenses above, we talked about the three tenses in their most basic forms, the **simple forms**. In their simple forms, the three tenses involve actions that merely occur at their respective places in time. Unless otherwise specified, we assume a tense to be simple. When we refer to the present tense, we are referring to the simple present. When we refer to the past tense, we are referring to the simple past. And when we refer to the future tense, we are referring to the simple future.

Sometimes, however, it becomes necessary to use the verb to imply action that ends. Here, we need to use the **perfect forms**. The perfect forms of the past, present, and future tenses have fixed ending points in terms of time.

In its perfect form (called the **present perfect**), the present tense expresses action or condition that is completed in the present. To form the present perfect tense of a verb, use **have** or **has** with the past participle of the main verb (**have** or **has** + verb + **-ed**).

I **have completed** my work.

The work is complete now, in the present. The verb phrase **have completed** is in the present perfect tense.

In the perfect form of the past tense (called the **past perfect**), the verb expresses action or condition that was completed before a certain time in the past. To form the past perfect tense of a verb, use **had** with the past participle of the main verb (**had** + verb + **-ed**).

I **had completed** my work.

Here, the work was complete at some point in the past. The verb phrase **had completed** is in the past perfect tense.

In the perfect form of the future tense (called the **future perfect**), the verb relates action that will be completed before a certain time in the future. To form the future perfect tense of a verb, use either **shall** or **will** and **have** with the past participle of the main verb (**shall** or **will** + **have** + verb + **-ed**).

> I **shall have completed** my work before we leave for our vacation.

The work will be complete in the future at some point before the speaker and his or her cohorts leave for their vacation. The verb phrase **shall have completed** is in the future perfect tense.

There is yet another form of tense that describes verbs whose action or condition is specifically ongoing, the **progressive form**. The action or condition of verbs in a progressive tense begins at some point in time, past, present, or future, and continues. A progressive tense verb adds a form of **be** to its present participle (**be** + verb + **-ing**). Like the future perfect, the future progressive also uses **shall** or **will** with the other pieces of the progressive tense verb.

PRESENT PROGRESSIVE	I **am loving** you.
PAST PROGRESSIVE	I **was loving** you.
FUTURE PROGRESSIVE	I **shall be loving** you.

Oddly enough, a tense can be both progressive *and* perfect. It may seem counterintuitive that a verb can involve an ongoing action or condition that has a fixed ending point, but a little clarification will reveal this to be true. That some event or feeling is ongoing does not imply that it will never end or has not ended. It simply means that the action or condition persisted for a notable period of time before it ended.

PRESENT PERFECT PROGRESSIVE	I **have been looking** for you.
PAST PERFECT PROGRESSIVE	I **had been looking** for you.
FUTURE PERFECT PROGRESSIVE	I **shall have been looking** for you.

The "looking" in each example began, continued for a time, and then ended. Each verb is in its respective perfect progressive tense.

FROM MY FILES: NOBODY'S PERFECT

Many parents are now turning to home schooling as an alternative to public education. A mother who had given her child a grammar test called and asked, "Is **am flying** in the past progressive active voice, present progressive active voice, or present progressive passive voice?" The materials she was using had been purchased from a parochial school that aided parents who were educating their children at home. The answer key put the verb in the past progressive tense, active voice. Her son had answered, "*Present progressive tense, active voice.*"

The child was right. The book was wrong. Remember that the first auxiliary verb in the verb phrase indicates the tense of the phrase. Since **am** is a present tense auxiliary, the phrase must be in the present tense. Books and other printed materials sometimes contain mistakes. Nobody is perfect. This mom was wise to call rather than to trust the answer key of the textbook blindly.

MUSICAL GRAMMAR

Q. A lover of musicals who was also a highly literate word sleuth called with a question about one of her favorite productions, *My Fair Lady*. She realized that much of Eliza's speech was written deliberately in the cockney dialect but wondered how one of the girl's responses to Professor Higgins would have differed had it been uttered by the refined Eliza we meet at the musical's end. Here is the passage in question:

Higgins: What does it matter what becomes of you?

Eliza: You don't care. I know you don't care. You wouldn't care if I was dead. I'm not so much as them slippers.

A. Eliza makes her first mistake in the third sentence of her reply. The verb in the clause **if I was dead** needs to be in the subjunctive mood. The sentence should read, "You wouldn't care if I were dead." Eliza's second mistake falls in the final sentence. She uses the personal pronoun **them** where she needs a demonstrative pronoun, such as **these** (see Chapter 6, p. 194). "I'm not so much as these slippers." Of course, Professor Henry Higgins made sure that Eliza knew her grammar before the curtain closed. Corrected, their dialogue reads as follows:

Higgins: What does it matter what becomes of you?

Eliza: You don't care. I know you don't care. You wouldn't care if I were dead. I'm not so much as these slippers.

SUBJECT-VERB AGREEMENT

Perhaps the most commonly made mistake in constructing a sentence or clause is the failure to create agreement between subject and verb. The subject names who or what the sentence is about (see Chapter 10, p. 284 for more information). The person and number of the verb must match the person and number of the subject noun(s) or pronoun(s). In other words, if I have a third person plural subject, such as **doctors**, I must use the third person plural form of an appropriate verb, such as **operate**.

> The *doctors* **operate** on their patient. (correct third person plural verb)

not   The *doctors* **operates** on their patient. (incorrect third person singular verb)

A plural subject requires a plural verb. A singular subject requires a singular verb. A subject in the first person requires a verb in the first person. A subject in the second person requires a verb in the second person. No matter what forms they come in, subject and verb must agree. In this agreement, you will find the key to the harmonious sentence, Grasshopper.

> *I* **see** the sign. (correct first person singular verb)

not   *I* **sees** the sign. (incorrect third person singular verb)

> *You* **know** better than that. (correct second person singular or plural)

not   *You* **knows** better than that. (incorrect third person singular verb)

Compound subjects are composed of several nouns or pronouns connected by **and, or, either-or**, or **neither-nor**. Subjects connected by **and** almost always form a plural subject and demand a plural verb.

> **Dogs and cats** *love* to have their ears scratched.

> **Cream cheese and tomato** *are* delicious on a bagel.

There are two exceptions to this rule. The first occurs when a seemingly compound and plural subject comes to be regarded as singular through popular usage.

> **Bacon and eggs** *is* my favorite breakfast.

> **Corned beef and cabbage** *is* an Irish tradition.

Under other circumstances, these subjects would be plural and take a plural verb. However, people have come to look at each set as a unit. These subjects have become singular and need singular verbs.

The other exception occurs when subjects connected by **and** describe a single person or thing.

> **The creator and champion** of the sport *is* injured.

> **The cause and solution** to our problem *is* this.

In the first sentence, the words **creator** and **champion** refer to a single person, so the verb is singular. In the second sentence, the words **cause** and **solution** refer to a single object or issue. The verb must also be singular.

When two singular subjects are connected by **either-or** or **neither-nor**, we regard the complete subject as singular. It then takes a singular verb.

> **Either the penguin or the seal** *eats* my tuna sandwich.

> **Neither Adam nor Dan** *takes* out the trash.

When a singular subject and a plural subject are connected by **either-or** or **neither-nor**, the verb takes the number of whichever subject is closer.

> Neither the manager nor the **workers** *were* responsible for the accident.

> Either the dogs or the **cat** *is* next in line for the bathtub.

In the first example, the plural subject **workers** is nearer to the verb, so the verb is plural. In the second example, the singular subject **cat** is closer to the verb. The verb then is singular.

DECEPTIVE AGREEMENT

Q. A high-ranking police official received this invitation and asked, "Is this correct? 'It is requested that a member of your staff attend this ceremony.'"

A. Believe it or not, the sentence is fine. I correctly guessed that the point of controversy was the verb in the clause **that a member of your staff attend this ceremony** (see Chapter 13 for information on clauses). In this special case, the singular noun **member** does not take a singular verb, **attends**. In **that**-clauses such as the one mentioned above, the verb is in the subjunctive mood and must appear in its base form. **Attend** is the correct base form of the verb. We will talk about base forms of verbs shortly.

COLLECTIVE NOUN AGREEMENT

Q. "How do I know whether a collective noun used as a subject takes a singular or plural verb?"

A. The number of the collective noun and the accompanying verb will depend on context. Remember that a collective noun names a group of individuals or things. If you speak of the group as a single entity, then use a singular verb.

The **audience** *is* listening.

The **band** *was* marching.

If for some reason you are alluding to separate individuals in the group, then use a plural verb.

The **audience** *were* listening.

The **band** *were* stumbling about the field.

To avoid criticism and confusion, use a singular verb whenever possible. Generally, Americans use a singular verb regardless of the situation. By contrast, the British tend to use a plural verb with a collective noun.

MISTAKEN SUBJECT

Q. " 'One of two remaining escaped convicts were captured today' is a sentence I'm using in a news release," said a prison warden. "I want to be absolutely sure of my English. Is it correct?"

A. The warden has mistaken the object of a preposition for the subject of the sentence. **Of two remaining escaped convicts** is a prepositional phrase. **Of** is a preposition. The verb **were captured** agrees with the plural object **convicts**. The true subject of the sentence is the singular pronoun **one**. The warden needs to rewrite his sentence so that it contains a singular verb. "One of two remaining escaped convicts was captured today."

HEAVENLY GRAMMAR

Q. Calling from her convent in the Pacific Northwest, an erudite nun was concerned about the subject-verb agreement in *The Liturgy of the Hours*, a prayer which her community recites. It reads, "The glorious company of apostles praise you. The noble fellowship of prophets praise you. The white-robed army of prophets praise you."

A. The author of the liturgy has made a common error. In each sentence, he or she has mistaken the object of a preposition for the subject of the sentence. In the first sentence, the plural object **apostles** is not the subject. The singular noun **company** is the subject. In the second sentence, the plural object **prophets** is not the subject. The singular noun **fellowship** is the subject. In the final sentence, the plural object **prophets** is not the subject. The singular noun **army** is the subject. Every one of these singular subjects needs a singular verb, **praises**. The liturgy should read, "The glorious company of apostles *praises* you. The noble fellowship of prophets *praises* you. The white-robed army of prophets *praises* you." After hearing my answer, the sister commented that she felt compelled to rewrite the entire liturgy. Although the sentiments were beautiful, she could not abide imperfect grammar.

CONJUGATION

The conjugation of a verb is the complete set of verb forms inflected across tense, mood, voice, person, and number. Since a complete conjugation table showing every possible form of a verb would be quite unwieldy, we often limit our conjugation to the **principal parts** of verbs: **present indicative**, **past indicative**, and **past participle**. Knowing these three forms alone, we can discern the rest.

PRESENT INDICATIVE	PAST INDICATIVE	PAST PARTICIPLE
awake	awoke	awoken
bare	bared	bared
bear	bore	borne
beat	beat	beaten
become	became	become
begin	began	begun
bite	bit	bitten

Present Indicative	Past Indicative	Past Participle
blow	blew	blown
break	broke	broken
bring	brought	brought
burst	burst	burst
catch	caught	caught
choose	chose	chosen
come	came	come
cost	cost	cost
creep	crept	crept
defend	defended	defended
discuss	discussed	discussed
dive	dived/dove	dived
do	did	done
draw	drew	drawn
drink	drank	drunk
drive	drove	driven
eat	ate	eaten
fall	fell	fallen
flee	fled	fled
fling	flung	flung
fly	flew	flown
forbid	forbade	forbidden
freeze	froze	frozen
get	got	gotten
give	gave	given
go	went	gone
grow	grew	grown
hang[†]	hanged	hanged
hang[†]	hung	hung
hurt	hurt	hurt
know	knew	known
lay	laid	laid
lead	led	led
lean	leaned	leaned
leave	left	left
lend	lent	lent
lie	lay	lain

[†] The verb **hang**, whose principal parts are **hang-hanged-hanged**, means "to punish by death at the gallows." *The criminals were **hanged** for their crimes.* The verb **hang**, whose principal parts are **hang-hung-hung**, means "to suspend." *The clothes were **hung** out to dry.*

Present Indicative	Past Indicative	Past Participle
lose	lost	lost
love	loved	loved
make	made	made
mean	meant	meant
opine	opined	opined
play	played	played
raise	raised	raised
ride	rode	ridden
ring	rang	rung
rise	rose	risen
run	ran	run
say	said	said
see	saw	seen
seek	sought	sought
set	set	set
shake	shook	shaken
shine[†]	shined	shined
shine[†]	shone	shone
sing	sang	sung
sink	sank	sunk
sit	sat	sat
slay	slew	slain
speak	spoke	spoken
spit	spat	spat
spring	sprang	sprung
steal	stole	stolen
strive	strove	striven
swear	swore	sworn
swim	swam	swum
swing	swung	swung
take	took	taken
tear	tore	torn
throw	threw	thrown
wear	wore	worn

Determining these three principal parts is not always a simple matter. Verbs can be **regular** or **irregular**. Regular verbs form their

---

[†] The verb **shine**, whose principal parts are **shine-shined-shined**, means "to polish." *I **shined** my shoes.* The verb **shine**, whose principal parts are **shine-shone-shone**, means "to give off light." *The stars **shone** in the sky.*

past indicative and past participle parts in a regular way; that is, **-ed** is added to their present indicative forms (also called the **base**). If the base of the regular verb ends in **e**, just add **-d**. In the chart above, **play** and **look** are regular verbs.

Irregular verbs form the past indicative and past participle parts in irregular ways. There is no easy method to use. A vowel can change. A consonant can be added. Or the form can remain the same across all three parts (**hurt-hurt-hurt**). Only a good memory can account for the many forms that irregular verbs can take. In the chart, the verbs **grow** and **make** are both irregular verbs.

To derive all the conjugated verb forms, we must start with the **base** of the verb. The base is the present indicative form: **wear, desire**. These are both verbs in their present indicative forms. Use these methods to make the inflected forms[†]:

THE PRINCIPAL PARTS

THE PRESENT INDICATIVE FORMS

Every verb in the **present indicative** except **be**, a special case, derives its first and second person singular forms and its first, second, and third person plural forms from the base, unchanged: I **run**, you **play**, we **sing**, they **fall**. To derive the third person singular forms, add **-s** or **-es** to the base: he **looks**, she **grows**, it **makes**, she **goes**, he **tries**.

THE PAST INDICATIVE FORMS

The **past indicative forms** of verbs are made by adding **-ed** or **-d** to the base forms of regular verbs and by making the necessary changes to irregular verbs: they **rode**, we **looked**, I **made**, it **glided**. Unfortunately, there is no formula with which to solve the irregular verb puzzle. Each form must be committed to memory.

THE PAST PARTICIPLE

To create the **past participle**, add **-ed** or **-d** to the base forms of regular verbs or make the necessary changes to irregular verbs: **broken, grown, looked, carried**. There is no rule that would allow us to create the past participles of all irregular verbs.

[†] Unless otherwise specified, a rule will apply to all persons and numbers of the verb.

THE REST OF THE PARTS

THE PRESENT PERFECT INDICATIVE FORMS

The **present perfect indicative** pairs the past participle of the verb with either **have** or **has**: we **have played**, he **has carried**. Use **has** when the subject of the verb is in the third person singular and **have** in the others.

THE PAST PERFECT INDICATIVE FORMS

The **past perfect indicative** consists of **had** followed by the past participle: you **had known**, they **had sipped**.

THE FUTURE INDICATIVE FORMS

To form the **future indicative**, use either **shall** or **will** with the base of the verb: we **shall change**, she **will make**.

THE FUTURE PERFECT INDICATIVE FORMS

To form the **future perfect indicative**, use **shall** or **will** with **have** and the past participle: I **shall have tried**, he **will have seen**.

THE IMPERATIVE FORMS

To create the **imperative** form of a verb, use its unchanged base. **Look** at it! **Help** me. **Carry** this package. Of course, the polite imperative speaker would include a "please" with any request or command.

THE PRESENT SUBJUNCTIVE FORMS

To create the **present subjunctive** form of a verb, use the unchanged base form of the verb regardless of person or number. Such verbs appear in subordinate clauses that begin with the conjunction **that**: that he **attend** the ceremony, that she **believe** my story. We also see present subjunctive verbs in colloquial expressions such as "God **save** the queen" and "He **let** the cat out of the bag." Again, the present subjunctive verbs must be in their base forms.

The Mythical Present Perfect Subjunctive Forms

There is no such thing as a **present perfect subjunctive** verb.

The Past Subjunctive Forms

The **past subjunctive** form of a verb, with two exceptions, is identical to the **past indicative** form. We often see past subjunctive verbs in subordinate clauses that begin with **if, as if, though**, or **as though**: (if) she **loved**, (if) we **came**. However, when the subject of such a subordinate clause is in the first person singular or the third person singular and its verb is **be**, use **were** rather than **was**: (if) I **were** in Boston, (if) she **were** here.

The Past Perfect Subjunctive Forms

The **past perfect subjunctive** is identical to the **past perfect indicative**. Use **had** with the past participle: (if) you **had shown**, (if) he **had arrived**. Like the past subjunctive verbs, past perfect subjunctive verbs often appear in subordinate clauses that begin with **if, as if, though**, or **as though**.

The Present Participle

To form the **present participle**, add -**ing** to the base form: **loving, gazing, carrying, seeing**. The present participle is used in the progressive form of a verb.

On the following pages are the conjugations of a few verbs, regular and irregular: **grow, look, run, have, do**, and **be**.

CONJUGATION TABLE: GROW

PRINCIPAL PARTS:

Present Indicative	Past Indicative	Past Participle
grow	grew	grown

INDICATIVE MOOD

	Singular	*Plural*

Present Tense

First Person	I grow	We grow
Second Person	You grow	You grow
Third Person	He, she, it grows	They grow

Past Tense

First Person	I grew	We grew
Second Person	You grew	You grew
Third Person	He, she, it grew	They grew

Future Tense

First Person	I shall grow	We shall grow
Second Person	You will grow	You will grow
Third Person	He, she, it will grow	They will grow

Present Perfect Tense

First Person	I have grown	We have grown
Second Person	You have grown	You have grown
Third Person	He, she, it has grown	They have grown

Past Perfect Tense

First Person	I had grown	We had grown
Second Person	You had grown	You had grown
Third Person	He, she, it had grown	They had grown

Future Perfect Tense

First Person	I shall have grown	We shall have grown
Second Person	You will have grown	You will have grown
Third Person	He, she, it will have grown	They will have grown

Imperative Mood

	Singular	*Plural*
Present Tense		
Second Person	(You) grow	(You) grow

Subjunctive Mood

	Singular	*Plural*
Present Tense		
First Person	(that) I grow	(that) we grow
Second Person	(that) you grow	(that) you grow
Third Person	(that) he, she, it grow	(that) they grow
Past Tense		
First Person	(If) I grew	(If) we grew
Second Person	(If) you grew	(If) you grew
Third Person	(If) he, she, it grew	(If) they grew
Past Perfect Tense		
First Person	(If) I had grown	(If) we had grown
Second Person	(If) you had grown	(If) you had grown
Third Person	(If) he, she, it had grown	(If) they had grown

CONJUGATION TABLE: LOOK

PRINCIPAL PARTS:

Present Indicative	**Past Indicative**	**Past Participle**
look	looked	looked

INDICATIVE MOOD

	Singular	*Plural*

Present Tense

First Person	I look	We look
Second Person	You look	You look
Third Person	He, she, it looks	They look

Past Tense

First Person	I looked	We looked
Second Person	You looked	You looked
Third Person	He, she, it looked	They looked

Future Tense

First Person	I shall look	We shall look
Second Person	You will look	You will look
Third Person	He, she, it will look	They will look

Present Perfect Tense

First Person	I have looked	We have looked
Second Person	You have looked	You have looked
Third Person	He, she, it has looked	They have looked

Past Perfect Tense

First Person	I had looked	We had looked
Second Person	You had looked	You had looked
Third Person	He, she, it had looked	They had looked

Future Perfect Tense

First Person	I shall have looked	We shall have looked
Second Person	You will have looked	You will have looked
Third Person	He, she, it will have looked	They will have looked

Imperative Mood

	Singular	*Plural*
Present Tense		
Second Person	(You) look	(You) look

Subjunctive Mood

	Singular	*Plural*
Present Tense		
First Person	(that) I look	(that) we look
Second Person	(that) you look	(that) you look
Third Person	(that) he, she, it look	(that) they look
Past Tense		
First Person	(If) I looked	(If) we looked
Second Person	(If) you looked	(If) you looked
Third Person	(If) he, she, it looked	(If) they looked
Past Perfect Tense		
First Person	(If) I had looked	(If) we had looked
Second Person	(If) you had looked	(If) you had looked
Third Person	(If) he, she, it had looked	(If) they had looked

CONJUGATION TABLE: RUN

PRINCIPAL PARTS:

Present Indicative	**Past Indicative**	**Past Participle**
run	ran	run

INDICATIVE MOOD

	Singular	*Plural*

Present Tense

First Person	I run	We run
Second Person	You run	You run
Third Person	He, she, it runs	They run

Past Tense

First Person	I ran	We ran
Second Person	You ran	You ran
Third Person	He, she, it ran	They ran

Future Tense

First Person	I shall run	We shall run
Second Person	You will run	You will run
Third Person	He, she, it will run	They will run

Present Perfect Tense

First Person	I have run	We have run
Second Person	You have run	You have run
Third Person	He, she, it has run	They have run

Past Perfect Tense

First Person	I had run	We had run
Second Person	You had run	You had run
Third Person	He, she, it had run	They had run

Future Perfect Tense

First Person	I shall have run	We shall have run
Second Person	You will have run	You will have run
Third Person	He, she, it will have run	They will have run

IMPERATIVE MOOD

	Singular	*Plural*
Present Tense		
Second Person	(You) run	(You) run

SUBJUNCTIVE MOOD

	Singular	*Plural*
Present Tense		
First Person	(that) I run	(that) we run
Second Person	(that) you run	(that) you run
Third Person	(that) he, she, it run	(that) they run

Past Tense

	Singular	*Plural*
First Person	(If) I ran	(If) we ran
Second Person	(If) you ran	(If) you ran
Third Person	(If) he, she, it ran	(If) they ran

Past Perfect Tense

	Singular	*Plural*
First Person	(If) I had run	(If) we had run
Second Person	(If) you had run	(If) you had run
Third Person	(If) he, she, it had run	(If) they had run

CONJUGATION TABLE: HAVE

PRINCIPAL PARTS:

Present Indicative	Past Indicative	Past Participle
have	had	had

INDICATIVE MOOD

	Singular	*Plural*

Present Tense

First Person	I have	We have
Second Person	You have	You have
Third Person	He, she, it has	They have

Past Tense

First Person	I had	We had
Second Person	You had	You had
Third Person	He, she, it had	They had

Future Tense

First Person	I shall have	We shall have
Second Person	You will have	You will have
Third Person	He, she, it will have	They will have

Present Perfect Tense

First Person	I have had	We have had
Second Person	You have had	You have had
Third Person	He, she, it has had	They have had

Past Perfect Tense

First Person	I had had	We had had
Second Person	You had had	You had had
Third Person	He, she, it had had	They had had

Future Perfect Tense

First Person	I shall have had	We shall have had
Second Person	You will have had	You will have had
Third Person	He, she, it will have had	They will have had

Imperative Mood

	Singular	*Plural*
Present Tense		
Second Person	(You) have	(You) have

Subjunctive Mood

	Singular	*Plural*
Present Tense		
First Person	(that) I have	(that) we have
Second Person	(that) you have	(that) you have
Third Person	(that) he, she, it have	(that) they have
Past Tense		
First Person	(If) I had	(If) we had
Second Person	(If) you had	(If) you had
Third Person	(If) he, she, it had	(If) they had
Past Perfect Tense		
First Person	(If) I had had	(If) we had had
Second Person	(If) you had had	(If) you had had
Third Person	(If) he, she, it had had	(If) they had had

CONJUGATION TABLE: DO

PRINCIPAL PARTS:

Present Indicative	Past Indicative	Past Participle
do	did	done

INDICATIVE MOOD

	Singular	*Plural*

Present Tense

First Person	I do	We do
Second Person	You do	You do
Third Person	He, she, it does	They do

Past Tense

First Person	I did	We did
Second Person	You did	You did
Third Person	He, she, it did	They did

Future Tense

First Person	I shall do	We shall do
Second Person	You will do	You will do
Third Person	He, she, it will do	They will do

Present Perfect Tense

First Person	I have done	We have done
Second Person	You have done	You have done
Third Person	He, she, it has done	They have done

Past Perfect Tense

First Person	I had done	We had done
Second Person	You had done	You had done
Third Person	He, she, it had done	They had done

Future Perfect Tense

First Person	I shall have done	We shall have done
Second Person	You will have done	You will have done
Third Person	He, she, it will have done	They will have done

IMPERATIVE MOOD

	Singular	*Plural*
Present Tense		
Second Person	(You) do	(You) do

SUBJUNCTIVE MOOD

	Singular	*Plural*
Present Tense		
First Person	(that) I do	(that) we do
Second Person	(that) you do	(that) you do
Third Person	(that) he, she, it do	(that) they do
Past Tense		
First Person	(If) I did	(If) we did
Second Person	(If) you did	(If) you did
Third Person	(If) he, she, it did	(If) they did
Past Perfect Tense		
First Person	(If) I had done	(If) we had done
Second Person	(If) you had done	(If) you had done
Third Person	(If) he, she, it had done	(If) they had done

CONJUGATION TABLE: BE

As mentioned before, the conjugation of the verb **be** is a special case. It does not follow the standard rules. Here is the complete conjugation of this verb.

PRINCIPAL PARTS:

Present Indicative	**Past Indicative**	**Past Participle**
am, is, are	was, were	been

INDICATIVE MOOD

	Singular	*Plural*

Present Tense

First Person	I am	We are
Second Person	You are	You are
Third Person	He, she, it is	They are

Past Tense

First Person	I was	We were
Second Person	You were	You were
Third Person	He, she, it was	They were

Future Tense

First Person	I shall be	We shall be
Second Person	You will be	You will be
Third Person	He, she, it will be	They will be

Present Perfect Tense

First Person	I have been	We have been
Second Person	You have been	You have been
Third Person	He, she, it has been	They have been

Past Perfect Tense

First Person	I had been	We had been
Second Person	You had been	You had been
Third Person	He, she, it had been	They had been

Future Perfect Tense

First Person	I shall have been	We shall have been
Second Person	You will have been	You will have been
Third Person	He, she, it will have been	They will have been

IMPERATIVE MOOD

	Singular	*Plural*

Present Tense

Second Person	(You) be	(You) be

SUBJUNCTIVE MOOD

	Singular	*Plural*

Present Tense

First Person	(that) I be	(that) we be
Second Person	(that) you be	(that) you be
Third Person	(that) he, she, it be	(that) they be

Past Tense

First Person	(If) I were	(If) we were
Second Person	(If) you were	(If) you were
Third Person	(If) he, she, it were	(If) they were

Past Perfect Tense

First Person	(If) I had been	(If) we had been
Second Person	(If) you had been	(If) you had been
Third Person	(If) he, she, it had been	(If) they had been

Principal Parts Questions

Many callers come to me with questions about the forms of verbs, especially their principal parts. Here are some of the most informative.

Begin, Began, Begun

Q. "My husband always says 'have began.' I've always thought that it sounds strange."

A. It should sound strange. This husband is mixing up his principal parts. He is using **have** with the past indicative form of the verb, but what he really needs is the past participle. **Begun** is the past participle of **begin**.

I **have begun** my Swedish class.

Began is the past indicative.

I **began** the game.

Sink, Sank, Sunk

Q. A corporate executive and avid reader called to report this travesty from a work of popular fiction. "I sunk down, and she sunk down." She said, "I simply can't believe this low level of literacy. How could the author and the editors let it get to print?"

A. Ay carumba! Such a sentence pains my eyes. Look back at the chart of principal parts. You will find that the past indicative form of **sink** is **sank**. **Sunk** is the past participle and must be used in conjunction with an auxiliary verb. The corrected quote should read, "I sank down, and she sank down."

Had Gone/Had Went

Q. A Dutch scriptwriter called to settle an argument she was having with her husband over whether **had gone** or **had went** was the correct verb form. She said, "I can't get my stubborn American husband to realize that **had gone** is the correct form of the verb. Will you settle the score?"

A. It was obvious that this woman knew more than her husband. Although she had received her education in Holland and he in the United States, she knew vastly more than he did. I verified that **had gone** was the correct choice. The true focus of their argument was over the past perfect form of the verb **go**. The past perfect includes the past participle with the auxiliary **had**. **Gone** is the past participle. **Went** is the past indicative. The Dutch woman won, hands down. Holland 1. America 0.

DIVE, DIVED, DOVE

Q. A member of the Navy SEALS was writing his memoirs. He asked, "Is it correct to say, 'We dove deep into the sea'?"

A. Both **dived** and **dove** are acceptable options for the past indicative form of **dive**. Some style manuals warn against using **dove**, but many experts feel it is a sound option. Use whichever your ears prefer. It's a matter of style.

SHRINK, SHRANK, SHRUNK

Q. A movie producer asked, "Can I use **shrunk** without any helping verbs?" The movie *Honey, I Shrunk the Kids* had just hit the theaters.

A. Unsure of myself, I consulted the dictionary. Much to my surprise, it listed **shrank** and **shrunk** as alternate past indicative forms of **shrink**. *Honey, I Shrank the Kids. Honey, I Shrunk the Kids.* Either is correct, but I prefer the former.

HANG AND HANG

Q. "Were people hanged or hung for committing murder?" asked one caller with rather morbid curiosity.

A. The verb **hang** has two meanings. With principal parts **hang-hanged-hanged**, it means "to punish by death at the gallows."

The law **hanged** the criminals at high noon.

With principal parts **hang-hung-hung**, it means "to suspend."

I **hung** the feeder from a branch of the willow tree.

Both involve some sort of suspension, but that of the **hang-hung-hung** series is much less gruesome.

OBJECTS AND COMPLEMENTS OF VERBS

Now that we have looked at the verb in its own right, it is time to turn to the verb in relation to the rest of the sentence. No verb works alone. There is always a subject, performing the action of the verb or exhibiting the state or condition that the verb indicates. Even the shortest imperatives, such as "Run!", have a subject. It is an understood "you," omitted for the sake of convenience. The subject, though, is not our concern here.

In many sentences, the subject and verb alone cannot express a complete idea. The idea only becomes whole with the help of other words. Different verbs are helped by different types of words or phrases, but these will always follow the verb. Action verbs may take **direct** and **indirect objects** while linking verbs take **subject complements**. We will deal with each in turn.

OBJECTS OF ACTION VERBS

The action verb takes two types of objects: **direct objects** and **indirect objects**. The **direct object** receives the action of the verb. It is the target of the verb action. The direct object answers the questions "Whom?" or "What?"

> She gave me a **present**.

> I saw **Tom** at the restaurant.

Each example contains a direct object that completes the meaning of the verb. In the first example, the direct object **present** tells *what* she gave. In the second example, the direct object **Tom** tells *whom* I saw. Look at each sentence without its direct object.

> She gave me.

> I saw.

Neither expresses a complete thought. The direct objects are essential for the whole meaning to come through.

The second type of object, the **indirect object**, receives and precedes the direct object in the sentence. It answers the questions "To whom?" or "For whom?" Most indirect objects refer to people.

> She gave **me** the evil eye.

> I made **her** dinner.

He gave the **chair** a fresh coat of paint.

The first example contains a direct object, **eye**, telling what was given, and an indirect object, **me**, telling to whom the evil eye was given. The second example has a direct object, **dinner**, telling what was made, and an indirect object, **her**, telling for whom the dinner was made. The third example contains a direct object, **coat**, also telling what was given, and an indirect object, **chair**, telling to what the fresh coat of paint was given.

Indirect objects often follow verbs of creation or giving. The action of these verbs has direction. It may occur *for* someone or it may occur so that something goes *to* someone else. Here are a few examples: give, offer, pay, send, write, paint, make.

Direct objects are fairly easy to recognize. They are usually nouns and sometimes pronouns, and they are the targets of the verb action. If there is only one object in a sentence, it is always a direct object. If in doubt, however, ask one of the questions "What?" or "Whom?" with the action verb in the sentence.

I sent the **postcard**.

I called my **parents**.

What did I *send*? The answer is "the postcard." *Whom* did I *call*? The answer is "my parents." They are the direct objects.

Indirect objects can be more difficult to spot. Once you find a direct object, see if there are any words that come between it and the verb. Since the indirect object, when present, always precedes the direct object, it is likely that one of these words is the indirect object. After you have found a candidate for indirect object, ask whether the sentence can be manipulated so that the word in question follows either of the prepositions **for** or **to**.

The child gave his **mother** quite a scare.

She wrote **me** a love letter.

In the first example, we deduce that the noun **scare** is a direct object. There are four words between the verb **gave** and the direct object. Only one of these words, **mother**, can be used with one of the prepositions **to** or **for**.

The child gave quite a scare **to** his **mother**.

In the second example, three words, **me**, **a**, and **love**, fall between the verb **wrote** and the direct object **letter**.

She wrote a love letter **for me**.

Please note that an indirect object placed in a prepositional phrase is no longer an indirect object. It becomes the object of a preposition (see Chapter 7, p. 230). In the phrases **to his mother** and **for me**, the words **mother** and **me** are not indirect objects. They are objects of prepositions.

It is also important to note that only the principal or main verb in a verb phrase takes the objects.

We have not seen that **movie**.

John is giving **them** a **ride**.

In the first example, the main verb **seen**, not the verb phrase **have seen**, takes an object, **movie**. In the second example, the main verb **giving**, not the verb phrase **is giving**, takes an indirect object **them** and a direct object **ride**.

TRANSITIVE VS. INTRANSITIVE VERBS

Any verb that requires a direct object is known as a **transitive verb**.

I **trim** the lawn.

The noun **lawn** receives the action of the verb, the trimming. The verb **trim** is a transitive verb.

I **taught** the children.

The noun **children** receives the action of the verb, the teaching. The verb **taught** is also a transitive verb.

Verbs that do not take objects are **intransitive verbs**.

We shall **run** when we get the chance.

No word receives the action of this verb. Therefore, **run** is an intransitive verb.

We **stayed** at the Ritz.

No noun or pronoun receives the action of this verb either. It is intransitive.

Some verbs can be either transitive or intransitive, depending on how they are used.

TRANSITIVE	INTRANSITIVE
I **work** the lathe in the workroom.	She **works** at the copy shop.
Bob **operates** the copy machines.	Dr. Blaum **operates** on her patients.
I **ran** yesterday.	I **ran** the marathon.

DO I NEED A DIRECT OBJECT?

Q. "I am terribly confused about the verb **do** and its past participle form **done**," said a fledgling English teacher. "I consulted the dictionary, but now I'm more confused than ever. My dictionary says that **do** is a transitive verb, so it requires a direct object. I would also expect the past participle, **done**, to require a direct object, but people are always saying things like 'We are done.' There isn't a direct object in that sentence. What's the story here?"

A. **Do** is one of those verbs that can be transitive or intransitive, depending on how it is used. In these sentences, **do** is a transitive verb.

I **do** that every day.

You **did** it yesterday.

I'll **do** it today.

In others, **do** can be intransitive.

That will **do**.

We were **done** a long time ago.

Whether the verb takes an object depends on the writer's needs.

Grammar is not a cut and dry topic. Her dictionary was merely offering its writers' opinions on the nature of the verb **do**. To be honest, some of the statements made in this book represent my opinions, and certain of my readers may disagree with them. While controversy will not make your studies any easier, it allows English to be a dynamic and engaging language. Do not fear conflict. Embrace it!

DICTIONARY ABBREVIATIONS

Q. "I found the abbreviations **vi.**, **vt.**, and **vl.** in my dictionary. What do they mean?" asked a high school sophomore from Kentucky.

A. These abbreviations stand for different kinds of verbs. The abbreviation **vi.** stands for "intransitive verb." Such verbs do not take direct objects.

The rain **fell**.

Fell is an intransitive verb because it has no object.

The abbreviation **vt.** stands for "transitive verb." These verbs do take direct objects.

The robbers **stole** the cash.

Stole is a transitive verb because it has a direct object, **cash**.

The abbreviation **vl.** stands for "linking verb." Remember that a linking verb joins the subject to some word or words in the predicate.

My cat **is** a calico.

That potion **smells** foul.

These dishes **are** clean.

The verbs **is**, **smells**, and **are** are linking verbs in these sentences.

OBJECT COMPLEMENTS

Direct objects themselves may take complements called **object complements**. These are nouns, pronouns, and adjectives which re-name or describe the direct object. An object complement always follows the direct object in the sentence.

The kids painted the wall **orange**.

The committee appointed him **treasurer**.

My kids call me **DoDa**.

In the first example, the adjective **orange** is the object comple-ment of the direct object **wall**. The complement describes the object. It indicates the color that the wall was painted. In the second example, the noun **treasurer** is the object complement of the direct object **him**. This complement renames the object. It indicates his new title. In the final example, the proper noun **DoDa** is the object complement of the direct object **me**. This complement also renames the object, telling what the speaker's children call him.

DOUBTS ABOUT OBJECT COMPLEMENTS

Q. "Is 'I found these paintings the most striking' a correct sentence?" asked an art critic who wanted to be sure he had phrased his idea properly.

A. The sentence is fine. The noun **paintings** is the direct object of the verb **found**. The present participle **striking** is an object complement since it functions as an adjective to modify the direct object. The adverb **most** modifies **striking**. As far as we can tell, our critic's grammar is flawless.

It isn't enough merely to speak and write correctly. One needs a knowledge of grammar to understand the inner workings of language and to speak without fear of reproach. Such freedom must seem especially important to those who work within a community of critics.

COMPLEMENTS OF LINKING VERBS

The linking verb is followed by another type of helping element, the **subject complement**. Subject complements rename or describe the subjects of sentences. In other words, they *complement* the *subjects*.

Many of these complements are nouns, pronouns, or other nominals that rename or provide additional information about the subject of the sentence. They always follow linking verbs. A less contemporary term for a noun, pronoun, or other nominal used as a subject complement is **predicate nominative**.

He is the **boss**.

Nancy is the **winner**.

This is **she**.

My friends are **they**.

In the first example, the subject complement **boss** explains the subject **he**. It tells what he is. In the second example, the subject complement **winner** explains the subject **Nancy**. It tells what Nancy is. In the third example, the subject complement **she** renames the subject **this**. It tells who this is. In the final example, the subject complement **they** identifies the subject **friends**. It tells who the friends are.

Other subject complements are adjectives that modify the subjects of sentences. They also follow linking verbs. A less contemporary term for an adjective used as a subject complement is **predicate adjective**.

> My coworkers are **friendly**.

> This story is **exciting**.

In the first example, the subject complement **friendly** modifies the subject coworkers. In the second example, the subject complement **exciting** modifies the subject **story**.

A Complement Question

Q. "Can a predicate nominative and a predicate adjective be found in the same sentence?" asked a writer.

A. They certainly can. Here is an example: "He is a house husband and quite content." The subject of the sentence is **he**. The verb **is** is a linking verb. The noun **husband** is a predicate nominative and the adjective **content** is a predicate adjective. Both types of subject complements follow a single linking verb. Contemporary grammarians view the entire phrase **a house husband and quite content** as a single subject complement.

From My Files: Verbal Obfuscation

Occasionally, I will help an attorney who is mired by his or her own verbal obfuscation. On one occasion, I was asked for a grammatical interpretation of a will. Mine was to have been a second opinion, but the case was called to court before the lawyer received my analysis. He entered the fray armed only with the first opinion and lost the case. The attorney's other expert focused on the wrong words and became so entwined in her tortuous explanation that she proved the opposition's case.

The portion of the will in question read, "I bequeath all of my memorabilia, effects, and property located at . . . ." The expert with the faulty opinion had foolishly concentrated on the word **located**, a past participle (see Chapter 5, p. 152), attempting to show that it only described the last of the three nouns preceding it, **property**. Why she would make such an argument, I cannot begin to say.

The key word in the sentence is **all**, the direct object of the verb **bequeath**. All is bequeathed. **Of my memorabilia, effects, and property** is a prepositional phrase used to describe **all**. Since each of the nouns in the prepositional phrase is of equal value, each represents an equal portion of the *all* that was *bequeathed*. In other words, the attorney's clients should have received all of their forebear's belongings. It is too bad that they didn't. It is too bad that the judge was in such a hurry to hear the case. And it is too bad that the attorney didn't ask for a postponement. If he had, his clients would have won. In the truest sense, this situation proved the value of precise grammar.

SOME OTHER THINGS YOU SHOULD KNOW ABOUT VERBS

English is a language full of complications. Like most other languages, it contains rules, distinctions, and other peculiarities whose origins are lost to antiquity but whose influences are still felt today. These complications, though sometimes troublesome, are part of our language, and the careful grammarian will pay attention to them. More than a few of the complications can be found within the realm of the verb.

Do

Expert writers and speakers have three broad uses for the auxiliary verb **do** and its accompanying forms (**did**, **does**, and **done**). We often use **do** to create the **emphatic forms** of verbs. The emphatic forms emphasize the action that the verb expresses by using a form of **do** as an auxiliary before the principal or main verb.

> I **do** know the answer.

> I **did** mail my tax forms.

> She **does** have a right to know.

We could have written any one of these sentences in a nonemphatic form.

> I know the answer.

> I mailed my tax forms.

She has a right to know.

However, the emphasis on the action of the verb disappears.

Please note: only verbs in the past and present tenses can be emphatic in the manner mentioned above. There is simply no way to construct a future tense verb that implies emphasis by using the emphatic **do**.

The auxiliary verb **do** does not always carry emphasis. English speakers often use this word idiomatically to ask questions.

Do you know who I am?

Does it hurt?

Did you do your homework?

We also use **do** with the adverb **not** to negate or deny the action of the verb.

I **do** not have a receding hairline.

It **does** not matter.

Brenda **did** not say that.

The main verb **do** may express completion, another idiomatic usage.

She **does** the crossword every day.

I **did** what I was told.

I have **done** this job.

In each of these three examples, **do** or one of its forms expresses a task accomplished or completed.

SHALL VS. WILL

Think back to the discussion of tenses. Remember that the future tenses require one of the auxiliary verbs **shall** or **will** as part of the verb construction. The choice is not an arbitrary one. **Shall** and **will** do serve different purposes, depending on what the speaker's intentions are.

SHALL

A speaker using **shall** in the **second** or **third person** obliges the subject of the sentence to complete the action of the verb.

She **shall** meet us here. (third person)

Because of the **shall**, you can bet that she will be here at the agreed-upon time.

You **shall** clean your room. (second person)

This is your mother speaking. Since she has used **shall**, you can be sure that the statement is more command than request.

In the **first person, shall** simply indicates future action without obligation.

I **shall** see you at the ball. (first person)

I **shall** accompany them to the Festival of the Harvest. (first person)

WILL

A speaker using **will** in the **first person** implies a certain strength of purpose in the action of the verb.

I **will** pass the test. (first person)

The word **will** in this sentence indicates that the speaker is determined to pass that test.

I **will** not fail.

Because of the **will**, it is clear that the speaker will stand for nothing less than success.

In the **second** and **third persons, will** simply communicates future action with no special strength of purpose.

You **will** love this movie. (second person)

They **will** follow my instructions to the letter. (third person)

MAY, CAN, AND MUST

My first grade teacher would not stand for the question "Can I go to the bathroom?" Any student unfortunate enough not to know the correct phrasing was met with an indignant reply. "I don't know. Can you?" The poor soul would stand flustered, possibly shifting from foot to foot, until he realized what needed to be said. "Oh. *May* I go to the bathroom?"

Though this used to annoy me to no end, my teacher was passing on a valuable lesson. We must choose our words carefully.

Meaning is specific, and even subtle differences can have important consequences. The word **can** is used in questions regarding ability. *Can* you finish your dinner? Are you able to finish your dinner? *Can* you come to the dance? Are you able to come to the dance? *Can* I go to the bathroom? The student's intention was not to question his ability to use the bathroom facilities. At that moment, he possessed an all-too-powerful capacity to complete the action.

Instead, the situation requires an auxiliary verb that involves permission. In the interrogative mood, **may** is such a verb. *May* I be excused? Will you grant me permission to be excused? *May* I go outside? Will you allow me to go outside? *May* I go to the bathroom? Will you give me permission to go to the bathroom?

The word **may** can carry other meanings as well. In the indicative mood, it can imply possibility. I *may* ask her to marry me. There is a possibility that I will ask her to marry me.

May, as part of an exclamation, can also express a wish or a hope. *May* all your Christmases be white! I wish that every one of your Christmases be white. *May* you live long and happy. I wish you a long and happy life.

Of course, the more direct student might have said, "I *must* use the bathroom." The word **must** denotes a life-or-death imperative. I *must* see the President. Our lives depend on my seeing the President. I *must* have a new outfit. I will not survive without a new set of clothes.

COULD, MIGHT, WOULD, AND SHOULD

Linguists choose to categorize their auxiliary verbs. While the resulting distinctions may not make much difference to the average English speaker, they are useful in an academic study of grammar, and one of those categories may help us to resolve a confusing issue involving four particular auxiliary verbs. The contemporary term for verbs in this category is **modal auxiliary**. These are the primary modals.

PRESENT TENSE	PAST TENSE
can	could
may	might
will	would

PRESENT TENSE	PAST TENSE
shall	should
must	had to
dare	dared
need	(no past tense form[†])
ought to	(no past tense form[†])
(no present tense form[††])	used to

A modal auxiliary verb indicates the subject's attitude toward the action of the verb. The modal auxiliaries **can** and **could** indicate the subject's ability to complete the action.

I **can** have those documents ready by Monday.

She **could** be here as early as eight o' clock this evening.

The modal auxiliaries **may** and **might** involve the subject's receiving permission to complete the action of the verb.

You **may** sharpen your pencil.

Might I ask you a question?

The modal auxiliaries **will** and **would** involve the subject's intention to complete the action of the verb.

She **will** move her car in the next ten minutes.

Otherwise, I **would** have paid you back.

The modal auxiliaries **shall, should**, and **ought to** indicate the subject's obligation or intention to complete the action of the verb. As an auxiliary, **ought** is always followed by **to**.

The knight **shall** slay the wicked beast.

I **should** leave now.

Bill **ought to** let us know his plans for the holidays.

The modal auxiliaries **must** and **had to** indicate the necessity of the subject's completing the action of the verb. As the past tense form of the modal auxiliary verb **must, had** is always followed by **to**.

I **must** get my hands on those plans.

We **had to** clean the pool.

[†] When **need** is used as a modal auxiliary verb, it does not have a past tense form. Neither does **ought to**. They are both auxiliaries of present urgency.

[††] As its **-ed** ending suggests, **used to** always denotes or describes habitual action or condition that existed only in the past, not in the present. Due to this semantic property, **used to** has no present tense form.

As modal auxiliaries, **dare**, **dared**, and **need** ask questions or express the intention of the subject not to complete the action of the verb.

> **Dare** we ask for more gruel?

> They **dared** not offend the Countess.

> **Need** I say more?

The modal auxiliary **used to** denotes an habitual action or condition that existed only in the past. Like **ought** and **had**, the modal auxiliary **used** is always followed by **to**.

> I **used to** race dachshunds.

> I **used to** be anemic.

A modal auxiliary verb may also indicate the possibility of an event.

> She **may** not be strong enough to speak.

> I **might** have known that you were behind those shenanigans.

> This **could** be the greatest night of my life.

> You **must** have known that we were planning some kind of surprise party.

> They **should** be here soon.

The confusing members of the modal auxiliary club are **could**, **might**, **would**, and **should**. A moment ago, you read that each of these is the past tense form of another modal auxiliary verb. Now, think about how you use each of these past tense forms. Does the action or being of the verb phrases of which these modals are parts necessarily occur in the past? No, it does not. Though we classify **could**, **might**, **would**, and **should** as past tense modal auxiliary verbs, we often use them to refer to time in the present and future. The tense of the modal auxiliary verb does not always correspond to the actual time spoken of in the real world.

> That guy **could** be your brother.

> I **might** be persuaded to change my mind.

> I **would** leave those bear cubs alone.

> You **should** visit the county fair this weekend.

On the other hand, we do use the modal auxiliaries in verb phrases that express action or condition in the past.

> You **could** have called me.

Ben **might** have lost his jacket.

Laura **would** never have agreed to that ridiculous plan.

I **should** have been paying better attention to the time.

If you are still feeling confused, don't worry. This is a confusing issue. The fault lies, in part, with the system itself. Grammar is only a model of language. Like any other model, it is useful for summarizing and explaining, but it falls short of encompassing the system as a whole. Creating a model that captures the language in its entirety would be like creating a life-size map of the world. Both products are of absolutely no use.

Take the time to reread the text and to ponder the issues. Take with you the information that enhances your personal grasp of the language, and leave behind that which gets in the way. And, if you can think of a better way to reconcile this dilemma or any other we might encounter, please let me know.

OFFENSIVE ENGLISH

Q. An erudite New Yorker called the Hot Line in horror and dismay about a sentence in a well-known national magazine. "Is this really correct? 'They treatied with us several years ago.' Can **treaty** be changed into a verb?"

A. This is just another example of the egregious modern proclivity to turn nouns into verbs. **Treatied** is not a legitimate word. The noun **treaty** has no corresponding verb form. The sentence should read, "They **negotiated** a treaty with us several years ago." There was a cartoon in *The New Yorker* recently. It depicted a CEO saying to his secretary, "I want this letter to look important. Change all the nouns to verbs."

Some say English is in a sorry state, and, quite often, I find it hard to disagree with them. People who find new ways to use words keep the language living and breathing, but the changes must enhance, not corrupt and oversimplify. Ever since the start of the Cold War, the military has been creeping through our televisions into our homes, and military-speak has followed right behind into our language. Most of this double-talk sounds awful, but as it enters popular usage, these words (or nonwords) become legitimized. **Surveil**, from **surveillance,** found its way into the diction-aries in 1949. I'm sure that George Orwell is spinning in his grave.

A Noun Becomes a Verb

Q. "Can the word **mentor** be used as a verb? Can I mentor a student?"

A. **Mentor** is usually a noun, but usage dictates acceptance. Given time, it just might become a verb. Of course, every mentor must have a protégé.

Contractions

English speakers are obsessed with brevity. Most of us are look-ing for the shortest possible way to express a complete thought, and, to this end, we have created the **contraction**. Many contrac-tions are abbreviated versions of verb phrases in the negative form. An apostrophe (') replaces the missing letters. A verb phrase in the negative form includes the word **not**. I have **not** seen the new building. Have you **not** seen enough?

The contraction combines the **not** and an auxiliary or linking verb into one word, replacing the **o** in **not** with an apostrophe.

is not → isn't	does not → doesn't
should not → shouldn't	have not → haven't

Please note that not every auxiliary contracts itself easily with **not**. Some require special manipulation to render the resulting contrac-tion easy-to-pronounce.

will not → won't (*not* willn't)	shall not → shan't (*not* shalln't)

We also contract certain verbs with pronouns and the verb **have** with some auxiliaries. The pronoun **I** can be contracted with the verbs **am** and **have**.

I am → I'm	I have → I've

The pronouns **you** (singular and plural), **we**, and **they** can be con-tracted with the verbs **are** or **have**.

you are → you're	we have → we've	they have → they've

The pronouns **he**, **she**, and **it** can be contracted with the verbs **is** and **has**.

he is → he's	she is → she's	it has → it's

The auxiliary verbs **might, should, could,** and **would** are often contracted with **have**.

might have → might've	should have → should've
could have → could've	would have → would've

Contractions may be appropriate and expeditious in casual writing, but they are to be avoided in more formal documents.

A RECURRING PROBLEM

Q. "My father really criticized me for using 'reoccur.' Is it a word?" asked a high school senior.

A. There is no such word as **reoccur**. The young man should have used the verb **recur**. I told him to surprise his father by using it correctly the next time.

TROUBLESOME VERBS

There are several pairs of verbs that are perpetually confused. Look at a few calls to the Hot Line that address these pairs.

LIE AND LAY

Q. "Would you like to go lay out on the beach?" a young man asked his girlfriend. The bright young woman promptly called our number to find out if her beau was using proper English.

A. Hunky as he may be, her man has fallen victim to the widespread Lie-Lay Problem. **Lie** means "to recline." It is intransitive and never takes an object. **Lay**, a transitive verb, means "to set down." It always takes a direct object, naming the thing that is set down. Since the two of them wish to recline on the sand, the young man should have asked her, "Would you like to go **lie** out on the beach?"

RAISE AND RISE

Q. "Chances of rain will raise tonite." This headline in a local newspaper bothered a young teacher and parent, so she called the Hot Line.

A. Obviously, **tonite** should be spelled **tonight**, but, even more disturbing is the use of **raise** instead of **rise**. **Raise**, a transitive verb, can only be done by someone to something.

The soldier **raises** the flag.

Rise, on the other hand, is an intransitive verb and can never affect something else.

The bread **rises**.

In the sentence the caller quoted, there is no object. Therefore, **rise** is the verb of choice.

Some newspapers, tabloids in particular, bastardize the language either for space reasons or to emphasize their editorial points. In mass media lingo, **doughnut** becomes **donut**, **borough** becomes **boro**, and **tickets** become **tix**. These are as unacceptable as the replacement **thru** is for **through**.

SIT AND SET

Q. "Why do **sit** and **set** often get confused?" asked a bowling instructor. "I am always instructing my students to 'set' a point on the alley where the ball is launched."

A. **Set** is a transitive verb, meaning "to place." It must be used with a direct object. In the caller's sentence, **point** is a direct object. Therefore, **set** is the correct verb to use. However, you could not say, "We set around all day." Instead, you would *sit* around all day. **Sit** is an intransitive verb meaning "to recline on the buttocks." The word **set** is used dialectically like **sit** in some parts of the South where folks might ask you to "set a spell."

BARE AND BEAR

Q. "What's the difference between the verbs **bare** and **bear**?" asked a caller.

A. **Bare**, whose principal parts are **bare**, **bared**, and **bared**, means "to show," "to open up," or "to disrobe."

The sunbather **bared** his hairy chest to the sky.

The president **bared** his guilty soul to the nation.

Bear, whose principal parts are **bear**, **bore**, and **borne**, means "to carry."

The old man **bore** his load courageously.

The child **has borne** her responsibilities well.

YOU SHOULD OF KNOWN BETTER.

One of the most egregious errors any English speaker can make is to replace the auxiliary **have** with the preposition **of** in a verb phrase.

INCORRECT	I should **of** seen it coming.
CORRECT	I should **have** seen it coming.
INCORRECT	Bob could **of** stopped on the way.
CORRECT	Bob could **have** stopped on the way.
INCORRECT	They might **of** seen the whole thing.
CORRECT	They might **have** seen the whole thing.

The error is a ridiculous one and easily avoidable. It occurs when a careless speaker contracts the auxiliary **have** with **could**, **might**, **should**, or **would**. Speaking rapidly, he fails to enunciate the **'ve** portion of the contraction, and a grammatically messy statement comes out.

The error feeds off itself when indiscriminate listeners hear an **of** in a hastily spoken verb phrase, assume it to be correct, and adopt it into their own speech and writing. Others then hear or read the mistake, and the circle of offenders grows. Only a rigorous approach to grammar can break this cycle.

 FROM MY FILES: PRAYER GRAMMAR

Occasionally, I get a call and cannot help but smile. This sweet twelve-year-old child called to ask about the verb **lay**. She explained that every night, before going to sleep, she recites this prayer:

Now I **lay** me down to sleep.
I pray the Lord my soul to keep.

If I should die before I wake,
I pray the Lord my soul to take.

Her seventh grade teacher had explained the difference be-tween the verbs **lie** and **lay** that day. The young lady asked me if **lay** was used correctly in the prayer. Her misgivings about its usage were apparent. As a present indicative verb, **lay** means "to place." It is also the past indicative form of the verb **lie**, which means "to recline." Her first inclination was to replace **lay** with **lie**, since the sleeper needs to lie down in the present to go to bed.

However, notice that the verb **lay** takes a direct object, **me**. The object, in this case, is the thing being laid down. The girl is stating that she is laying herself down. This is an odd way to describe going to bed, but it is not an incorrect one. The prayer's grammar is solid.

TEST YOUR KNOWLEDGE

Questions

1. Verbs express _____ , _____ ,

   or _____ .

2. The _____ joins the subject with a word or words

   in the predicate.

3. What is the final verb in the verb phrase called?

4. Which voice do grammarians prefer?

5. In which mood are verbs that express a condition contrary to fact?

6. In what tense is the verb in the sentence "I am running"?

7. What number verb is used in a sentence with singular subjects separated by **either-or**?

8. What is a direct object?

9. What is an indirect object?

10. Which verb takes a direct object, **rise** or **raise**?

(SEE ANSWERS ON FOLLOWING PAGE)

ANSWERS

1. action, existence, condition

2. linking verb

3. This verb is the principal or main verb.

4. Grammarians prefer the active voice, although the sciences sometimes demand the passive voice for the description of a process.

5. These verbs are in the subjunctive mood.

6. The verb phrase **am running** is in the present progressive tense.

7. Such a sentence needs a singular verb.

8. A direct object is the word that receives the action of the verb.

9. An indirect object is a noun or pronoun that precedes and receives the direct object.

10. **Raise**, a transitive verb, takes a direct object. **Rise**, an intransitive verb, does not.

3.

Adjectives

Adjectives are words that modify nouns or pronouns.

One task of language is to paint a picture. If verbs and nouns are outlines and shapes, then adjectives are colors and textures. Adjectives fall into a broad class of words called **modifiers**. A modifier is any word that acts to describe or qualify another word in such a way that it changes the other word's meaning. Describing and qualifying nouns and pronouns are the primary functions of adjectives.

Here is a simple example: "I watched a movie on television." This sentence is not terribly informative or inspirational because it lacks adjectives. To accurately describe the wonders of modern technology, we need to add some color: "I watched the **greatest action** movie of all time, *Star Wars*, on my **new, digitally-enhanced** television." The addition of the adjectives changes what we know of the nouns.

TYPES OF ADJECTIVES

There are two main flavors of adjective: **descriptive** and **limiting**.

DESCRIPTIVE ADJECTIVES

Descriptive adjectives describe the nouns and pronouns they modify. They point out color, shape, texture, scent or any other quality that entities named by nouns and pronouns can possess. This is the function of the adjective with which we are the most familiar.

> The **hot** pan burnt my fingers.
>
> I'll have a **tall** glass of lemonade.
>
> I am **thirsty**.

In the first example, the adjective **hot** describes the noun **pan**. In the second example, the adjective **tall** describes the noun **glass**. In the third example, the adjective **thirsty** describes the pronoun **I**.

Some of the descriptive adjectives are also **proper adjectives**, derived from proper nouns. Usually, the proper noun undergoes some mild change in form on its way to becoming an adjective. The proper noun **America** changes into the proper adjective **American**. The proper noun **Orwell** turns into the proper adjective **Orwellian**.

> **America** had no idea what one day would be **American**.
>
> **Orwell** imagined a bleak, **Orwellian** future.

Proper adjectives need to be capitalized as are the proper nouns in which they have their origins. If you have forgotten the capitalization rules, please refer back to Chapter 1, p. 5.

CHOOSING THE CORRECT ADJECTIVE

Q. "My boyfriend said to me, 'That is heaven.' Shouldn't he have said, 'That is heavenly'?" asked a young woman.

A. The young lady was, indeed, correct. **Heaven** is a noun. It names the place in which her boyfriend found himself. **Heavenly** is an adjective. It describes the feelings her boyfriend had. He should have said, "That is heavenly."

THE NATURE OF *MANIFEST*

Q. "Is **manifest** a verb or an adjective?" inquired a historian who frequented the Hot Line.

A. **Manifest** can be a verb or an adjective. As an adjective, it means "evident or obvious."

His destiny is **manifest**.

We discussed the **manifest** content of my dream.

As a verb, it means "to become obvious."

Her happiness **manifested** itself in her smile.

His curiosity **manifests** itself in his questions.

Be aware that there is another adjective, **manifestable**, derived from the verb.

His guilt was **manifestable** because of the strong evidence.

Your unconscious desires are **manifestable** under the therapist's tutelage.

Manifestable means "able to become obvious."

LIMITING ADJECTIVES

Limiting adjectives restrict the definitions of the nouns and pronouns they modify. The demonstrative pronouns we will see in Chapter 6 (p. 194) sometimes function as limiting adjectives because they point out certain objects from a group.

This dog is mine.

Which dog is mine? This dog is mine. Not that dog or that dog. That other dog over there isn't mine either. This dog here in front of me is mine. The demonstrative pronoun **this** limits the meaning of the noun **dog** by identifying it with a single animal.

Most standard limiting adjectives describe quantity. These include the numbers, **one**, **two**, **three**, etc., and assorted quantity words such as **half**, **double**, **daily**, and **weekly**, among others.

I found **five** dollars in my pocket.

I read the **daily** paper.

The adjective in the first example answers the question "How many dollars did I find?" The answer is "five dollars." The adjective **five** limits the meaning of the noun **dollars** by telling how many were found. Because of its influence, we know that five, and not one, ten, or twenty dollars, was found.

The adjective in the second example answers the question "What kind of paper do I read?" The answer is "a daily paper." The adjective **daily** limits the meaning of the noun **paper**. It tells us that the paper is the daily kind, not the biweekly, monthly, or yearly kind.

FROM MY FILES: POLITICALLY CORRECT GRAMMAR

I recently heard the mayor of a major American city speak about the battle raging between grammatical and political correctness. What are the differences between words or phrases that are politically correct and their grammatically correct counterparts? There need not be any differences at all. Speech can be both grammatically correct and socially aware. What identifications do you make with each of these pairs of labels: a blind Indian vs. a visually impaired Native American, a barmaid vs. a bartender, a third-world country vs. a developing nation, ignorant vs. educationally disadvantaged, a salesman vs. a salesperson, a chairman vs. a chair? The first in each pair is outdated and politically incorrect, whereas the second is sensitive, modern, *and* grammatically correct.

While it is important that our words show respect, we must not let our desire not to offend carry our speech to a ridiculous extreme. Author Sue Grafton twits political correctness in her book *L is for Lawless* by deliberately forming some strange constructions. She names a girl stewardperson instead of a stewardess, places a bellhuman in place of a bellboy, and asks that desks be "personed" instead of "manned." Whichever words you choose, be aware that they can elicit a smile or a frown.

DEGREES OF COMPARISON

The primary characteristic of the adjective is its lack of characteristics, its ease of use. Unlike nouns, pronouns, and verbs, which trouble us with form changes and gender and number and case and person, adjectives are a very static bunch. English, unlike almost all other languages, has smartly decided that modifiers should not be affected by those troublesome properties. The word **beautiful** remains the same whether it applies to a man or a woman, a boy or a girl, a dog or a cat, a car or a painting. So it is with the rest of the adjectives.

The one characteristic that adjectives do possess is that of comparison. Many times, it is necessary to express the degree of a quality that one object possesses in relation to other objects. We can manipulate the form of an adjective to express this relationship. There are three levels of comparison: **positive**, **comparative**, and **superlative**.

POSITIVE DEGREE

The positive degree, the adjective in its most basic form, indicates a lack of comparison. An adjective in the positive degree expresses the pure quality of an object without making a comparison with other objects.

The night is **warm**.

Anna's dress is **beautiful**.

Her **long** hair shimmers in the moonlight.

In each example, the adjective names a quality of a single object without making any comparison.

COMPARATIVE DEGREE

In the comparative degree, one object holds a greater or lesser degree of a quality than the object(s) with which it is compared. Often, this degree compares just two objects.

This house is **smaller** than that one.

This painting is **more beautiful** than that one.

The waves today are **less violent** than the ones yesterday.

In the first example, one house possesses the quality of smallness to a greater degree than another house. In the second example, one painting possesses a greater degree of beauty than another painting. In the final example, one set of waves is seen as possessing a lesser degree of violence than another set.

Comparison in the comparative degree is often created after the adjective by the conjunction **than**. This conjunction sets up the object or objects with which the main object is compared.

I think ice cream is tastier **than** cake.

Beth believes that movies are less enjoyable **than** books.

In the first example, **than** sets up a comparison between ice cream and cake. The adjective **tastier** modifies the noun **ice cream**. Ice cream possesses the quality of tastiness to a greater degree than cake does. In the second example, **than** sets up a comparison between movies and books. The adjective phrase **less enjoyable** modifies the noun **movies**. Movies possess the quality of enjoyability to a lesser degree than books do.

That the conjunction **than** is absent, however, does not mean that the sentence cannot contain adjectives in the comparative degree. Sometimes, **than** and the items of comparison that follow are implied. They are so obvious that they need not be mentioned.

I like **larger** cars **better**.

In this example, the speaker claims to prefer cars that possess a greater degree of largeness over cars that do not. We could have written the sentence in this way:

I like **larger** cars **better** than smaller cars.

As you can see, the additional information is not particularly illuminating. The sentence was fine without it. Other sentences are constructed to create the comparison without the word **than**.

The **juicier** the burger is, the **higher** the calories are.

The comparative degree is exclusive. The main object of comparison is seen as distinct from the objects to which it is compared by virtue of the different degree of its quality. It would be a mistake to say, "I enjoy swimming more than anything." Such a statement includes swimming in the group of objects being compared. The comparative degree is exclusive. Swimming is enjoyed more, so it must be separate. Such a sentence should read, "I enjoy swimming more than anything *else*." The addition of the word **else** separates swimming from the other objects.

SUPERLATIVE DEGREE

The superlative degree is the highest degree of comparison for adjectives. An object modified by an adjective in the superlative degree holds the greatest or least degree of the quality of that adjective. No object can possess a quality to a degree higher than the superlative. This degree compares more than two objects.

That was the **most disgusting** movie I have ever seen.

Theirs is the **largest** house in our city.

That was the **saddest** story I've ever heard.

Hers must be the **least believable** excuse I have ever received from a student.

In the first example, one movie possesses the most disgustingness of any movie seen by that movie-goer. In the second example, one house possesses the most largeness of any house in the city. In the third example, one story possesses the most sadness of any story heard by that listener. In the final example, one excuse possesses the least believability of any excuse the speaker has ever received.

The superlative degree often carries a prepositional phrase beginning with **of, among,** or **in,** to define the objects among which the comparison is made.

She is the most beautiful girl **in** the ballroom.

His story is the best **of** all the stories submitted.

In the first example, the preposition **in** begins the prepositional phrase **in the ballroom**. This phrase defines the area within which the comparison of all the girls was made. Of those girls in the ballroom, *she* was the most beautiful. In the second example, the preposition **of** begins the prepositional phrase **of the stories submitted**. The phrase defines the group of stories among which the selection of the best story was made. Of those stories, *his* story was the best.

The superlative degree is inclusive. It includes the main object in the total group of objects that is compared. It is perfectly reasonable to say, "I like swimming the best of anything." Since swimming is a part of the group of objects compared, we do not have to use a word such as **else** to create separation. Swimming is included.

FORMS OF COMPARISON

There are several ways to create the different comparison forms for adjectives. We will talk about each of them in turn.

SUFFIX COMPARISON

Most one-syllable and a few two-syllable adjectives have forms of comparison made by the addition of a suffix. To make the comparative form, add **-er** to the positive. To make the superlative form, add **-est** to the positive. The positive form itself requires no change.

DEGREES OF COMPARISON BY SUFFIX

POSITIVE	He is **angry**.
COMPARATIVE	He is **angrier** than she is.
SUPERLATIVE	He is **angriest** of them all.
POSITIVE	That shirt is **cheap**.
COMPARATIVE	That shirt is **cheaper** than this one.
SUPERLATIVE	That shirt is **cheapest** of them all.
POSITIVE	January is **rainy**.
COMPARATIVE	January is **rainier** than February.
SUPERLATIVE	January is **rainiest** of all the months.

Please notice that it is not always a simple matter to add the suffix. Most words require special changes to make the suffix stick. See Chapter 14 pp. 388–389 for information on spelling and suffixes.

ADVERB COMPARISON

Other adjectives, mostly multi-syllabled, require the addition of an adverb to create the forms of comparison. An adverb, as we will see in the next chapter, is a modifier that describes a verb, an adjective, or another adverb. The adverbs we need will precede the adjectives they modify. To create the comparative forms, use one of the adverbs **more** or **less**. To create the superlative forms, use one of the adverbs **most** or **least**. Again, the positive degree requires no change in form.

DEGREES OF COMPARISON BY ADVERB

POSITIVE	This is **bizarre**.
COMPARATIVE	This is more **bizarre**.
SUPERLATIVE	This is most **bizarre**.
POSITIVE	That is **dangerous**.
COMPARATIVE	That is more **dangerous** than this.
SUPERLATIVE	That is most **dangerous**.
POSITIVE	I feel **tranquil**.
COMPARATIVE	I feel more **tranquil**.
SUPERLATIVE	I feel most **tranquil**.

There is no set rule to follow that will let you know whether your adjective needs an adverb or a suffix to create the form of comparison. Some one-syllable words need an adverb. Some multi-syllable words may take a suffix. Your ear is the best judge. Use the version that sounds correct.

Please avoid redundancy in your forms of comparison. Never use a suffix and an adverb with a single adjective. One car is never more cheaper than another. It is simply cheaper. One joke is not the most funniest joke ever. It is simply the funniest. One modification of the adjective will suffice.

FORMING THE COMPARISON

Q. A high-ranking government official spouted, "We need more bolder approaches." A member of the press corps called to ask if the adverb **more** was necessary.

A. In order to determine whether **more** was used correctly, it would be necessary to see the punctuation. If a comma appears between **more** and **bolder**, then each describes the noun **approaches**. "We need more, bolder approaches." The politician is asking for approaches that are bolder and greater in frequency. His statement is correct.

Without a comma, **more** is redundant. The adjective **bolder** alone expresses the comparative degree of **bold**. It is sufficient unto itself and does not require the adverb **more**. Under this interpretation, the politician should have said," We need bolder approaches."

MUCH MORE SIMPLE VS. SIMPLER

Q. A member of the Presidential cabinet spoke a few weeks ago about taking some of the frills out of government. He stated, "Let's make this much more simple."

A. In the sentence, **much more simple** describes the pronoun **this. Much** is an adverb describing **more**. This cabinet member chose to use the adverb **more** to create the comparative form of the adjective **simple**. Couldn't he have used **simpler** instead? The sentence then would have read, "Let's make this much simpler." Either construction is grammatically correct, but the second is more concise and easier to comprehend.

STRICT, STRICTER, STRICTEST

Q. Often, a fine line separates the meaning of one word from another. A defense attorney called to ask for an interpretation of a sentence from a document that was crucial to her argument. The sentence read, "The information will be kept in stricter confidence." She asked, "What difference does the form of **strict** make to the sentence?"

A. All adjectives have three forms of comparison: the positive (**strict**), the comparative (**stricter**), and the superlative (**strictest**). The use of the comparative form, **stricter**, creates a weak construction. It tells us nothing about how strict the confidence is because we have nothing to compare it to. Is the confidence stricter than that kept by a man who shares information freely with anyone he meets on the street? If so, it may not be strict at all. Or is it stricter than the confidence kept by a tight-lipped Pentagon general? If so, it may be quite strict.

The author's intent probably was to indicate that the information would be put under the tightest security. He should have used either the positive or the superlative form. The sentence could read, "The information will be kept in the strictest confidence" or "The information will be kept in strict confidence." Both imply tight-lipped secrecy.

IRREGULAR COMPARISON

Other adjectives have forms of comparison that defy any attempt at formulization. These forms are irregularly compared. Their changes are case-specific, and you must memorize each in turn. Here is a partial list:

DEGREES OF IRREGULAR COMPARISON

POSITIVE	COMPARATIVE	SUPERLATIVE
bad	worse	worst
end	no form	endmost
far	farther/further	farthest/furthest
fore	former	foremost
good/well	better	best
no form	inner	inmost/innermost
late	later/latter	latest/last
little	less/lesser	least
many/much	more	most
mid	no form	midmost
old	older/elder	oldest/eldest
no form	outer	outmost/outermost
top	no form	topmost
no form	upper	upmost/uppermost

IRREGULAR DISTINCTIONS

Q. "What is the difference between the adjectives **farther** and **further**?" asked a sixth-grade teacher from Pennsylvania.

A. Some readers may have noticed that a few of the irregularly compared adjectives have different forms in the comparative and superlative degrees. One of these is the adjective **far**. The adjectives in the **far → farther → farthest** progression refer to physical distance.

> We reached the **farther** shore.

The adjectives in the **far → further → furthest** progression refer to a mental or physical distance.

> We drove the **furthest** distance that we could in a day. (physical distance)
>
> That is the **furthest** thing from my mind. (mental distance)

Other adjectives carry similar distinctions in their forms of comparison. The adjectives in the **old** → **older** → **oldest** progression refer to age.

I am **older** than my sister.

The adjectives in the **old** → **elder** → **eldest** progression also refer to age but with the implication of advanced age.

My **eldest** brother is in his eighties.

The adjectives in the **late** → **later** → **latest** progression refer to order in time.

The time is **later** than I thought.

The adjectives in the **late** → **latter** → **last** progression refer to a physical order in space.

Tom took the **last** flight home.

BETTER THAN BEST

Q. In a recent election, one party ran an advertisement that began with the line "The Incumbent vs. The Challenger: Who is Best?" Several callers asked if **best** was the correct form of comparison to use.

A. Since there are only two people contrasted here, the incumbent and the challenger, the spin doctors should have used the comparative form, **better**. "The Incumbent vs. The Challenger: Who is Better?" Superlative forms, such as **best**, are reserved for situations that compare three or more objects.

BAD, WORSE, WORST

Q. A sports enthusiast called to question a statement made by a star athlete. He said, "One of my favorite baseball players said, 'We're badder than them.' I know that **badder** is not correct, but what could he have said instead?"

A. The caller was correct. The statement needed work. The forms of comparison for the adjective **bad** are **bad** → **worse** → **worst**. There is no word **badder**. Taking proper form and intended meaning into account, he should have said, "We are *better* than they are."

The National Grammar Hot Line recognizes that **bad, badder**, and **baddest** are slang for "terrific or wonderful," the exact opposite of the literal definitions of the words. The athlete was not trying to say that his team was worse than the opposition. Most slang is faddish, and some may become acceptable parts of the lexicon, but avoid it until it is.

ADJECTIVES BEYOND COMPARISON

A number of adjectives are beyond comparison. The qualities that these adjectives express exist in only one degree. To compare objects according to one of these qualities creates a moot point since all objects with the quality possess it to an equal degree. Here is a partial list of uncomparable adjectives:

absolute	final	square
alone	full	supreme
blind	eternal	straight
circular	incomparable	total
complete	instantaneous	ultimate
dead	mortal	unique
deadly	perfect	universal
empty	perpendicular	vertical
fatal	single	wrong

How can one line be more perpendicular than another or the most perpendicular of all lines? There is but one degree of perpendicularity, and, to this degree, all things perpendicular are equal. In the same way, one accident cannot be more fatal than another. Their consequences are identical. They have both caused death. These adjectives and others like them are beyond comparison.

Please note that this uncomparability applies to these adjectives under their strictest definitions. English is a flexible language to say the least, and many people, expressing themselves in a creative way, have uttered one of these adjectives in the comparative or superlative degree. A grief-stricken man might say, "I have never felt **more alone** than I do now." A flea market shopper, using the adjective **unique** to mean "unusual or distinct," could say, "This is the **most unique** lamp I have ever seen." These sentences contain uncomparable adjectives in comparative and superlative forms. Often, the speaker's intention is to indicate that one object more closely approximates the perfect state described by the adjective than another. We normal speakers are allowed this same poetic license, but take care that each usage is a sensible one.

LESS OR FEWER

Q. "How can I keep **less** and **fewer** straight? I always confuse them, and I don't understand the difference," stated an irritable copywriter.

A. Both words are adjectives. **Less** modifies nouns that name a whole or a collection but are singular in number. **Fewer** modifies nouns that name a number of separate objects and are plural. For instance, one would have **less** knowledge but **fewer** facts, **less** time but **fewer** minutes, **less** heat but **fewer** fires, **less** congestion but **fewer** cars, **less** traffic but **fewer** accidents, and **less** inclement weather but **fewer** storms.

POSITIONING THE ADJECTIVE

The conscientious grammarian needs to know where to place his or her adjectives. An adjective can either precede or follow the noun that it modifies, depending upon a number of factors which we will now consider.

TYPICAL USAGE

Adjectives typically precede the nouns that they modify.

My **tired** feet need a massage.

The birds' calls blended into a **sweet** song.

I appeal to your **keen** intellect.

In the first example, the adjective **tired** precedes the noun modified, **feet**. In the second example, the adjective **sweet** precedes the noun modified, **song**. In the third example, the adjective **keen** precedes the noun modified, **intellect**.

SPECIAL USAGE

Some adjectives are placed after the nouns they modify for no discernible reason. This is merely the way it is done. For instance, we speak of a notary public, a court martial, and an attorney general. The adjective **public** describes the noun **notary**, the adjective **martial** describes the noun **court**, and the adjective **general** describes the noun **attorney**. Typical adjective usage suggests that we say "public notary" or "martial court" or "general attorney," but actual usage dictates otherwise. These instances you must learn on a case-by-case basis.

EMPHATIC USAGE

Place the adjective after the noun modified to emphasize the qualities described by the adjective.

A man, **old** and **wise**, gave me these instructions.

Can you hear the emphasis that the alternative placement puts on the adjectives **old** and **wise**? Their position highlights the man's age and wisdom. The sentence could just as well read, "An old, wise man gave me these instructions." But such a construction removes the emphasis from the adjectives.

USAGE AS OBJECT COMPLEMENTS

Adjectives that serve as object complements follow the direct objects that they modify.

Have you heard anything **new**?

I asked you to bring something **blue**.

We found her **tiresome**.

That made me **hungry**.

In the first example, the adjective **new** is the object complement of the direct object **anything**. In the second example, the adjective **blue** is the object complement of the direct object **something**. In the third example, the adjective **tiresome** is the object complement of the direct object **her**. In the fourth example, the adjective **hungry** is the object complement of the direct object **me**.

USAGE AS SUBJECT COMPLEMENTS

Adjectives used as subject complements must follow linking verbs and so, by necessity, follow the nouns and pronouns that they modify.

My feet are **cold**.

The cat looks **frightened**.

The milk smells **rotten**.

In the first example, the adjective **cold** follows the linking verb **are** and complements the noun **feet**. In the second example, the adjective **frightened** follows the linking verb **looks** and complements the noun **cat**. In the third example, the adjective **rotten** follows the linking verb **smells** and complements the noun **milk**.

MISPLACED MODIFIER

Q. A chuckling newspaper editor called to tell me about an ad that was to appear in the next day's edition. The ad read, "Huge Fan Sale!"

A. Whoa! Those are some big fans! I wondered exactly how large the devices were. So did he. We generally assume that an adjective describes the noun it is nearest to. In this case, the adjective **huge** is nearest to the noun **fan**. It appears that **huge** modifies **fan**, but the meaning is quite absurd. Who ever heard of a sale of oversized fans? **Huge** actually modifies the noun **sale**. Corrected, the ad should read, "Huge Sale of Fans."

In a similar grammar gaffe, I was recently offered a hot cup of coffee. I refused, fearing that it might burn my fingers, and, instead, asked for a cup of hot coffee. Take care that you don't misplace your modifier.

SOME OTHER THINGS TO REMEMBER ABOUT ADJECTIVES

Please pay careful attention to these additional adjective issues.

NOUNS AS ADJECTIVES

English speakers often use nouns in such a way that they modify other nouns. In these cases, the nouns function as adjectives.

My father built a **log** cabin in the woods.

The outlaw stepped through the **saloon** door.

Our **tile** roof is leaking.

The words **log**, **saloon**, and **tile** are nouns, but they function in these sentences as adjectives. **Log** modifies **cabin**. It indicates what kind of cabin was built. **Saloon** modifies **door**. It describes what kind of door was stepped through. **Tile** modifies **roof**. It explains what kind of roof was leaking.

Possessive case nouns frequently function as adjectives while retaining their ability to show possession.

My **sister's** car was stolen.

Bob's painting is beautiful.

In the first example, the possessive noun **sister's** modifies **car**. It indicates whose car was stolen. In the second example, the possessive noun **Bob's** modifies **painting**. It tells whose painting is beautiful. Each of these examples shows a typical noun working at the job of an adjective.

DESCRIBING A SALES POSITION

Q. "Should I be called 'Northwest Regional Manager' or 'Northwestern Regional Manager'?" asked a newly-promoted executive.

A. There are several directions in which to go. **Northwest** is a noun. As you know, nouns can be used as adjectives, and this noun is in the title **Northwest Regional Manager**. **Northwestern**, on the other hand, is an adjective and can describe a noun such as **manager** in the title **Northwestern Regional Manager**. With the same adjective, we could also use the title **Northwestern Region Manager**, where **Northwestern** describes the noun **region**. Any one is acceptable. An oddity to note: Northwestern University in Evanston, Illinois, is not in the northwestern portion of the country at all but was in the Northwest Territory when the school opened in 1851.

UNGRAMMATICALLY PLEASANT

Q. A realtor questioned a description he had written of a house. He asked, "Is it OK for me to write, 'Two story house for sale.' "

A. Since there are two *stories* to this house, the description should read, "Two stories house for sale." There are two, so the noun **story** must be plural. Of course, "two story house" is colloquial. Through common usage, it has become an accepted and agreeable construction, but it is not correct. As much as I wanted to instruct the realtor to use the version with proper grammar, I could not do so in good conscience. A man who wants to sell houses needs to please his customers. Here, it is the ungrammatical version that pleases most ears.

Overused Adjectives

Q. A troubled high school sophomore called with this to say: "My English teacher marks me down for using certain words in my papers. If I say something is 'nice' or 'funny,' she takes points off, and I'm ending up with too many C's. They seem like okay words. Why is she doing this to me?"

A. This young man's teacher and I must share a pet peeve. I am continually being irked by word choices such as the ones this fellow has just described. Too many speakers and writers make annoyingly uninformative adjective choices. Adjectives such as **nice** or **cute** are used in so many different contexts that their presence tells us nothing about the nouns that they modify. I may mention that we had a **nice** afternoon or that she was wearing a **cute** dress, but have I revealed anything interesting? No, I have not. If I had been thinking, I would have mentioned our **wonderful** afternoon and her **stunning** dress. Now *that* is information. These adjectives better communicate the meanings desired. Some other overused adjectives are **cute, funny, good, great**, and the currently popular **awesome**.

Do not be overzealous in your use of adjectives either. Over-description, redundancy, and ambiguity have ruined many a fine sentence. Be wise in your choices. Select only those adjectives that truly add color or flavor to your words and leave the remainder of the description to context.

The prevailing literary posture, which has existed since pen was first put to paper and still exists today, that nouns and verbs should carry the action and that the overuse of adjectives weakens prose, is one that Ernest Hemingway took seriously. To be sure that he didn't overuse adjectives, he often took his writings to the poet Ezra Pound for proofing. Despite his vigilance, Hemingway couldn't do without adjectives entirely. In fact, he used seven in the first two sentences of his novel *A Farewell to Arms*.

"In the **late** summer of that year we lived in a house in a village that looked across the river and the plain to the mountains. In the bed of the river there were pebbles and boulders, **dry** and **white** in the sun, and the water was **clear** and swiftly **moving** and **blue** in the channels."

ANOTHER MISUSE

Q. "I heard a famous defense lawyer say, 'I need to concise this.' Can you change an adjective into a verb like this?" asked a caller.

A. **Concise** is an adjective. It is not a verb. One cannot *concise* anything. The attorney could have asked his aid to make this concise, whatever "this" was. Famous or not, the attorney gets an "F" in grammar.

DETERMINERS

Grammar is by no means cut and dry. As depth of understanding increases, the old, familiar ways of approaching a topic become inadequate and the need for new principles arises. At the beginning of the chapter, we discussed a class of adjectives called **limiting adjectives**. While this category is certainly descriptive of the functions of its members, there is a more sophisticated way of viewing these words. Modern grammarians define a class of words called **determiners**. A determiner is a word that determines the reference of a noun phrase. The category of determiners includes the articles, **a, an,** or **the;** the demonstrative pronouns, **this, that, those,** or **these;** the possessive pronouns, such as **my, her,** or **their;** and the interrogative pronouns, such as **who, which,** or **what;** among others (please see Chapter 6 for more information on demonstrative, possessive, and interrogative pronouns). Words of this type aid the reader or listener in determining which person, place, thing, or idea is named by the noun phrase that the writer or speaker has written or spoken.

I sat on **the** porch.

This idea is not a good one.

She left **her** coat at the skating rink.

Which movie did you decide to see?

In the first example, the article **the** is a determiner that modifies the noun **porch**. In the second example, the demonstrative pronoun **this** is a determiner that modifies the noun **idea**. In the third example, the possessive pronoun **her** is a determiner that modifies the noun **coat**. In the fourth example, the interrogative pronoun **which** is a determiner that modifies the noun **movie**.

Number or quantity words, such as **one**, **all**, **third**, or **three-fifths**, also function as determiners. These determiners are often used in conjunction with other determiners so that two or more precede the noun modified.

Buddy drank **all the** milk.

The runners have completed **the first three** laps.

In the first example, **all** and **the** are determiners that modify the noun **milk**. In the second example, **the**, **first**, and **three** are determiners that modify the noun **laps**.

When using number words, it is important to keep the difference between **cardinal numbers** and **ordinal numbers** in mind. Cardinal numbers are counting numbers. They express absolute number without any implication of position. The following is a brief list of cardinal numbers:

one	thirty-two	one million	one quintillion
five	seventy-eight	one billion	one sextillion
nine	one hundred	one trillion	one septillion
fourteen	one thousand	one quadrillion	one decillion

The ordinal numbers, on the other hand, are position numbers. They correspond to the cardinal numbers but indicate position in relation to other numbers. The ordinal numbers all carry a suffix: **nd**, **rd**, **st**, or **th**. The following is a brief list of ordinal numbers.

first	thirty-second	one millionth	one quintillionth
fifth	seventy-eighth	one billionth	one sextillionth
ninth	one hundredth	one trillionth	one septillionth
fourteenth	one thousandth	one quadrillionth	one decillionth

When a cardinal number and an ordinal number modify the same noun, the ordinal number always precedes the cardinal number.

The **first two** operations were the most difficult to watch.

The **second three** innings were quite dull.

In the first example, the ordinal number **first** precedes the cardinal number **two**. Both **first** and **two** are determiners. In the second example, the ordinal number **second** precedes the cardinal number **three**. Both **second** and **three** are determiners. Try reading the sentences with the ordinal and cardinal numbers reversed. They simpy sound wrong.

APPROACHING INFINITY

Q. "What is the largest counting number word that you have ever heard of?" asked an elementary school math teacher from Phoenix, Arizona.

A. The largest word for a cardinal number or counting number that I've heard of is the word **googolplex**. One **googol** is ten raised to the power of one hundred or 10^{100}. One googolplex is 10 raised to the power of googol:

$$10^{10^{100}}.$$

To write this number the long way, you would write a numeral **1** followed by a googol of **0**s. Believe me, it's not worth it. This is an inconceivably large number.

ARTICLES

Our discussion of determiners would not be complete without mention of **articles**. This class has only three members: **a, an**, and **the**. Their function is to determine the references of nouns. Traditionally, the trio has been included among adjectives, but contemporary grammarians have begun viewing articles as a separate part of speech and include them among the category of words called **determiners**[†]. The function of an article, after all, is to limit, point out, or *determine* a noun.

POSITIONING ARTICLES

In most cases, the article directly precedes the noun that it determines or modifies.

An alligator crawled from **the river**.

The baby cried for **an hour**.

[†] Remember! A **determiner** is a word that determines the reference of a noun phrase.

A woman left **the package an hour** ago.

Sometimes, however, a modifier or a series of modifiers will separate the article and the noun.

A tall, dark **stranger** walked into **the** cluttered **office**.

The smaller **version** is **a** better **bargain**.

INDEFINITE AND DEFINITE ARTICLES

There are two types of articles: **indefinite** and **definite**. The indefinite articles are **a** and **an**. We use **a** before words that begin with consonant sounds: **a house, a car, a motorcycle, a brilliant scientist**. We use **an** before words that begin with vowel sounds: **an airplane, an umbrella, an exit, an admirable goal**. These articles are indefinite because they do not point to any noun in particular. When we speak of "a destination," we aren't speaking of any destination in particular. Similarly, if we write of "an idea," we don't have any specific idea in mind.

Determining which indefinite article to use is not as simple as seeing whether the following word begins with a consonant or a vowel. The article **an** sometimes precedes words that begin with a consonant but that are pronounced with an initial vowel sound: **an honor, an hour**. The article **a** sometimes precedes words that begin with a vowel but that are pronounced with an initial consonant sound: **a unicorn, a unit**. Both of these words begin with the /y/ sound in y$\overline{oo}$. A few words are pronounced with either an initial consonant or an initial vowel sound: **a** or **an history, a** or **an hotel**. In these cases, choose the article that fits your pronunciation.

The definite article **the**, on the other hand, points to particular people, places, things, and ideas. When we speak of "the dog," we are referring to one dog in particular. When we say "the closet," there is only one closet that we could mean. We use the definite article when we are certain that the reader or listener knows which person, place, thing, or idea the noun names.

The man you just mentioned stopped by.

The car is in the garage.

In the first example, we use the definite article **the** with the noun **man** because the individual named by the noun has already been mentioned. In the second example, we use the definite article **the** with the noun **car** because this particular car is so familiar to the person or people to whom the sentence is directed that it needs no other identification.

The pronunciation of the definite article changes, depending upon the initial sound of the word that it precedes. If the word begins with a consonant sound, the **e** in **the** is pronounced "uh": **the** (thuh) **ball, the** (thuh) **bat.** If the word begins with a vowel sound, the **e** makes a long vowel sound like in **sweet: the** (thee) **automobile, the** (thee) **exorcist.**

AN ARTICLE QUESTION

Q. One perturbed caller commented, "If the President doesn't know the right word, how should we know it? As a highly educated person, shouldn't the country's leader know his grammar? I heard him say 'an historic event' at a press conference."

A. The caller should have kept his pants on. The President could have been correct. **Historic** is a word with two pronunciations. In certain regional dialects, the **h** can be silent, so that the word is pronounced "istoric," or the **h** can be vocalized in standard pronunciation, so that the word begins with a strong, breathy /**h**/ sound, "historic." In the former case, the word begins with a vowel sound, so the article needed is **an.** In the latter case, the word begins with a consonant sound, so the article needed is **a.** I'm guessing that the President chose the former option and used the correct article.

Folks, the **a-an** distinction exists only to make our lives easier, not to confuse us. Try saying "a inner tube" out loud. It's awkward. Now use the correct article, **an.** The words flow smoothly. We use the article that allows us to speak in an easier manner. The President selected the option that worked the best for him.

ARTICLES AND ABBREVIATIONS

Q. Should I put **a** or **an** before our company's abbreviation?" asked an executive secretary. "The abbreviation is S.P.U."

A. The rule dictates that **a** precedes words that begin with a consonant sound and that **an** precedes words that begin with a vowel sound. The answer to the question depends on how one says the company's name. If each letter is pronounced, then the first sound in the letter **s** is a vowel sound (the short /e/ sound in ĕs). The article **an** would be appropriate: an S.P.U. If one pronounces the three letters as a single word (spoo, perhaps), then the first sound is a consonant sound. The article **a** would be appropriate: a S.P.U.

EUCHARIST

Q. "Should **a** or **an** be used before **Eucharist**?" asked a church member.

A. Although the noun **Eucharist** begins with a vowel, it is pronounced with an initial consonant sound, the /y/ sound in yo͞o. Therefore, we say, "*a* Eucharist." We make the same choice with words such as **unicorn** and **eunuch**. By the way, the term **Eucharist** refers to the sacrament of Holy Communion and to the sacred elements of Holy Communion, the bread and wine, in the Christian Church.

ADJECTIVES, ARTICLES, AND NOUNS

Q. A businessman called with an intriguing question. He asked, "What happens to an adjective when you put an article in front of it? I was watching TV with my kids and the announcer said that they would be broadcasting 'a special' shortly. **Special** is an adjective in the dictionary, but it was being used like a noun on TV."

A. This fellow's consternation was understandable. We often see words that we associate with one part of speech used as other parts of speech. In this case, the word **special**, which we typically associate with adjectives, was being used as a noun. Its unusual function was due to the presence of the article before it.

Each article possesses the amazing ability to transform an adjective into a noun. Place **a**, **an**, or **the** in front of an adjective and suddenly it has the effect of a noun in the sentence. We see **a Western** at the movies, and we watch **a special** on television. We attend **a spectacular** at the local civic arena, and, at baseball games, we sing of the land of **the free** and the home of **the brave**. Doctors treat **the sick**, humanitarians help **the poor**, and Catherine **the Great** ruled Russia. The words **Western**, **special**, **spectacular**, **free**,

brave, **sick**, **poor**, and **Great** (an epithet) are all adjectives doing the jobs of nouns, thanks to articles.

FROM MY FILES: THE EVOLUTION OF NICE

Few words have gone through as many changes as the adjective **nice**. Through the years, **nice** has meant "silly," "simple," "ignorant," "foolish," "wanton," and even "lascivious." Old French lent the word to English in the thirteenth century when it meant "silly" or "simple." It was based on the Latin, **nescius**, meaning "ignorant," from **nescire**, "to be ignorant." Obviously, there has been an extreme shift since then!

At first, the English meaning was the same as the French with a shade of "stupid" or "foolish." In the fourteenth century, the meaning of **nice** changed to "wanton," and even "indecent" or "lewd." In the fifteenth century, **nice** acquired the sense of "coy" and "shy," but all of these meanings are now obsolete.

In the sixteenth century came a shift in connotation to "sensitive, critical discernment," as in "a nice distinction" or "a nice piece of craftsmanship." This Renaissance meaning lasted until the eighteenth century, when it finally evolved into the modern **nice**, meaning "pleasing," "agreeable," or "delicately discriminating."

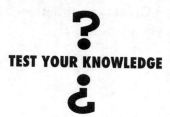

TEST YOUR KNOWLEDGE

QUESTIONS

1. Adjectives describe _____ or _____.

2. Which type of adjective restricts the definition of the word it modifies?

3. Are proper adjectives capitalized?

4. Where are adjectives that modify pronouns placed?

5. Where would you place an adjective to emphasize it?

6. Is the superlative degree exclusive or inclusive?

7. What are the two primary ways of creating the forms of comparison?

8. Why is it inappropriate to use the adjective **vertical** in the comparative or superlative degrees?

9. What is the difference between cardinal and ordinal numbers?

10. Is it correct to say "a universe" or "an universe"?

(SEE ANSWERS ON FOLLOWING PAGE)

ANSWERS

1. nouns, pronouns

2. The limiting adjectives restrict definitions.

3. Proper adjectives are always capitalized.

4. Adjectives follow the pronouns they modify.

5. Place the adjective after the noun for emphasis.

6. The superlative degree is inclusive.

7. Create the forms of comparison by adding a suffix (**-er/-est**) or an adverb (**more/less, most/least**).

8. **Vertical** is superlative by definition.

9. Cardinal numbers are counting numbers. Ordinal numbers are position numbers.

10. Since the word **universe** begins with a consonant sound, "a universe" is the correct choice.

4.

Adverbs

> **Adverbs** are words that modify verbs, adjectives, or other adverbs.

Adjectives are not the only modifiers in the world of grammar. Just as nouns and pronouns sometimes require description, so do verbs and adjectives. For this descriptive purpose, language includes adverbs. Adverbs modify verbs, adjectives, and even other adverbs. As modifiers of verbs, they indicate when, where, how, or how often an action is performed.

They'll arrive **soon**. (when)

Put the flowers **here**. (where)

She dances **awkwardly**. (how)

Cynthia travels **frequently**. (how often)

In the first example, the adverb **soon** modifies the verb **arrive**. It tells when the arrival will occur. In the second, the adverb **here** modifies the verb **put**. It tells where the flowers should be placed. In the third, the adverb **awkwardly** modifies the verb **dances**. It tells how she dances. In the final example, the adverb **frequently** modifies the verb **travels**. It tells how often Cynthia travels.

As you now know, adverbs do not modify only verbs. They also describe adjectives and other adverbs.

Kareem Abdul Jabar is **extremely** tall.

Anthony sings **quite** exquisitely.

In the first example, the adverb **extremely** modifies the adjective **tall**. It indicates how tall Kareem is. In the second example, the adverb **quite** modifies the adverb **exquisitely**. It indicates how exquisite Anthony's singing is. Incidentally, the adverb **exquisitely** modifies the verb **sings**. It tells how Anthony sings.

AN ADVERB QUESTION

Q. An editor of a dictionary was writing its foreword. He called about the sentence "The world is a much different place from what it was fifty years ago." The editor asked, "What do you think of the use of **much** in the sentence? I think it sounds funny."

A. I see no problem with the use of the word **much**. The word **different** is an adjective, describing **place**, a noun. The word **much**, an adverb, modifies **different**, an adjective. Each of the parts of speech is in its proper place.

The phrase **much different** may look or sound strange to some readers, although it is grammatically correct. **Much** is an adverb and has been since the thirteenth century when it came into being. Therefore, **much** can describe **different**. If your ears still resist, try **very different** or **extremely different**. Both **very** and **extremely** are also adverbs, capable of modifying an adjective such as **different**.

ANOTHER ADVERB QUESTION

Q. "Is **interesting enough** or **interestingly enough** correct?" asked one caller.

A. Either one will work, depending on how you use the words. Many people use the phrase **interestingly enough** as an introductory expression. In this context, **enough** is an adverb modifying another adverb, **interestingly**.

Interestingly enough, the burglars were never caught.

We can also use the phrase **interesting enough** in a grammatically correct sentence.

The book was **interesting enough** to attract the attention of the censor.

In this context, **interesting** is an adjective modified by the adverb **enough**.

YET ANOTHER ADVERB QUESTION

Q. One caller heard a radio personality say, "It took twenty years to evolve this highly." He asked, "Has the announcer used **highly** in the right way? I think he has, but I need some validation."

A. The radio personality did use **highly**, an adverb, in the correct way. It describes the infinitive **to evolve**. Since infinitives are forms of verbs, they can be modified by adverbs.

However, the sentence falls short of squeaky clean. The adverb **highly** is modified by the demonstrative pronoun **this**. Grammar allows us to use pronouns to modify nouns or other pronouns. An adverb requires an adverb modifier. Let's change **this** to **so**. The announcer could have said, "It took twenty years to evolve *so* highly."

CREATING ADVERBS

Q. "Do I just need to add **-ly** to an adjective to change it into an adverb?" asked an inquiring seventh-grader.

A. The adverbs we know the best are those ending in **-ly**, and most of these are based on adjectives. We add **-ly** to these adjectives and the result is an adverb (adjective + **-ly** → adverb). Note that for those adjectives ending in **y**, change the **y** to **i** before adding **-ly**.

angry → angrily	magnificent → magnificently
awkward → awkwardly	numb → numbly
careful → carefully	petulant → petulantly
clever → cleverly	ready → readily
crazy → crazily	sober → soberly
fanciful → fancifully	strange → strangely
final → finally	sure → surely
fond → fondly	thoughtful → thoughtfully
greedy → greedily	truthful → truthfully
indignant → indignantly	wise → wisely

However, not every adjective has an adverb counterpart. There is no word **bigly** based on **big** and no word **tinily** based on **tiny**, but there is **sillily** based on **silly**.

Do watch out for adverbs that do not end in **-ly** at all. They are their own words without origins in the world of adjectives. Here are a few examples: again, away, now, quite, seldom, then, too, very. This list is by no means complete, and, if ever in doubt, you should consult your dictionary. It is the definitive source for identifying parts of speech.

ADJECTIVES ENDING IN -LY

Q. The same young man called back the next day and asked, "What about **lovely**? That's an adjective, isn't it?"

A. This fellow had made another excellent point. The wary grammarian must never let his or her guard down. There are several adjectives that end in **-ly**: homely, lonely, lovely, manly, womanly. These are adjectives and adjectives only. Please note that this list is not complete.

ADJECTIVE OR ADVERB?

Q. A teacher at a Portland elementary school asked, "Is **early** an adjective or an adverb?"

A. You must be careful with the modifier **early**. It is both an adjective *and* an adverb. Here are a few more words that can be either adjectives or adverbs: cowardly, deep, early, friendly, hard, kindly, leisurely, lively, long, loud, only, and timely.

> We stopped at Bob's Pancake House for an **early** lunch. (adjective)
>
> We rose **early**. (adverb)
>
> The band played a **lively** tune. (adjective)
>
> Step **lively**, soldiers! (adverb)

HARD VS. HARDLY

Q. An English major at a Colorado college asked, "What is the difference between the words **hard** and **hardly**?"

A. The caller was wondering about the difference between the *adverbs* **hard** and **hardly**. Remember that **hard** can also be an adjective. It is easy to think that **hardly**, the adverb form of the adjective **hard**, retains the implication of rigidity or diligence of the adjective.

In fact, the definitions of the two words in question are quite different. As an adverb, **hard** means "firmly or diligently."

The novice skier fell **hard**.

Jennifer thought **hard** on the matter.

The adverb **hardly** usually means "barely or scarcely."

I **hardly** know her.

The mirror was **hardly** scratched.

Hardly can be used to mean "firmly or diligently," but the usage is rare. For this purpose, we most often use the shorter version, **hard**.

CATEGORIES OF ADVERBS

According to what meanings they convey, adverbs can fall into one of a number of general categories. Please note that the word lists that follow each category title are only partial ones.

Time: again, early, never, now, often, soon, then, today, tomorrow

The plane landed five minutes **early**.

Our ship will come in **soon**.

Location or **direction**: above, away, below, down, here, in, inside, out, there, up

The sound intensity rose **above** my threshold of pain.

We plan to stop **here** for the night.

Manner: cheerfully, cunningly, fast, quickly, right, slowly, well

The tortoise moves **slowly**.

The fox hunts **cunningly**.

Degree: almost, entirely, little, much, rather, too, very

I am **almost** certain that she will be there.

There are **too** many bagel shops in my neighborhood.

Reason: so, why

>   I don't think **so**.
>
>   **Why** did she say that?

Number: first, once, second, twice, third, thrice

>   We were here **first**.
>
>   I will only say this **once**.

Lot

Q. A travel agent asked, "What kind of word is **lot**? Someone asked me, 'Are a *lot* more Californians traveling this year?' It got me thinking, and I wanted to find out."

A. **Lot** is usually a noun, meaning "a large amount," "one's fortune," or "a share."

>   My uncle has a **lot** of money.
>
>   Accept your **lot** in life.
>
>   I inherited the **lot** on the corner.

Lot can also be used as an adverb in sentences such as the one our travel agent offered. There, it means "very many." In her sentence, the adjective **more** modifies the noun **Californians**. The adverb **lot** modifies **more**.

DEGREES OF COMPARISON

Like adjectives, adverbs are a simple bunch. They do not trouble us with gender, number, person, or case issues. These properties do not command confusing form changes in adverbs.

Adverbs do change with comparison. Like adjectives, they have three forms of comparison: **positive**, **comparative**, and **superlative**. The functions and characteristics of each category are the same as they were for the adjectives. The positive degree expresses the quality without comparison. The comparative degree compares two verbs, adjectives, or adverbs. The superlative degree compares three or more verbs, adjectives, or adverbs. Please refer back to Chapter 3, pp. 100–103 if a review is necessary.

Adjectives and adverbs are compared by the same methods. The forms of comparison for adverbs can be created by using a suffix or an adverb.

ADVERB COMPARISON

Most adverbs are compared by using another adverb. Use **more** or **less** for the comparative forms and **most** or **least** for the superlative forms.

DEGREES OF COMPARISON BY ADVERB

POSITIVE	He behaves **capriciously**.
COMPARATIVE	He behaves more **capriciously** than she.
SUPERLATIVE	He behaves most **capriciously**.
POSITIVE	They dance **gracefully**.
COMPARATIVE	They dance more **gracefully** than we.
SUPERLATIVE	They dance most **gracefully**.
POSITIVE	Judy sings **horribly**.
COMPARATIVE	Judy sings more **horribly** than Bob.
SUPERLATIVE	Judy sings most **horribly**.

SUFFIX COMPARISON

There are a few adverbs that are compared by using a suffix. Use **-er** for the comparative forms and **-est** for the superlative forms. These appear identical to their adjective counterparts, but, as adverbs, they are different in function.

DEGREES OF COMPARISON BY SUFFIX

POSITIVE	We left **early**.
COMPARATIVE	We left **earlier** than they.
SUPERLATIVE	We left **earliest**.
POSITIVE	Tom drives **fast**.
COMPARATIVE	Tom drives **faster** than I.
SUPERLATIVE	Tom drives **fastest**.
POSITIVE	Betty will arrive **soon**.
COMPARATIVE	Betty will arrive **sooner** than Sheila.
SUPERLATIVE	Betty will arrive **soonest**.

IRREGULAR COMPARISON

There are a number of adverbs compared irregularly. These, you must learn case by case.

DEGREES OF IRREGULAR COMPARISON

POSITIVE	COMPARATIVE	SUPERLATIVE
badly	worse	worst
far	farther/further	farthest/furthest
fore	former	foremost/first
late	later	latest/last
little	less	least
much	more	most
well	better	best

IRREGULAR DISTINCTIONS

Q. The same Pennsylvania teacher we met in Chapter 3 said, "I know that the adjective **far** and its forms of comparison can also be adverbs. Do they have the same meanings as they did when they were adjectives?"

A. This delightful woman had brought up a great point about the forms of adverbs irregularly compared. In some cases, adverbs in the comparative and superlative degrees can take different forms. Which form you use depends on the meaning you want to convey.

The adverbs in the **far → farther → farthest** progression refer to physical distance.

I ran **farther** than I ever had before.

The adverbs in the **far → further → furthest** progression refer to a mental or physical distance.

We cannot travel any **further** tonight. (physical distance)

Each day of my vacation, thoughts of work are drifting **further** from my mind. (mental distance)

The adverbs in the **late → later → latest** progression refer to order in time.

We arrived **later** than usual.

The adverbs in the **late** → **latter** → **last** progression refer to a physical order in space.

Bob stood **last** in line for the concert tickets.

ADVERBS BEYOND COMPARISON

There are many adverbs that are never compared. They describe one-dimensional qualities unfit for comparison. Here are some examples.

again	ever	now	thus
almost	here	past	too
back	never	so	twice
before	no	then	very
by	not	there	yes

How can one event occur "more twice" than another? The concept of comparison just doesn't make sense when applied to these adverbs.

MORE THOROUGHLY TESTED?

Q. "Can you say that one product is more thoroughly tested than another?" asked a chemist for a large pharmaceutical company.

A. The adverb **thoroughly** means "completely." Some might express concern over the logic behind the phrase **more thoroughly tested**. These critics will claim that the quality expressed by this adverb has only one degree. All things thorough are equally thorough, and all things done thoroughly are done equally thoroughly. If Product A has been "more thoroughly" tested than Product B, Product B was not thoroughly tested to begin with. Under this interpretation, the chemist should change his phrasing to indicate that one product was tested thoroughly while another was not.

However, language is a tool, and the purpose of this tool is to communicate. The phrase **more thoroughly tested** communicates a very clear idea. One product has been better tested than another. Though **thoroughly** is, in a rigid way, beyond comparison, the phrase **more thoroughly** does not mislead. The testing of one product more closely approximates the perfect state of thoroughness than another. The chemist may state that one product is more thoroughly tested than another without fear of reproach.

POSITIONING THE ADVERB

Adverbs are mobile words. Where an adverb is positioned depends on what type of word it modifies and on how the speaker wishes to communicate his or her idea. When an adverb modifies an adjective or another adverb, the modifying adverb will precede the word modified.

We are **quite** happy with the new apartment.

My sister drives **so** recklessly.

In the first example, the adverb **quite** precedes the adjective that it modifies, **happy**. In the second, the adverb **so** precedes the adverb that it modifies, **recklessly**.

The plot thickens when the adverb modifies a verb. These adverbs may occupy a number of different positions within the sentence. They may directly follow the verbs modified.

Lara aimed **carefully** at the target.

Jack stepped **gingerly** across the broken glass.

In these two examples, the adverbs **carefully** and **gingerly** follow the verbs that they modify, **aimed** and **stepped**.

Though the adverb may follow the verb, an object or phrase can sometimes come between the two. Here, the adverb will not *directly* follow the verb.

The bomb squad lifted the explosive **carefully**.

I watched the game **intently**.

In the first example, the adverb **carefully** modifies the verb **lifted**. An article, **the**, and a direct object, **explosive**, separate **carefully** from the verb. In the second example, the adverb **intently** modifies the verb **watched**. An article, **the**, and a direct object, **game**, separate **intently** from the verb.

The adverb may also lie within a verb phrase although it is not a part of the verb phrase.

The syndicate does **not ordinarily** give refunds.

They will **definitely** feel offended.

In the first example, the adverbs **ordinarily** and **not** fall inside the verb phrase that they modify, **does give**. In the second example, the adverb **definitely** lies within the verb phrase that it modifies, **will feel**.

The adverb may precede the verb. It can begin the sentence, or it can appear just after the subject. In either case, the positioning emphasizes the quality described by the adverb.

> **Often**, I take a nap during my lunch break.

> She **always** arrives earlier than is necessary.

In the first example, the adverb **often** modifies the verb **take** and begins the sentence. In the second example, the adverb **always** modifies the verb **arrives**. It falls after the subject but before the verb. In both examples, the positions emphasize the particular qualities of the adverbs.

As a general rule, it is wise to place the adverb as near as possible to the word that it modifies. Tightening the space between the modifier and the word modified reduces the chance of mistakenly linking the modifier with a word it was not intended to modify. Look at how the placement of the adverb in the following two sentences affects their meanings.

> I lost **almost** a full pint of blood.

> I **almost** lost a full pint of blood.

In the first example, it appears that the adverb **almost** modifies the adjective **full**. The sentence indicates that someone lost a little less than a full pint of blood. In the second example, the adverb **almost** appears to modify the verb **lost**. The sentence indicates that someone came close to losing a pint of blood but did not lose any at all. The position of the adverb has a drastic effect on the meaning of the sentence. Be sure that your choice of placement creates the meaning you intend.

POOR MODIFICATION

Q. A teacher asked, "What would you do with this sentence? 'Many people enjoy eating simply for pleasure.' One of my students wrote it in a health report."

A. It's difficult to tell which word the adverb **simply** modifies. It could modify the gerund **eating**. We would then assume that many people enjoy eating in a simple manner. The adverb could also modify the prepositional phrase **for pleasure**. The phrase serves an adverb function since it modifies **eating**. It tells why people eat. If **simply** modifies this phrase, then we assume that many people eat just for the pleasure of it. The adverb **simply** is synonymous with the adverb **just** in this context. Whatever the case, the sentence needs rewording to create a clearer meaning. It could read, "Many people enjoy eating just for the pleasure of it."

MORE POOR MODIFICATION

Q. When a close friend's mother passed away, the funeral home sent him some literature explaining embalming. He shared the pamphlet with the Hot Line and asked for elucidation. A sentence in the pamphlet read, "The consent form is required to be completed when obtaining the necessary express authorization to embalm orally by telephone."

A. **By telephone** is a prepositional phrase. It appears to modify the adverb **orally**. The adverb appears to modify the infinitive **to embalm**. As limited as my knowledge of mortuary science is, I am certain that one cannot embalm the body over the phone. The process is quite complex. The adverb **orally** should modify the gerund phrase **obtaining the necessary express authorization**. We need to move the adverb and clean up a bit of messy writing. The sentence should read, "The consent form must be completed when orally obtaining the necessary express authorization to embalm."

FROM MY FILES: COLLOQUIALISMS

Language is full of irregularities. Carelessness and common usage often bring statements with serious grammatical flaws into everyday speech. When they become common, we assume that they are correct. Two of these, **rest easy** and **clear-cut**, have been inspirations for numerous calls to the Hot Line. **Easy** and **clear** are both adjectives, capable of modifying nouns and pronouns only.

Rest and **cut** are both verbs. Each requires an adverb modifier. **Rest easy** becomes **rest easily,** and **clear-cut** becomes **clearly-cut.**

The dictionary does list **clear-cut** as an adjective, first used in 1855, but **clearly-cut** and **rest easily** are technically correct. However, **clear-cut** and **rest easy** are also acceptable simply because they are in common use. Colloquial expressions such as these challenge the grammarian who must walk a narrow line between colloquially and grammatically correct English. In school, as well as in the professional world, colloquial English should always take a back seat to that which is grammatically correct.

THE TRUTH ABOUT ADVERBS AND ADJECTIVES

Because they are both modifiers, it can be difficult to determine whether to use an adverb or an adjective. The first step in making the decision is determining what you need at that point in the sentence. Do you need a word to modify a noun or a pronoun? If so, use an adjective. Do you need a word to modify a verb, an adjective, or an adverb? If so, use an adverb.

There are situations, however, where such simple problem solving is not enough. Most adverb/adjective mistakes are made when the modifier follows the verb. Here are two tips that will help the watchful grammarian avoid this pitfall.

TIP 1   Do not use an adjective immediately after an action verb. Only adverbs modify action verbs. These sentences have been written incorrectly.

My brother walks **strange**. (incorrect)

Wendy writes **careful**. (incorrect)

Sue talks **soft**. (incorrect)

In each example, the author has mistakenly modified an action verb with an adjective. We need to change the adjectives into adverbs. These sentences should appear as follows.

My brother walks **strangely**. (correct)

Wendy writes **carefully**. (correct)

Sue talks **softly**. (correct)

TIP 2   Beware of action verbs posing as linking verbs. Think back to our discussion of verbs. Some action verbs, such as **smell, taste,**

look, and **appear,** can be used as linking verbs. A modifier that follows a linking verb is a subject complement. It complements or modifies the subject of the sentence, a noun, pronoun, or other nominal, and, therefore, must be an adjective.

> The ivy grew **high**.

> The ivy grows **quickly**.

In the first example, the verb **grew** is a linking verb. The modifier that follows, a subject complement, refers to the subject. The adjective **high** describes the noun **ivy**. It indicates how large the ivy grows. The usage is correct.

In the second example, the verb **grows** is an action verb. The modifier that follows refers to the verb and should be an adverb. Here, the adverb **quickly** describes the verb **grows**. It indicates the manner in which the plant grows. This usage is correct as well but instills the sentence with a very different meaning.

The Death of Adverbs

Q. One of the "A" students in my English class asked, "Are adverbs being subjugated by adjectives?"

A. I am sorry to say that, in common language, adverbs are being overrun by adjectives. Look at this sentence written on a final essay for one of my classes: "Everyone seems to think higher of the President now." **Higher** is an adjective. It cannot modify the infinitive **to think**. The sentence should read, "Everyone thinks more highly of the President now."

Adjectives have not yet taken over, but we do need to concentrate on the proper use of adverbs. One caller heard an actor in a commercial say, "Does your scalp itch so bad?" The adjective **bad** has taken the place of an adverb. The actor should have asked if her friend's scalp itched *badly*. By the way, this caller commented that his scalp didn't itch so badly that he'd trade an adjective for an adverb.

Biblical vs. Biblically

Q. A Bible school instructor needed an interpretation. He said, "I heard the phrase 'to think and act biblical.' Should it be **biblical** or **biblically**?"

A. The adjective **biblical** modifies nouns and pronouns, informing us that they are related to the bible. The adverb **biblically** modifies verbs, adjectives, and other adverbs. An act done biblically is done in a biblical manner. In the caller's phrase, the word in question modifies a compound infinitive, **to think and act**. Since an infinitive is a verbal or verb form, it requires an adverb modifier. The correct phrasing, therefore, is "to think and act biblically."

FAIR VS. FAIRLY

Q. "Can people be treated fair?" asked a studious caller who was working on a term paper.

A. **Fair** is an adjective. The modifier in question describes a verb phrase, **be treated**. The sentence requires an adverb to modify this action verb. People are treated *fairly*.

HEALTHY, HEALTHIER, OR HEALTHILY

Q. The owner of a health food store asked, "Which is correct? 'They are eating healthy' or 'They are eating healthier'?"

A. BOTH sentences are wrong. Each uses an adjective to describe the manner in which people eat. In the first sentence, the adjective **healthy**, in the positive degree, modifies the verb phrase **are eating**. In the second, the adjective **healthier**, in the comparative degree, modifies the verb phrase **are eating**. Only adverbs modify verbs. The store owner can use "They are eating healthily" or "They are eating more healthily." **Healthily** is an adverb. If he insists on using the adjectives, he can say, "They are eating healthy foods" or "They are eating healthier foods."

QUICK VS. QUICKLY

Q. A nurse at a local medical center wanted to know if her supervising doctor knew his grammar. She said, "Yesterday, when we were examining a patient, he said, 'It's happening too quick.' Did he speak correctly?"

A. The doctor made a common mistake. He used an adjective, **quick**, in place of an adverb. The doctor should have said,

"It's happening too *quickly*." The word **quickly** is an adverb. It modifies the verb phrase **is happening**.

DRINKING, DRIVING, AND ADVERBS

Q. A caller with a social conscience called to ask if the slogan for a prominent organization contained an error in grammar. She said, "You know that line 'Friends don't let friends drive drunk.' Is "drunk" correct?"

A. The author of the saying used an adjective, **drunk**, to describe a verb, **drive**. He needs an adverb. With perfect grammar, the slogan might read, "Friends don't let friends drive drunkenly."

However, some might claim that the modifier is not acting on the verb at all. Instead, it modifies an understood but unwritten pronoun, **they**. If the slogan were written without the missing words, it might read, "Friends don't let friends drive when they are drunk." In this sentence, the adjective **drunk** is a subject complement. It complements the subject of the subordinate clause, **they**. The new sentence makes for an awkward slogan, so we would quite rightly eliminate the added words. This does not change the fact that the adjective **drunk** could be correct.

TIGHT VS. TIGHTLY

Q. " I have a sign on the door of my library that reads, 'Please close the door tight,' " commented a librarian from a mountain community. "It gets cold up here in the Rockies in the winter, and we don't need anyone letting in the ice and snow. A client told me that the sign should say, 'Please close the door tightly.' Which do you think is right?"

A. This modifier puzzle has no right or wrong answer. Both the client and the librarian are correct but for different reasons. Which version to choose is a matter of preference. If we prefer the librarian's version, then the adjective **tight** is an object complement, describing the direct object **door**. The complement indicates the condition of the door once it is closed. If we prefer the client's version, then **tightly** is an adverb, modifying the verb **close**. The adverb describes the manner of the closing action. In either case, the important thing is not to let the door swing open.

KEY ADVERB/ADJECTIVE DISTINCTIONS

There are several pairs of related adjectives and adverbs that can puzzle even the most studious grammarian. Let's allow a few calls to The National Grammar Hot Line to clarify the issues.

BAD VS. BADLY

Q. "Do children behave *bad* or *badly*?" asked a weary, but still grammar-conscious parent.

A. I told the caller that children behave *badly* and wished her well with the incorrigible youths. Her question had hit upon an important distinction that most of us fail to make. Too many amateur grammarians use the adjective **bad** to modify an action verb when they need the adverb **badly**.

The children behaved **bad** in school today. (incorrect)

In this sentence, the adjective **bad** modifies the action verb **behaved**. Modifiers of verbs are adverbs, but the word **bad** is not and will never be an adverb. The sentence should read as follows:

The children behaved **badly** in school today. (correct)

This sentence uses an adverb, **badly**, the proper part of speech, to modify a verb, **behaved**.

GOOD VS. WELL

Q. "Should I say, 'We played well' or 'We played good'?" inquired a caller with a penchant for basketball.

A. After commending her on a game well played, I informed her that she should say, "We played well." **Good** and **well** may be the two most misused words in the English language. **Good** is an adjective. It can only modify nouns and pronouns. **Well** is an adverb. It can only modify verbs, adjectives, and other adverbs. Too many people use **good**, the adjective, when they need **well**, the adverb.

I scored **good** on my spelling test. (incorrect)

The new car runs **good**. (incorrect)

In each example, the adjective **good** modifies a verb, **scored** and **runs**, respectively. Only adverbs modify verbs. These situations call for the adverb **well**.

I scored **well** on my spelling test. (correct)

The new car runs **well**. (correct)

A frequently used expression, "to feel well," in American parlance, implies that one's touching ability is in excellent condition.

Good vs. Well Revisited

Q. "Is 'We did good' a correct statement? My grandma keeps telling me that **good** is wrong," said a high school student.

A. Grandmas are very wise. **Good** is an adjective. It can only describe a noun or a pronoun. The sentence needs a modifier to describe the verb **did**, an action verb. The correct word choice would place the adverb **well** after the verb. The student amended his statement to "We did well." Of course, the Hot Line understood that he was speaking colloquially, but why not use the right form?

Real vs. Very

Q. A parent concerned about his son's grammar called to ask, "How do I explain to my son the difference between **real** and **very**? I don't want him to say things like 'I played real well,' but I don't know how to explain the distinction between the words."

A. I love it when I get calls from parents concerned about their children's grammar. It gives me hope for the future and a strong sense of purpose. I thanked the man for his call and gave him the words to make the distinction. **Real** is an adjective meaning "actual or genuine." **Very** is an adverb meaning "quite or extremely." It is an all too common error to use **real** when the situation demands **very**.

I am **real** glad you made it. (incorrect)

The pie smells **real** good. (incorrect)

In these examples, the adjective **real** is used to modify other adjectives, **glad** and **good**, but an adjective can only modify a noun or a pronoun. The sentences should look like the following:

I am **very** glad you made it. (correct)

The pie smells **very** good. (correct)

In these examples, the adverb **very** modifies the adjectives as only an adverb can.

The adverb **really** is derived from the adjective **real**. It means "actually or truly" but is frequently used in place of the adverb **very**.

I am **really** glad you made it. (acceptable)

The pie smells **really** good. (acceptable)

While this usage is not incorrect, the adverbs **very** and **really** have subtle differences in meaning that are worthy of note. **Very** involves an extreme, while **really** involves truth. They are similar but not the same. Be aware of the difference. Say what you mean!

SOME OTHER THINGS TO REMEMBER ABOUT ADVERBS

These are a few points to note about adverbs on your journey to becoming a grammar maven.

OTHER KINDS OF ADVERBS

Some adverbs fall into one of two special classes: **interrogative adverbs** and **negative/affirmative adverbs**.

INTERROGATIVE ADVERBS

The interrogative adverbs are used at the beginnings of sentences to ask questions. The words **how, when, where,** and **why** are the most common of this type.

How much do you know about this insidious plot?

When do you expect the plane to arrive?

Where did she say she was going?

Why do you think that?

In the first example, the adverb **how** asks the question and modifies the adverb **much**. The question is one of degree. The adverb **how** can also ask questions of manner or quality as in "How did you do that?" or "How was the play?" In the second example, the adverb **when** asks the question and modifies the verb **expect**. The question involves time. In the third example, the adverb **where** asks the question and modifies the verb phrase **did say**. The question is one of location. In the final example, the adverb **why** asks the question and modifies the verb phrase **do think**. The question involves cause.

NEGATIVE/AFFIRMATIVE ADVERBS

The negative and affirmative adverbs answer questions. The negative adverbs are **no** and **not**. The affirmative adverb is **yes**. The adverbs **yes** and **no** stand independently from the remainder of the sentence and are usually set off by commas.

No, you may not pet the cheetah.

Yes, I saw the preliminary report.

No, that is not what I meant.

Yes, Carol is joining us for dinner.

As independent elements, **yes** and **no** can express complete ideas on their own. For instance, if someone asks me, "Do you enjoy baseball?" I can respond, "Yes," and still express a complete idea. I could have answered, "I enjoy baseball" or "Yes, I enjoy baseball," but the simple, one-word, adverb answer imparts an identical message.

The negative adverb **not** is often positioned between words in a verb phrase but is not a part of the verb phrase. It is an independent adverb whose function is to switch the meaning of the verb to its exact opposite.

Brian will **not** tell me where we are going.

I have **not** given my approval to the project.

Clarisse was **not** the culprit.

In the first example, the adverb **not** modifies the verb phrase **will tell**. Because of **not**, Brian refuses to reveal their destination. In the second example, **not** modifies the verb phrase **have given**, and its presence indicates that I have yet to offer any approval. In the final example, **not** modifies the verb **was**. Clarisse's innocence hangs on the presence of the adverb.

INDEPENDENT ADVERBS

Q. A fan of war movies wondered, "What part of speech is **forward** when the captains yells, 'Forward! March!' at his troops?"

A. In that command, the word **forward** is an adverb. English speakers have been known, on occasion, to use single adverbs as independent exclamations. The practice is not common. The last such utterances I heard came from a grizzled sea captain and a sergeant major in the United States Marine Corps. The captain yelled, "Away!" and his crew set sail. The sergeant major hollered, "Forward!" and his troops marched into the desert. The adverbs **away** and **forward** are complete thoughts unto themselves. They are abbreviated versions of more traditionally complete sentences, and their meanings are obvious in the contexts in which they are spoken. The sea captain is actually telling his crew, "Sail away!" The sergeant major is commanding his troops, "March forward!" Captains and commanders are often people of few words and prefer the shortened or elliptical approach to speech.

DOUBLE NEGATIVES

One of the defining characteristics of nonstandard English is the use of the double negative. In the double negative construction, two negative words are used to make a positive. Used correctly with the adverbs **no** and **not**, the double negative can place emphasis on an idea or a phrase.

There is **no** way we can **not** go on this trip.

Using the sentence above is equivalent to writing, "We must go on this trip." The writer has chosen to emphasize the fact that no way exists to prevent him and his compatriots from traveling, so he uses the double negative. Such usage is justifiable.

However, the double negative is too often used with the intention of expressing a negative idea. Speakers forget that one negative word expresses one negative idea and that two negative words express a positive idea.

We **can't hardly** wait for Christmas. (incorrect)

I **haven't barely** started to think about the wedding.
(incorrect)

In the first example, the speaker intends to say that he or she is eager for Christmas, but the double negative formed by the two negative words **can't** and **hardly** indicates that he or she doesn't much care when the holiday comes around. In the second example, the speaker wants to say that he or she has not thought about the wedding yet, but the double negative formed by the negative words **haven't** and **barely** indicates that he or she has spent a great deal of time thinking over the matter. Here are the sentences correctly written with a single negative:

> We **can hardly** wait for Christmas. (correct)

> I **have barely** started to think about the wedding. (correct)

PERPETUATING THE DOUBLE NEGATIVE

Q. The caller, a widely-syndicated writer, had read a paraphrase of a quote. The original quotation read, "They won't never talk." The paraphrase read, "They said that they won't never talk." The columnist asked, "Should he have perpetuated the grammatical error in the original quote?"

A. This wily columnist recognized the misuse of the double negative found in both the paraphrase and the original quotation. The double negative in the phrase **won't (will not) never talk** reverses the intended meaning of the statement. The original author meant to say that they will never talk. With the double negative, it is certain that they will.

The columnist and I both agreed that the paraphrase should have been written with correct grammar. If the writer wanted to quote directly and keep the error, he could have used the notation [*sic*]. The presence of [*sic*] within a quotation indicates that a passage, sentence, phrase, or word was written as intended, even though it may contain an error or peculiarity. The amended paraphrase would read, "They won't never [*sic*] talk." Notice that [*sic*] is enclosed in brackets. By the way, did you know that a *metaphrase* is a word-for-word translation while a *paraphrase* is simply an interpretation and general rewording?

ADVERBIALS

Contemporary grammarians use the term **adverbial** to describe sentence elements that perform the same functions as normal adverbs[†]. This element commonly appears in the form of an adverb

---

[†] Adverbs and adverbials are similar but not the same. Though they share the same modifying function, their characters are different. An adverbial is a sentence element or functional category. It is a part of a sentence that performs a certain function. An adverb, on the other hand, is a type of word or part of speech. We can say that an adverb may serve as an adverbial, but an adverbial is not necessarily an adverb. There are many other types of words or parts of speech apart from the adverb that we might include in a sentence to perform the modifying function of adverbials.

phrase[†], a noun phrase, or a prepositional phrase (see Chapter 7, p. 230 for more information on prepositional phrases) and often indicates time, place, manner, or reason.

Our plane lands **late Tuesday night**.

We rode our bikes **to the beach**.

She sings **quite dreadfully**.

Exhausted, the triathlete collapsed a mere fifty yards from the finish line.

In the first example, the adverbial **late Tuesday night**, a noun phrase, modifies the verb **lands**. It tells us when the plane will land. In the second example, the adverbial **to the beach**, a prepositional phrase, modifies the verb **rode**. It indicates the place we rode our bikes to. In the third example, the adverbial **quite dreadfully**, an adverb phrase, modifies the verb **sings**. It indicates the manner in which she sings. In the fourth example, the adverbial **exhausted**, a past participle, modifies the verb **collapsed** (see Chapter 5, p. 152 for more information on participles). It indicates the reason that the triathlete collapsed.

When a sentence is incomplete or ungrammatical without an adverbial, we call this element an **adverbial complement**.

They are **in the gym**.

The town lies **one hundred miles north of Los Angeles**.

In each example, the adverbial complement is a necessary part of the sentence. In the first example, the adverbial complement **in the gym** completes the meaning of the verb **are**. In the second example, the adverbial complement **one hundred miles north of Los Angeles** completes the meaning of the verb **lies**.

ADVERBS MODIFYING PRONOUNS

On occasion, we find a word that we would typically identify as an adverb functioning as an adjective or, as contemporary grammarians would have it, a determiner to modify a pronoun.

We lost **almost** everything.

Hardly anyone recognizes me with this new hairstyle.

[†] An adverb phrase consists of a simple adverb and a number of optional modifiers.

She dances **quite well**.

Tom runs **quickly**.

Both **quite well** and **quickly** are adverb phrases.

In the first example, **almost**, a word which we would typically call an adverb, modifies the pronoun **everything**. In the second example, **hardly**, another word which we would typically call an adverb, modifies the pronoun **anyone**.

REDUNDANT MODIFIERS

Q. A very sick patient heard his doctor say, "You have a cough that's always chronic." The patient asked, "Did he need to use **always**? It sounds unnecessary to me."

A. The use of **always** is redundant. Both **chronic** and **always** mean "continuing or constant." If something is chronic, it is *always* present by definition. The doctor only needed to say, "You have a chronic cough."

FROM MY FILES: TOO MANY ADVERBS

Author Woolcott Gibbs once complained, "Writers always use too damn many adverbs. On one page recently, I found eleven modifying the verb." Woolcott went on to say that "a writer who can't make his context indicate the way his character is talking ought to be in another line of work." Watch your adverbs. Only modify those words that need modifiers (as reported in James Thurber's *The Years with Ross*).

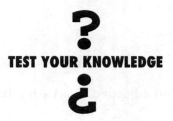

TEST YOUR KNOWLEDGE

QUESTIONS

1. What three types of words can adverbs modify?

2. Is the word **leisurely** an adjective or an adverb?

3. What do interrogative adverbs do?

4. Is the negative adverb **not** ever a part of a verb phrase?

5. What are the three degrees of comparison for adverbs?

6. Name the three forms of comparison for the adverb **almost**.

7. Why are adverbs sometimes placed before the verb?

8. Do adverbs typically follow linking verbs?

9. What is a double negative?

10. What type of word is **evening** in the sentence "She called home yesterday evening?"

(SEE ANSWERS ON FOLLOWING PAGE)

ANSWERS

1. Adverbs can modify verbs, adjectives, or other adverbs.

2. **Leisurely** can be an adjective or an adverb.

3. They ask questions.

4. No, the adverb **not** is never a part of a verb phrase.

5. Adverbs are compared in the positive, comparative, and superlative degrees.

6. **Almost** is an adverb that is beyond comparison. It has no forms of comparison.

7. Adverbs are placed before verbs to emphasize the qualities of the adverbs.

8. No, adverbs typically follow *action* verbs, since it is action verbs that adverbs modify. Adverbs never follow linking verbs. *Adjectives* often follow linking verbs and function as subject complements.

9. A double negative is a construction that uses two negative words to express a positive idea.

10. **Evening** is a part of the adverbial **yesterday evening** (a noun phrase). It tells us when she called home. By itself, **evening** is a noun.

5.

Verbals

Verbals are forms of verbs that are used as other parts of speech.

Riddle me this, dear reader: When is a verb not a verb? The answer: when it's a verbal. The verbal is a verb form used as another part of speech. It is a powerful grammatical construct that allows us to use words derived from verbs in non-verb roles. There are three of these in English: **participles**, **gerunds**, and **infinitives**.

Because they are derived from verbs, verbals retain some of the abilities of verbs. They can carry objects or take modifiers and complements. At the same time, verbals possess abilities unknown to the typical verb, the abilities of other parts of speech. In this way, verbals may perform the duties of two parts of speech simultaneously.

In spite of these new powers, the verbal must give up one of the abilities of its original verb form. No verbal can assume the role of a true verb to express action or condition in a sentence.

PARTICIPLES

The first verbal we will discuss is the **participle**, a verb form that may be used as an adjective or an adverbial[†]. There are two main classes of participle: **present** and **past**.

To form the **present participle**, add **-ing** to the base form of the verb. This form implies action that is ongoing at the time of the action of the main verb in the sentence.

> **Seeing** you again, I feel so nostalgic.

The seeing and the feeling of nostalgia occur simultaneously.

To create the **past participle**, add **-ed** to the base form of a regular verb or make the necessary change to an irregular verb. This form implies action now completed but that may have been ongoing at the time of the main verb.

> He wandered from town to town, **persecuted** wherever he went.

Though the persecution is now over, it was in progress while the man was wandering.

How to Use a Participle

Q. An attorney representing a labor union asked, "Is **conflicting** the right word to use in the statement 'There are conflicting reports.' "

A. **Conflicting** is a present participle. In the sentence, it describes the noun **reports**. The participle is used as it should be. It functions as an adjective. The sentence is acceptable, but the author might also have written, "There are reports which conflict."

Verbal Rhetoric

Q. A student in my rhetoric class, having just been taught present participles, came forth with this wonderful quotation. She said, "I'm not a human being but a human becoming." Several other students in the class asked me to parse the part of this beautiful sentence dealing with participles.

A. **Being** and **becoming** are present participles. They both modify the noun **human**. The grammar of the sentence is

---

[†] Remember that we can also use a participle form as the main verb in a verb phrase. However, since this chapter is about verbals, forms of verbs used as other parts of speech, that usage is not a part of this definition.

impeccable. The student has a mind of quicksilver. The professor and the rest of the class now look upon her with great respect. If only more of us could know and practice her philosophy of personal growth . . . .

A Financial Matter

Q. "Is compound interest the same as compounded interest?" asked a caller on the verge of opening a new savings account.

A. The key to resolving this matter is to find the meaning of the word **compound** in terms of economics. In such a context, **compound** is a verb. It means "to pay interest on the accrued interest and the principal." **Compounded** is the past participle form of the verb **compound,** so *compounded interest* is interest paid on accrued interest and the principal. *Compound interest* is a colloquial version of the same term. Though we recognize the meaning as economic, the standard adjective **compound** has no definition in terms of finances. Interest is not simply compound. However, brokers are not necessarily grammarians, and most will accept either term.

Placement of Participles

Participles used as adjectives have the same versatility of placement that normal adjectives do. A participle can come directly before the noun it describes, just as a standard adjective would.

The lawyer's **closing** argument was unconvincing.

Late fall sometimes brings **freezing** rain.

Both **closing** and **freezing** serve as standard adjectives in these two examples. The former describes the subject **argument**, and the latter describes the direct object **rain**.

The participle can also fill in for a **subject complement**, completing the meaning of a linking verb. Remember that a linking verb cannot stand on its own like an action verb. It needs a complement to make the predicate complete.

His performance was **convincing**.

Her injury is **debilitating**.

The present participles in the above examples, **convincing** and **debilitating**, function as subject complements, completing the meanings of the linking verbs **was** and **is**, respectively.

The previous examples were all of present participles. The following are examples of past participles used as adjectives:

> The **excited** puppy nearly bowled the child over.
>
> The army used a **forgotten** tactic to surprise the enemy.
>
> The children are **thrilled**.

In the first example, the past participle **excited** modifies the noun **puppy**. In the second example, the past participle **forgotten** modifies the noun **tactic**. In the third example, the past participle **thrilled** is a subject complement. It completes the meaning of the linking verb **are** and complements the subject **children**.

Many past participles appear in participle phrases (which we will discuss shortly) that function as adverbials of reason. Such phrases tell us *why* the action or condition of the verb is so. These participle phrases often appear at the beginnings of sentences and are set off by commas.

> **Hunted** to extinction, the dodo is a lost treasure.
>
> **Accustomed** to luxury, the millionaire was uncomfortable in the shabby hotel.

In the first example, the past participle phrase **hunted to extinction** is an adverbial of reason. It modifies the verb **is** and tells us why the dodo is a lost treasure. In the second example, the past participle phrase **accustomed to luxury** is also an adverbial of reason. It modifies the verb **was** and tells why the millionaire was uncomfortable.

PARTICIPLES AND CURSES

Q. One caller, an enemy of bureaucracy, asked if it was proper for him to exclaim, "This damn meeting!" during corporate powwows.

A. I'm not sure if such exclamations are proper, but they are understandable. To damn is to condemn. To grant the verb **damn** the modifying powers of an adjective, we need its past participle form, **damned**. For grammar's sake, a sharper expression is

"This *damned* meeting!" However, a curse is colloquial by nature, and the use of **damn** as an adjective is common enough.

I too find that most meetings are *damnable*. Don't forget to say the **n**. This surprising pronunciation introduces us to the phlegm-phlegmatic syndrome. In **phlegm**, the **g** is silent. In **phlegmatic**, the **g** is pronounced. There are no grammar laws, only guidelines. Keep your ears open for exceptions and your mind open to change.

PARTICIPLE PHRASES

The astute reader will remember that several of the above-mentioned participles were included in phrases. These phrases, which include a participle as well as its objects, complements, and modifiers, are called **participle phrases.**

MODIFIERS IN PARTICIPLE PHRASES

First, we turn to the **modifiers** of participles. A modifier, as you know, is any word that acts to describe or qualify another word in such a way that it changes the meaning of that other word. Adjectives modify or describe nouns. Adverbs modify or describe verbs, adjectives, or other adverbs. Participles may be modified by adverbs or adverbials.

Flying into the storm, Superman risked life and limb.

This sentence contains the present participle phrase **flying into the storm** which modifies the verb **risked**. The entire phrase functions as an adverbial, telling where Superman risked life and limb. The prepositional phrase **into the storm**, an adverbial, modifies the present participle **flying** and indicates where Superman flew.

Here is a second example of a modified participle:

We came upon a lost child **weeping uncontrollably**.

The present participle phrase **weeping uncontrollably** modifies the noun **child**. It describes the state of the child. The adverb **uncontrollably** modifies the present participle **weeping**. It tells how the child wept.

A Misused Modifier

Q. "Here's a beauty I discovered in a history textbook," said a physician and close friend. "Allenby's troops included 200 rangers mounted on camels and D. H. Lawrence."

A. Poor D. H. Lawrence! No poet has the material fiber to carry so many rangers through the desert. It's sheer brutality! The sentence contains an odd past participle phrase, **mounted on camels and D. H. Lawrence**. The fault lies with the prepositional phrase **on camels and D. H. Lawrence**. It modifies the participle as an adverbial would, telling where the rangers were mounted. **D. H. Lawrence** appears to be an object of the preposition **on**, so both he and the camels would have carried rangers. The author intended to include D.H. Lawrence among the rangers *on* the camels. I believe a bit of rearrangement is in order. The sentence should read, "Allenby's troops included D.H. Lawrence and 200 rangers mounted on camels."

Objects and Complements in Participle Phrases

Next, we look at the **objects** and **complements** of participles. Remember that the participle retains some of the abilities of its ancestor, the verb. The participle can take an object or precede a subject complement, just as a verb can.

The following examples illustrate the objects of participles:

> **Tipping his hat**, the stranger went on his merry way.

> **Giving her the message**, the boy felt a weight lift from his shoulders.

In the first example, the present participle phrase **tipping his hat** is an adverbial that modifies the verb **went**. It tells how the stranger went on his merry way. The present participle **tipping** takes a direct object, **hat**. It indicates what the stranger tipped.

In the second example, the present participle phrase **giving her the message** is an adverbial that modifies the verb **felt**. It tells why the boy felt the weight lift. The present participle **giving** takes an indirect object, **her**, and a direct object, **message**. **Message** tells what was given, and **her** indicates to whom it was given.

The following are examples of participles used with subject complements:

> **Being the king**, he would never allow his subjects to go hungry.

> **Feeling strong**, the runner fell into a rapid pace.

The first example contains a present participle phrase, **being the king**, that modifies the verb phrase **would allow**. It tells why he would never allow his subjects to go hungry. The phrase contains a subject complement, **king**, which completes the meaning of the present participle **being**[†].

In the second example, the present participle phrase **feeling strong** modifies the verb **fell**. It tells why the runner fell into a rapid pace. The phrase contains a subject complement, **strong**, which completes the meaning of the present participle **feeling**.

Subject complements in participle phrases always complete the meanings of participle forms of linking verbs. In these examples, **being** is the present participle form of the linking verb **be**, and **feeling** is the present participle form of the linking verb **feel**. Depending upon its usage, the verb **feel** can be either an action or a linking verb.

PARTICIPLES LONG PAST

Q. The owner of a very well-known eastern seaboard restaurant asked, "On my menu, should I write 'ice tea'?"

A. Colloquially, "ice tea" is acceptable. Grammatically, it needs some work. Many have commented that the drink is not ice tea, but *iced* tea. **Iced** is the past participle of the verb **ice**[††]. This example illustrates a wide variety of verbal misdemeanors. Power steering should be *powered* steering, although "power steering" first appeared in print in 1932, possibly before it appeared in cars. Link sausages should actually be called *linked* sausages, and pancakes should technically be panned cakes, although the noun **pancake** dates back to the fifteenth century. The weight of history is against the grammarians on this one. Similarly, roast beef would become *roasted* beef, and ice cream, grammatically speaking, should be *iced* cream. Then, of course, no bagel is complete without a slathering of *creamed* cheese, although cream cheese was around in 1853.

[†] Any participle phrase has an implied subject, and it is this implied subject that the subject complement in the participle phrase is complementing. In this example, the implied subject of the present participle phrase **being the king** is the subject of the sentence, **he**.

[††] Not to be confused with the noun **ice**.

Why, in all these examples, did Americans drop the participle ending **-ed**? It seems to The National Grammar Hot Line that creamed cheese has much more pizzazz than cream cheese. English speakers are inclined to shrink the number of words or letters it takes for them to speak or write a statement. This penchant for brevity exists in England as well. Australia has even gotten into the act, replacing the ol' standard barbecue with the newfangled "barbie."

TROUBLESOME PHRASING

Q. A teacher called to say, "Listen to this winner written by the principal of our school: 'Being inclined to bark, whine, have embarrassing accidents, and noisily lick themselves, students should not bring their dogs to class.' "

A. I've had some troublesome and whiney students, but none have ever barked, licked themselves, or had embarrassing accidents. The present participle phrase **being inclined to bark, whine, have embarrassing accidents, and noisily lick themselves** is an adverbial of reason that tells us why students should not bring their dogs to class.

Any participle phrase has an implied subject. In this sentence, the structure suggests that the implied subject of the participle phrase is the subject of the sentence, **students**. We know, however, that the principal intended the implied subject of his participle phrase to be the direct object **dogs**. Let's reword the sentence so that it reads, "Students should not bring their dogs to class, as pets are inclined to bark, whine, have embarrassing accidents, and noisily lick themselves."

PARTICIPLES IN VERB PHRASES

Q. A troubled caller asked, "Is a participle used in a verb phrase still a verbal?"

A. This caller has brought us to an important distinction that must be made in the use of the participle. Recall that a verb phrase is made up of one or more auxiliary verbs and a principal or main verb. The participle is the principal or main verb component of the verb phrase. A participle in this role, because it is functioning as a verb, is *not* a verbal. Verbals are forms of verbs that have the functions of *other* parts of speech.

The winter is **growing** longer.

My sister has **graduated** from college.

In these examples, we see a present participle and a past participle, respectively, used as main verbs in two verb phrases.

However, it is not always clear that the participle is part of a verb phrase, especially if it follows a linking verb. Is the participle a main verb or is it a subject complement?

Her manner is **endearing**.

She is **tired** of your demands.

The man is **running** for his life.

The first two examples contain participles used as subject complements. The present participle **endearing** complements the subject **manner**. It tells what her manner is. The past participle **tired** complements the subject **she**. It indicates how she feels. The third example includes a participle as part of a verb phrase. The present participle **running** is the main verb in the verb phrase **is running**. The participle completes the verb phrase. Though we quickly discerned the purposes of these participles, this task is not always so easy.

Fortunately, there is a simple rule with which we can make this distinction. Any participle that 1) follows a linking verb and that 2) describes the subject of the sentence functions as a **subject complement**. A participle that 1) follows a linking verb, but 2) denotes action, is probably the **main verb** in a verb phrase.

Your flowers are **blooming**. (main verb in verb phrase)

My house is **freezing** during the winter. (subject complement)

We have **tried** to remain calm. (main verb in verb phrase)

We were **drenched** after the downpour. (subject complement)

ANIMATION AND GRAMMAR

Q. A movie critic questioned whether this sentence animates the animators. "The animators are animating."

A. To animate is to enliven. The present participle **animating** could describe the animators or it could complete a verb phrase. In the descriptive role, **animating** is a subject complement.

It informs us that the animators are such captivating characters that they give life and energy to the people around them. As a friend of several, I find the interpretation believable. However, common sense makes the other option more likely. The participle completes the verb phrase **are animating**. It expresses an action that animators perform. They animate cartoons.

THE KING NEEDS A PARTICIPLE

Q. An English professor at a Midwestern university called with a question about pronunciation and told us, "I was *shook up* by some of the students in my classes."

A. Even though "shook up" is a colloquialism, The National Grammar Hot Line was "shaken up" by what he said. After all, the caller was the head of an English department! The word in question, **shook**, is the main verb in the verb phrase **is shook** and is supposed to be a past participle. However, **shook** is the past indicative form of **shake**. The sentence requires the true past participle, **shaken**.

Also, it is enough simply to be *shaken* by students. The word **up** is extraneous. Incidentally, "shook up" has been in print since 1897, nearly sixty years before Elvis Presley became "All Shook Up."

DANGLING PARTICIPLES

One of the most insidious but also the most amusing of the common grammar errors is that of the dangling participle. As you know, participles often modify words in sentences. As it is with other modifiers, the word that the participle modifies must be clear. When it is difficult to determine what word a participle modifies or when there is no word that the participle can modify, we say that the participle *dangles*.

As disconcerting as the dangling participle can be to those concerned with clear speech, it does provide many amusing errors. Here are some calls to the Hot Line that illustrate the danger and the humor of the problem.

RUNNING WATER

Q. One caller asked, "Is this a dangling participle? 'He left the water running.'"

A. Does this sentence truly contain an example of a dangling participle? The question gave me pause. In a strict and narrow sense, I suppose that it does. Someone unfamiliar with English idiom might read this sentence and notice that the participle **running** could modify either **water** or **he**. Is the *water* running or is *he* running? Ignoring context, there is no way to tell. Under this interpretation, the sentence would contain a dangling participle. Our hypersensitive critic might insist that the sentence read, "He left the running water" or "Running, he left the water." By placing the participle next to the noun that it modifies, he or she will eliminate the confusion.

However, a participle dangles because it is used in a manner that obfuscates the meaning of the sentence. No person familiar with the English language would flinch at hearing someone say, "He left the water running." It is obvious that the *water*, and not *he*, was running. No one constructs sentences that read, "He left the running water" or "Running, he left the water." Both amended versions sound quite unnatural. Since the meaning of the original sentence is clear as written, the participle, in this writer's mind, does not dangle.

FREE LIVING

Q. "They live in the guest house of a home given to them at no charge," quoted a realtor. "The sentence sounds funny. Can it be fixed?"

A. From the sentence, it is impossible to tell whether it was the guest house or the home that was given to the people. The past participle phrase **given to them at no charge** could modify either noun. I guessed that it was the guest house that they received at no charge and suggested a rewrite, so that the sentence reads, "They lived in a guest house given to them at no charge."

PARKING GRAMMAR

Q. "Don't go into darkened parking lots unless well lighted," reported Denver's Channel 4. Three callers asked, "What does this sentence mean?"

A. This is murky thinking all around. What word does the past participle phrase **well lighted** modify? It could modify the understood subject of the sentence, **you**, but this meaning is ridiculous. How can the driver be well lighted? The participle could also modify the plural noun **lots**. Then the sentence would indicate that you shouldn't enter a darkened parking lot unless it is well lighted. How can a darkened lot have light? The sentence needs serious attention. It should read, "Only enter well lighted parking lots."

PIT BULLS AND PARTICIPLES

Q. "I just wrote this sentence in a report," said a police officer. " 'A nine-year-old girl has been attacked by a pack of pit bulls returning home from school.' My sergeant laughed and gave me your number. What's wrong with it? It tells what happened!"

A. The present participle phrase **returning home from school** appears to modify the noun **pack**. The sentence implies that the pit bulls were returning home from school, not the girl. We can remedy the situation by writing, "A nine-year-old girl returning home from school has been attacked by a pack of pit bulls."

CULINARY GRAMMAR

Q. "What can we do with this ridiculous sentence?" asked a chef at a Los Angeles hotel. "I'm reading from the proposed menu for an upcoming banquet. It reads, 'The chef will not serve sponge cake until thoroughly saturated with wine.' "

A. The sentence does create a vivid picture. The chef is soaked with wine and wondering whether or not to serve the sponge cake! **Saturated** is a past participle. The current wording leads us to believe that the past participle phrase **thoroughly saturated with wine** modifies the subject, **chef**. It should modify the direct object, **cake**. The sentence cries for change. Why not write, "The chef will not serve sponge cake until it is thoroughly saturated with wine."

AIRLINE MAGAZINES

Q. "I read funny things in airline magazines. What do you think of this: 'He was walking off with my attaché case filled with Las Vegas winnings'?"

A. It's funny, all right! **Filled** is a past participle, but, as part of the past participle phrase **filled with Las Vegas winnings**, does it describe the subject, **he**, or the object of a preposition, **case**? The journalist should have written, "He was walking off with my attaché case which was filled with Las Vegas winnings."

That reminds me of the wayward husband who, sneaking home late one night, stumbles on almost every step and makes an awful racket. His wife calls down to see if he's all right. "Yes," he slurs, "but I'm carrying a case of beer." "Well, leave it downstairs," she says. "I can't," he replies. "It's in my stomach."

TAXES

Q. "What's the matter with the sentence?" asked a news hound. " 'The President plans to tax all households bringing in over $30,000 a year.' "

A. **Bringing in over $30,000 a year** is a dangling participle phrase. It could apply to the subject **President** or to the direct object **households**. If the former is correct, our elected officials will soon be paupers. A mere thirty grand is pocket change to those federal monoliths. The government needs more money than that to stay afloat. We should rewrite the sentence so that it reads, "The President plans to tax all households that earn over $30,000 a year."

PARTICIPLES UNVEILED

Q. "I just graduated from law school, and I was handed this notice about advanced courses available to me. It said, 'We have introduced new programs for lawyers unveiled in 1994.' Since I have never worn veils, I'm wondering if I am eligible."

A. Does the past participle phrase **unveiled in 1994** describe **lawyers** or **programs**? Who can say? The sentence should probably read, "In 1994, we unveiled new legal programs for lawyers." Anywho, **unveiled** is a poor word choice. Wouldn't **announced** have been better?

Birthday Bash

Q. Several members of the English department called in this one. "James Dickey, poet and professor, was a guest of honor at a surprise luncheon with a birthday cake thrown by several close friends in the English department."

A. Duck, James! **Thrown by several close friends in the English department** is a dangling participle phrase. It sounds as if this past participle phrase modifies the noun **cake**. In reality, James Dickey was a guest of honor at a *luncheon* thrown by his friends in the English Department. Dickey was *honored* with a birthday cake. It wasn't thrown at him! The author should have written, "James Dickey, poet and professor, was honored with a birthday cake at a luncheon thrown by several of his close friends in the English department."

Newspaper Grammar

Q. "This headline is silly. I read it in the newspaper this morning. Check it out: 'British Arrest 126 Protesting Missiles,' " offered a caller from Indiana.

A. In their quest for brevity, the newspaper editors have omitted a noun that the present participle **protesting** might logically modify. We can't tell whether it describes the 126 (people) or the missiles. The headline should read, "British Arrest 126 Missile Protesters."

GERUNDS

The second type of verbal that we are to discuss is the **gerund**, a verb form that takes the place of a noun in a sentence. Contemporary grammarians include gerunds under the category of nominals[†]. Gerunds can function anywhere in a sentence that a standard noun can. As with the present participle, the gerund is created by adding **-ing** to the base form of the verb.

> **Knowing** is half the battle. (functions as subject)
>
> His favorite pastime is **sailing**. (functions as subject complement)
>
> She loves **skiing**. (functions as direct object)

[†] A nominal is any noun or pronoun or any word, phrase, or clause that performs the same function as a noun.

The timid seventh-grader would not give **dancing** a chance. (functions as indirect object)

The brace keeps the tree from **falling**. (functions as object of a preposition)

GERUND PHRASES

As a verbal, the gerund retains the ability of verbs to take objects, complements, and adverb or adverbial modifiers. As a nominal, it gains a new ability, one unavailable to the adjective-/adverbial-like participle. The gerund can also be modified by adjectives. A gerund, its objects, its complements, and its modifiers together constitute a **gerund phrase**.

USE OF THE GERUND

Q. A caller asked, "What's wrong here? I heard something weird on the radio. The announcer said, 'Eating fruits decrease heart attacks.' "

A. The sentence contains a plural verb, **decrease**, that agrees with the plural noun **fruits**, but that noun is not the subject of the sentence. **Eating fruits**, a gerund phrase, is the singular subject of the sentence. It needs a singular verb, **decreases**. The announcer should have said, "Eating fruits *decreases* heart attacks."

MODIFIERS IN GERUND PHRASES

Gerunds, in a nod to their verb ancestry, retain the right to be modified. Like the participle, the gerund may carry adverb or adverbial modifiers.

Eating quietly can be difficult.

Traveling to the desert requires careful preparation.

The crashing of the waves lulled me to sleep.

Each of these examples is of a gerund modified by an adverb or an adverbial. The gerund phrases **eating quietly, traveling to the desert**, and **the crashing of the waves** function as the subjects of the sentences. The adverb **quietly** modifies the gerund **eating**. The prepositional phrase **to the desert** functions as an adverbial to modify the gerund **traveling**. The prepositional phrase **of the**

waves functions as an adverbial to modify the gerund **crashing**[†] (the article **the** also modifies **crashing**).

Gerunds, like normal nouns but unlike their relatives, the participles, may also be modified by adjectives. These modifiers may be standard adjectives, as well as possessive case nouns or possessive pronouns used as adjectives.

> **Her quick thinking** saved us all a lot of trouble.

> **Slow dancing** is one of life's greatest pleasures.

> My **mom's cooking** is reason enough for me to travel back to Illinois.

The first sentence contains a gerund, **thinking**, modified by the adjective **quick** and the possessive pronoun **her**. Here, the possessive pronoun serves as a modifier. The second sentence contains a gerund, **dancing**, modified by the adjective **slow**. In the final sentence, the gerund **cooking** is modified by the possessive case noun **mom's**.

Objects and Complements in Gerund Phrases

Gerunds may take both indirect and direct objects. As former verbs, this is their right and privilege.

> **Knowing your enemy** is the best defense.

> **Telling her the secret** took a big load off my chest.

The first example contains the gerund phrase **knowing your enemy**. It functions as the subject of the sentence. The noun **enemy** is the direct object of the gerund **knowing**.

In the second example, the gerund phrase is **telling her the secret**. It is this telling of a secret that is the subject of the sentence. The gerund **telling** takes both an indirect and a direct object. The indirect object is a pronoun, **her**, and the direct object is a noun, **secret**.

Gerunds formed from linking verbs may take subject complements. Since the gerunds are based on linking verbs in these cases, the complements are necessary for the gerunds to acquire complete meanings. Remember that linking verbs cannot stand alone.

> **Being a cook** is the best job I can imagine.

[†] In this case, to see that the prepositional phrase does modify the gerund, perform a small manipulation to change the modifier into a possessive noun. *The waves' crashing lulled me to sleep*. Such a manipulation only works with prepositional phrases that begin with **of**.

She cannot help **looking beautiful**.

In the first sentence, the subject complement **cook** completes the meaning of the gerund **being**. The phrase **being a cook** is the subject of the sentence. In the second sentence, the subject complement **beautiful** completes the meaning of the gerund **looking.** The phrase **looking beautiful** is the subject complement of the subject of the sentence, **she**.

Notice that without these complements, the sentences would leave you hanging.

Being is the best job I can imagine.

She cannot help **looking**.

Lacking complements, the two sentences are incomplete and unclear in meaning.

USE OF THE GERUND

Q. A philosophy teacher was confounded by a sentence she had read in a philosophical journal. She said, "Look at this sentence: 'Being involved with reality and improving it is important to me.' Is it legal to use gerunds like that?"

A. I'm sure that the sentence is legal in the eyes of the law. As much as we might need them, there are no grammar police to punish the offenders, only watchdogs like me to advocate change. **Being involved with reality** and **improving it** are gerund phrases used as the compound subject of the sentence. They name that which the sentence is about. There is a problem in the sentence, but it is not with the gerunds.

We know that subject and verb must agree in number. A singular subject needs a singular verb. A plural subject needs a plural verb. A compound subject is plural, but this sentence has a singular verb, **is**. It should read, "Being involved with reality and improving it *are* important to me." The gerunds were fine, but the verb was off.

POSSESSION AND THE GERUND

Q. "My boss handed me back a report with this sentence under-lined, highlighted, and circled: 'I approved Jim leaving.' She said that she won't stand for this sort of sloppy writing anymore. What's the problem with it? The mistake has made me kind of edgy at work."

A. I commend the caller's boss for her devotion to proper grammar, but maybe she should switch to decaf. The caller's mistake was an honest one that even the wiliest grammarian may be prone to make. It is certainly not worth the discomfort the boss's harsh words caused. Here, though, is the explanation of the problem.

As we saw in the discussion above, possessive case nouns and possessive pronouns can modify gerunds. The caller, however, has used a noun to modify a gerund without putting that noun in the possessive case. After all, he did not approve Jim. The caller approved his leaving. The sentence should read, "I approved *Jim's* leaving."

Here are two sentences with the same flaw:

She hates to ignore **them suffering**. (incorrect)

I object to **him winning** that point. (incorrect)

In each sentence, the author has created an incorrect and illogical construction by failing to use the appropriate possessive pronoun. She does not hate to ignore them; she hates to ignore their suffering. And I do not object to him; I object to his winning. Here are the correct constructions:

She hates to ignore **their** suffering. (correct)

I object to **his** winning that point. (correct)

In the grammatically correct versions, the modifying pronouns are possessive pronouns.

INFINITIVES

We end our discussion of verbals with the most powerful of the three, the **infinitive**. The infinitive combines the abilities of its relatives. Like the gerund, the infinitive can function as a nominal. And like the participle, the infinitive can function as an adjective or an adverbial. In this way, the infinitive is the most functional of the three verbals.

It is hard to miss an infinitive. Most are marked by a single word, the word **to**. To make a complete infinitive, combine this marker, **to**, with the base form of the desired verb: **to love**, **to play**, **to dream**. Infinitives can also make use of the present perfect verb form: **to have been**, **to have seen**, **to have given**. Some special cases do exist where inclusion of the word **to** would create awkward phrasing, and there we choose to omit the marker. We will talk about these in more detail later on.

Notice that the infinitive bears a striking resemblance to the prepositional phrase. **To** is sometimes a preposition, but infinitives and prepositional phrases are quite different. In order to distinguish between the two, remember that the infinitive always consists of the word **to** followed by a verb. No true verb will *ever* follow the preposition in a prepositional phrase.

FUNCTIONS OF INFINITIVES

The infinitive, unlike its verbal counterparts, can be used as a nominal, an adjective, or an adverbial. We first turn to its nominal uses. As a nominal, the infinitive can fill almost any role that a standard noun would. We can use infinitives as subjects, objects, and subject complements.

> His goal is **to climb** Mt. Everest. (functions as subject complement)
>
> **To swim** is my greatest love. (functions as subject)
>
> My friend Bud loves **to ski**. (functions as direct object)

The infinitive can go almost anywhere a noun can.

Infinitives also work well as modifiers. Some infinitives modify nouns as standard adjectives would. They follow the nouns that they modify.

> We need clean air **to breathe**.

There are no good movies **to see**.

He doesn't have anything **to lose**.

In the first example, the infinitive **to breathe** modifies the noun **air**. In the second example, the infinitive **to see** modifies the noun **movies**. In the third example, the infinitive **to lose** modifies the pronoun **anything**.

Other infinitives function as adverbials to modify verbs and adjectives. Infinitives in this role follow the verbs and adjectives that they modify.

We are looking **to buy** a car.

The man lied **to save** his neck.

In the first sentence, the infinitive **to buy** modifies the verb **looking**. In the second sentence, the infinitive **to save** modifies the verb **lied**. Infinitives modifying verbs often express a purpose. They describe the reasons behind the actions of the verbs.

The following are examples of infinitives functioning as adverbials to modify adjectives. Again, the infinitive follows the word that it modifies.

The couple was happy **to leave**.

The kids were ready **to go**.

In most cases where an infinitive modifies an adjective, the adjective modified follows a linking verb. This is certainly true in the examples above. The infinitive **to leave** indicates what the couple was happy about. It modifies the adjective **happy**. The adjective follows the linking verb **was**. The infinitive **to go** tells what the kids were ready for. It modifies the adjective **ready**. This adjective follows the linking verb **were**.

To Make Amends

Q. "What does 'to make amends' mean?" asked a caller. "Isn't amend a verb?"

A. Amend is a verb, meaning "to fix, correct, or change." To make amends is to compensate for injury or loss. It's an infinitive phrase with **amends** as the direct object of the infinitive **to make**. While **amend** began life as a verb, common usage has shaped the word into a noun. As a noun, **amends** means "recompense or payment." The use of **amends** as the object of an infinitive is acceptable. Please note that we always use **amends** in the plural form. One can never make *an amend*.

INFINITIVE PHRASES

The infinitive, accompanied by objects, complements, or modifiers, is called an **infinitive phrase**.

I do not want **to eat this food**.

In this sentence, the infinitive phrase **to eat this food** is the direct object of the verb **want**.

MODIFIERS IN INFINITIVE PHRASES

As a verbal, an infinitive may have adverb or adverbial modifiers.

We would like you **to return quickly**.

I want you **to come with me**.

In the first example, the infinitive phrase **to return quickly** carries the adverb modifier **quickly**. In the second example, the infinitive **to come** is modified by the adverbial **with me**.

OBJECTS AND COMPLEMENTS IN INFINITIVE PHRASES

Infinitives are capable of taking any objects or complements that normal verbs can. These include direct objects, indirect objects, and subject complements.

I need **to hear the broadcast**.

I have **to tell her the news**.

No one likes **to be the last person in line**.

We just want **to be happy**.

The infinitive in the first example, **to hear,** takes the noun **broadcast** as its direct object. In the second example, the infinitive **to tell** takes an indirect object, **her**. and a direct object, **news**. The infinitive in the third example, **to be**, takes a subject complement, the noun **person**. The infinitive in the final example, **to be**, also takes a subject complement, the adjective **happy**. Notice that the subject complements complete the meanings of the infinitive forms of a linking verb, **to be**.

INFINITIVE INTERPRETATION

Q. The first line of a front-page story in a large metropolitan newspaper read, "Police took away two teenage boys to try to settle the situation." Several readers called, wondering about the meaning of the sentence.

A. **To try to settle the situation** is an infinitive phrase. It consists of an infinitive, **to try**, followed by a direct object, **to settle the situation**. The direct object is another infinitive phrase. It consists of an infinitive, **to settle**, followed by a direct object, **situation**.

The statement is open to interpretation. The police might have taken the boys away, so that the boys might work together to resolve a conflict. They might also have taken the boys away as a means to resolve a conflict. The sentence should be rewritten for clarification. Under the former interpretation, the sentence could read, "The police took the teenage boys away so that the two of them could settle the situation." Under the latter interpretation, the sentence could read, "In an attempt to settle the situation, the police took the two teenage boys into custody."

INFINITIVES IN OTHER ROLES: DELAYED SUBJECTS

Q. "What's the relationship between **it** and the infinitive phrase in the sentence 'It took so long **to get there**'?" asked a caller. "My daughter said this once after a long car trip. I thought you might be able to help me out. I'm just curious."

A. It does my heart good to get a call from someone who is merely curious. It's good to know that the love of grammar is still alive in the world. One role that an infinitive can fill is that of the **delayed subject**. Sentences with delayed subjects always begin with the dummy **it**, a **dummy element** that takes the place of some word(s) in a sentence. Dummy elements were once called **expletives**. The word **expletive** comes from the Latin **explere**, meaning "to fill up," and this is what it does. The dummy element or expletive fills the place of the subject.

In the caller's sentence, the dummy **it** fills the place of the subject **to get there**. The true subject, the infinitive phrase, is delayed till the end of the sentence. To verify that this is truly a delayed subject, replace the dummy **it** with the infinitive phrase.

To get there took so long.

The infinitive phrase moves easily from its place at the end as a delayed subject to the front of the sentence where it becomes a normal subject.

FROM MY FILES: GRAMMAR DRAMATICS

A New York drama critic always praised the first Broadway show of the new season. He explained that he was reluctant to stone the first cast. **To stone the first cast** is an infinitive phrase. **Cast** is the direct object of the verb **to stone**. The Hot Line admires this critic's clever play on words.

BARE INFINITIVES

As mentioned earlier, it is sometimes possible to omit the infinitive marker **to** for the sake of a more harmonious-sounding construction. Grammarians call such infinitives without markers **bare infinitives**. The English language only allows us to omit the marker in infinitives placed after certain verbs in the active voice.

The following list of sentences illustrates a few of the verbs after which we may omit the infinitive marker[†]. The verbs in italics are the verbs to note (they have been written again in parentheses in their present indicative forms at the ends of the sentences). The words in bold are bare infinitives. The marker **to** is missing in each. Read every sentence twice, first without the marker and then with the marker restored. The bare versions are clearly preferable.

They *bade* us **depart** with all due haste. (bid)

I *felt* her heart **beat**. (feel)

We *heard* the birds **whistle** a merry tune. (hear)

Why not *let* him **cook** dinner? (let)

[†] Infinitives used after the verb **help** (active voice) may or may not be bare. The choice belongs to the writer or speaker.

We *helped* them **clear** the debris
We *helped* them **to clear** the debris.

The guards *made* the crowd **disperse** peacefully. (make)

I *saw* you **hide** in the bushes. (see)

The detective *watched* him **cross** the street. (watch)

When these verbs are used in the passive voice, the marker **to** returns.

They were *bade* **to depart** with all due haste. (bid)

Her heart was *felt* **to beat**. (feel)

The birds were *heard* **to sing** a merry tune. (hear)

Most of us omit **to** when we encounter situations such as these without a second thought. The practice is an inseparable part of the way we write and speak, but understanding our instincts makes us stronger. These constructions are indeed infinitives in spite of their unusual forms.

A MISUSED VERBAL

Q. During a sermon, a pastor opined, "I hate hurting people." A member of the congregation called to say, "I think there's a more sensitive wording for this sentence. I know what the pastor meant, but he needs to think about his grammar. What would you change?"

A. In the sentence, **hurting** could be a present participle. It would modify the noun **people**. The pastor's message would be that he dislikes people in pain, a troublesome statement for a holy man to make. More likely, **hurting** is a gerund, part of the gerund phrase **hurting people**. In this case, the pastor would be saying that he dislikes causing harm to others, a reasonable sentiment for such a man to express. Unfortunately, the structure of the sentence does not indicate the correct interpretation. A better choice of grammar would be to use the infinitive **to hurt** in place of **hurting**. The sentence would read, "I hate to hurt people."

SPLIT INFINITIVES

Perhaps the most notorious of all grammatical mistakes is the **split infinitive**. English teachers have railed against this offense since time immemorial, but it is one that not even the most astute student of grammar is immune from making. Even starship captains are guilty of this crime. In the original *Star Trek* television show, Captain James T. Kirk, in his opening monologue, declares the Enterprise's five-year mission to be "**to boldly go** where no man has gone before."

Captain Kirk has split his infinitive, **to go**, straight down the middle with the adverb **boldly**: **to** *boldly* **go**. A split infinitive is any infinitive phrase construction that separates the infinitive marker **to** from the verb. The most common splits occur when modifiers are misplaced: **to** *thoroughly* **wash**, **to** *loudly* **sing**, **to** *joyfully* **dance**. This was Captain Kirk's mistake.

As a general rule, the marker and the verb should be consecutive items in the infinitive phrase: **to wash** *thoroughly*, **to sing** *loudly*, **to dance** *joyfully*. Here are a few sentences that violate the rule:

> The workers need **to** *completely* **redo** our driveway. (incorrect)
>
> Tell Beth **to** *quickly* **come** here. (incorrect)
>
> He would like **to** *often* **visit**. (incorrect)

The adverb **completely** splits the infinitive **to redo**. The adverb **quickly** splits the infinitive **to come**. And the adverb **often** splits the infinitive **to visit**. These split infinitives make for awkward sentences. Here are the same examples with infinitives restored:

> The workers need **to redo** our driveway *completely*. (correct)
>
> Tell Beth **to come** here *quickly*. (correct)
>
> He would like **to visit** *often*. (correct)

Without the split infinitives, the sentences are much easier to digest. Captain Kirk should have stated his mission to be "**to go** *boldly* where no man has gone before."

The split infinitive is not always an act of grammatical mayhem. Some well-known writers have taken artistic license to split infinitives, but they have done so carefully and judiciously. They use split infinitives to emphasize certain points or simply to create more poetic constructions.

FROM MY FILES: LITERARY SPLITS

"When I split an infinitive, God damn it, I split it so it stays split."

—Raymond Chandler (1888-1959). American novelist and screenwriter (*The Big Sleep*) in a letter to his publisher.

PERFECT FORMS: A LAST POINT ABOUT VERBALS

Like verbs, verbals can be expressed in perfect form. Recall that the perfect form implies action that ends. To create the perfect form of a present participle, use **having** with the past participle form of the verb. The past participle has no perfect form.

> **Having said** his peace, the man departed. (perfect form of present participle)

> **Having seen** the results, Bob vowed never to cook again. (perfect form of present participle)

> **Having felt** an earthquake, we moved to another state. (perfect form of present participle)

In each of these examples, the present participle in perfect form is an adverbial of reason, telling why the action of the verb was so.

To create the perfect form of a gerund, use **having** with the past participle of the verb.

> **Having seen** the albino gorillas is an honor and a privilege.

> **Having known** her gives me great satisfaction.

In the first example, the gerund **having seen** in the gerund phrase **having seen the albino gorillas** is in the perfect form. The entire phrase serves as the subject of the sentence. In the second example, the gerund **having known** in the gerund phrase **having known her** is in the perfect form. This phrase also serves as the subject of the sentence.

To create the perfect form of an infinitive, use the infinitive marker **to** followed by **have** and the past participle of the verb.

> **To have won** the award is a great honor.

> I was fortunate **to have seen** the forests before they were paved over.

In the first example, the infinitive **to have won** in the infinitive phrase **to have won the award** is in the perfect form. The entire phrase is the subject of the sentence. In the second example, the infinitive **to have seen** in the infinitive phrase **to have seen the forests before they were paved over** is in the perfect form. The entire phrase is an adverbial, modifying the adjective **fortunate**.

TEST YOUR KNOWLEDGE

QUESTIONS

1. What can verbs do that verbals cannot?

2. Which type of participle implies action that is now complete but that may have been ongoing at the time of the main verb?

3. Would a grammarian ever order a glass of ice tea?

4. What type of word or sentence element can modify a participle?

5. Which type of verbal can be modified by adjectives?

6. What role do gerunds play in sentences?

7. Noun that modify gerunds must be in what case?

8. Why is the infinitive the most powerful verbal?

9. When can we omit the infinitive marker?

10. What is a split infinitive?

(SEE ANSWERS ON FOLLOWING PAGE)

Answers

1. Verbs can express action or condition. Verbals have lost this ability.

2. The past participle implies this sort of action.

3. No, a grammarian would order a glass of *iced* tea.

4. An adverb or an adverbial can modify a participle.

5. Gerunds can be modified by adjectives.

6. Gerunds play the roles of nouns in sentences. Contemporary grammarians call gerunds nominals.

7. They must be in the possessive case. Also, only *possessive* pronouns can modify gerunds.

8. The infinitive is the most powerful verbal because it can function as a nominal, an adjective, or an adverbial.

9. We can omit the infinitive marker when the infinitive is used after certain verbs, such as **bid**, **feel**, or **make**.

10. A split infinitive is a grammatical construction that separates the marker from the base form of the verb with some intervening word.

6.

Pronouns

Pronouns take the places of nouns in sentences.

All ears crave variety. A varied array of words and sentences are candies for our brains. Repetition and overuse are chopped livers and spoons full of castor oil. Nouns can grow especially cumbersome when we discuss the same person, place, or thing over a period of time. The discriminating listener cringes at hearing one noun used twice in the same sentence or even twice in consecutive sentences. He or she would prefer that one occurrence be replaced with another word. To this end, the English language has incorporated the pronoun.

It is impossible not to understand pronouns. Look in your dictionary and you will quickly discover that the prefix **pro-** means "in place of," "in favor of," "supporting," or "acting as." Knowing this, you will never forget the function of pronouns. They stand in for nouns.

The last time I saw Jack, I gave **him** a black eye.

Sally is impossible. I wish **she** would move away.

Instead of using **Jack** again, we use the pronoun **him**. Instead of using **Sally** again, we use the pronoun **she**. The pronouns please our ears by eliminating repetition. Read these same examples without the pronouns.

> The last time I saw Jack, I gave **Jack** a black eye.

> Sally is impossible. I wish **Sally** would move away.

They sound terrible, don't they?

The pronoun has no identity in and of itself. Instead, it takes meaning from the context in which it is found. This meaning usually comes from the word for which the pronoun stands, called its **antecedent**. In the above examples, **Jack** is the antecedent of the pronoun **him**, and **Sally** is the antecedent of the pronoun **she**.

> George Washington picked up **his** waistcoat and admired **its** golden buttons.

Here, **George Washington** is the antecedent of **his** and **waistcoat** is the antecedent of **its**. These antecedents put faces on the generic pronouns.

Since pronouns take the places of nouns, they can fill any role that nouns might fill and have the same four properties as nouns: **gender**, **person**, **number**, and **case**. Refer back to Chapter 1 on nouns for definitions of these terms. We will look at each property in greater detail as it becomes relevant to your understanding of pronouns.

TYPES OF PRONOUNS

Pronouns can be of eight different types: **personal**, **possessive**, **reciprocal**, **reflexive**, **demonstrative**, **interrogative**, **relative**, and **indefinite**. We will look at each in turn.

PERSONAL PRONOUNS

Personal pronouns indicate a person speaking, spoken to, or spoken of. Each personal pronoun refers to a specific individual or group.

> **I** am too tired to drive.

> **You** saw the meteor shower last weekend.

> **She** taught the kids to speak Japanese.

> Bob saw **them** at the new burger joint.

The pronoun **I** refers to the person speaking. The pronoun **you** refers to the person spoken to. The pronouns **she** and **them** refer to persons spoken about.

The following is a complete declension of the personal pronouns:

NOMINATIVE CASE

	Singular	*Plural*
First Person	I	we
Second Person	you	you
Third Person	he, she, it	they

OBJECTIVE CASE

	Singular	*Plural*
First Person	me	us
Second Person	you	you
Third Person	him, her, it	them

Notice that only the third person makes any distinction according to gender. The remaining pronouns have an unknown gender. Their genders are not explicit in their forms but come from the contexts in which the pronouns are used.

CASE AND PERSONAL PRONOUNS

Always choose your pronouns carefully. Many unnecessary mistakes occur because speakers and writers use a pronoun in the wrong case, substituting a nominative case pronoun for an objective case pronoun or an objective case pronoun for a nominative case pronoun. Here are a few examples of poor use of pronouns.

Sheila and **me** love to ride motorcycles. (incorrect)

Bob's friend took a picture of Jen and **he**. (incorrect)

The dog chased my friend and **I** to the edge of its yard.
(incorrect)

The first example uses the objective case form, **me**, but needs the nominative case form, **I**. The second two examples use the nominative case forms of the pronouns, but need the objective case forms, **him** and **me**. Here are the same sentences written correctly:

Sheila and **I** love to ride motorcycles. (correct)

Bob's friend took a picture of Jen and **him**. (correct)

The dog chased my friend and **me** to the edge of its yard.

(correct)

Many callers have rung the Hot Line with questions about case and personal pronouns. Here are a few of the most informative:

A CASE QUESTION

Q. "My teacher said this isn't okay. What do you say?" inquired a caller. "The sentence is 'Give it to us, you and I.' "

A. Your teacher is correct. **Us** is the object of the preposition **to** and is in the objective case. Therefore, the pronouns referring to **us**, **you** and **I**, must also be in the objective case. **You** is fine, but **I** is the nominative case form of the first person, singular personal pronoun. The sentence should read, "Give it to us, you and *me*."

ANOTHER CASE QUESTION

Q. "Is it correct to say, 'He opened the door for you and I'?" asked an inquisitive English student.

A. This is a terrible sentence. **For you and I** is a prepositional phrase. The objects of the preposition **for** both need to be in the objective case. Again, **you** is fine, but please change **I**, the nominative case form, to **me**, the objective case form.

Sometimes a trick is necessary to help determine the right form to use. If you are unsure of whether to use the nominative or objective case forms of pronouns when two are used together, examine each one separately. Take the sentence "She opened the door for him and I." I can tell you that there is a mistake with a pronoun in there. To figure out which one, let's look at each pronoun in isolation. "She opened the door for him." This sounds fine, so try the other. "She opened the door for I." Does this make your ears ring? It should. We need an objective case pronoun, not a nominative case pronoun. Rewritten, the sentence should read, "She opened the door for him and *me*."

YET ANOTHER CASE QUESTION

Q. A private secretary called about her telephone grammar. She asked, "Should I say, 'This is me' or 'This is I'?"

A. One aspiring to literacy would say, "This is *I*" or "This is *she*" or "This is *he*." The pronoun following the linking verb **is** in each sentence is a subject complement, renaming the subject **this**. Therefore, each pronoun needs to be in the nominative case form. The response "This is me" uses a pronoun, **me**, in the objective case form.

STILL ANOTHER CASE QUESTION

Q. A choir member called about her church's slogan: "The Church is We." She said, "This sounds ridiculous. I know there's a grammar problem in there somewhere."

A. The slogan is perfectly correct. **We** is a subject complement, correctly in the nominative case form. It renames the subject, so it must share the properties of the subject. Bravo or brava to the grammarian who composed that slogan.

ONE MORE CASE QUESTION

Q. A gentleman who had just returned from a family reunion called his mother to request that she send him doubles of the pictures she had taken. He said to his mother, "Please send the good doubles to Sheila and I." His mother responded, "I'll send you the pictures if you promise to brush up on your grammar." The man called the Hot Line to find out what was wrong with his sentence.

A. This gentleman has made the mistake of using a pronoun in the wrong case. **Sheila** and **I** are both objects of the preposition **to**. The proper noun **Sheila** is fine, but the personal pronoun **I** is incorrect. Our caller has used the nominative case form of the singular, first person personal pronoun when he should have used the objective case form, **me**. He should have said, "Please send the good doubles to Sheila and *me*."

GENDER AND PERSONAL PRONOUNS

English is a sexist language. Everyday speech is full of male-biased words such as *mankind, repairman,* and *chairman* that blatantly disregard the places that females hold in society. The same sexism is evident in our use of the masculine pronouns **he, him,** and **his** in language that attempts to speak unpreferentially to males and females, while avoiding troublesome word constructions, such as **he or she**.

> If someone sees my dog, **he** should call me at once.

Here, the speaker has used the masculine pronoun **he** to refer to both men and women. The speaker does not intend to imply that only men who see his lost dog should call. (There, even I have used the masculine pronoun unfairly when I referred to *"his* lost dog.") The poor soul wants *anyone* who sees his dog to call, male or female. He has simply done what he was taught to do, to use the masculine pronoun.

Is this practice fair? I think not! The sentence could have been written as follows:

> If someone sees my dog, **he or she** should call me at once.

But this is awkward wording. Why not create a gender neutral pronoun that applies strictly to people? (I do not think that anyone wants to fall under the heading of the neuter pronoun **it**.) This new neutral pronoun might seem strange at first, but, in the end, our language would be stronger and less-biased.

English also contains another gender peculiarity by which speakers simply disregard gender and use the neuter pronoun **it**. This typically occurs when a speaker refers to animals or infants. Such statements do not imply that their subjects have no normal gender, but that the gender just isn't important or isn't known.

> The baby sucked **its** thumb.

> The dog tucked **its** tail between **its** legs and ran when **it** saw the vacuum cleaner.

The pronouns **it** and **its** are neuter pronouns. We assume that the sexes of the baby and the dog are unknown or unimportant.

NUMBER AND PERSONAL PRONOUNS

There are two points to remember about number in personal pronouns. The first is that the pronoun **you**, whether it is singular or plural, always takes a plural verb.

> **You** are late for the meeting. (correct)

> **You** were late for the meeting. (correct)

Both **are** and **were** are plural forms of the verb **be**. The proper English speaker would never use the singular forms.

You is late for the meeting. (incorrect)

You was late for the meeting. (incorrect)

These sentences are unacceptable!

The second point to remember is that the plural pronoun **we** can be used in a singular manner as a **royal we**. Traditionally, a monarch, for reasons known only to the monarchy, will refer to himself or herself with the pronoun **we**.

We will permit you to kiss the ring.

We are not amused!

Monarchs supposedly rule with God's blessing and guidance, so maybe the monarchs are including their deity in this royal **we**. Or perhaps it is an ego issue. The monarchs' heads are swollen enough that they look upon themselves as multiple people. The royal **we** sounds a bit silly, but this is how it is done.

We can also be used as a singular pronoun in the **editorial we**. A journalist may refer to himself or herself with the pronoun **we** to distance himself or herself from his or her writing. Please note, however, that even though the royal and editorial **wes** refer to single individuals, we still use them with plural verbs. Queen Victoria would never say, "We *is* not amused."

DUMMY IT

The neuter pronoun **it** is the most malleable of the personal pronouns. **It** can function as the subject of a sentence without standing for any specific noun or nouns. Contemporary grammarians refer to this pronoun as the **dummy it** (one of the **dummy elements**).

It snowed last night.

It is cold outside.

Neither of these pronouns has a discernible antecedent. They both introduce the sentences without referring to specific nouns.

The dummy **it** can also fill the place of a delayed subject. The true subject, some phrase or clause, is delayed until the end of the sentence.

It is true that Wendy has a new job.

It took us a long time to get there.

In the first example, **it** stands in for the clause **that Wendy has a new job**. In the second example, **it** stands in for the infinitive phrase **to get there**. To see that the clause and phrase are the true subjects, substitute each one for the pronoun **it**.

That Wendy has a new job is true.

To get there took us a long time.

These versions may sound awkward, but they are grammatically correct.

THE MORE PERSONAL PERSON

Q. An insurance supervisor filling out an evaluation for one of her employees was stumped. The form listed several traits which the worker was expected to possess. These were expressed as "maintains the system, contributes to morale, encourages fellow workers, etc." The supervisor needed to add her own comments and wondered whether to write them in the third person, as the authors of the form had, or in the second person, which would make her notes seem more personal.

A. The National Grammar Hot Line advised her to address the employee in the second person. Though she would be breaking with corporate tradition by establishing a more personal tone in her report, we at the Hot Line felt that if there is one thing corporate America needs, it's a bit of personality. Those cold dark giants, who refer to people as resources and who spy on employees with closed circuit cameras and computer key stroke monitors, need to rediscover their humanity.

This story has an encouraging postscript. The supervisor called several weeks later to report blissfully that the employee had been very pleased with the tone of the evaluation. The supervisor had written, "You are showing more incentive with your everyday responsibilities. You need, however, to be a little more punctual. However, your overall performance is quite acceptable." She informed us that this personal approach to business was to become a part of her repertoire.

POSSESSIVE PRONOUNS

The possessive pronouns are pronouns that show possession. The following chart lists them according to person and number.

	Singular	*Plural*
First Person	my, mine	our, ours
Second Person	your, yours	your, yours
Third Person	his, her, hers, its	their, theirs

Some possessive pronouns are used to modify nouns in the same manner as adjectives are. Modern grammarians would say that they function as determiners. These are:

	Singular	*Plural*
First Person	my	our
Second Person	your	your
Third Person	his, her, its	their

Take a look at a few examples:

My dog has fleas.

Our vacation was a disaster.

Her speech was brilliant.

Their car has a flat tire.

Each possessive pronoun limits the noun it modifies as an adjective might do. It tells whose dog, vacation, speech, or car the speaker is talking about. Please note that the possessive pronouns are never written with apostrophes.

Other possessive pronouns are used as personal pronouns would be, only to represent nouns, while still showing possession. They do not modify nouns as adjectives do. These pronouns are: **mine, ours, yours, his, hers, its**, and **theirs**.

The gold is **mine**.

The title is **yours**.

Victory is **theirs**.

This shoe is **his**.

Each of them represents a noun possessed by someone.

mine → my gold

yours → your title

theirs → their victory

his → his shoe

Sometimes members of this second group of possessive pronouns are used after the preposition **of** as double possessives.

That kid **of yours** has got to settle down.

This coat **of mine** needs to be cleaned.

That dog **of theirs** never stops barking.

The combination of the preposition **of** and a possessive pronoun (**yours, mine, theirs**) in each noun phrase above doubles each instance of possession. Remember that we sometimes use phrases beginning with **of** to express possession (see Chapter 1, p. 30).

A POSSESSIVE QUESTION

Q. "Do I use an apostrophe **s** with possessive pronouns to show possession?" asked an alert high school senior with an appetite for learning.

A. Never! Never! Never! Do *not* use apostrophe **s** ('s) with a possessive pronoun to show possession. The most commonly apostrophied possessive pronoun is **it**. Sentences such as "This is it's food" and "We know it's location" are all too common. **It's** is a contraction of **it is**. This is not what the authors of these sentences were looking for. Please, when you are using the possessive pronouns, especially **its**, do not add an apostrophe (').

BITE YOUR TONGUE

Q. An editor was in a quandary over whether or not to pluralize a noun in his sentence. "Here is my sentence," he said. " 'The Hindus were told to bite their tongue by a spiritual leader.' Should **tongue** be singular or plural?"

A. The colloquial expression "bite your tongue" only applies to one person. Many Hindus would have to bite their *tongues*, for they, as a group, do not possess a single tongue that can be bitten collectively. His sentence should read, "The Hindus were told to bite their *tongues* by a spiritual leader."

RECIPROCAL PRONOUNS

The pronoun phrases **each other** and **one another** are known as **reciprocal pronouns**. The action of each member of the group that the pronoun phrase stands for affects all the other members of that group. Thus, we use the name "reciprocal." Use **each other** when the group consists of just two people, animals, or things.

> The two friends helped **each other** through tough times.

> You and I have told **each other** all of our secrets.

Use **one another** when the group consists of more than two people, animals, or things.

> The four of us will help **one another** out of our current predicament.

> The people in my office need to learn to cooperate with **one another**.

The reciprocal pronouns seem quite similar to the personal pronouns. The pronouns in both sets may stand for a person speaking, spoken of, or spoken to. Unlike a personal pronoun, however, a reciprocal pronoun cannot be the subject of a sentence.

REFLEXIVE PRONOUNS

There is another set of pronouns, the **reflexive pronouns**, with the same liability as the reciprocal pronouns. No reflexive pronoun can be the subject of a sentence. The reflexive pronouns are formed by adding either **-self** or **-selves** to the appropriate possessive pronoun:

	Singular	*Plural*
First Person	myself	ourselves
Second Person	yourself	yourselves
Third Person	himself[†], herself, itself	themselves[†]

Reflexive pronouns also lack possessive forms.

The reflexive pronouns often refer or *reflect* back to the subject of the sentence.

> I gave **myself** the day off.

> My parents treated **themselves** to a night on the town.

[†] These two reflexive pronouns are based on the objective case forms, **him** and **them**, of the appropriate personal pronouns. **Hisself** and **theirselves** are just too awkward.

In the first sentence, the pronoun **myself** refers back to the subject **I**. In the second sentence, the pronoun **themselves** refers back to the subject **parents**. In a sense, these pronouns are turning the action of the verb back to the subject of the sentence.

The reflexive pronouns may also fill an *emphatic* role. Here, these pronouns place emphasis on another noun or pronoun in the sentence.

> You **yourself** told me to ask for a raise.

> Janet built the house **herself**.

In the first example, the pronoun **yourself** emphasizes the subject **you**, and in the second, the pronoun **herself** emphasizes the subject **Janet**.

Never use a reflexive pronoun in place of a standard personal pronoun. They are correctly used only in the reflexive or emphatic roles. The following sentences are incorrect:

> John and **myself** repaired the copy machine. (incorrect)

> Jane drove Sherry and **myself** to the movies. (incorrect)

They should read:

> John and **I** repaired the copy machine. (correct)

> Jane drove Sherry and **me** to the movies. (correct)

This problem most often occurs when someone substitutes the singular, first person reflexive pronoun **myself** for one of the singular, first person personal pronouns **I** or **me**. Be careful!

A REFLEXIVE ERROR

Q. "My friend said, 'Ms. Jones and myself went to lunch.' Is this correct?" asked a secretary.

A. Her friend has used a reflexive pronoun, **myself**, when she needs a singular, first person personal pronoun in the nominative case form. A reflexive pronoun only performs a reflexive or emphatic role and is never the subject of a sentence. Corrected, the sentence should read, "Ms. Jones and I went to lunch." Never, never use any of the reflexive pronouns without a reference in the same sentence to a prior noun or pronoun.

ANOTHER REFLEXIVE ERROR

Q. "I'm writing a memo. Can I say, 'Tension is loosening between ourselves and Russia'?" asked a public relations executive.

A. Again, the reflexive pronouns are only used in reflexive or emphatic roles. The executive needs a plural, first person personal pronoun in the objective case form. His memo should read, "Tensions are loosening between Russia and *us.*"

YET ANOTHER REFLEXIVE ERROR

Q. "I heard this mortgage company advertising on the radio. One of their lines was 'We're lending money to people like yourself.' Is that the right way to use **yourself**?" asked a caller.

A. This caller's sharp ear recognized the problematic usage of a reflexive pronoun in the advertisement. As you already know, reflexive pronouns are only kosher in reflexive or emphatic roles. **Yourself** does not refer back to or emphasize any noun in this sentence. The jingle needs a new object for the preposition **like**. The radio announcer should have said, "We're lending money to people like *you.*"

STILL ANOTHER REFLEXIVE ERROR

Q. "Can a legal team squabble among itself?" asked a listener to a widely publicized trial. She was questioning the grammar of a news anchor reporting on the trial.

A. The singular **it** cannot hold a squabble. Only a schizophrenic team could squabble among itself. Multiple individuals, however, can squabble among *themselves.* The sentence should read, "Members of the team squabbled among themselves." Since the reflexive pronoun **themselves** refers back to the subject of the sentence, **members of the team**, it can function as the object of the preposition **among** (see Chapter 7, p. 230 for information on objects of prepositions.)

DEMONSTRATIVE PRONOUNS

Demonstrative pronouns point to the nouns that they are replacing. There are just two demonstrative pronouns: **this** and **that**. The plural form of **this** is **these**, and the plural form of **that** is **those**.

This is going to be a great year.

That was one crazy summer.

These are the only good shoes I own.

Those are the largest strawberries I have ever seen.

USES OF DEMONSTRATIVE PRONOUNS

Use **this** and **these** to refer to objects that are nearby in space or time.

This is my ruler in my hand.

These are my crayons on my desk.

Use **that** and **those** for objects that are farther away in space and time.

That is my ruler across the room.

Those are my crayons on the other desk.

The demonstrative pronouns may also function as adjectives to modify nouns. Modern grammarians classify demonstrative pronouns in this role as determiners.

This house is beautiful.

That dog is vicious.

Those flowers are gorgeous.

These eggs are cracked.

These pronouns limit the nouns that they modify by telling which of the many houses, dogs, flowers, and eggs the speaker is talking about.

A DEMONSTRATIVE QUESTION

Q. A winner of a state lottery, writing to her mom, wanted to know if she should write, "This sweepstakes saved my life" or "These sweepstakes saved my life."

A. According to my files, **sweepstakes** can be singular or plural. Therefore, she should write, "This sweepstakes saved my life," if she won a single sweepstakes, or "These sweepstakes saved my life," if she won multiple sweepstakes, the lucky devil. Her choice of pronoun would determine whether **sweepstakes** is singular or plural.

INTERROGATIVE PRONOUNS

Interrogative pronouns are words of interrogation. They ask questions. The interrogative pronouns are **who**, **which**, and **what**. Their forms stay constant across person, gender, and number, but **who** does change form with case:

Nominative	who
Objective	whom
Possessive	whose

USES OF INTERROGATIVE PRONOUNS

Each interrogative pronoun refers to a certain type of noun. It can refer to people or animals or things or some combination thereof.

Who and its accompanying forms refer strictly to people. They are general in terms of reference, referring to one or a few out of all possible people.

Who stole my car?

Whom were you dancing with?

Whose book is this?

Be careful to choose the correct form of **who**. If the interrogative pronoun replaces the subject, use the nominative case form:

Who stole the cookies from the cookie jar?

Who ate all of my brussel sprouts?

If the interrogative pronoun replaces the object of a verb or the object of a preposition, use the objective case form.

To **whom** did you lend my car?

For **whom** did you buy those flowers?

The interrogative pronoun **which** can refer to people, animals, or things, but is selective in its questioning. It refers to one or a few out of a specified group.

> **Which** of you broke my front window?

> **Which** puppy should we take home?

> **Which** car do you like best?

Each instance asks for one out of a small and select group of people, puppies, or cars.

The final interrogative pronoun **what** may apply to people, animals, or things. With people, **what** asks for a description.

> **What** are they?

> **What** am I?

In context these pronouns could be used to ask questions of occupation, character, appearance, or of any other topic that could describe a person.

With animals and things, **what** is general in terms of reference, similar to **who**. It refers to one out of all possible animals or things.

> **What** do you see?

> **What** color is that?

> **What** did they find at the bottom of the lake?

Any of the interrogative pronouns may also be used as an adjective to modify a noun.

> **Whose** story do you believe?

> **What** time is it?

> **Which** blouse do you like better?

Interrogative pronouns used in this way are classified as determiners.

Notice that an interrogative pronoun will never have an antecedent. Since it asks a question, there is no way to know which noun an interrogative pronoun refers to. The antecedent remains a mystery until the question is answered.

FROM MY FILES: REFORM SCHOOL

Several years ago, a tough-looking twenty-five year old male sauntered into my office midway through the semester. He had been sitting in class staring at me for about eight weeks and had done reasonably well on his tests and essays but had never really spoken out about anything. He always wore shirts opened from his neck all the way down to his belly-button. A casual observer could see the scars and tattoos that covered his skin and the gang letters written across his knuckles. Although he had started the semester with a fairly cocky attitude, his indifferent demeanor had changed and had been replaced by one of serious intent. As he stood at the door of my office, I noticed that he held an ugly-looking club in his left hand. He looked at me and said, "Strumpf, this is for you. I've used it to hurt a lot of people in my life. In the time I've been in your class, I've learned that words are much more powerful than clubs. I want you to keep this club as a momento of one of your students who changed as a result of your teaching." I thanked him, corrected his pronunciation—he should have said "memento," not "momento"—and took the club. I still have it in the bottom drawer of my desk. The young man has gone on to law school and is well on his way to becoming a successful attorney. Every once in a while, he reappears at the door of my office, smiles at me, and leaves without ever saying a word.

RELATIVE PRONOUNS

Relative pronouns perform two functions at the same time. They take the places of nouns as normal pronouns would, but they also connect those replaced nouns to subordinate clauses. Briefly, a subordinate clause is a group of words that has a subject and a predicate, but that does not make sense on its own. When a subordinate clause begins with a relative pronoun, we call it a **relative clause** or a **nominal relative clause**. See Chapter 13 for more information on clauses.

The relative pronouns are: **who, which, that, what, when, where,** and **why**. They do not change form with gender, person, or number. Only **who** changes form with case:

Nominative	who
Objective	whom
Possessive	whose

Here are a few examples:

The person **who** finds my dog will receive a reward.

The car **which** struck mine was stolen.

The story **that** we read last week was a great one.

I know **what** you are talking about.

They don't know the time **when** they will be here.

Do you know the place **where** we're going?

Tell me the reason **why** you left the firm.

There is also a group of compound relative pronouns formed by adding **-ever** or **-soever** to one of the standard relatives.

whoever	whatever	whosesoever
whomever	whosoever	whichsoever
whichever	whomsoever	whatsoever

Those formed with **soever**, with the exception of **whatsoever**, are archaic and no longer in common use.

The prize goes to **whoever** reaches the finish line first.

Whoever said that did not have his or her facts straight.

You can choose **whichever** prize you want.

USES OF RELATIVE PRONOUNS

Each relative pronoun refers to a certain type of noun—a person, a place, or a thing—or some combination of the three.

Who and its accompanying forms only refer to people.

The people **who** climbed that mountain are crazy.

The people **whom** we saw earlier looked concerned.

I saw the woman **whose** book won the literary award.

Which refers to animals and things, never to people.

The dog **which** tipped over my garbage needs a shorter leash.

The crowd cheered as the plane **which** had flown around the world landed.

Please note that English grammar allows the use of **whose** as a replacement for **which**.

We encountered animals the ferocity of **which** was frightening.

We encountered animals **whose** ferocity was frightening.

Both sentences are grammatically correct, but the second is easier on the ears.

That refers to people, animals, or things.

The woman **that** witnessed the shooting will testify tomorrow.

The camel **that** carried us through the desert has died.

The explorers found the cave **that** hid the treasure for so many years.

What refers only to inanimate objects, never to people or animals.

I saw **what** happened to your wallet.

The expert mountaineer knew **what** he was talking about.

The pronoun **what** never has a specific antecedent; it implies its own antecedent.

What is interchangeable with the pronoun phrase **that which**.

I saw **that which** happened to your wallet.

The expert mountaineer knew **that which** he was talking about.

When refers to times.

Do you remember the time **when** we filled the pool with lime jello?

The day **when** I will have my revenge is coming soon.

Where refers to places or locations.

We returned to the place **where** we fell in love.

This is the spot **where** he was last seen.

Why refers to reasons.

> No one knows the reason **why** the boss blew his top.

> I cannot tell you the reason **why** they behaved as they did.

Kids Are People Too

Q. The assistant manager of a Midwestern ballet company was writing a press release for a Christmas performance and faxed the Hot Line a copy. At the bottom, he had written, "How is my grammar?" Alas, we found an error.

A. The offending sentence read, "*The Nutcracker* has 60 children which were chosen to perform." People are never **which**. They are always **who**, **whom**, **whose**, or **that**. The relative pronoun **which** refers to animals and things. We quickly faxed back our correction, hopeful that the faulty statement had not yet gone to press. The sentence should have read, "*The Nutcracker* has 60 children who were chosen to perform."

Real Relative Pronouns vs. Relative Adverbs

Within the category of relative pronouns, grammarians make a distinction between **real relative pronouns** and **relative adverbs**. The distinction is based on how the two types of relative pronoun are used within relative clauses. The real relative pronouns are **who, which, that**, and **what**. We call these the real relative pronouns because they play nominal roles, such as subject, object, or subject complement, within the clauses of which they are parts. These are roles which we readily associate with pronouns.

> The present **that** we bought you was too large to wrap.

In this example, the relative pronoun **that** begins the relative clause **that we bought you**. **That** refers to the subject of the sentence, **present**. Within the relative clause, **that** is the direct object of the verb **bought**. It answers the question "What?" What did we buy you? We bought you *that*.

Relative adverbs play different roles within relative clauses. Instead of being subjects, objects, or subject complements, they function as adverbials. Even so, they still refer back to nouns in main clauses[†] and so, in a sense, replace those nouns in relative

---

[†] A main clause is a group of words with both a subject and a predicate that can stand alone as a complete thought.

clauses. However, their adverbial role is not one that most of us readily associate with pronouns.

This is the place **where** I saw her for the first time.

In the above example, the relative adverb **where** begins the relative clause **where I saw her for the first time**. **Where** refers to the subject complement **place** in the main clause **this is the place**. Within the relative clause, **where** is an adverbial. It indicates the place in which the writer first spotted this woman. I spotted her *where* for the first time? I spotted her *here* for the first time. The relative adverb **where** is an adverbial within the relative clause. Still, we say that **where** stands in for the noun phrase **the place** in the relative clause, so we must acknowledge that it does have the characteristics of a pronoun.

Here is yet another of those fuzzy grammatical issues. Grammarians want to place **who, which, that, what, where, when,** and **why** into the same category because they all stand in for nouns. But these grammarians also see that different pronouns have subtly different functions within relative clauses. There is no easy solution to this dilemma, but I think that the distinction made above should make things easier.

RELATIVE PRONOUNS IN RELATIVE CLAUSES

Many of the subordinate clauses that relative pronouns introduce modify the antecedents of these same relative pronouns. Contemporary grammarians refer to subordinate clauses that modify nouns, pronouns, or other nominals as **relative clauses**. Relative pronouns used in relative clauses always have antecedents.

The guy **who** took our tickets gave me the creeps.

We saw the plane **that** broke the air speed record.

In the first example, the relative pronoun **who** introduces the relative clause **who took our tickets**. The relative clause describes the subject of the sentence, **guy**. That ticket-taker is creepy.

In the second example, the relative pronoun **that** introduces the relative clause **that broke the air speed record**. The relative clause modifies the direct object **plane** in the main clause. The plane is a record-breaker.

RELATIVE PRONOUNS IN NOMINAL CLAUSES

Other subordinate clauses that are introduced by relative pronouns function as nominals. Contemporary grammarians call these clauses **nominal clauses**. Recall that the term **nominal** applies to any noun or pronoun or any word, phrase, or clause that performs the same function as a noun. Nominal clauses do not always begin with relative pronouns, but we may call nominal clauses that do **nominal relative clauses**. We will examine the other flavors of the nominal clause in Chapter 13 (p. 360).

We can find nominal clauses anywhere that we might find any other nominal. Relative pronouns that introduce these clauses never have antecedents. Since the entire clause stands for a noun, there is nothing for the pronoun to refer back to.

A nominal clause might be the **subject** of a sentence:

What they need is not my concern.

The relative pronoun **what** introduces the nominal clause **what they need**. The entire nominal clause is the subject of the sentence.

A nominal clause may also be the **direct object** of the verb:

I know **what** you are talking about.

The relative pronoun **what** introduces the nominal clause **what you are talking about**. The entire nominal clause serves as the direct object of the verb **know**. It answers the question "What do I know?"

A nominal clause could be a **subject complement**:

This is **what** I set out to do.

The relative pronoun **what** introduces the nominal clause **what I set out to do**. The nominal clause follows a linking verb, **is**, and complements the subject, **this**. (Do you remember what kind of pronoun **this** is?)

A nominal clause can also be the **object of a preposition**:

We need to talk about **what** we should do next.

Here, the relative pronoun **what** introduces the nominal clause **what we should do next**. The entire nominal clause is the object of the preposition **about**.

INDEFINITE PRONOUNS

Indefinite pronouns have no specific antecedents. They do not point to any one person, place, animal, or thing. Instead, these pronouns stand for an individual or group in a general or *indefinite* way. The indefinite pronouns are:

all	each	neither	one
another	either	nobody	other
any	few	none	some
both	many	nothing	such

There are also a number of **compound indefinite pronouns**:

anybody	everybody	somebody
anyone	everyone	someone
anything	everything	something

Here are a few examples of indefinite pronouns in use:

That is **all** she wrote.

Did **somebody** say **something**?

Few shall return from the perilous quest.

Everything she has said is true.

NUMBER AND CASE OF INDEFINITE PRONOUNS

The forms of the indefinite pronouns stay the same while gender and person may change. With number and case, however, these pronouns become difficult.

NUMBER

Some indefinite pronouns are **only singular**: another, anybody, anyone, anything, each, either, everybody, everyone, everything, neither, nobody, nothing, somebody, someone, something.

Each is responsible for his or her own books.

Nobody knows where my dog has gone.

Some are **only plural**: both, few, many, several.

Many have heard this story before.

Few survive an attack of the Ebola virus.

Others may be **singular or plural**: all, any, none, some, such.

> **Such** is life. (singular)
>
> **Such** are the ways of the world. (plural)
>
> **None** is as happy as I am for the both of you. (singular)
>
> **None** are expected to return from the dangerous mission.
>
> (plural)

Still other indefinite pronouns have **different singular and plural forms**:

one → ones   other → others

> **One** needs to wear comfortable shoes on long trips.
>
> **Others** from my home town did not fare so well when the floods came.

Be careful that the pronoun you choose has the number appropriate to your sentence.

EVERYBODY

Q. "What is wrong with the sentence 'Everybody are not happy'?" asked an exchange student, perfecting her English.

A. The sentence contains a number problem. The pronoun **everybody** is singular, but here it is used with a plural verb. The sentence should read, "Everybody *is* not happy," meaning that there are some who are unhappy. To see that the pronoun is singular, think of it as two separate words. "Every body is not happy." **Body** is a singular noun, is it not? Therefore, **everybody** must be a singular pronoun.

NONE

Q. "I just answered a call for help by saying, 'None are available,' " said a dispatcher on his cellular phone. "Should I have said, 'None is available'?"

A. The dispatcher was wondering whether the indefinite pronoun **none** is singular or plural. **None** is a condensation of the pronoun phrase **no one**. Since **one** is a singular pronoun, the phrase **no one** is also singular. One might conclude that **none** is singular as well, but such a conclusion would be incorrect. The truth of the matter is that **none** can be singular or plural.

Remember that usage determines grammar. Over time, English speakers have begun to use this pronoun in a plural manner, so our present grammar allows it to be a plural pronoun. The dispatcher may use whichever version of the sentence he chooses.

CASE

All indefinite pronouns take the same forms in both the nominative and objective cases. Only some of the indefinite pronouns, however, have possessive forms. These are formed in the same way as the possessive forms of nouns are. Add apostrophe s ('s) to the nominative/objective form. They are: another's, anybody's, anyone's, everybody's, everyone's, nobody's, one's, and somebody's.

What happened here is **anybody's** guess.

Everyone's mood was lifted when the sky cleared and the sun came out.

INDEFINITE PRONOUNS USED AS DETERMINERS

Any of the indefinite pronouns except **none** may function as an adjective to modify a noun. Indefinite pronouns that function in this way are classified as determiners.

Neither student can solve the calculus problem.

Any person who dislikes camping is a fool.

Many ships went down in the storm.

Instead of the pronoun **none**, use **no** when circumstances demand a negative adjective.

No explorer has ever found the lost city of Atlantis.

I will drink **no** wine before its time.

INDEFINITE PRONOUN PHRASES

Sometimes a group of words can function as a single indefinite pronoun: any one, each one, every one, no one, some one. These are called **indefinite pronoun phrases**.

No one heard our cries for help.

Any one of you could be the murderer.

When we use the adverb **else** with a pronoun phrase or compound pronoun, the entire word group can function as a single indefinite pronoun. Technically, these are noun phrases.

Someone else needs to accompany him to the store.

No one else's car is as fast as yours.

I will not accept **anyone else's** help.

In these examples, the phrases **someone else**, **no one else's**, and **anyone else's** all function as indefinite pronouns. The apostrophe **s** ('s) is added to **else** to create the possessive form.

FROM MY FILES: SLOGAN GRAMMAR

A national coffee company advertises with the slogan "This is them . . . and this is us." However street smart it is, their advertisement is not grammatically correct. The proper wording is "This is they . . . and this is we." It sounds a bit strange, but it is 100% correct. So much of our time is spent either listening to poor grammar on the television and radio or reading it in magazines and on billboards that it becomes difficult, though not impossible, to stick to the straight and narrow. Isn't it about time that the copy editors, if there are any left, returned to a higher form of English? Isn't it just as easy to use the correct grammar as it is the incorrect? The coffee company's line appears over opposing pictures of a competitor's coffee can and its own can. What's wrong with "This is theirs . . . this is ours."

AGREEMENT BETWEEN PRONOUNS AND ANTECEDENTS

The word **antecedent** comes from two Latin words, **ante**, meaning "before," and **cedo**, meaning "go." The antecedent is the noun that the pronoun refers back to. It frequently appears *before* the pronoun in the sentence. Because antecedent and pronoun have such a strong connection, it is essential that they agree in person, number, and gender.

PERSON AGREEMENT

Just as pronoun and antecedent must agree in gender, so must they agree in person. A person or object spoken of requires a third person pronoun. A person spoken to requires a second person pronoun[†]. A person speaking requires a first person pronoun. Most of the time creating this agreement is quite simple.

Take extra care when using pronouns that refer to indefinite pronoun antecedents in the third person. Many people mistakenly use a second person pronoun as in the following:

> If anyone would like to come with us, **you** should get ready now. (incorrect)

The sentence should look like this:

> If anyone would like to come with us, **he or she** should get ready now. (correct)

NUMBER AGREEMENT

Pronouns and their antecedents should always agree in number. A singular antecedent needs a singular pronoun. A plural antecedent needs a plural pronoun. Here are a few special cases that you should watch out for:

INDEFINITE PRONOUN USED AS ANTECEDENTS

Be careful with pronouns whose antecedents are indefinite pronouns. Some indefinite pronouns are plural. Some are singular. Some are both plural and singular. Some take different forms, depending on their usage. The number of the pronoun should always match the number of its antecedent. Take another look at the section on indefinite pronouns if you have any questions (p. 203).

COMPOUND ANTECEDENTS CONNECTED BY *AND*

Compound antecedents connected by **and** almost always require a plural pronoun.

> My mother and father took **their** time getting here.

> Bill and I need **our** morning coffee.

[†] The second person deals only with *people* spoken to in the strictest grammatical sense. However, creative speakers, especially easily frustrated computer users, often find themselves speaking to objects. "You blasted machine! Where on God's green earth did you put that file?!?" Please remember that grammar is just a model or set of guidelines and that human creativity and expressiveness allow us to transcend the model when the need arises.

My sister and brothers spent all **their** money on my present.

There is an exception to this rule. If singular antecedents connected by **and** all refer to one person, animal, or thing, the referring pronoun is singular.

The king and conqueror looked over **his** kingdom.

Though the antecedent is compound, both items refer to a single man. The referring pronoun needs to be singular.

COMPOUND ANTECEDENTS CONNECTED BY *OR, EITHER-OR, OR NEITHER-NOR*

It can be unclear what to do when the compound antecedents of a pronoun are connected by **or, either-or**, or **neither-nor**. These two rules should clear things up:

RULE 1   If the antecedents connected by these four conjunctions are all singular, then they are treated separately and the pronoun that refers to them is singular.

Either the cat or the dog left **its** mark on my new sofa.

Neither John nor Bill agreed to tell **his** story to the reporters.

RULE 2   If the antecedents connected by these four conjunctions differ in number, then the pronoun should agree with the nearest of the antecedents.

Neither the father nor his sons knew **their** way out of the deep dark forest.

Neither my brothers nor my sister knows **her** manners.

ANTECEDENTS PLURAL IN FORM BUT SINGULAR IN MANNER

Some nouns take plural form, but are used in a singular manner and need a singular pronoun. Many of these nouns express weight or quantity.

Ten *miles* takes **its** toll on even the seasoned runner.

That fifty *dollars* should be returned to **its** rightful owner.

In the first example, the singular pronoun **its** refers to the seemingly plural pronoun **miles**. In this case, however, we see a single bundle of ten miles rather than ten separate miles. In the second example, the singular pronoun **its** refers to the seemingly plural noun

dollars. However, we view the fifty dollars as a group, not fifty individual dollars, and so use a singular pronoun.

COLLECTIVE NOUNS USED AS ANTECEDENTS

A pronoun that refers to a collective noun may be singular or plural, depending on how we view the members of the collective noun. If the members act together as a unit, then the pronoun is singular.

> The marching band took **its** time warming up.

The singular pronoun **its** refers to the collective noun **band**. Here, we look at the band as a single unit and use a singular pronoun, **its**.

If the members of the collective noun act separately, as individuals, we use a plural pronoun.

> The band tuned **their** instruments for several minutes.

Here, the plural pronoun **their** refers to the collective noun **band**. We see each of the band members acting separately, so we use a plural pronoun.

ANTECEDENTS MODIFIED BY ADJECTIVES WITH SPECIAL IMPLICATIONS

If a singular antecedent is modified by two or more adjectives that imply different types or varieties of that antecedent, the referring pronoun is plural.

> Szechwan and Cantonese food are different in **their** use of spice.

The plural pronoun **their** refers to the seemingly singular antecedent **food**. However, the modifiers **Szechwan** and **Cantonese** imply different types of food, so we need a plural pronoun. The sentence could have been written as follows:

> Szechwan food and Cantonese food are different in **their** use of spice.

A NUMBER PROBLEM

Q. "Why do so many Americans play God with pronouns, changing singular to plural at will?" asked an irate caller from Great Britain.

A. This call focused on one of the most common language errors in the United States. The National Grammar Hot Line receives questions about pronouns and number almost every day. People have problems with the numbers of pronouns for all sorts of reasons. They may be careless or ignorant or distracted by more important matters. In any case, be sure that your pronouns agree with their antecedents in number.

Actually, it is the lack of a gender-neutral pronoun that is responsible for much of the confusion. Not wanting to use the masculine gender and unwilling to refer to a coworker as "it," many turn to the plural, but gender-neutral, pronoun **they** as a substitute for a singular noun. These befuddled souls realize that they are still talking about single individuals, so they match their plural pronouns with singular verbs. This will not do. Where is our gender neutral pronoun?

ANOTHER NUMBER PROBLEM

Q. A social worker was concerned about this sentence she was using in a letter. She asked, "How does this sound to you? 'Do you know someone who lives alone and who worries about their life?' "

A. I answered, "It sounds to me as if you have a problem with number." The National Grammar Hot Line knows a lot of people who live alone, but wishes there were more who were worried about their use of language. *Someone,* a singular indefinite pronoun, cannot worry about *their* life. He or she can worry about his or her own life, and that should be burden enough. Why borrow trouble? The sentence should read, "Do you know someone who lives alone and worries about his or her life?"

YET ANOTHER NUMBER PROBLEM

Q. Right on the heels of the question above came this one from a neighborhood watch group. "We want to put this sentence in a flier. 'If you know somebody who has broken the law, you should report them.' What do you think?"

A. Here is another number problem. The indefinite pronoun **somebody** is singular. You cannot report *them,* plural. You may report *him or her,* and it's your civic duty to do so. The flier should read, "If you know somebody who has broken the law, you should report him or her."

STILL ANOTHER NUMBER PROBLEM

Q. The National Grammar Hot Line received 15 calls in one morning from people complaining about this obvious infraction in a radio spot. "Pamper your baby. Keep them dry and happy."

A. The secret of having more children is to wrap them in these diapers, and, voilà, one has doubled his or her offspring. One baby, he or she, suddenly becomes many babies, "them." The spot is obviously in need of some work. Had the announcer used a singular pronoun in his second sentence, he would have been correct! "Pamper your baby. Keep *him or her* dry and happy." He could also have changed the object to **babies**! "Pamper your *babies*. Keep them dry and happy." By the way, the average number of children per household in America is 1.8.

GENDER AGREEMENT

The grammatical concept of gender refers to the classification of words according to sex. English uses a natural gender by which words that involve females are feminine, words that involve males are masculine, and words that do not have any obvious sex are neuter (with a few exceptions). This system may seem natural, but believe me, not all languages have been constructed so logically.

Knowing the gender of the antecedent, we can then choose a pronoun that has the matching gender. A masculine antecedent requires a masculine pronoun. A feminine antecedent requires a feminine pronoun. A neuter antecedent requires a neuter pronoun.

The **boy** brought **his** turtle to class for show-and-tell.

Susan told me that **she** would like to move to Florida.

The old **truck** lost **its** muffler about two miles ago.

In the first example, the masculine pronoun **his** refers back to the masculine noun **boy**. In the second example, the feminine pronoun **she** refers back to the feminine noun **Susan**. In the third example, the neuter pronoun **its** refers back to the neuter noun **truck**. These are easy.

The sex of the antecedent is not always so clear, however, and it is then that problems arise. To resolve the issue, English, rather unfairly, turns to the masculine pronouns **he, him,** and **his** to refer to both sexes.

As we saw in the discussion of personal pronouns, some sentences need to refer to both sexes in a single word. To do so, some writers and speakers use the masculine gender. An author might write, "The reader should disregard all **his** previous assumptions." This author knows that a substantial portion of the readers are women, but has used the pronoun **his** to refer to both men and women.

Other sentences might contain pronouns whose antecedents are indefinite pronouns. Since indefinite pronouns do not specify gender in their forms, it may be unclear what gender the pronouns referring to them should take. Again, we may use masculine pronouns.

If **anyone** saw the crash, **he** should call the police A.S.A.P.

The indefinite pronoun **anyone** is the antecedent of the personal pronoun **he. Anyone** could refer to both men and women, so we use the masculine **he.**

However, sensitive grammarians typically recommend that we use the unbiased but awkward **he or she** when the pronoun needs to refer to both genders.

A professional athlete rapidly loses **his or her** ability to compete as **he or she** ages.

Before **anyone** attempts to windsurf, **he or she** should buy a life jacket.

These constructions sound strange, but better a funny sound than a sexist remark. This discussion gives us yet another reminder of the necessity of bringing a gender neutral pronoun to the English language.

In other sentences where a personal pronoun has an indefinite pronoun antecedent, the sex of the personal pronoun may be obvious from the context of the sentence.

Anyone in the Secret Society of Women Only knows **her** secret handshakes.

Here, it is clear that **anyone** refers to females. Would you expect to find men in a society of women only? Accordingly, we pick a feminine pronoun.

Other questionable cases arise when there is a series of two or more antecedents, joined by a conjunction. We will call these **compound antecedents**. The elements of the compound antecedents may differ in gender. In this case, simply use a plural pronoun. Gender is not an issue.

> The brother and sister gave **their** dog a bath.

> We investors and you executives need to coordinate **our** efforts.

There is one complicating factor to this rule. When items of different sexes are connected by **or, nor, either-or**, or **neither-nor**, a single pronoun cannot logically refer to all of the items. The writer or speaker may do one of two things. The writer or speaker may use the awkward construction **he or she**:

> A man or a woman has driven **his or her** car into the arena.

The writer or speaker may also pick a pronoun that matches the gender of the nearest item:

> A man or a woman has driven **her** car into the arena.

> A woman or a man has driven **his** car into the arena.

In the first example, the feminine noun **woman** is closer, so we use a feminine pronoun, **her**. In the second example, the masculine noun **man** is closer, so we use a masculine pronoun, **his**. While this second option is perfectly acceptable, in the interests of equality, the Hot Line recommends that you use the first.

VAGUE ANTECEDENTS

Some people write as if they think that finding the antecedent of a pronoun is an amusing guessing game. A pronoun should not have more than one possible antecedent.

> Bob gave his father **his** pocketknife.

We have no idea whose pocketknife was given. Did Bob give his father his father's pocketknife? Or did Bob give his father Bob's own pocketknife? Looking at this sentence, we have no way of knowing. It needs to be rewritten.

If the former interpretation is correct, then the sentence should read as follows:

Bob returned his father's pocketknife to his father.

By using the verb **returned**, we know that Bob gave back an object that did not belong to him. We also apply the possessive noun **father's** to the noun **pocketknife**. The knife must belong to Bob's father.

If the latter interpretation is correct, then the sentence should read as follows:

Bob loaned his father Bob's pocketknife.

Here we do two things to clarify the meaning. The first is to use the verb **loaned**, implying that Bob is giving out something that belongs to him. The second is to replace the second **his** with the possessive noun **Bob's**. With these two corrections, it becomes clear who the knife belongs to.

While the first example was downright murky and needed to be rewritten, other sentences are phrased in such a way that the antecedent of a pronoun contained therein can be inferred. If the sentence structure doesn't illuminate the antecedent of a pronoun, the context of the sentence should. For instance, take this sentence:

John told Mary that they should leave right away.

The pronoun **they** could refer to the people named in the sentence, John and Mary, or it could refer to some other group of people that John and Mary had been speaking of. Taken out of context, we have no idea who to choose. However, very few sentences are spoken or written without context. In real life, the sentences spoken or written previously would let us know the identities of the individuals that the pronoun **they** refers to.

ANTECEDENT WOES

Q. A registered nurse became quite agitated when a supervising physician left her directions which read, "The tray can be placed below the bed if it is dry." Giggling, she called the Hot Line to ask, "What would I do with this sentence to make the instructions clear?"

A. **If it is dry** is an adverbial clause, modifying the verb **can be placed** (see Chapter 13, p. 351 for information on adverbial clauses). The subject of the clause is the pronoun **it**, but which word does **it** refer back to? Is the antecedent **tray** or **bed**? A little thinking will illuminate the correct answer, **tray**, but the doctor should have placed his pronoun nearer to its antecedent. The best sentence would read, "If the tray is dry, it can be placed below the bed."

GRAMMAR AND THE COMMON COLD

Q. A teacher found this sentence in an educational journal and passed it on to the Hot Line for perusal. "My dad asked me to walk the dog because he had a bad cough."

A. Has the author of this sentence found a miraculous cure for the canine cough? Will a simple walk relieve this doggie of what ails him? I don't think so. What we have here is a vague antecedent. **Because he had a bad cough** is an adverbial clause, modifying the verb **asked** (see Chapter 13, p. 351 for information on adverbial clauses). The problem lies with the subject of the clause, **he**. What is its antecedent? Is it **dog** or **dad**? One assumes that the answer must be **dad**—sick dogs do not like to go on walks any more than sick dads do—but the reference is obscure. The sentence should read, "Because my dad had a bad cough, he asked me to walk the dog."

GRAMMATICAL CANNIBALS

Q. A professor at a local university sent us this gem written in a term paper by one of his students. The sentence read, "The farmers have to raise the cattle so they will be strong and healthy enough to eat."

A. Yikes! Who is eating whom in this farming community? Are the ranchers fattening up their own for shipment to the dog food plant? Is cannibalism alive and well somewhere in rural Iowa? Of course not! The sentence contains a vague antecedent. Does the personal pronoun **they** apply to the farmers or the cattle? It certainly refers to the cattle. The sentence should read, "The farmers have to raise their cattle to be strong and healthy enough to eat." It behooves us all to practice the art of clear and concise writing and speech.

SLAUGHTERHOUSE GRAMMAR

Q. A Chicago resident called about this ridiculous sign in her local butcher shop:

FRESH MEAT
THE BUTCHER KILLS HIMSELF TWICE WEEKLY

A. Someone needs to get that poor butcher some help . . . with his grammar. The butcher is not making biweekly suicide attempts. He is slaughtering his livestock twice a week so that the merchandise remains fresh. A better sign would read as follows:

FRESH MEAT
THE BUTCHER SLAUGHTERS HIS STOCK TWICE WEEKLY

SOME PRONOUNS DON'T NEED ANTECEDENTS

Remember that not all pronouns have antecedents. Some pronouns take the places of nouns and fill the roles of nouns, but do not refer to any nouns in particular. We have seen several of these cases before.

PERSONAL PRONOUNS

Some personal pronouns do not require antecedents. The first person pronouns **I** and **we** point to the speaker as antecedent by virtue of the fact that they are in the first person. No specific noun antecedent is necessary. Also, the second person pronoun **you**, singular and plural, and the third person pronoun **it**, in its use as a dummy element, are often used without antecedents.

INTERROGATIVE PRONOUNS

The interrogative pronouns never have antecedents. Since they ask questions, the nouns they refer to are unknown. If we could give an interrogative pronoun an antecedent, we would have no use for the pronoun in the first place.

THE RELATIVE PRONOUN *WHAT*

The relative pronoun **what** never has an antecedent. Instead, it implies its own antecedent.

I saw **what** (that which) you did.

The implied antecedent is the demonstrative pronoun **that** within the phrase **that which**.

INDEFINITE PRONOUNS

None of the indefinite pronouns have antecedents. That is why they are indefinite.

SOME OTHER THINGS YOU SHOULD KNOW ABOUT PRONOUNS

Here are a few points to remember when you use pronouns.

PRONOUNS AND CONTRACTIONS

Several of the pronoun-verb contractions sound just like possessive pronouns. Take care not to confuse them.

Its vs. It's: The possessive pronoun **its** is never spelled with an apostrophe.

The cat drank **its** milk.

The milk belongs to the cat. The possessive pronoun needs no apostrophe.

With an apostrophe, this word is a contraction of the personal pronoun **it** and one of the verbs **is** or **has**.

It's raining. → **It is** raining.

It's rained. → **It has** rained.

Whose vs. Who's: The possessive pronoun **whose** is never spelled with an apostrophe.

Whose ball is this?

To whom does the ball belong? The question asks for the possessor of the ball.

With an apostrophe, **who's** is a contraction of the personal pronoun **who** and one of the verbs **is** or **has**.

Who's this? → **Who is** this?

Who's been here before? → **Who has** been here before?

Your vs. You're: Without an apostrophe, **your** is a possessive pronoun.

> **Your** idea sounds great.

The idea belongs to you. The pronoun shows possession.

With an apostrophe, **you're** is a contraction of the personal pronoun **you** and the verb **are**.

> **You're** the greatest. → **You are** the greatest.

Their vs. They're: Without an apostrophe, **their** is a possessive pronoun.

> **Their** new car is gorgeous.

The car belongs to them. The pronoun shows possession.

With an apostrophe, **they're** is a contraction of the personal pronoun **they** and the verb **are**.

> **They're** here. → **They are** here.

Theirs vs. There's: The possessive pronoun **theirs** never carries an apostrophe.

> The tennis court is **theirs**.

It is their tennis court. The pronoun takes the place of a noun and shows possession.

Spelled **there's**, this word is a contraction of the dummy element **there** and one of the verbs **is** or **has**.

> **There's** too much violence on TV. → **There is** too much violence on TV.

> **There's** been an accident. → **There has** been an accident.

A MISTAKEN CONTRACTION

Q. A law student asked me to proofread a portion of his closing argument. I found mistakes in the sentence "A person is presumed innocent until their found guilty."

A. The law student used a possessive pronoun when he needed a contraction. **Their** is a possessive pronoun.

> **Their** words are honorable.

He needs a contraction of a personal pronoun and a verb, such as **they're**. His sentence could read, "A person is presumed innocent until they're found guilty."

However, a major error remains. The singular noun **person** is the antecedent of the plural pronoun **they**. There has been a number shift. The law student needs to adjust the number of the pronoun so that it agrees with its singular antecedent. His sentence should read, "A person is presumed innocent until *he or she* is found guilty."

A Brain Teaser

Q. A speech writer called in a quandary. "I've got three sentences, and I'm not sure which one is right. Do I use 'It's who's ever writing it,' 'It's whosever writing it,' or 'It's whoever's writing it'?" he asked.

A. Whoa! Hearing those makes my head spin. I must say that none are very euphonious, but on a second, third, fourth, and fifth examination, I can say that either the first or the third sentence could work. The subject and verb of all three are the pronoun **it** and the verb **is**, encapsulated in the contraction **it's**. The first and third options work because the remainder of the sentence in each is a nominal clause complete with subject and predicate and introduced by a relative pronoun. The clauses serve as subject complements (see Chapter 13, p. 355 for more information on nominal clauses).

In the first sentence, the clause is **who's ever writing it**. **Who** is the subject of the clause and **is**, the verb. The two are combined in the contraction **who's**. The complete sentence could be written, "It is who is ever writing it."

In the third sentence, the clause is **whoever's writing it**. **Whoever** is the subject and **is**, the verb. The two are combined in the contraction **whoever's**. The sentence could be written, "It is whoever is writing it."

The second sentence does not work because **whosever** is not a real word. This is a ridiculous sentence and should never have been written. It simply does not make sense.

To be honest, all three need work. It is possible that one may make more sense in context, but I wouldn't count on it. The style is poor, and the audience is bound to be confused. I advised this fellow to take some time to rework one of the sentences into a more comprehensible form.

A Word of Caution With Demonstrative Pronouns

Q. A man from New Mexico called to comment, "I said, 'Those type of berry is poisonous.' My daughter told me the sentence is wrong. What do you say?"

A. I warned the man to be careful with demonstrative pronouns that modify words that refer to classes of objects, such as **kind**, **sort**, or **type**. If the noun is singular, such as **kind**, it needs a singular modifier, **this** or **that**. If the noun is plural, such as **sorts**, it needs a plural modifier, **those** or **these**. It is all too easy to do as he did and match a singular noun to a plural modifier or a plural noun to a singular modifier. This gentleman's sentence should have read, "That type of berry is poisonous."

Here are a few more examples of incorrectly used demonstrative pronouns and the corrections needed:

These sort of behavior will never do. (incorrect)

This sort of behavior will never do. (correct)

That kinds of berries are juicy. (incorrect)

Those kinds of berries are juicy. (correct)

Verb Agreement with Indefinite Pronouns

Do not forget about the numbers of your indefinite pronouns. Some are singular. Some are plural. Some are singular or plural. Some take different forms, depending on whether they are singular or plural. When an indefinite pronoun is the subject of the sentence, that pronoun and the verb must agree in number.

Singular

Somebody is coming to unlock the door.

The singular pronoun **somebody** takes a singular verb, **is**.

PLURAL

Few travel this far into the mountains.

The plural pronoun **few** takes a plural verb, **travel**.

SINGULAR OR PLURAL

Some is left in the container.

Some are going to leave shortly.

The pronoun **some** can be singular or plural. In the first example, it is singular and takes a singular verb, **is.** In the second example, it is plural and takes a plural verb, **are.**

SINGULAR AND PLURAL FORMS

Some **other** in my department knows where the keys are.

Others in my department know where the keys are.

The indefinite pronoun **other** changes form, depending on whether it is singular or plural in usage. In the first example, it is singular, **other**, and so takes a singular verb, **knows**. In the second example, it is plural, **others**, and so takes a plural verb, **know**.

POSSESSIVE PRONOUNS USED AS DETERMINERS

Recall from our discussion of determiners in Chapter 3 that possessive pronouns are often used as determiners. A determiner is a word that determines the reference of a noun phrase. It aids the reader or listener in determining which person, place, thing, or idea is named by the noun phrase that the writer or speaker is writing or speaking. Though the functions of possessive pronouns in this role are similar to those of adjectives, we choose the more precise classification of determiner. Take a look at the following examples of possessive pronouns used as determiners:

His shirt is muddy.

Your quick mind has helped you escape from many sticky situations.

As you might expect, the reference that possessive pronouns provide is one of ownership. They inform us to whom some piece of property or attribute belong. In the first example, the possessive pronoun **his** is a determiner. It modifies the noun **shirt** and tells us whose shirt it is that is muddy. In the second example, the posses-sive pronoun **your** is a determiner. It modifies the noun **mind** and indicates whose quick mind helped its possessor escape from the sticky situations.

Please note that when a series of determiners modifies the same noun, the possessive pronoun precedes the other determiners in the series. Take a look at these two examples:

> **My** first three children were boys.

> Tell us what **your** first choice is.

In the first example, the determiners **my**, **first**, and **three** modi-fy the noun **children**. The possessive pronoun **my** is at the head of the series. Also note that the ordinal number **first** precedes the car-dinal number **three**. In the second example, the determiners **your** and **first** modify the noun **choice**. The possessive pronoun **your** precedes the ordinal number **first** in the series.

Aha! A Determiner!!

Q. A college student called to ask, "In the sentence 'His man-ners left me cold,' what do you call the word **his**? I mean, I know it's a pronoun, but it seems to be doing the same thing that an adjective does. Do you call it an adjective or would you call it something else?"

A. The answer to the question our young friend has posed is contained in the lesson previous, and you, dear reader, should know the answer to his question. The word **his** is indeed a possessive pronoun, but its function is that of a determiner. It helps us determine *whose* manners the sentence is addressing. Such words were once classified as adjectives, but we now look at them more precisely as possessive pronouns that function as determin-ers. Take a look at some more examples of sentences that contain possessive pronouns functioning as determiners:

> **His** feet are huge.

> **Your** paper was excellent.

In the first example, the possessive pronoun **his** is a determiner. It modifies the noun **feet** and indicates whose feet are huge. In the second example, the possessive pronoun **your** is a determiner. It modifies the noun **paper** and tells us whose paper was excellent.

FROM MY FILES: MRS. MALAPROP

Writing for the magazine *Smithsonian*, James J. Kilpatrick added to the lore of hospital solecisms with this report.

"I commend to you patients' charts in any hospital in the nation, and you will find Mrs. Malaprop alive and well. The lode is inexhaustible."

- "He was eating his tray, so I didn't examine him."

- "For impotence, we will discontinue the meds, and let his wife handle him."

- "He was advised to force fluids through his interpreter."

- "Patient has an electric chair for transportation."

- "She slammed the phone down on the nurse."

- "When she fainted, her eyes rolled around the room."

- "Patient walks six blocks now. The doctor told him it may take a year to come back."

- "Many children in the trauma center have witnessed death. This can be very painful."

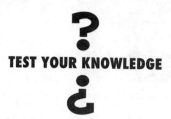

TEST YOUR KNOWLEDGE

QUESTIONS

1. What are the eight types of pronouns?

2. What does a reflexive pronoun do in a sentence?

3. What number verb does one use with the second person personal pronoun **you**?

4. With personal pronouns, when does one use the nominative case form? When does one use the objective case form?

5. Name the demonstrative pronouns in their singular and plural forms.

6. Do interrogative pronouns have antecedents?

7. Which relative pronoun refers only to people?

8. **Anyone, somebody,** and **everybody** are examples of what kind of pronoun?

9. Which type of pronoun has the most number problems associated with its use?

10. Does the possessive pronoun **its** ever need an apostrophe?

(SEE ANSWERS ON FOLLOWING PAGE)

ANSWERS

1. Personal, possessive, reciprocal, reflexive, demonstrative, interrogative, relative, indefinite

2. A reflexive pronoun refers back to the subject or emphasizes a particular noun or pronoun.

3. One uses a plural verb regardless of whether **you** is singular or plural.

4. One uses the nominative case form when the pronoun is a subject or a subject complement. One uses the objective case form when the pronoun is an object of a verb, a preposition, or a verbal.

5. The demonstrative pronouns are **this**, **that**, **these**, and **those**. The plural of **this** is **these**. The plural of **that** is **those**.

6. No, they do not. Since an interrogative pronoun asks a question, the antecedent is unknown until the question is answered.

7. The relative pronoun **who** refers only to people.

8. They are indefinite pronouns.

9. Indefinite pronouns cause the most number problems. Some are only singular. Some are only plural. Some can be either singular or plural. Some take different singular and plural forms. Be sure of the number of the indefinite pronoun that you use.

10. No, it does not. With an apostrophe, **it's** is a contraction for **it is**.

7.

Prepositions

Prepositions are words that show the relationships between two words or phrases in a sentence.

Now we arrive at prepositions; tasty morsels for the grammar gourmet. Chew them slowly and swallow them carefully, for they are troublesome but immeasurably useful little words. With all credit to Gertrude Stein, "Then come the things that can of all things be most mistaken, and they are prepositions." Fear not my friends! With a little discussion and a few questions and answers, we will chew, swallow, digest, even understand these crumbs without any undue indigestion.

Prepositions are relationship words. They relate some word or phrase to another word or phrase, most often in terms of location, direction, or time.

A loathsome troll lurks **under** the bridge. (location)

The train **to** Oxford always runs late on Fridays. (direction)

Barnes was imprisoned twice **during** his lifetime. (time)

Here is a list of the most commonly used prepositions:

aboard	beside	like	till
about	between	near	to
above	betwixt	notwithstanding	toward
across	beyond	of	under
after	but	off	underneath
against	by	on	until
along	down	out	unto
among	during	outside	up
around	except	over	upon
at	for	past	via
before	from	per	with
behind	in	since	within
below	inside	through	without
beneath	into	throughout	

COMPLEX PREPOSITIONS

In some cases, the relationship that the preposition needs to express is too complicated for a single preposition. Here, we use a combination of two or three words that function together as a unit. These are called **complex prepositions**. The following is a partial list:

across from	because of	in addition to	in spite of
along side of	by way of	in case of	instead of
along with	from under	in front of	on account of

Here are a few examples of sentences containing complex prepositions:

The sounds are coming **from under** the front porch.

My house sits **across from** the cemetery.

The mower is **in front of** the shed.

In the first example, the sounds do not come *from* the porch, and they do not come *under* the porch. They come *from under* the porch. In the second example, the house does not sit *across* the cemetery, and it does not sit *from* the cemetery. It sits *across from* the cemetery. In the third example, the mower is not *in* the shed, and it is not *of* the shed. It is *in front of* the shed. The combination of prepositions in each of the three examples creates a complete meaning.

PARTICIPLE PREPOSITIONS

Q. "What is the word **concerning** in the sentence 'I have called concerning the lawsuit'?" asked a paralegal. "Someone said this to me this afternoon, and it got me thinking."

A. Excellent question! Though **concerning** looks much like a present participle, it is actually a preposition. There are a number of other prepositions that look like verb participles but are truly prepositions. Here is a partial list:

barring	considering	pending	respecting
concerning	excepting	regarding	saving

The following sentences contain examples of such prepositions:

The concert will start at nine **barring** rain.

Considering his status in the community, it was surprising that the scandal was not more devastating.

PARTNERS OF PREPOSITIONS

No true preposition can work alone. A preposition needs partners to carry on the relationship that it establishes. These partners are the **object** and the **referent**†. The first partner, the **object** of the preposition, is usually a noun or a pronoun and is usually located right after the preposition.

My friend bought flowers for **me**.

The peasants paid their tribute to the **king**.

I saw a UFO in the **sky**.

In the first example, the object of the preposition **for** is the pronoun **me.** In the second example, the object of the preposition **to** is the noun **king.** In the third example, the object of the preposition **in** is the noun **sky.**

The second partner, the **referent**, is the word that the preposition and object, acting together, describe or modify. The referent may be a nominal, a verb, an adverbial, or an adjective.

The car **smashed** into the telephone pole.

The **puppy** with the spots is my favorite.

Juggling swords without cutting your hands off is quite a challenge.

---

† The term **referent** most often plays a fairly esoteric role in philosophical linguistics. We use the term in the context of prepositions because it is descriptive of the word that the preposition and object modify.

In the first example, the referent of the preposition **into** is the verb **smashed**. In the second example, the referent of the preposition **with** is the noun **puppy**. In the third example, the referent of the preposition **without** is the gerund phrase **juggling swords**.

From My Files: Irregular Hours

A friend called to inform me that a record store was open from ten to five. I asked if it was open at ten to five in the morning or in the evening. He laughed and clarified his former statement saying, "It's open from ten in the morning to five in the evening." Why would a shop open at ten minutes to five in the morning or ten minutes to five in the evening?

PREPOSITIONAL PHRASES

As we saw before, no preposition works alone. In fact, any preposition must participate in a word construction called the **prepositional phrase**. This phrase consists of a preposition, the object of the preposition, and any modifiers of that object.

All eyes were locked **on the giant screen**.

We left the theater **after the first act**.

The first example contains the prepositional phrase **on the giant screen**. The preposition **on** creates a relationship between the object **screen** and the referent **locked**. The phrase indicates where the eyes were locked. The adjective **giant** describes the screen.

The second example contains the prepositional phrase **after the first act**. The preposition **after** creates a relationship between the object **act** and the referent **left**. The phrase tells us when we left. The adjective **first** describes the act.

Objects of Prepositions

The object of a preposition is usually a noun or a pronoun, always in the objective case. Though case has no significant implications for standard nouns, it is quite important to pronouns. Pronouns that function as objects of prepositions must take their objective case forms.

We returned the faulty merchandise to **them**. (correct)

She arrived before **him**. (correct)

I would like to go to the dance with **her**. (correct)

As you can see, each of these pronoun objects is in the objective case form. It would never do to use them in their nominative case forms.

We returned the faulty merchandise to **they**. (incorrect)

She arrived before **he**. (incorrect)

I would like to go to the dance with **she**. (incorrect)

Oh, the humanity!

Notice that the object is *usually*, not always, a noun or a pronoun. Objects may also be words from other parts of speech that function as nouns. These noun substitutes are called **nominals**[†].

• **Nominal Adjectives:**

His mood changed from **angry** to **morose**.

This day is somewhere between the **sublime** and the **ridiculous**.

• **Nominal Adverbs:**

Light fell on us from **above**.

We will take care of the problem at **once**, Sir!

• **Gerunds:**

The object could also be a gerund, a verbal or verb form that takes the place of a noun. The gerund always ends in **-ing**.

I have nothing against **dancing**.

Running is near **swimming** on the gamut of exhausting sports.

Remember that another verbal, the infinitive, uses **to** as its infinitive marker: **to** smile, **to** fly. Infinitives, however, *are not* prepositional phrases. Though **to** is a part of the infinitive, it does not have the prepositional ability to establish a relationship between words. The verb portions of infinitives (i.e., **smile** or **fly**) are not objects.

[†] The title **nominal** describes any noun or pronoun or any word, phrase, or clause that functions as a noun.

OBJECT QUESTIONS

Q. Even presidents make mistakes. Maybe the White House staff needs a grammar coach to watch over it so that these errors do not occur? A recent President inspired seventy-one callers to dial the Hot Line with this gaffe. "It is time for Congress and I to make amends, to make a budget."

A. **For Congress and I** is a prepositional phrase. The objects of prepositions are always in the objective case. Nouns do not change form with case, so **Congress** is fine. Personal pronouns, on the other hand, do. The objective case form of the first person, singular pronoun is **me**. **I** is the nominative case form. The President should have said, "It is time for Congress and *me* to make amends, to make a budget."

ANOTHER OBJECT QUESTION

Q. "Should I ask for 'Always in our heart' or 'Always in our hearts'?" asked a widow wanting to know how to phrase the words on her husband's tombstone.

A. The answer to this woman's question requires a judgment call. Both **in our heart** and **in our hearts** are prepositional phrases. The word in question is the object of the phrase. If her husband were loved collectively, she should choose "Always in our heart." A heart can be shared figuratively. If, on the other hand, he were loved in different ways by different people, then she should choose "Always in our hearts."

YET ANOTHER OBJECT QUESTION

Q. A businessman wondered, "Can a product advertised 'for free' also be marketed 'freely'?"

A. To offer something **for free** is to offer it without charge. **For free** is a prepositional phrase with an adjective as an object. Though the adjective is not a typical object, the colloquial nature of the expression allows us to treat **free** as a nominal. The expression is acceptable. To give freely is to give without any fetters attached. This adverb is more appropriate to emotions than it is to advertising. Advertisers should use **for free** when they are offering a product with no expectation of compensation.

USES OF PREPOSITIONAL PHRASES

Grammar defines a **phrase** as a group of words lacking subject and predicate that functions as a single part of speech. Accordingly, we treat the prepositional phrase as a unit, filling the role of one specific part of speech in the sentence. It may act as a modifier or a nominal.

PREPOSITIONAL PHRASES USED AS MODIFIERS

Many prepositional phrases modify nouns, pronouns, or other nominals in sentences. In these cases, the preposition creates a relationship between its object and the noun, pronoun, or nominal referent in the sentence. The prepositional phrase describes or qualifies this noun, pronoun, or nominal. The phrase may follow the modified word(s) or it may appear in the predicate after a linking verb.

> The restaurant **at the beach** serves excellent burgers.

> My dad bought the beach house **near the marina**.

> The girl **under the umbrella** is **with me**.

In the first example, the prepositional phrase **at the beach** modifies the noun **restaurant**. The preposition **at** establishes a relationship between the nouns **beach** and **restaurant**. The relationship indicates where the restaurant that serves the good, greasy food is.

In the second example, the prepositional phrase **near the marina** modifies the noun **house**. The preposition **near** establishes a relationship between the nouns **marina** and **house**. The relationship indicates where the house my dad bought is.

In the third example, the prepositional phrase **under the umbrella** modifies the noun **girl**. The prepositional phrase **with me**, a subject complement, complements the noun **girl**, the subject of the sentence. **Under the umbrella** follows this noun and indicates the girl's location. **With me** follows the linking verb **is** and indicates whom the girl is with.

Some prepositional phrases function as adverbials, modifying verbs, adjectives, and adverbs. The prepositions in these phrases establish relationships between their objects and verb, adjective, or adverb referents in the sentences. These phrases will follow the words that they modify.

Jill's present arrived just **after her birthday**.

The smog is thick **in the early morning**.

Carl runs awkwardly **in these shoes**.

The first example contains the prepositional phrase **after her birthday**, modifying the verb **arrived**. It tells when the present arrived. The second example contains the prepositional phrase **in the early morning**, modifying the adjective **thick**. It indicates when the smoke is thick. The final example contains the prepositional phrase **in these shoes**, modifying the adverb **awkwardly**. It tells how Carl runs awkwardly.

PREPOSITIONS AT GRADUATION

Q. A recent secondary school graduate proudly announced that he received his degree when he "graduated high school." His mother called to ask us whether there was a prepositional phrase missing from his sentence.

A. First, he received a diploma, not a degree, from high school. A degree can only be presented by a college or university. Second, one cannot "graduate high school." Taken literally, this means that the student sends the high school out into the world to embark on life's long journey. The young man should amend his statement to say that he "graduated from high school." The prepositional phrase **from high school** is an adverbial that modifies the verb **graduated**.

PREPOSITIONAL PHRASES USED AS NOMINALS

There is one case in which the preposition acts without a referent—when the prepositional phrase is a nominal. Remember that a nominal is any noun or pronoun or any word, phrase, or clause that performs the same function as a noun. Nominals have no descriptive or qualifying abilities, so they do not refer to other words. Nominals put names on people, animals, and things. Similarly, a prepositional phrase used as a nominal will have no referent. Its function will be to name.

Beyond the stars is where I would like to fly.

At noon is when we decided to meet.

In the first example, the prepositional phrase **beyond the stars** names a place, a place where I would like to fly. In the second example, the prepositional phrase **at noon** names a time, a time that we decided to meet.

Positioning the Preposition

The word preposition comes from two Latin words, **prae** meaning "before," and **ponere**, meaning "to put." The preposition is usually placed right before its object.

We drove **through** the **woods**.

Tim trained his binoculars **on** the **eagle**.

In each of these examples, the preposition comes almost directly before its object, separated only by a modifier. Occasions do arise, however, when it is appropriate to place the preposition somewhere else. When you encounter such an occasion, proceed with caution.

Contrary to popular belief, it is not a mortal sin to end a sentence with a preposition, as long as the sentence sounds natural and its meaning is clear.

We found the earring you were looking **for**.

I know the place you are thinking **of**.

These sentences are fine.

Such constructions become dangerous, however, when their objects are pronouns. Separated from the preposition, the object is less distinctively an object and easily mistaken for a pronoun in the nominative case form. Warning! Warning! Warning! It is of the utmost importance that objects be in the objective case form.

Whom are you looking **for**? (correct)

Whom are they staring **at**? (correct)

These sentences correctly put the pronoun objects of the prepositions **for** and **at** in objective case forms. If only all objects could be so lucky.

Who are you looking **for**? (incorrect)

Who are they staring **at**? (incorrect)

These sad pronouns used as objects are in the nominative case form. With the prepositions far, far away at the ends of the sentences, the author did not even recognize these pronouns as objects. If in doubt, remember that it is always possible to reunite an object with the preposition that governs it.

> **For whom** are you looking? (correct)

> **At whom** are they staring? (correct)

The ideas expressed in these questions are identical to those expressed before, but their forms are different. Here, the preposition is restored to its usual position before the object, and the object is clearly an object again, correctly in the objective case form.

ENDING A SENTENCE WITH A PREPOSITION

Q. "Is it all right to end a sentence with a preposition?" asked an admirer of Winston Churchill. She and her supervisor were arguing about the sentence "This is one which I cannot find the answer for."

A. If a sentence that ends with a preposition sounds fine and makes sense, by all means, write the sentence. It is absolutely antiquated to forbid ending a sentence with a preposition. However, it is always possible to reword the sentence. "This is one for which I cannot find the answer."

Incidentally, Winston Churchill, whose pen and voice so many admire, was an advocate of this principle. He had a stock answer that he used to justify his reasoning. He would purposely end a sentence with a preposition. "Overzealous grammarians are people whom I will not put up with." Then Churchill would joke that he'd rather end every sentence with a preposition than trip over the clumsy alternative. "Overzealous grammarians are people up with whom I will not put."

SOME THINGS YOU SHOULD KNOW ABOUT PREPOSITIONS

Prepositions have a few peculiarities and trouble spots about which the serious student of grammar will want clarification.

PREPOSITIONS OR ADVERBS?

You may have noticed words that seem to be prepositions working outside of prepositional phrases. Do not be fooled! These are not prepositions. In some places, they may still function as prepositions, but, in others, they function without objects and are adverbs.

The astronomy instructor asked her students to look **up**.

The rescue team was told to stand **by**.

The office turned **down** my request for a vacation.

The highlighted word in each example is an adverb. In the first example, the adverb **up** modifies the infinitive **to look**. It tells where the students were asked to look. In the second example, the adverb **by** modifies the infinitive **to stand**. It tells us where the team was told to stand. In the third example, the adverb **down** modifies the verb **turned**. It indicates where the request was turned.

ONTO

Q. "I know there is a word **into**, but is there a word **onto**, spelled as one word?" asked a high school student.

A. There certainly is a word **onto**. Just take a glance at your dictionary. It means "on top of."

My parakeet jumped **onto** the cage.

It can also be spelled as two words, where **on** is an adverb and **to** is a preposition.

The army marched **on to** its destination.

To its destination is a prepositional phrase modifying **on**. **On** is an adverb modifying the verb **marched**.

SOAP OPERA GRAMMAR

Q. "One of my writers submitted a script with this sentence," said a soap opera director. " 'There hasn't been a day gone by that I haven't felt you dying inside Helen.' It sounds funny, don't you think?"

A. The sentence was meant to be spoken in the second person to a dying woman named Helen. **Inside Helen** (no comma) is a prepositional phrase. It suggests that someone is actually dying within Helen other than Helen herself. If we insert a comma between **inside** and **Helen**, the intent of the sentence becomes clear. It then reads, "There hasn't been a day gone by that I haven't felt you dying inside, Helen." **Inside** is an adverb modifying the verb

dying. It describes where Helen is dying. **Helen** is the name of the person to whom the sentence is spoken. On a stylistic note, I might also change the beginning of the sentence to read, "Not a day has gone by . . . ."

Common Usage Errors with Prepositions and Other Parts of Speech

English is a complex, but flexible language. It grants us powers of expression that a less sophisticated language could not provide but burdens us with the responsibility of using those powers wisely. Prepositions are a subject on which many readers and writers slip and fall. Some use unnecessary words with the prepositions, and others use inappropriate words in place of true prepositions. Whatever the case may be, the resulting grammatical constructions are incorrect. The following calls to the Hot Line will illustrate a few of the most commonly made errors:

The Unnecessary Preposition Error

Q. A caller from Cincinnati asked, "Can I say, 'I didn't know where it was at'?"

A. Do not use a preposition unless the sentence requires it. The preposition **at** in this sentence is superfluous. Try to re-arrange the words so that **at** is reunited with its referent. You may have trouble finding one. Should the sentence read, "I don't know at where it was"? No, it should not. Please remove the preposition so that the sentence does read, "I didn't know where it was."

Here are a few more examples of sentences containing unneeded prepositions:

Stay off **of** the grass. (incorrect)

Where are we **at**? (incorrect)

Where is she driving **to**? (incorrect)

The picture is over **with**. (incorrect)

The prepositions in bold print are unneeded and unwanted. They provide no useful information and give the sentences a rather vulgar sound. Take them away!

Stay off the grass. (correct)

Where are we? (correct)

Where is she driving? (correct)

The picture is over. (correct)

These are much sweeter.

A WORD OF CAUTION

Q. "Could the word **from** be deleted in this sentence?" asked the owner of a stable. "It reads, 'As he dismounted from his horse, the animal spooked.' " The owner was posting a notice on his bulletin board about a rider who had been injured the previous week.

A. **From his horse** is a prepositional phrase. If **from**, a preposition, were deleted, it would be possible to interpret the sentence as meaning that the horse was being dismounted from some other creature. Keep **from**. Writers, take care not to remove necessary prepositions. Of course, you could say, "As he dismounted, the horse spooked," leaving **from his horse** out. The meaning is still clear.

THE DIFFERENT-THAN ERROR

Q. "Is it appropriate to say that one thing is *different than* another?" asked a teacher from Utah.

A. When your intention is to describe the differences between people, animals, or things, use **different from**. **Different than** is never correct.

She is **different than** the rest. (incorrect)

She is **different from** the rest. (correct)

THE IN-BACK-OF ERROR

Q. "My husband just told me that 'the kids are in back of the house.' I told him that he was using incorrect grammar by saying 'in back of,' and he told me to get a life. Was I right?"

A. This woman was correct in a sense. You shouldn't use the wordy compound preposition **in back of** when you can say **behind**. The simple preposition is more concise.

The kids are **in back of** the house. (wordy)

The kids are **behind** the house. (excellent)

However, her husband wasn't incorrect. His version was just wordier. It sounds as if they could both use a night away from the kids.

THE OUTSIDE-OF ERROR

Q. "Is **outside of** a synonym for **except**?" asked a would-be word sleuth from Baltimore.

A. The compound preposition **outside of** is not a suitable substitute for **except**.

> I know no one who plays the accordion **outside of** Anthony.
> (incorrect)

> I know no one who plays the accordion **except** Anthony.
> (correct)

The use of **outside of** even sounds a little creepy. Can you imagine playing the accordion *inside of* poor Anthony?

THE INSIDE-OF ERROR

Q. "I was also wondering about **inside of** and **within**," asked the same would-be word sleuth.

A. Many people mistakenly use the compound preposition **inside of** to speak of time. The correct preposition to use in this context is **within**.

> Our project must be complete **inside of** the week. (incorrect)

> Our project must be complete **within** the week. (correct)

Only use the construction **inside of** when **inside** is used as a noun.

> The **inside of** the house was worn and dirty. (correct)

> The doctor examined the **inside of** my mouth. (correct)

In both examples, **inside** functions as a noun, naming the inside portions of a house and a mouth. The preposition **of** begins a prepositional phrase in each.

THE REGARDS ERROR

Q. "My boss is always saying 'in regards to,' and I keep telling him that he should say 'in regard to,' but he doesn't believe me. What do you think?"

A. This caller knows her grammar. The use of the plural **regards** in the phrases **in regards to** and **with regards to** is incorrect. Since each phrase shows its speaker regarding just one issue, the **regard** is singular: **in regard to** and **with regard to**.

> I am calling **in regards to** your memo. (poor)

> I am calling **in regard to** your memo. (excellent)

> **With regards to** our meeting, I cannot attend. (poor)

> **With regard to** our meeting, I cannot attend. (excellent)

AMBIGUOUS PREPOSITIONS

Prepositions and prepositional phrases are subtle pieces of grammar. Used carelessly, they can communicate faulty, misleading, even horrifying ideas. When you use a prepositional phrase, make sure that the meaning of the phrase is the meaning you intend to communicate and that the word modified by the phrase is clear to the listener or reader. Take a look at some of the problems that have crossed my desk at the Hot Line.

PREPOSITIONAL PHRASE PLACEMENT

Q. A newscaster asked, "Is placement of a prepositional phrase in a sentence of any great importance?"

A. The placement of a prepositional phrase has severe consequences for the meaning of a sentence. The phrase must be so placed that its referent is clear. If the referent is uncertain or missing, we say that the phrase dangles. Take a look at this example:

> I cleaned the room **with my pal Joseph**. (unclear)

The referent of the prepositional phrase **with my pal Joseph** is uncertain. If the phrase modifies the noun **room**, then the meaning of the sentence indicates that the speaker cleaned the room occupied by his or her pal Joseph. The phrase is supposed to function as an adverbial, modifying the verb **cleaned**. This meaning indicates that the speaker cleaned with the help of his or her pal Joseph. To clarify things, place the phrase at the beginning of the sentence:

> **With my pal Joseph**, I cleaned the room. (clear)

A Hairy Question

Q. An attorney phoned me with this dandy of a dangling prepositional phrase: "People in front of me cleaning their faces with beards amused me." He said, "Some sentence, hmmm?"

A. **Cleaning their faces** is a present participle phrase. **With beards** is a prepositional phrase. The placement of the words is a mess. It is unclear whether the prepositional phrase modifies the present participle **cleaning** or the noun **people**. Do people with beards who are cleaning their faces amuse the speaker? Do people who clean their faces with their beards amuse the speaker? We don't have the slightest idea. Immediately, change the sentence to "People with beards cleaning their faces amused me" or, even better, "Bearded people cleaning their faces amused me."

Sentence Contamination

Q. Writing in *Smithsonian* magazine, William R. Appel reported that residents of Marshville, North Carolina, received a frightening notice in the mail. It read, "You probably got a letter warning you about the dangers of lead-contaminated water in your mail."

A. I don't really care whether the water in my mail is contaminated or not. My letters and bills, even my junk mail, should not be wet! **In your mail** is a dangling prepositional phrase. In its current position, the phrase seems to modify the noun **water**. Evidently, contaminated water has seeped into the mail. To make sense of the situation, we should move the phrase. The sentence should read, "You probably got a letter in your mail warning you about the dangers of lead-contaminated water."

Time Ambiguity

Q. A number of people heard this on a national radio news program and called my number. "A drop of silver nitrate within twenty minutes of birth prevents blindness."

A. Horrified at the news writers' carelessness, the Hot Line automatically replied that the drug would have to be administered *after* birth. My Lord! It would have been brutal any other way. As it stands, the statement suggests that the drug could also be administered before birth. **Within 20 minutes** and **of birth** are prepositional phrases.

BETWEEN WHAT TIMES?

Q. "Does this make sense: 'The injured baby was between one-and-a-half years old'?" asked a skeptical newspaper reader.

A. The baby must be between two ages. This sentence only lists one. The clearest way of expressing the idea is to write, "The injured baby was between twelve months and eighteen months old." **Between twelve months and eighteen months** is a prepositional phrase.

THE COPIOUS DRINKER AND HER PILE

Q. "Is this ad correct?" asked an astute beer drinker. "It reads, 'She is sitting among a pile of beer cans.' "

A. **Among a pile** is a prepositional phrase. Structurally, it is correct, but logically, it doesn't make sense. You cannot sit *among* a pile, which is defined as a single heap. You can sit *on* a pile or *next to* a pile or *between* two piles, but not *among* one. The sentence needs to be reworded.

> She is sitting **among** many beer cans.

> She is sitting **on** a pile of beer cans.

> She is sitting **in the midst of** many beer cans.

Any of these will work. Why was she there anyway? Doesn't she have better things to do with her time? And who drank all that beer? The possibilities boggle the mind.

CLARIFYING SOME DEFINITIONS

Q. A frequent Hot Line caller asked, "What's the difference between **between** and **among**? I feel like I know the answer, but I just can't put it into words."

A. There are several pairs of prepositions whose definitions are easily confused. The pair **between-among** is certainly one of these. The preposition **between** refers to just two people, animals, or things. The preposition **among** refers to more than two.

> The cotton candy was divided **between** the two children.

The rumor was spread **among** the townspeople.

Here are a few other pairs of prepositions whose definitions could use some clarification:

• **Beside-Besides**

One places a spoon *beside* or *next to* the knife. One plays tennis *besides* or *in addition to* golf.

My dog waited **beside** my bed while I was sick.

Besides me, only four other people came to the first meeting.

• **By-With**

By refers to the individual taking the action. **With** refers to the instrument used to create the action.

The book was written **by** Hemingway.

The tree was felled **with** a sharp ax and a quick stroke.

• **During-For**

During refers to a small set of times within a larger period, while **for** refers to the entire period named.

I went to the bathroom four times **during** the first act.

The thief was sent to prison **for** twenty-five years.

• **In-Into**

The preposition **in** denotes motion or action *within* a certain area. The preposition **into** refers to motion *toward* an area from the outside.

We swam **in** the pool.

We dove **into** the pool.

• **Of-Off**

The words **of** and **off** may look similar, but their meanings are quite different. The preposition **of** indicates distance, origin, cause, material, possession, or inclusion, among other definitions.

The balloon touched down three miles south **of** the landing sight. (distance)

Charles is the Prince **of** Wales. (origin)

The miners died **of** oxygen deprivation. (cause)

The ring is **of** the purest gold. (material)

You are one **of** us now. (inclusion)

The preposition **off** implies removal or departure.

That took the weight **off** my shoulders.

Take your feet **off** the table.

Stay **off** my lawn, you kids!

Off can also be an adverb, again implying removal or departure.

I took **off** my shirt.

The thieves took **off** the car's hubcaps.

• With-From

The prepositions **with** and **from** can both imply separation, but the types of separation implied differ. **With** indicates an active separation, one where some person, place, or thing actively moves away from another.

Let's dispense **with** the social niceties.

I had to part **with** many of my prized possessions when we moved.

The separation of the preposition **from** is passive. It is a matter of fact, such as the distance from one place to another or from one time to another, rather than the result of an active will.

The fireworks will start twenty minutes **from** now.

We are seventy miles **from** the nearest telephone.

AN ADDITIONAL CLARIFICATION: TO-TOO

Q. I received a fax one afternoon with a question from a frustrated high school biology student. She wrote, "In my lab reports, I often don't use the word **to** correctly. I put in an extra **o**, and I get points knocked off my grade even though the rest of the report is fine. What is the correct way to use **to** and **too**?"

A. This caller is not alone in her frustration. The preposition **to** and the adverb **too** are often misused. People err in their uses of these words for two reasons: 1) they write without thinking or 2) they are not clear on the definitions. Only you can rectify the first situation, but I can help with the second.

The word **to**, as we have seen before, is a preposition. It usually means "toward" or "in the direction of."

We decided to go **to** the movies.

My family traveled **to** Europe last summer.

To, as you well know, is also the marker of infinitives. In this role, it does not have the true power of the preposition to create relationships between words.

I love **to** ski.

To run a marathon is one of my dreams.

On occasion, you may encounter **to** as an adverb, meaning "toward a certain point."

The saloon door swung **to** and fro.

The submariner pulled the hatch **to**.

The word **too** is an adverb and only an adverb. It can mean "also," "extremely," or "excessively."

I would like to come **too**. (also)

That is **too** much lasagna for one person to eat. (extremely)

It is **too** bright in this room. (excessively)

To-With

Q. "Should I say, 'It's been a pleasure talking **to** you' or 'It's been a pleasure talking **with** you'?" a CEO asked.

A. **To you** and **with you** are both prepositional phrases. **To** is a one-directional preposition. It implies that you did most of the talking. **With** implies a joining together, a give and take. **To** is a soliloquy, whereas **with** is a colloquy. Either is correct, but the meanings are different, and **with** is just a bit more couth.

In-On

Q. A publicist for a year-round resort asked, "Are sports played *in* or *on* the water?"

A. Some sports, such as water polo and swimming, can only be played *in* the water. In these activities, the participants' bodies are surrounded by the water. Other sports, such as water-skiing and rafting, are done *on* the water. Here, the participants' bodies remain above the water. Klutzier water-skiers, however, may find themselves *in* the water more often than *on*.

IN-WITHIN

Q. "What's the difference between **in an hour** and **within an hour**?" asked an attorney.

A. An event that will take place **in an hour** will occur at the end of sixty minutes. An event that will take place **within an hour** may occur any time between the present and sixty minutes from the present. The difference is crucial, especially if you are to meet someone at a specific place and time. Both **in an hour** and **within an hour** are prepositional phrases.

BUT-EXCEPT

Q. "Can **but** be a preposition in the sentence 'No one but me knows the material so well'?" The caller, a scholar from Biloxi, wanted clarification.

A. The usage of **but** is perfectly acceptable. **But** can be a preposition but only when it means "except."

All of us will go **but** Jim.

All of us will go **except** Jim.

In the caller's sentence, **but** is a preposition, meaning "except."

No one **except** me knows the material so well.

No one **but** me knows the material so well.

FROM MY FILES: POLITICAL GRAMMAR

A political ad a few years ago showed photographs of six potential candidates. It asked the reader, "Between these, whom would you choose?" Grammatically, **between** can only involve two entities. The writer implied that only two of the individuals were worthy of being considered. If he had wanted the readers to consider all six of them, he should have written, "Among these, whom would you choose?" Or perhaps some clever spin doctor knew exactly what was being said. Did the two front-runners also know? If so, what a devious use of grammar this was to eliminate the competition!

COLLOCATIONS AND PREPOSITIONS

Q. A legal secretary complained that her boss always uses constructions which sound and look awkward. "Is there a prescribed list of which prepositions go with which words?" she asked plaintively.

A. Yes, there is. Grammarians call regular pairings of words **collocations**. That one word is collocated with another does not mean that both words must be used together or not at all. A collocation is simply a common and expected usage of that pair of words. This list of collocations will indicate which prepositions we use in conjunction with particular words. It's a good idea to keep the list near your computer as it can be a great boon in settling petty arguments. Here's the list:

Abhorrence *to*

Hypocrisy is abhorrent **to** one.

Abide *with*

One abides **with** his wife.

Absolve *by, from*

One is absolved **by** the judge. One is absolved **from** all penalties.

Accede *to*

One accedes **to** a request.

Accommodate *to, with*

One accommodates **to** circumstances. One accommodates a friend **with** a loan.

Accompany *by, with*

One is accompanied **by** companions. One accompanies a speech **with** slides.

Accord *with*

One is in accord **with** the new office regulations.

According *to*

Everything is going according **to** my plan.

Account *to, for*

One has to account **to** the principal. You must account **for** your actions.

Accountable *to, for*

> One is accountable **to** the boss for one's work. You are accountable **for** the entire loss.

Accuse *of*

> One may accuse another **of** wrongful actions.

Acquiesce *in, to*

> One acquiesces **in** a decision. She acquiesced **to** the demands.

Acquitted *of,*

> One is acquitted **of** a misdemeanor.

Adapted *to, for, from*

> One adapts oneself **to** a situation. One is not adapted **for** heavy lifting. A movie is adapted **from** a best-selling book.

Admit *of, to*

> Some words admit **of** two meanings. He admits **to** the accusation of improper behavior.

Advantage *in, of, over, to, with*

> There is an advantage **in** early tax filing. You have the advantage **of** me. You have an advantage **over** me. There is an advantage **to** keeping your promises. The advantage lay **with** the movie director.

Adverse *to*

> He is adverse **to** his move to the city.

Advise *of, about*

> She advised me **of** the new regulations. Advise me **about** the issue before deciding.

Agree *in, with, on, to*

> We agree **in** principle. You must agree **with** me that the letter must be rewritten. I agree **on** that point. Agree **to** honor the contract.

Agreeable *to, with*

> Oysters may not be agreeable **to** your stomach. Your plan is agreeable **with** our future plans.

Analogous *to*

This situation is analogous **to** mine.

Angry *at, with*

She is angry **at** her boss. She is also angry **with** my friendly attitude toward him.

Answer *to*

He must answer **to** his parents.

Appeal *to, against*

He appealed **to** his parents' sense of fair play, but he also appealed **against** their unjust criticism.

Apply *to, for*

Apply **to** the office for a day off. Apply **for** social security.

Answer *to, for*

Nevertheless, she must answer **to** her parents. You must answer **for** your shortcomings.

Apropos *of*

Apropos **of** your statement, let me say I agree.

Argue *about, against, for, with*

Let's not argue **about** it any more. I shall not argue **against** you. Let's argue **for** a better way of doing things. I do not like to argue **with** you.

Behalf *in, on, of,*

One uses one's influence **in** behalf **of** another person and acts **on** behalf **of** that person. One might also influence a panel **in** another person's behalf or act **on** that person's behalf.

Capable *of*

One is capable **of** running a marathon.

Care *about, for*

One does not care **about** unimportant things. One cares **for** the good opinion of others.

Careless *about, of*

One should not be careless **about** or **of** details.

Cause *for*

Adam's words were cause **for** violence.

Center *upon*

Center your attention **upon** the important facts.

Characteristic *of*

Those remarks are characteristic **of** my mother.

Compatible *with*

One should be compatible **with** one's fellow workers.

Compliance *with*

One attempts compliance **with** requests.

Concur *in, with*

I concurred **in** the demand. That doesn't concur **with** my understanding.

Connect *by, with*

They are connected **by** marriage. Their good manners are connected **with** their upbringing.

Consideration *for, of*

It's nice to have consideration **for** others. In consideration **of** the circumstances, he was overly polite.

Consist *in, of*

The decision consists **in** weighing the facts. The book consists **of** sixteen chapters.

Contend *against, for, with*

I contended **against** the passage of the bill. I contended **for** a more equitable policy. I contended **with** his ugly disposition.

Contrast *to, with*

One thing is contrasted **to** or **with** another thing.

Convenient *to, for*

The bus stop is convenient **to** my work, which makes commuting convenient **for** me.

Conversant *with*

He is conversant **with** the material.

Correspond *to, with*

This does not correspond **to** or **with** the facts.

Defer *to*

I always defer **to** the officer in charge.

Depend *on, upon*

That depends **on** or **upon** his testimony.

Desirous *of*

He is desirous **of** a promotion at his firm.

Die *from, of*

He died **from** or **of** kidney failure.

Differ *from, with*

Twins may differ **from** each other in appearance, but they may also differ **with** each other about the best course of action.

Different *from*

He is different in person **from** his pictures.

Dispense *with*

Let's dispense **with** the formalities.

Dispute *with, about, over*

I will not dispute **with** you **about** or **over** the facts in the case.

Dissent *from*

I dissent **from** the argument you proposed.

Distinguish *between, among, from*

One distinguishes **between** two things and **among** several, but one distinguishes a camel **from** a chicken.

Divide *between, among*

One divides anything **between** two and **among** three or more.

Enamored *of*

He is enamored **of** his fiancee.

Enter *into*

A person enters **into** an agreement.

Entrust *to, with*

> One entrusts one's finances **to** a business manager. One entrusts one's business manager **with** one's money.

Free *from, of*

> It's nice to be freed **from** responsibilities and to be free **of** them.

Furnish *with*

> One furnishes another **with** a recommendation.

Give *to, for*

> One gives a donation **to** the church **for** its upkeep.

Grieve *at, for, over, with*

> It's normal to grieve **at** or **for** or **over** the death of a pet. You can grieve **with** someone.

Guard *against, from*

> One guards **against** or **from** unnecessary risks.

Happen *on, upon, to*

> Sometimes, one happens **on** or **upon** good buys by chance. Good luck can happen **to** anyone.

Identical *to, with*

> Twins may be identical **to** or **with** one another.

Incorrect *in*

> He was incorrect **in** his answer.

Independent *of*

> He's lucky to be independent **of** any kind of financial pressure.

Infer *from*

> One infers **from** another person's implication.

Initiated *into*

> One is initiated **into** a new club.

Inseparable *from*

> They are inseparable **from** each another.

Instill *into, in*

> He has had discipline instilled **into** him by his father. I shall instill **in** you certain virtues.

Intercede *for, with*

He intercedes **for** his parents **with** the tax assessor.

Interest *in*

He has a great interest **in** art.

Join *with, in, to*

Join **with** the others **in** the fun. Join this plug **to** the outlet.

Jump *at, to*

One jumps **at** a generous offer. One jumps **to** conclusions.

Liable *for, to*

Life makes us all liable **for** our actions. Indiscretions are liable **to** catch up with us.

Live *in, at, on*

One may live **in** or **at** a house of his or her own. One may also live **on** the coast.

Meddle *in, with*

She likes to meddle **in** or **with** other peoples' affairs.

Necessity *for, of*

There is no necessity **for** you to attend. There is no necessity **of** your attending.

Need *for, of*

There is no need **for** you to go. There is no need **of** your going.

Object *to*

He objects **to** the change in plans.

Oblivious *of*

He is oblivious **of** his shortcomings.

Overcome *by, with*

He was overcome **by** the play. She was overcome **with** emotion.

Parallel *to, with*

Lines may be parallel **to** or **with** one another.

Part *from, with*

One does not like to part **from** or **with** one's former companions. One does not like to part **with** one's money.

Ponder *on, upon, over*

He ponders **on** or **upon** or **over** his future course of action.

Preferable *to*

Employment is preferable **to** unemployment.

Prejudiced *against*

One is prejudiced **against** a matter.

Preside *at, over*

The chairman presides **at** or **over** the meeting.

Prevail *against, on, upon, with, over*

It's sometimes difficult to prevail **against** hard times. But one can prevail **on** or **upon** or **with** one's boss for a raise. One can certainly prevail **over** a situation.

Provide *against, for, with*

One must provide **against** the future **for** one's senior years to be sure one is provided **with** the necessities. Your pension will provide **for** your needs.

Quarrel *over, with*

One should not quarrel **over** small things. One should not quarrel **with** one's siblings.

Reason *with, about*

One reasons **with** one's spouse **about** a matter.

Reckon *with*

One must reckon **with** inflation.

Reconcile *to, with*

One must reconcile oneself **to** or **with** many changes in life.

Rejoice *with, at, in*

It's nice to rejoice **with** a friend **at** or **in** his or her good luck.

Result *from, in*

The argument resulted **from** a lie the boy told and eventually resulted **in** a fight.

Retire *from, into*

One retires **from** office. A turtle retires its head **into** its shell.

Seek *after, for, out*

> Gold miners seek **after** wealth. Ponce de Leon was seeking **for** the Fountain of Youth. One can seek **out** justice.

Strive *against, with, for*

> One strives **against** or **with** difficulties **for** a positive outcome.

Supply *to, with*

> One can supply goods **to** the army. One can also supply the army **with** goods.

Trade *in, on, with*

> She trades **in** stocks and bonds. She trades **on** the stock exchange. She trades only **with** reliable brokers.

Variance *with*

> His bank records are at variance **with** his accountants.

Vary *from, in, with*

> His opinions vary **from** the norm. Opinions may vary **in** intensity. The flavor of wine varies **with** age.

Vexed *at, by*

> One is vexed **at** one's girlfriend or boyfriend. One is vexed **by** her or his attitude.

Vie *for, with*

> He vied **for** her affections. He vies **with** his opponents.

Wait *by, for, on*

> One waits **by** the telephone. One waits **for** the bus. A waiter or waitress waits **on** a table or a customer.

Yield *to*

> Don't yield **to** temptation.

BEHALF

Q. "What is the difference between **in behalf of** and **on behalf of**?" asked a Pittsburgh judge.

A. Some experts argue that the two are interchangeable. I am not among them. **On behalf of** means "as the agent of."

On behalf of Smith, Smith, & Jones, I thank you for this honor.

In behalf of means "in the interest of."

In behalf of the well-being of our society, I ask you not to run for another term.

PREPARE YOURSELF WITH PREPOSITIONS

Q. " 'One of two remaining escaped convicts were captured today' is a sentence I'm using in a news release," said a prison warden. "I want to be absolutely sure of my English. Is it correct?"

A. Of two remaining escaped convicts is a prepositional phrase. Of is a preposition and convicts is its object. The warden took the plural noun convicts for the subject of the sentence and used a plural verb, were. He has made a mistake. The object of a preposition cannot be the subject of a sentence. The singular subject one needs a singular verb, was. The corrected sentence reads, "One of two remaining convicts was captured today."

A knowledge of prepositional phrases not only increases writing efficiency but also enhances reading comprehension. Not knowing that of two remaining convicts is a prepositional phrase, it would be easy to mistake convicts for the subject of the sentence. Knowing that convicts is the object of the preposition, we realize that it cannot be the subject. The only other choice for subject is the pronoun one. I teach grammar in my reading classes; lo and behold, my scholars in training automatically do better in all of their endeavors!

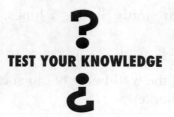

TEST YOUR KNOWLEDGE

QUESTIONS

1. A preposition is a _____ word.

2. What two partners do prepositions work with?

3. What grammatical construction are prepositions always part of?

4. The word or phrase modified by the prepositional phrase is called the _____.

5. Is the object of the preposition always a noun?

6. Which verbal do we sometimes see as an object of a preposition?

7. How might a prepositional phrase function in a sentence?

8. Is it a mistake to place a preposition at the very end of a sentence?

9. Identify the problem in this sentence: "Where are we taking him to?"

10. What is the difference in meaning between the prepositions **between** and **among**?

(SEE ANSWERS ON FOLLOWING PAGE)

ANSWERS

1. relationship

2. Prepositions always work with objects and referents.

3. Prepositions are always part of prepositional phrases.

4. referent

5. The object of the preposition is always a nominal (a word, phrase, or clause that functions as a noun), but it is not necessarily a standard noun.

6. The gerund is frequently the object of a preposition.

7. A prepositional phrase may function as a nominal or a modifier.

8. No, it is OK to place a preposition at the end of a sentence as long as the sentence sounds fine and makes sense.

9. The sentence contains an unnecessary preposition. Remove **to**. It should read, "Where are we taking him?"

10. **Between** applies to just two people, animals, or things, while **among** applies to more than two.

8.

Conjunctions

> **Conjunctions** are the connections between words and groups of words.

Language is composed of many elements. We take words and put them together to make simple ideas. We then take these simple ideas and put them together to make more complicated ones. The simple ideas that make up the more complicated ones do not stick together on their own, however. For this, we need some tape.

Conjunctions are language's Scotch™ tape. They connect words, phrases, clauses, and sentences.

Bill **and** I saw the concert last weekend.

My friend Dana can paint, **but** she really loves to sculpt.

I would like Italian **or** Chinese food for dinner.

In each example, a conjunction connects one word to another word or one group of words to another group of words. The following is a list of some commonly used conjunctions:

although	because	if	nor
and	before	lest	only
as	for	neither	or

provided	that	whereat	whereupon
save	though	whereby	wherever
since	unless	wherefore	whether
so	when	wherein	while
than	whereas	whereof	yet

Sometimes two or three words can be used together as a single conjunction.

I took this class **so that** I could learn more about genetics.

I will be there **as soon as** I can.

These examples use two- and three-word conjunctions: **so that** and **as soon as**.

COORDINATE AND SUBORDINATE CONJUNCTIONS

Conjunctions also show the relationships between the words and word groups that they connect. These connected elements may be of equal importance, but they may also differ in importance in relation to one another. With this relating function in mind, conjunctions are divided into two general categories: **coordinate** and **subordinate**.

COORDINATE CONJUNCTIONS

Coordinate conjunctions connect elements of equal importance.

My cats **and** dogs are great friends.

Sam loves to cook, **but** he loves to eat more.

I think that Susan **or** Mary will ask me to the dance.

In the first example, the conjunction **and** connects the nouns **cats** and **dogs**. In the second example, the conjunction **but** connects two simple sentences: **Sam loves to cook** and **he loves to eat more**. In the third example, the conjunction **or** joins the names **Susan** and **Mary**. In each example, the elements connected are of equal importance. One does not depend on the other to substantiate its meaning. Each could function just as well without the other.

We can divide coordinate conjunctions further into **conjunctive conjunctions** and **disjunctive conjunctions**. Conjunctive conjunctions bring elements together. They have an additive function. The conjunction **and** is the most famous of the conjunctive conjunctions.

The frog sings **and** dances.

Jane **and** I went to the movies.

I need a hammer **and** chisel to cut this stale bread.

In each example, the conjunctive conjunction **and** adds elements of the sentences together: the frog's abilities, the people going to the movies, and the tools needed to cut the bread.

The other and, by far, the larger class of coordinate conjunctions is that of the disjunctive conjunctions. While they may tie words and groups of words together, they also imply an opposition or separation. Some disjunctive conjunctions are **but, or, nor,** and **yet**.

They will stay, **or** they will go.

The sports car was beautiful **but** expensive.

I never called her back, **nor** have I regretted it.

Do you see how the connected elements of each sentence are in opposition, be they words or groups of words? Instead of being added together, the elements on either side of these disjunctive conjunctions almost seem to defy one another.

A COORDINATE QUANDARY

Q. "My associate and I are having a minor confrontation over a sentence. We're confused about whether we should use a preposition or a conjunction. Here's the sentence that's giving us trouble: 'We will celebrate its anniversary with a luncheon in a salute to women of achievement.' Now, can we replace **in** with **and**? If we do, does it change the meaning of the sentence?"

A. Either **in** or **and** is acceptable at this spot in the sentence, but the choice of word will have drastic effects on meaning. Which word the coworkers select will depend on how they view the "salute to women of achievement." If the celebration is being held as a salute to women of achievement, then the sentence should read, "We will celebrate its anniversary with a luncheon *in* a salute to women of achievement." The prepositional phrase **in a salute to women of achievement** functions as an adverbial of reason to modify the verb phrase **will celebrate**. It gives us the reason for celebrating.

If, however, the luncheon and the salute are regarded as two separate events that will take place at the celebration, the sentence should read, "We will celebrate its anniversary with a luncheon *and* a salute to women of achievement." The coordinate conjunction **and** has an additive effect within the phrase. It adds the noun **salute** to the noun **luncheon** so that both are objects of the preposition **with**. The entire prepositional phrase **with a luncheon and a salute to women of achievement** functions as an adverbial of manner to modify the verb phrase **will celebrate**. It tells us the manner of the celebrating.

Whew! Do you see how a simple word change can have a severe effect on meaning? Grammar is the interior framework of language. Change the interior and there are bound to be consequences for the exterior, the meaning. Thank you, callers, for bringing these lovely quandaries to my attention. Please keep calling.

SUBORDINATE CONJUNCTIONS

Subordinate conjunctions connect elements of differing importance. One element is always a **main clause**. The other is a **subordinate clause**. The main clause has a subject and predicate and may stand on its own as a complete thought. For this reason, grammarians sometimes refer to it as an **independent clause**.

The subordinate clause also has a subject and predicate, but it cannot stand alone and make sense. It depends on the main clause. This element contains the subordinate conjunction. The function of the subordinate clause is to modify the main clause in some way, rather than to express a primary idea. This is why we view it as less important, and this is why we have assigned it the title of **subordinate clause**. The word **subordinate** implies a lower rank. The subordinate conjunction binds the words of the subordinate clause to those of the main clause (see Chapter 13, p. 334 for more information about main and subordinate clauses).

Here is a list of the most familiar subordinate conjunctions:

after	because	for	since
although	before	if	than
as	even if	lest	that
as if	even though	provided	though
as though	except	save	till

unless	when	where	whether
until	whenever	wherever	while

The relationship that the subordinate conjunction creates between main and subordinate clauses may carry one of several meanings:

PLACE

Subordinate conjunctions such as **where** and **wherever** can imply a sense of **place**.

Where there is smoke, there is fire.

I will go **wherever** you ask me to go.

TIME

Subordinate conjunctions such as **after, before, since, until, when, whenever,** and **while** can imply a sense of **time**.

It has been years **since** I saw you last.

I saw dolphins swim past the end of the pier **while** I was waiting for you.

MANNER

Subordinate conjunctions such as **as** and **as if** can imply a sense of **manner**.

You look at me **as if** I were from another planet.

She treats me **as** an equal.

REASON

Subordinate conjunctions such as **as, because, in order that, since, so that,** and **that** can provide a **reason**.

I came **because** I want to see you.

I stopped running **so that** my knee could heal.

POSSIBILITY OR CONDITIONALITY

Subordinate conjunctions such as **although, if, even if, provided, though,** and **unless** can state **possibility** or **conditionality**.

If you go, I will go too.

Sammy will not go to bed **unless** we read her a story.

COMPARISON

Subordinate conjunctions such as **as** and **than** can make a **comparison**.

I like summer more **than** I like winter.

She does not want to do anything else **than** to play pinball.

CORRELATIVE CONJUNCTIONS

Q. One blustery afternoon, a caller telephoned to say, "There's this quote that I hear all the time: 'As ye sow, so shall ye reap.' I think it's from the Bible. My question is this. What is the structure of the sentence? It looks like it's just two subordinate clauses, each one beginning with **as** or **so**. What's the explanation of this?"

A. The quote is indeed Biblical, Galatians 6:7 to be exact. This particular phrasing of that Biblical quote makes use of a special type of conjunction. Conjunctions of this class are called **correlative conjunctions**, and they come in pairs. Some correlative conjunctions function as coordinate conjunctions. Others function as subordinate conjunctions. In the caller's sentence, the pair **as-so** is a correlative conjunction. It links a subordinate clause, **as ye sow**, to a main clause, **so shall ye reap**.

The following are common examples of correlative conjunctions:

as-as	neither-nor
as-so	not-but
both-and	not only-but also
either-or	not so much-as
if-then	whether-or

Some of these words do not normally fall under the heading of conjunction. The word **both**, for instance, is a determiner[†]. However, the pairings change the functions of these words into those of conjunctions. Take a look at some more examples:

Neither Tom **nor** Harry knows where the report went.

Both Jack **and** Jill went up the hill.

[†] A **determiner** is a word that determines the reference of a noun phrase. Determiners are words, such as **a, an, the, other, that, few,** or **many**, that aid the reader or listener in determining which person, place, thing, or idea is named by the noun phrase that the writer or speaker has written or spoken.

Either the cat goes **or** I go.

If you hadn't called, **then** I would never have heard about the accident.

Whether you want to finish your homework **or** not is not my concern.

As you wish, **so** do I.

Not only am I a fisherman, **but also** I am a fabulous chef.

The washer never gets my clothes **as** clean **as** I would like.

When using the correlative conjunctions **either-or** or **neither-nor**, remember that **either** is always paired with **or** and that **neither** is always paired with **nor**. These words are not interchangeable.

FROM MY FILES: THE PRESIDENT'S CABINET

One Wednesday morning, I heard the CBS news reader state, "The President or his cabinet are going to meet this afternoon." What savage language! The broadcasting industry must be made to recognize its responsibility as a bearer of standards. Unconsciously, we mimic what we hear, and, with the average American watching three to four hours of television a day, the voices of the media are the voices often mimicked. It is vital that all media personalities, before they are allowed to speak to the public, be trained in the rudiments of grammar. Before any network employs a newscaster, he or she should be tested for basic grammar and pronunciation. It is unfortunate that the networks do not pay experts to monitor and correct their broadcast scripts.

This newscaster had implied that either the President or his cabinet was to meet. The cabinet can certainly meet, but the President alone, assuming he is sane, cannot. He needs others to meet with. The reader should have said, "The President **and** his cabinet are to meet this afternoon."

SOME OTHER THINGS TO REMEMBER ABOUT CONJUNCTIONS

Here are a few additional issues about conjunctions that any skilled grammarian needs to address.

CONNECTIONS

One of the most important things to remember when using conjunctions is that they must connect like parts of speech or sentence elements. Adjectives should be connected to adjectives, adverbs to adverbs, nouns to nouns, and verbs to verbs. It would never do to connect an adverb to a noun or a noun to a verb. A noun, verb, adjective, or adverb can be connected to a phrase as long as the phrase is of the same functional type as the word that it is connected to.

> You must choose hot coffee at dinner **or** sleeping at night.

> Terry played well **and** without error.

In the first example, the conjunction **or** connects the noun phrase **hot coffee at dinner** to the gerund phrase **sleeping at night**. Both elements function as nominals so we can connect them. In the second example, **and** connects the adverb **well** to the prepositional phrase **without error**. Both play adverbial roles in the sentence, so we can correctly connect them, as well.

CONJUNCTIVE ADVERBS

Q. "What part of speech is **eventually**?" asked a late-night caller. "My dictionary says that it's an adverb, but that doesn't quite seem right."

A. This is a significant question because it highlights an entity known as the **conjunctive adverb**. Remember that a standard adverb modifies a verb, an adjective, or another adverb.

> The snow fell **mercilessly**.

In this example, **mercilessly** describes the verb **fell**. Its role is that of a standard adverb.

Conjunctive adverbs share characteristics with two parts of speech. They are similar to standard adverbs because of the meanings that they can convey, but they are also similar to coordinate conjunctions because they connect main clauses.

Conjunctive adverbs are unlike standard adverbs in one very important way. While the meaning implied by a standard adverb affects only a single word or phrase, the meaning implied by a conjunctive adverb concerns the entire clause of which it is a part.

These are the most common conjunctive adverbs:

accordingly	eventually	in like manner	on the contrary
afterwards	finally	in short	on the other hand
again	for example	instead	otherwise
also	for instance	in the meantime	perhaps
anyhow	furthermore	later	so
as a result	hence	likewise	still
at last	however	meanwhile	subsequently
at the same time	in addition	moreover	that is
besides	in any case	namely	then
consequently	indeed	nevertheless	therefore
earlier	in fact	next	thus

As we just discussed, conjunctive adverbs carry meanings that are similar to those of standard adverbs. The possible meanings of these special adverbs number six.

1. **Time**: afterwards, earlier, eventually, later

2. **Addition**: also, for example, furthermore, moreover

3. **Cause**: as a result, consequently, hence, therefore

4. **Manner**: anyhow, in like manner, in short, likewise

5. **Contrast**: however, in fact, on the contrary, on the other hand

6. **Example**: for instance, for example

Examine these examples of conjunctive adverbs in action. Remember that each possesses a modifying and a connecting function.

> Tom wanted to buy the leather jacket; **however**, his empty wallet persuaded him not to.

> Grandma took the kids to the zoo. **Afterwards**, they stopped for ice cream.

In the first example, the conjunctive adverb **however** joins the main clauses **Tom wanted to buy the leather jacket** and **his empty wallet persuaded him not to**. The meaning of the conjunctive adverb affects the latter clause. It implies a sense of contrast, indicating that the second clause exists in contrast with the first.

In the second example, the conjunctive adverb **afterwards** forms a connection between the main clauses **Grandma took the kids to the zoo** and **they stopped for ice cream**. Again, the meaning of the conjunctive adverb affects the latter clause. It implies a sense of time, indicating that the event described by the second clause occurred after the event described by the first.

We can see that adverbs and conjunctions are related. In some places, a single word may perform the functions of both. We will complete our discussion of conjunctive adverbs in Chapter 13, p. 337, on compound and complex sentences.

CONJUNCTIONS AND COMMAS

So far, our discussion has been limited to connections between pairs of items, but sometimes it is necessary to connect more than two items. When several items in a series are connected by the same conjunction, you can replace that conjunction with a comma between all but the last two items.

> The movie is long, silly, **and** boring.

> Leslie, Karl, **and** I went skiing last weekend.

It is not a grammatical crime to leave the conjunctions between all the items. In some situations, they can add flavor or emphasis to a sentence.

> The movie is long **and** silly **and** boring.

> Leslie **and** Karl **and** I went skiing last weekend.

If you choose this stylistic option, the commas are unnecessary.

ONLY

Q. A caller from Ann Arbor, Michigan, asked, "Is **only** an adverb or a conjunction?"

A. **Only** can be an adverb or conjunction. In fact, it can even be an adjective. **Only** is a versatile word. With this versatility, however, comes a greater potential for confusion. When you put **only** to use, be sure that it is used in the way that suits your needs. If an adjective, it should clearly modify a noun or pronoun.

> John is our **only** child.

If an adverb, it should clearly modify a verb, an adjective, or an adverb.

> My little brother **only** eats pickles.

If a conjunction, it should connect phrases and clauses.

I would have finished, **only** I broke my leg.

LIKE

Speakers of American English use the word **like** far too loosely. Statistics could show that one thousand four hundred and twenty-three teenagers utter the word **like** every second. Sadly, many of these utterances present **like** as a conjunction. **Like** is NOT a conjunction. It is a preposition. These poor souls unwittingly use incorrect sentences such as those below:

He acts **like** he is already the Homecoming King.

I wish I was popular **like** they are.

I want to be famous **like** Brad Pitt is.

Oh, no, no, no! These sentences all use **like** as a conjunction to join main and subordinate clauses.

There are two things we can do to correct the problem. We could change those subordinate clauses into true prepositional phrases:

He acts **like** the Homecoming King.

I wish I was popular **like them**.

I want to be famous **like Brad Pitt**.

With the verbs removed and the pronouns changed where necessary, we create prepositional phrases:

We could also replace the word **like** with true conjunctions.

He acts **as if** he were already the Homecoming King.

I wish I was **as** popular **as** they are.

I want to be **as** famous **as** Brad Pitt.

Some solutions work better than others. Pick the one that works best for your sentence.

LIKE VS. AS

Q. Adding to the Like-As Controversy was this call from a high school senior on the East Coast. (Mom, please don't quibble over the long-distance phone bill.) His teacher marked him off on a term paper for writing, "High school is valuable like any experience in life should be." Our troubled senior asked, "What's wrong with my sentence?"

A. **Like** is a preposition. It must be used in a prepositional phrase. In his sentence, **like** begins an adverbial clause, a group of words containing a subject and a predicate that functions as an adverb. Any adverbial clause begins with a subordinate conjunction, but **like** is not a subordinate conjunction. The young man needs to replace the preposition with the subordinate conjunction **as**. Corrected, his sentence would read, "High school is valuable *as* any experience in life should be."

LIKE VS. AS AGAIN

Q. "Is **like** a preposition in the sentence 'Like I said, we do not offer a next-day service'?" asked a post office worker.

A. The word **like** is a preposition, but in the sentence above, it is being used as a subordinate conjunction. This usage is unacceptable. The sentence needs a true conjunction, such as **as**. "As I said, we do not offer a next-day service."

In colloquial speech, **like** is accepted by many as a subordinate conjunction. Language is forever changing, and usage ultimately determines what is right and what is wrong despite the protestations of the purists. Purist though I am, I do not stubbornly resist change, even if it occasionally rankles! The use of **like** as a conjunction in contemporary English is so widespread that no one can deny that the word has found a new role. Few would argue with the grammar of a sentence such as "It looks like rain," but the sentence contains a subordinate clause introduced by **like**. The verb has been omitted from the subordinate clause **like rain** (see pp. 369–372 for more information on verbs omitted from subordinate clauses). Even *The American Heritage Dictionary* acknowledges the legitimacy of using **like** as a conjunction when the verb has been removed from the subordinate clause. Those who avoid using **like** as a conjunction across the board will find their sentences to be tortured.

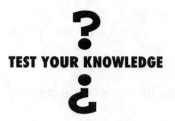

TEST YOUR KNOWLEDGE

QUESTIONS

1. What is the primary function of the conjunctions?

2. Which conjunctions connect pieces of equal importance?

3. Which type of coordinate conjunction has an additive function?

4. What meaning do the disjunctive conjunctions imply?

5. Why do we label a subordinate conjunction "subordinate"?

6. Name the six relationships that subordinate conjunctions can create between clauses.

7. What do adverbs have to do with conjunctions?

8. Could a conjunction connect an adverb to an adjective?

9. Must you use commas in a series of three or more items connected by the same conjunction?

10. Is **like** a conjunction?

(SEE ANSWERS ON FOLLOWING PAGE)

ANSWERS

1. The conjunctions join words, phrases, and clauses.

2. The coordinate conjunctions connect pieces of equal importance.

3. The conjunctive conjunction has an additive function.

4. The disjunctive conjunctions imply a separation between the elements connected.

5. The subordinate conjunction takes its label from its duties. It joins a subordinate clause, the clause of lesser importance, to a main clause, the clause of greater importance. It is subordinate to the main clause.

6. These six relationships are: place, time, manner, reason, possibility or conditionality, comparison.

7. Certain words, called conjunctive adverbs, carry the functions of both conjunctions and adverbs.

8. No, conjunctions only connect words of the same type. For instance, they connect adjectives to adjectives and adverbs to adverbs.

9. No, the comma is not essential. Some people leave the conjunctions to place emphasis on each item.

10. No, **like** is not a conjunction. It is a preposition.

9.

Interjections

Interjections are words that express strong feelings or grab attention.

Have you ever listened carefully to a James Brown song? His tunes are positively littered with exclamations such as "Hah," "Huh," "Ow," "Uh," or "Hep." Overcome by emotion and the music, he cannot help but exclaim something such as "Howwhh!" Independently, these may sound silly, but in the context of the music, they build excitement and hold the listener's interest.

Writers and speakers frequently find themselves in need of the same sort of words. These little firecrackers of prose are called **interjections**. The word comes from two Latin words, **inter** and **jacere**, which together mean "to throw between." Interjections are thrown between sentences or words to grab attention, create interest, or highlight the speaker's strong emotions.

The following is a list of common interjections:

Ah	Eh	Hallo	Horrors
Alack	Good	Heavens	Humph
Alas	Good grief	Hey	Indeed
Bah	Good heavens	Ho	Mercy

Mmm	Oh	Pshaw	Whew
Never	Oops	Well	Whoops
O	Pish posh	What	Zounds

Interjections come in many forms. They may be nonsense words similar to those in the songs of Mr. Brown, they may be real words, often nouns or adjectives, or they may even consist of more than one word.

Zoiks! You scared me.

Heavens! Get the poor man some help.

Good grief! Lucy, you should leave poor Schroeder alone!

Interjections always function independently of the other parts of speech. An interjection is an independent element because it lacks a grammatical relation to any other part of the sentence; it is a complete thought unto itself. Only when quoted does such a word take on any larger meaning in grammar.

"**Never**" was the last thing anyone heard him say.

Here the quoted interjection **never** serves as the subject of the sentence.

FROM MY FILES: COLLECTIVE POTTY MOUTH

Many people of my generation are appalled at the younger generation's collective potty mouth. At any coffee shop and on any street corner, we can find a young person punctuating each declarative sentence with all manner of foul language. If these cretins must use vulgarity, why not revert back to Elizabethan prose and send an adversary reeling with one of those fine sixteenth century expressions? Here are a few dated curses for the language buffs.

Thou beslubbering, beef-witted baggage!

Thou cockered, clapper-clawed bugbear!

Thou gleeking, flap-mouthed foot-licker!

Thou pribbling, ill-nurtured maggot-pie!

Thou quailing, motley-minded measley!

You beetle-headed, flap-eared knave!

Ods bodkins! What folderol, balderdash, and poppycock that is.

PUNCTUATION OF INTERJECTIONS

Interjections can be punctuated in one of two ways, depending on how strong they are. If the interjection is mild, it can be included in a single sentence, separated from the rest of the words by a comma.

Well, did you find the hotel?

Indeed, that is the strangest looking dog I have ever seen.

Stronger interjections, however, should stand alone. These are punctuated with an exclamation mark.

Heavens! You're covered with blood.

What! Who told you I can't dance?

You must choose the method appropriate to your own words.

TEST YOUR KNOWLEDGE

QUESTIONS

1. What are the functions of interjections?

2. What interjection might one utter to express dismay or disbelief?

3. If one includes an interjection in a sentence, how is it punctuated?

(SEE ANSWERS ON FOLLOWING PAGE)

Answers

1. Interjections can grab attention, create interest, or highlight the speaker's strong emotions.

2. One might utter "Zounds," "Zoiks," "Pshaw," or "Heavens," among others.

3. The interjection is separated from the rest of the sentence by a comma.

Part II
Dissecting the Sentence

10.

Subjects
& Predicates

The **subject** names whom or what a sentence is about. The **predicate** indicates action performed or existence expressed by the subject.

With the knowledge gained from chapters past, the budding grammarian should now be able to recognize, understand, and utilize any of the eight parts of speech. Grammar, however, is more than a means of classifying individual words and phrases. It is the internal framework of language and the key to complete thought and effective communication.

The concept of complete thought is not as simple as it might seem. While everyday speech may appear to send messages with whole meanings intact, such expressive completeness does not always include grammatical completeness. Complete conversational thought and complete grammatical thought are different entities. In normal conversation, I might respond, "Yeah, a great time!" to a question such as "Did you have a good time in Tahoe?" The meaning is clear, but my response lacks the appropriate elements to constitute a complete grammatical thought. In the larger world of grammar beyond the parts of speech, the complete sentence is the most basic unit of complete thought. To qualify as a complete sentence, a group of words must possess both a **subject** and a **predicate**.

SUBJECTS AND PREDICATES DEFINED

What, then, are subjects and predicates? The **subject** is the **naming part** of the sentence. It represents the person, place, or thing that performs the action of the verb or expresses the condition or state of the verb. It is the topic about which the speaker or writer is speaking or writing. The **predicate** is the **doing** or **being part** of the sentence. It represents the action taken by the subject or the existence or state of the subject. The predicate is a claim made about the subject by the speaker or writer. Here are a few simple examples of both subjects and predicates:

> Harriet ran.
>
> Factories pollute.
>
> Ignatius was tan.
>
> Camels swim?

Though short, each of these is a complete sentence because it contains a subject and a predicate. In the first sentence, the proper noun **Harriet** is the subject, and the verb **ran** is the predicate. **Harriet** performs the action of **ran**. In the second sentence, the noun **factories** is the subject, and the verb **pollute** is the predicate. **Factories** performs the action of the verb **pollute**. In the third sentence, the proper noun **Ignatius** is the subject, and the linking verb **was** and the subject complement **tan** form the predicate. **Ignatius** expresses the condition indicated by **was**. In the final sentence, the noun **camels** is the subject, and the verb **swim** is the predicate. **Camels** performs the action of **swim**.

HEAD AND COMPLETE SUBJECTS AND PREDICATES

Not all sentences are as simple as the ones mentioned above. Most subjects and predicates consist of two or more words. In the subject, there is always one word that names the entity spoken of. This is the **head**[†] **subject**. The head subject and its attendant modifiers together are called the **complete subject**.

> **The long, bitter winter** took its toll on the soldiers.

[†] Please note that the term **head** does not imply that the particular head subject is the first word in the complete subject.

In this example, the head subject is the noun **winter**. The complete subject is **the long, bitter winter**. **Winter** is the particular thing about which the sentence speaks. The article **the** and the adjectives **long** and **bitter** modify the head subject.

In the predicate, there is one word that unlocks the central meaning of the predicate. This word is always a verb and is called the **head[†] predicate**. If the word is a verb phrase, then the pieces of the verb phrase together constitute the head predicate. The head predicate along with its modifiers, objects, and complements is called the **complete predicate**.

> The hound dog **led us quickly out of the woods**.

> Our family **will be leaving town soon**.

In the first example, the head predicate is the verb **led**. The complete predicate is **led us out of the woods**. The central assertion made about the simple subject, **dog**, is that it *led*. The direct object **us** complements the head predicate. The adverb **quickly** and the adverbial **out of the woods** modify the head predicate.

In the second example, the head predicate is the verb phrase **will be leaving**. The complete predicate is **will be leaving town soon**. The central assertion made about the simple subject **family** is that it *will be leaving*. The direct object **town** complements the head predicate. The adverb **soon** modifies the head predicate.

Subjects and predicates are often single words. If just one word constitutes a subject or a predicate, then that word alone is both the head and complete subject or the head and complete predicate. This is often the case with pronouns used as subjects and with verbs or verb phrases used as predicates.

> **We** saw the eclipse.

> **Tigers** are on the list of endangered species.

> The doors **opened**.

> The crowd **has dispersed**.

In the first example, a single pronoun, **we**, is the head subject and the complete subject. In second example, the noun **tigers** is the head subject and the complete subject. In the third example, the verb **opened** is both the head predicate and the complete predicate.

[†] Please note that the term **head** does not imply that the particular head predicate is the first word in the complete predicate.

In the final example, the verb phrase **has dispersed** is the head predicate and the complete predicate.

IDENTIFYING THE PREDICATE

Q. "I often have a hard time locating the predicate. Is there any easy way to find it in a sentence like this one: 'Should the police have been patrolling the neighborhood?' " asked a caller.

A. The predicate is unclear because the sentence is interrogative. It asks a question. And, as we shall see in Chapter 11 (p. 301) on sentence types and structures, interrogative sentences frequently contain a subject-verb inversion. Here, the modal auxiliary verb **should** has been placed before the complete subject **the police**. The best way to find the predicate is to rearrange the words so that the order is that of a declarative sentence. Declarative sentences just make statements. Reworded, this sentence would read, "The police should have been patrolling the neighborhood." Now the sentence structure becomes clear. The complete subject is **the police**. The head subject is **police**. The complete predicate is **should have been patrolling the neighborhood**. The head predicate is **should have been patrolling**.

SIMPLE OR COMPOUND SUBJECTS AND PREDICATES

Simple sentences are not always as simple as they appeared in the discussion above. Previous examples had **simple subjects** and **simple predicates**. The writer was naming just one topic in the subject and making just one claim about the subject in the predicate. Some sentences contain two or more subjects or two or more predicates, each set joined by a conjunction. A sentence with two or more subjects is said to have a **compound subject**. A sentence with two or more predicates is said to have a **compound predicate**.

> **Bob and Doug** are funny guys.
>
> **Eating pie and swimming laps** together may cause trouble.
>
> Shelby **enjoys biking but loves swimming**.
>
> My pets **sleep on the couch together and eat from the same bowl**.

The first and second examples illustrate the compound subject. In the first example, the compound subject is **Bob and Doug**. The conjunction **and** connects the two proper nouns. In the second example, the compound subject is **eating pie and swimming laps**. The conjunction **and** connects the two gerund phrases.

The third and fourth examples illustrate the compound predicate. In the third example, the compound predicate is **enjoys biking but loves swimming**. The conjunction **but** connects the verbs **enjoys** and **loves**. The gerund **biking** is the direct object of **enjoy**, and the gerund **swimming** is the direct object of **loves**. In the fourth example, the compound predicate is **sleep on the couch together and eat from the same bowl**. The conjunction **and** connects the verbs **sleep** and **eat**. The adverb **together** and the adverbial **on the couch** modify **sleep**. The adverbial **from the same bowl** modifies **eat**.

We can also talk about the head and complete forms of compound subjects and predicates.

> **My sister Laurie and her friend Katie** are traveling through Europe.

> **Playing the lottery and burning your money** are equivalent activities.

These two sentences contain compound subjects. In the first sentence, the complete compound subject is **my sister Laurie and her friend Katie**. The head compound subject is **Laurie and Katie**. Since the subject is compound, we include the conjunction **and** in the head version. In the second sentence, the complete compound subject is **playing the lottery and burning your money**. The head compound subject is **playing and burning**.

> She **drives the car and sings along with the radio**.

> I **will run the marathon and win the medal**.

These sentences contain compound predicates. In the first sentence, the complete compound predicate is **drives the car and sings along with the radio**. The head compound predicate is **drives and sings**. We include the conjunction **and** in the head version because the predicate is compound.

The second sentence takes a shortcut that may need a bit of clarification. The complete compound predicate is **will run the marathon and win the medal**. The head compound predicate is **will run and win**. Notice that at least one head element of this compound predicate is a verb phrase, **will run**. The other element, at first glance, seems to be the lone verb **win**, but is, in fact, also a verb phrase, **will win**.

When a compound predicate is composed of verb phrases and those phrases share auxiliary verbs, it is not necessary to repeat the auxiliary verbs in the latter elements of the compound predicate. This sentence contains a predicate composed of two verb phrases, **will run** and **will win**, that share the modal auxiliary verb **will**. We could have written, "I will run the marathon and *will* win the medal." However, repetition of an auxiliary verb in a compound predicate can grow unwieldy, so we often choose to omit it. The sentence "I will run the marathon and win the medal" is kinder to the tongue and easier on the ears.

DIAGRAMMING: THE LOST ART

During my years as a teacher, I have recognized one practice that has helped my students become expert, grammar-conscious writers more than any other. To the studious grammarian, learning this practice is akin to discovering King Solomon's Mines, the Fountain of Youth, and the Holy Grail. Find it and be lifted out of darkness. I speak of **sentence diagramming**.

A sentence diagram is a pictorial representation of a sentence. It is a cluster of lines and curves, configured so that each word in the sentence fills a particular spot according to its part of speech and function. The basis of any sentence diagram is a single horizontal line divided in half by a much smaller vertical line. On one side of the small line sits the subject. On the other side sits the predicate.

| subject | predicate |

The most simple sentences consist of a single noun, a head and complete subject, and a single verb, a head and complete predicate.

✏ Birds call.

| Birds | call |

✏ We have arrived.

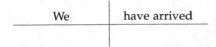

As we discussed earlier, few sentences are this simple. To serve any significant purpose, the system of sentence diagramming must accommodate such complications as modifiers, compound subjects, and compound predicates, among others. These things, our system does handle well.

Modifiers appear on right-slanted lines below the words that they modify, adjectives and articles below nouns, and adverbs below verbs.

✏ The small dog barks continuously.

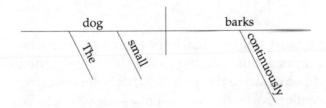

Compound subjects and compound predicates fit into a multi-tiered structure. The number of tiers depends upon the number of subjects or predicates. A vertical, dotted line represents the conjunction that connects the elements of the compound.

✏ The clever squirrel and the sly fox formed an alliance.

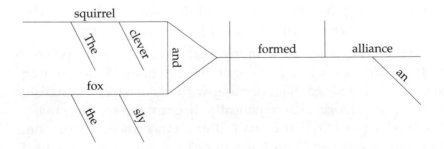

✏ The students sleep or relax.

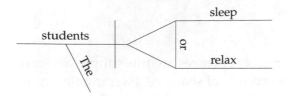

✏ Mike, Joe, and Dave surf, skate, and skydive.

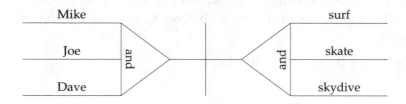

A generation ago, most English teachers used sentence diagramming to teach grammar, but, starting in the 1960s, misguided educators began to de-emphasize the practice. It's been amazing how many Hot Line callers, over the last twenty-four years, have asked about diagramming and why it is fast becoming a lost art.

At the University of Southern California, this grammarian's alma mater, the late Dr. Julia Norton McCorkle insisted that undergraduates in the English department know how to diagram sentences, and, thankfully, there are schools across the United States that are keeping sentence diagramming alive. In fact, a teacher from Washington, DC, informed me that her students are in the process of diagramming the Constitution and that she would send The National Grammar Hot Line a copy of the finished product.

Sentence diagramming is an invaluable tool. No less a personage than Winston Churchill spent his boyhood diagramming sentences and credited diagramming with his mastery of English. When I speak or write, I automatically diagram the sentence in my mind, making certain that I won't utter an incorrect construction. The worst mistake an English teacher can make is a grammatical error. While our discussion may not make you an expert in sentence diagramming, it will give you a solid foothold in the art. Ours will be a good start, but you must practice on your own.

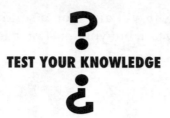

TEST YOUR KNOWLEDGE

QUESTIONS

1. Are conversational and grammatical complete thoughts the same thing?

2. What must any complete sentence possess to be complete?

3. What do we call the doing or being part of the sentence?

4. What is the head subject?

5. Are modifiers ever a part of the complete predicate?

6. What kind of subject do we see in the sentence "Swimming and diving are strenuous sports"?

7. Name the head compound predicate in the sentence "My brother enjoys driving and loves cars."

8. When are we allowed to omit a portion of a verb phase?

9. What is a sentence diagram?

10. Fill in the diagram for the sentence "The carpenter hammers carefully."

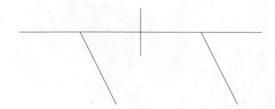

(SEE ANSWERS ON FOLLOWING PAGE)

ANSWERS

1. No, they are not. Even if we comprehend an idea communicated in casual conversation, it does not mean that the idea was expressed in a grammatically correct form.

2. A complete sentence must have a subject and a predicate.

3. This part is called the predicate.

4. The head subject is the particular word in the subject that names the person or thing spoken of.

5. Yes, the complete predicate is the head predicate along with its modifiers.

6. The sentence contains a compound subject, **swimming and diving**.

7. The head compound predicate is **enjoys and loves**.

8. We can omit a portion of a verb phrase in the latter elements of a compound predicate where the head elements are verb phrases that share the same auxiliary verbs.

9. A sentence diagram is a pictorial representation of a sentence.

10.

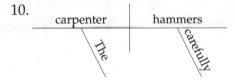

11.

Sentence Types & Structures

Sentence types are categories used to classify sentences according to function. **Sentence structures** are formulas used to build sentences.

Many people think of language use in speech and in writing as a purely creative process. What they do not realize is that language is highly regular, almost formulaic. Any grammatically complete thought will fit one of seven basic **sentence structures** and one of four **sentence types**. The structures and types are flexible and allow room for creativity, but they still indicate a common, underlying form given to us by grammar. Subjects and predicates are the base of both structures and types. We will now build upon that base.

SENTENCES TYPES

Every sentence falls into one of four categories, depending on the intentions of the speaker or writer and the manner of expression. A sentence can be **declarative**, **interrogative**, **imperative**, or **exclamatory**. We can often distinguish among the different types by looking at the punctuation of the sentences.

A **declarative sentence** makes a statement of fact or possibility. Most sentences are declarative.

> My name is Eric.
>
> We traveled through India.
>
> My dog had puppies last Thursday.
>
> I did not order the duck à l'orange.
>
> We may never see each other again.

Declarative sentences end with periods.

An **interrogative sentence** asks a question.

> Who gave you that information?
>
> What happened at the club?
>
> Where did the detective go?
>
> When did the lights flicker?
>
> Why didn't you come forward earlier?

Interrogative sentences always end with question marks.

An **imperative sentence** makes a request or gives a command.

> Take your shoes off!
>
> Don't talk so loudly.
>
> Bring me the paper, please.
>
> Help me lift this box.
>
> Hurry up!

Imperative sentences can end with periods or exclamation marks, depending on the urgency of the command or request.

An **exclamatory sentence** expresses a thought with strong emotion.

> How wonderful you have all been to me!
>
> What a beautiful day this has been!

Exclamatory sentences end with exclamation marks.

FORM VS. FUNCTION

Unfortunately, identifying sentence types may not be as simple as this past discussion has made it seem. To understand the issue, one must understand the difference between **form** and **function**. The form of a sentence is its appearance or shape. The order in which the elements that make up a sentence appear and the end punctuation determine the form. In contrast to form, sentences are written or spoken with particular functions in mind. The way a sentence is spoken or read (placement of emphasis and changes of intonation), its intended meaning, its purpose, and the end punctuation will determine its function. For instance, one may create a sentence that is declarative in form but interrogative in function.

You went on a date with Harry?

The appearance of the sentence, end punctuation aside, would suggest that it is declarative, but the tone with which the sentence is spoken or read carries a note of incredulity or questioning. Add to this the presence of the question mark at the end, and we realize that this sentence, though declarative in form, has an interrogative function.

The following sentence provides another illustration of the difference between form and function:

Who do they think they are!

The sentence is interrogative in form, but exclamatory in function. In appearance, it looks like a question. However, the speaker or writer does not expect an answer as he or she would if this were a standard interrogative sentence. Instead, the sentence expresses strong feeling or emotion, possibly indignation, and ends with an exclamation mark as an exclamation would. The specific forms of each sentence type will become clear as the chapter continues.

FROM MY FILES: TEACHING GRAMMAR

Several years ago, I received a call from an ambitious highway patrol officer who wanted help with her grammar. She was competing for a promotion to a position requiring strong communication skills, and, in order to be considered for the new job, she needed to score well on a series of examinations, one of which involved grammar. The prospect of such testing, she felt, was quite intimidating.

We met, and I tested her. Her scores were rather low, so we agreed to meet a number of times to strengthen her areas of weakness. In the weeks that followed, she worked diligently. A few days after our last session, she entered the examination room, confident and well-prepared. Several months later, she received a call telling her that she had been selected for the job.

What was the job? She was going to teach report writing. The two key elements of a good police report are accuracy and clarity. Only a competent grammarian can navigate the many intricacies and subtleties of language involved in writing these reports. A teacher of the process must be an expert. I wish this studious officer well and salute her for recognizing her deficient skills and finding the help to correct them.

WORD ORDER

Every sentence has an identifiable structure or arrangement of words. Take another look at the examples of the different sentence types on p. 296. Do you see any common word order within a given sentence type? You should identify four distinct word orders for declarative, interrogative, imperative, and exclamatory sentences.

DECLARATIVE WORD ORDERS

Declarative sentences are far and away the most commonly uttered of the basic sentence types. The declarative word order that we know best is the **canonical**[†] **order**. In canonical order, the subject of the sentence appears first, followed by the predicate.

> Your tire is flat.

> I gave her the ring for Christmas.

> We saw your dog in the park.

In each example, the subject is the first thing to appear in the sentence. The predicate follows immediately after.

If all speech and writing were this simple, the people of the world would soon die of boredom. Our brains crave a variety of word choices and also a variety of word orders. We must speak and write with diversity to maintain the interest of our peers. To support the human desire for novelty and change, English grammar permits alternative word orders.

[†] The word **canonical** means "orthodox, sanctioned, authoritative, or regular."

In some alternatively ordered sentences, the subject is not the first element to appear in the sentence. Some element of the complete predicate is **fronted** or placed at the beginning of the sentence in front of the subject. Fronting shifts emphasis from the subject to the fronted element in the sentence.

At the beach, I always feel content.

Never could I have imagined the horrors that awaited us.

The first sentence begins with the adverbial **at the beach**. Though the phrase precedes the subject **I**, it is still a part of the complete predicate. **At the beach** modifies the verb **feel**. The placement of the adverbial at the beginning of the sentence emphasizes the place where the speaker or writer feels content. The second sentence begins with the adverb **never** and the modal auxiliary verb **could**. Though it precedes the subject, **could** is still a part of the verb phrase **could have imagined**. The adverb **never** modifies **could**. Placement of the adverb at the beginning of the sentence emphasizes the negative quality of the verb phrase. That **could** is brought to the front of the sentence with **never** is because the latter modifies the former. Keeping them together maintains the integrity of the sentence.

A declarative sentence that includes a fronted element may also contain a **subject-verb inversion**. In such an inversion, we place the subject after the verb.

Into the street bounced the ball.

Under the table ran the cat.

Each of these sentences begins with an adverbial and contains a subject-verb inversion. The first sentence begins with the adverbial **into the street**, and the subject **ball** follows the verb **bounced**. The second sentence begins with the adverbial **under the table**, and the subject **cat** follows the verb **ran**.

Diagrams of declarative sentences are very straightforward. The normal order does not present any challenges we haven't already met.

☞ Those four, small dogs dug the holes.

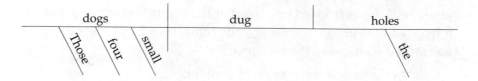

The alternative word orders may seem tricky, but they are not. Sentence diagrams care not for word order. We place words on a diagram by their functions, not their order. Though an adverbial may appear at the beginning of the sentence, it is still a part of the predicate, and the diagram displays it there.

☞ On the spur of the moment, he makes his decisions.

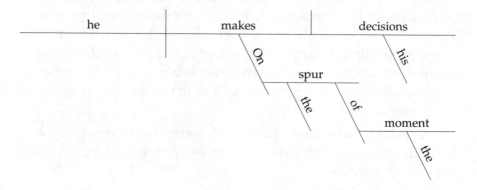

Notice the special structure that we use to handle prepositional phrases.

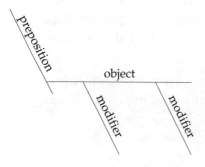

As modifiers, prepositional phrases appear below the words that they modify. **On the spur of the moment** modifies **makes**. **Of the moment** modifies **spurs**.

INTERROGATIVE WORD ORDERS

Most interrogative sentences contain a subject-verb inversion. They may start with auxiliary verbs.

> **Did** you see the comet?

> **Is** he going to ask her?

In the first example, the subject **you** follows the auxiliary verb **did**. In the second example, the subject **he** follows the auxiliary verb **is**.

Interrogative sentences may start with interrogative adverbs.

> **Where** did you buy that coat?

> **When** will you be here?

The interrogative adverb **where** begins the first sentence. The interrogative adverb **when** begins the second. In both sentences, an auxiliary verb appears before the subject.

Interrogative sentences sometimes begin with interrogative pronouns. These pronouns may or may not stand for the subjects of the sentences, and the sentences may or may not contain subject-verb inversions.

> **Whom** are you here to see?

> **What** did you say?

> **Who** threw the spit ball?

The interrogative pronoun **whom** begins the first sentence. **Whom** is the unknown object of the infinitive **to see**. The pronoun **what** begins the second sentence. It is the direct object of the verb **say**. The pronoun **who** begins the final sentence. It replaces the subject of the sentence. The first two sentences contain subject-verb inversions. The last does not.

Diagrams of interrogative sentences are no more complex than those of the declarative sentences. They may contain inversions, but this does not matter to the sentence diagrams. Do be careful with the interrogative words that sometimes begin interrogative sentences. Whether they are adverbs, such as **where** or **when**, or pronouns, such as **who** or **which**, these words will play particular roles. Their placements in diagrams should reflect those roles.

✏ Why did the commissioners cancel the game?

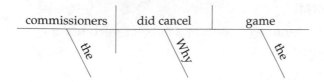

✏ Which of you stole the candy bar?

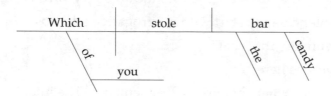

✏ What have you told the police?

you | have told | police | What
the

IMPERATIVE WORD ORDERS

Imperative sentences can provide especially confusing word orders. Often, these sentences do not appear to contain subjects. While it is true that the subjects may be unwritten or unspoken, they are not absent. The subjects are understood. As a command or request, an imperative sentence is always in the second person, spoken to an individual or a group. Therefore, we are allowed to assume the subject of an imperative sentence to be **you**. We say that the assumed subject is elliptical, understood, or implied.

> Shut the door!
> You shut the door!

Take my hand.
You take my hand.

Do not be afraid.
You do not be afraid.

We can write each example with the subject expressed or with the subject understood. Both constructions represent acceptable grammar. Sometimes, the written subject sounds fine and adds emphasis. At other times, it makes the sentence sound awkward and even quite rude. You must decide what is needed to remain a courteous speaker and writer, while conforming to the demands of your own linguistic style.

The diagrams of imperative sentences seem problematic. If the subject, **you**, is expressed, then we have no problem. If it is understood, what do we place in the spot reserved for subjects? Never fear! The engineers of the sentence diagrams have an answer. Simply place a parenthetical **(you)** in the subject slot. The parentheses indicate that the subject is understood.

✏ Take out the trash!

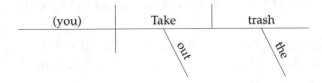

✏ You leave him alone!

You	leave	him	alone

EXCLAMATORY WORD ORDERS

While many declarative, interrogative, and imperative sentences are made with an exclamatory function, true exclamatory sentences are limited in number. Modern grammarians contend that only non-interrogative sentences beginning with **how** or **what** are of the exclamatory type.

How lovely your eyes are in the moonlight!

What a mess we have made!

Here is a diagram of the first sentence:

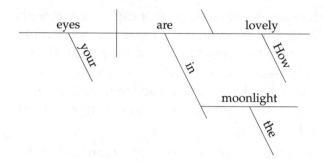

FROM MY FILES: THE MEDIA ASSASSINS

At times, reading a newspaper or a popular magazine makes my head hurt. Too many contemporary journalists do not know the English language. It almost seems as if they are out to assassinate English grammar.

The following sentences have appeared in national newspapers. The mistake in each is in bold. The words which should have been used are listed on the right.

INCORRECT	CORRECT
He waited with **baited** breath.	bated
I am against **capitol** punishment.	capital
Less than fifteen people attended.	fewer
If the Battle of Bull Run **was** fought today	were
He was arrested for **wreckless** driving.	reckless
He told it to Mary and **I**.	me
We'll drive you around when you get **hear**.	here
Please **portrait** her in a dignified manner.	portray
It was disappointing for **we** who predicted the outcome.	us

DIAGRAMS AND BASIC SENTENCE STRUCTURES

There is a set of seven fundamental sentence structures, based not on the word order, but on the essential structure of the sentence. Any complete sentence will include some combination of a number of common elements: subject, verb, adverbial complement, subject complement, object, and object complement. We have discussed each of these elements in chapters past. Here, we will look at the possible combinations of elements and diagrams of each combination.

SUBJECT-VERB

The S-V sentence structure consists of a noun, pronoun, or other nominal as the subject of the sentence and an intransitive verb or verb phrase as the predicate. Please note that modifiers are not necessary elements of any of the following structures. Any modifiable word is allowed to be modified, but modifiers are not essential elements.

☞ The horses can swim.

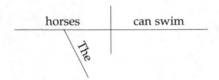

SUBJECT-VERB-ADVERBIAL COMPLEMENT

In the S-V-AC sentence structure, the verb is a linking verb, and the adverbial complement is an adverbial (see Chapter 4, p. 146) that complements (modifies) the verb in the sentence.

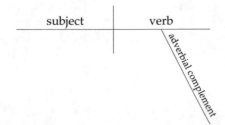

✏ Bill is outside the house.

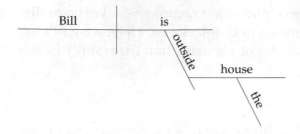

SUBJECT-VERB-SUBJECT COMPLEMENT

In the S-V-SC sentence structure, the verb is a linking verb and is followed by a subject complement that complements (modifies) the subject of the sentence.

subject	verb	subject complement

✏ Janet is the president.

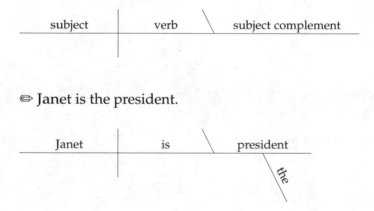

SUBJECT-VERB-DIRECT OBJECT

The verb in the S-V-dO sentence structure is a transitive verb and takes a direct object.

subject	verb	direct object

✏ Who painted your house?

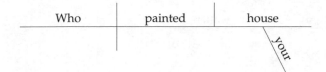

SUBJECT-VERB-INDIRECT OBJECT-DIRECT OBJECT

The verb in the S-V-iO-dO sentence structure is a transitive verb and takes a direct object *and* an indirect object.

✏ The realtor sold us a money pit.

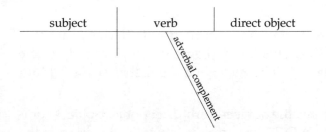

SUBJECT-VERB-DIRECT OBJECT-ADVERBIAL COMPLEMENT

The verb in the S-V-dO-AC sentence structure is a transitive verb and takes a direct object and an adverbial complement.

subject	verb	direct object

adverbial complement

☞ I put my wallet on the table.

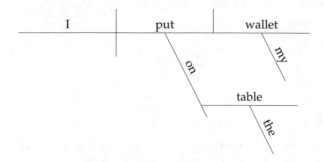

SUBJECT-VERB-DIRECT OBJECT-OBJECT COMPLEMENT

The verb in the S-V-dO-OC sentence structure is a transitive verb and takes a direct object and an object complement.

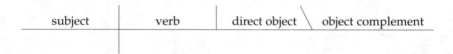

☞ My friends call me Skippy.

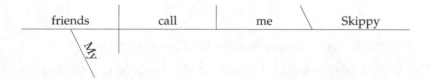

THE RIGHT STRUCTURE

Q. A disappointed restaurant patron asked, "Have I said this correctly? 'I find this food disgusting.' I said it to the maitre d'. His chef wouldn't know a good bouillabaisse if it bit him on the neck."

A. The sentence uses the subject-verb-direct object-object complement (S-V-dO-OC) sentence structure. The subject is the pronoun **I**. The verb is **find**. The direct object is the noun **food**. The object complement is the present participle **disgusting**. This patron knows her grammar.

HULA GRAMMAR

Q. An elementary school teacher said, "One of my students gave me this sentence in a report: 'Hawaii is my favorite island.' Is **island** a direct object?"

A. The teacher mistakenly thought that his student was using the subject-verb-direct object (S-V-dO) sentence structure. The proper noun **Hawaii** is the subject. **Is** is the verb. **Island** is *not* a direct object. It is a subject complement, specifically, a predicative nominative. We know this to be true because it follows a linking verb. A linking verb needs a complement in the predicate to complete its meanings. The noun **island** complements the linking verb **is** and renames the subject **Hawaii**. The sentence structure used here is subject-verb-subject complement (S-V-SC).

SOME OTHER THINGS TO REMEMBER ABOUT SENTENCE STRUCTURES

The following are additional issues to remember when evaluating sentence structure.

NOUNS IN DIRECT ADDRESS

Interrogative and imperative sentences often include a noun in direct address. Such nouns name the person to whom the question is directed or to whom the command or request is given. These are always set off by commas because they are independent elements. A noun in direct address has no grammatical relation to any part of the sentence and is never the subject of the sentence.

☞ Bosco, fetch the newspaper.

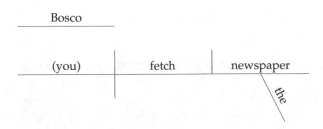

The subject of the sentence is an understood **you**, not **Bosco**. This proper noun is an independent element. We place independent elements on a horizontal line above the subject to separate them grammatically from the rest of the sentence. The sentence is imperative and has the S-V-dO structure.

Please note that in a diagram, we treat interjections, another type of independent element, in the same way that we treat nouns in direct address.

☞ Ouch! Watch your feet.

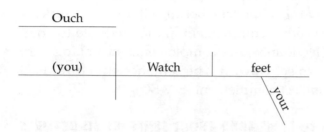

DUMMY ELEMENTS AND DELAYED SUBJECTS

By now, the concepts of dummy elements and delayed subjects should be familiar ones. We examined them during our discussions of pronouns in Chapter 6 (p. 187) and of infinitives in Chapter 5 (p. 172). A delayed subject appears in the predicate, and its normal position is filled by a dummy element, such as **it** or **there**, as the true subject.

Delaying the subject often creates an easier sentence construction, but any sentence with a delayed subject has an alternative wording. Here is a sentence with the subject delayed:

There was a robbery last weekend.

Here is the same sentence with the subject restored:

A robbery was last weekend.

Both are grammatically correct, but the first is more appealing to the ears.

Study this example of a sentence containing a dummy element and a delayed subject.

☞ There are too many clowns in this circus.

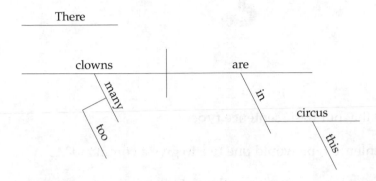

A dummy element serves no grammatical purpose in the sentence other than to fill the space left by the delayed subject, so we place it on a separate horizontal line above the subject slot, much like an independent element. The delayed subject fills the same space in the sentence diagram that a normal subject would. In this sentence, the complete delayed subject is **too many clowns**. The dummy element **there** is perched above the subject. The sentence is declarative and has a S-V-AC structure.

A WORD OF WARNING

This discussion of sentence structures has dealt with the structures in their most basic forms. Real-world sentences are complex, creative, and beautiful. They may even seem to deny the existence of any set of structures. Take a closer look at a tangled construction of your own, however. Underneath all the clauses, phrases, and modifiers, you will find a regular and quite mundane structure.

That such structures exist does not detract from the beauty of language. Any creation, artistic or not, must possess an underlying structure, and understanding this structure will not tarnish the final product. Instead, it will enhance your artistry as a writer and speaker.

TEST YOUR KNOWLEDGE

QUESTIONS

1. What are the four basic sentence types?

2. Which sentence type would one use to give a command?

3. Why are speakers and writers allowed to use any of several alternative word orders when constructing a sentence?

4. In most interrogative sentences, how are the subject and verb positioned?

5. Is the subject of an imperative sentence missing if it is not expressed?

6. Is it possible to diagram an understood subject?

7. What basic sentence structure does the sentence "You can call me Bruce" use?

8. Can a noun in direct address be the subject of a sentence?

9. What is a dummy element?

10. Why would we delay a subject?

(SEE ANSWERS ON FOLLOWING PAGE)

ANSWERS

1. The four basic sentence types are: declarative, interrogative, imperative, and exclamatory.

2. A command is issued in the form of an imperative sentence.

3. Alternative word orders satisfy the brain's craving for novelty and change.

4. In most interrogative sentences, the subject and verb are inverted.

5. No, the subject is implied or understood.

6. Yes. Place the understood subject in parentheses in the subject slot of the diagram.

7. The sentence uses the subject-verb-direct object-object complement (S-V-dO-OC) sentence structure.

8. No, such nouns are independent elements.

9. A dummy element fills the place of a delayed subject.

10. We would delay a subject to create a smoother construction.

12.

More Diagramming

Before we move on to more complicated sentences, it would be wise to strengthen our understanding of diagramming. Any part of speech or grammatical construct can find a place in a diagram, and there are several of the most basic that we have yet to cover fully. In this brief chapter, we will discuss prepositional phrases, contractions, verbals, and appositives.

PREPOSITIONAL PHRASES

A prepositional phrase can play one of two roles in a sentence, functioning as a modifier or a nominal. We looked at a diagram of a prepositional phrase briefly in Chapter 11 (p. 300).

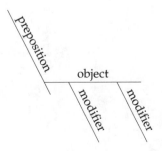

Prepositional phrases used as modifiers can function as standard adjectives or as adverbials. A prepositional phrase that functions as an adjective appears below the noun, pronoun, or other nominal that it modifies.

✏ The man of the hour has arrived.

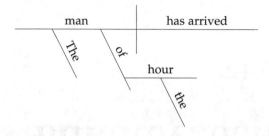

In this sentence, the prepositional phrase **of the hour** modifies the subject **man**.

A prepositional phrase that functions as an adverbial appears below the verb, adjective, or adverb that it modifies. The arm holding the preposition is connected to the slot filled by the modified word.

✏ The thief drove the stolen car into the ocean.

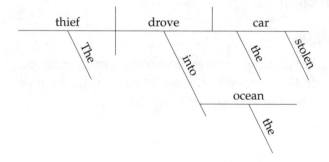

✏ I inherited a house full of ghosts.

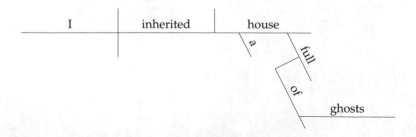

✏ She behaved responsibly under those circumstances.

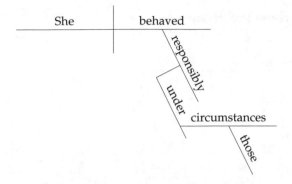

In the first example, the prepositional phrase **into the ocean** modifies the verb **drove**. In the second example, the prepositional phrase **of ghosts** modifies the adjective **full**. In the third example, the prepositional phrase **under those circumstances** modifies the adverb **responsibly**.

Notice the odd connections between the structures in the second diagram that hold the prepositional phrase **of ghosts** and the adjective that the prepositional phrase modifies, **full**, and between the structures in the third diagram that hold the prepositional phrase **under those circumstances** and the adverb that the prepositional phrase modifies, **responsibly**. In sentence diagrams, convention dictates that lines on which prepositions rest must slant to the left. The lines on which **full** and **of** rest in the second diagram and the lines on which **responsibly** and **under** rest in the third diagram cannot all slant to the left if the former in each pair connects directly to the latter, so we insert the right-slanting connector to make the connection and maintain the convention.

On occasion, we find a prepositional phrase working as a nominal. These are typically subjects of sentences.

✏ Beneath the waves is where the treasure lies.

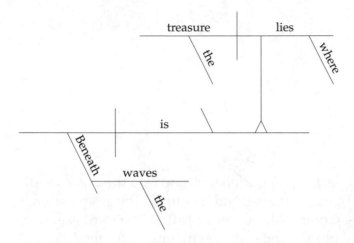

In this example, the prepositional phrase **beneath the waves** is the subject of the sentence. For now, do not concern yourself with the platform that holds the clause **where the treasure lies**. We will deal with the diagramming of clauses when we reach Chapter 13.

CONTRACTIONS

The issue of contractions in diagrams is not an issue at all. Simply expand the contracted words before placing them in the diagram.

✏ He's not stopping for anyone.

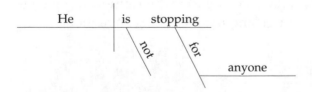

✏ I won't worry.

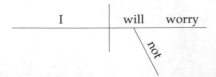

In the first example, **he's** becomes **he is**. In the second example, **won't** becomes **will not**.

VERBALS

Grammarians have created a unique structure for each of the verbals. Remember that there are three types of verbals: participles, gerunds, and infinitives.

PARTICIPLES

Participles are verbals which function as adjectives or adverbials. We place the participles on curved lines beneath the words that they modify.

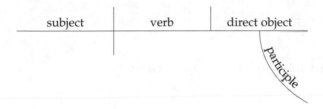

➥ There are overwhelming odds against us.

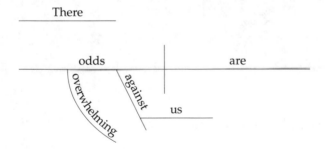

As former verbs, participles can take modifiers, objects, and complements. When these extra elements are added, we have a participle phrase. We diagram the modifiers, objects, and comple-

ments of each of the verbals in almost the same way that we would
the modifiers, objects, and complements of normal verbs.

✏ Our boat eased down the slowly flowing river.

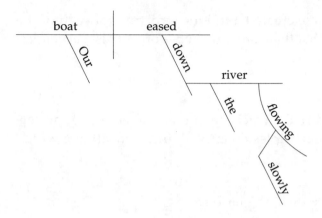

✏ Having told me the tale, he lost his composure.

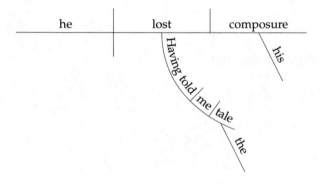

✏ Feeling groggy, he climbed immediately into bed.

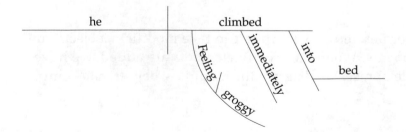

In the first example, **slowly flowing** is a present participle phrase. The adverb **slowly** modifies the present participle **flowing**. In the second example, **having told me his tale** is a present participle phrase. **Me** is an indirect object. **Tale** is a direct object. Both complete the perfect form of the participle **having told**. In the third example, **feeling groggy** is a present participle phrase. **Groggy** is a subject complement that completes the meaning of the present participle **feeling**.

Please note the strange connection between the participle **flowing** and the adverb **slowly**. By convention, the lines on which modifiers rest must slant to the left. The line on which the adverb **slowly** rests cannot slant to the left *and* connect directly to the line on which the present participle **flowing** rests, so we insert a connector between them.

GERUNDS

Gerunds are verb forms that function as nominals. The structure that holds the gerund in a diagram is a zigzagged line on a stick.

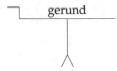

The forked base of the stick rests in the slot on the diagram corresponding to the place of the gerund in the sentence.

☞ Running is my favorite sport.

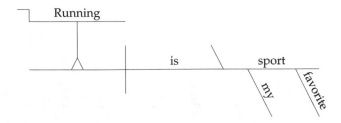

The gerund **running** functions as the subject of the sentence, so the base of the stick rests in the subject slot in the diagram.

Gerunds, utilizing their verb heritage, may take modifiers, objects, and complements. When we add these additional parts, we have a gerund phrase.

✏ I have never enjoyed professional wrestling

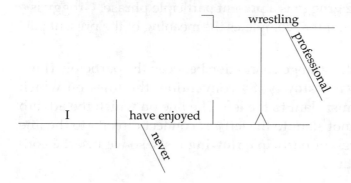

✏ Selling them the story is not an easy proposition.

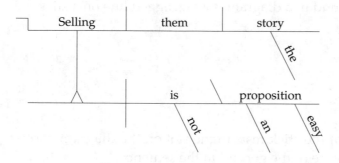

✏ Herman is obsessed with being fit.

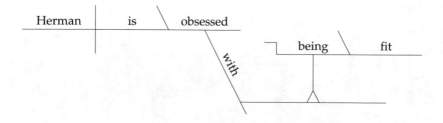

In the first example, **professional wrestling** is a gerund phrase. The adjective **professional** modifies the gerund **wrestling**. In the second example, **selling them the story** is a gerund phrase. The pronoun **them** is an indirect object of the gerund **selling**, and the noun **story** is a direct object of the same gerund. In the third example, **being fit** is a gerund phrase. The subject complement **fit** completes the meaning of the gerund **being**.

INFINITIVES

Our most powerful verbal is the infinitive. Recall that infinitives can function as nominals, adjectives, or adverbials. In a diagram, the infinitive looks like a prepositional phrase on a stick.

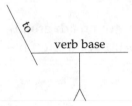

The base of the stick rests in the slot corresponding to the role that the infinitive plays in the sentence.

Many infinitives fill the same slots that standard nouns fill.

☞ I love to ski.

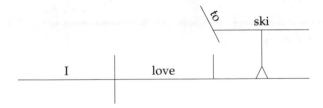

✏ To sing is my natural talent.

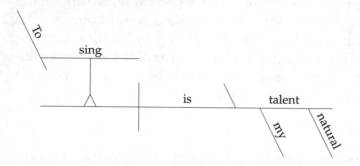

In the first example, the infinitive **to ski** is the direct object of the verb **love**. In the second example, the infinitive **to sing** is the subject of the sentence.

When the infinitive is a modifier (an adjective or an adverbial), the base of the stick rests on the horizontal portion of a shelf beneath the word modified.

✏ I am always the last to know.

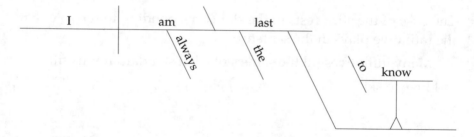

✏ The kids are ready to leave.

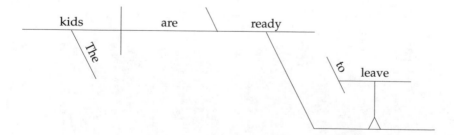

In the first example, the infinitive **to know** modifies the noun **last**. In the second example, the infinitive **to leave** modifies the adjective **ready**.

Like their verbal counterparts, infinitives may take modifiers, objects, and complements. With these extras, we call the verbal an infinitive phrase.

☞ I decided to write them a song.

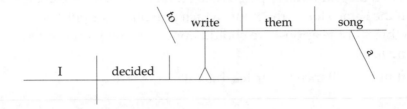

☞ We are anxious to see you in Denver.

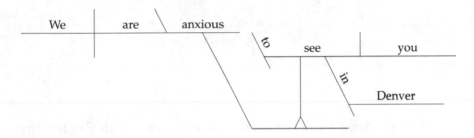

☞ Oscar's ambition is to be the king.

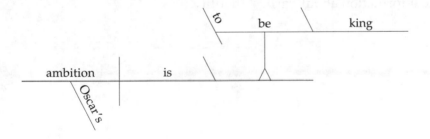

In the first example, **to write them a song** is an infinitive phrase. **Them** is an indirect object of the infinitive **to write**, and **song** is a direct object of the same infinitive. In the second example, **to see you in Denver** is an infinitive phrase. The pronoun **you** is the direct object of the infinitive **to see**. The adverbial **in Denver** (a prepositional phrase) modifies the same infinitive. In the third example, **to be the king** is an infinitive phrase. **King** is a subject complement, completing the meaning of the infinitive **to be**.

APPOSITIVES

It would never do to forget about appositives. They are such useful bits of grammar. The appositive is some nominal that enhances or explains another noun. In a sentence, it is often set off by commas. In a diagram, the appositive is set off by parentheses. It is placed in the same slot as the noun which it explains or enhances. Any modifiers of the appositive should appear below it on slanted modifying lines.

✏ He left his inheritance to Farfles, his cat.

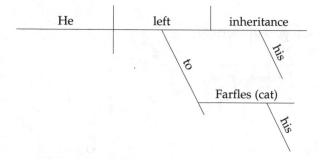

In this sentence, the noun **cat** is in apposition with **Farfles**, the object of the preposition **to**. The appositive tells us who this lucky Farfles is. The appositive enhances the noun **Farfles** by providing more information about Farfles' identity.

TEST YOUR KNOWLEDGE

QUESTIONS

Fill in the diagrams of the following sentences:

1. My name is of no importance to you.

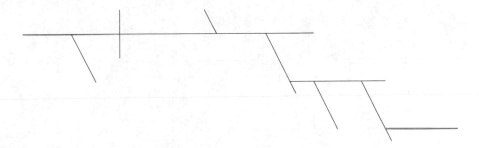

2. Amy hasn't seen snow for three years.

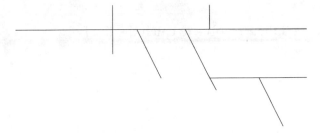

3. I ordered an iced tea.

4. Playing an instrument is a rewarding experience.

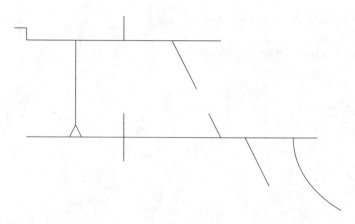

5. The police strengthened their resolve to catch the thief.

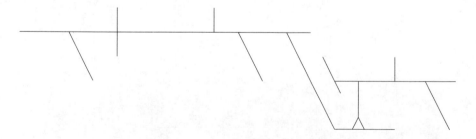

6. I enjoy baseball, the ultimate sport.

(SEE ANSWERS ON FOLLOWING PAGES)

ANSWERS

1.

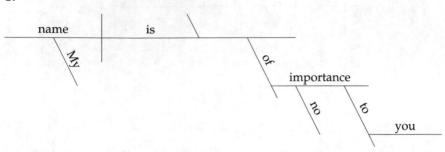

2.

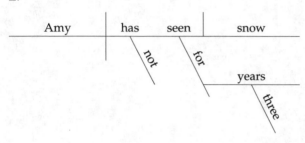

3.

4.

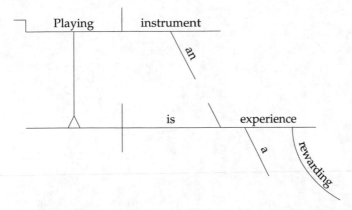

5.

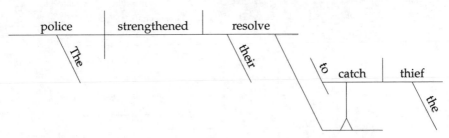

6.

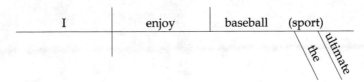

13.

Compound & Complex Sentences

> A **clause** is any group of words with a subject and a predicate.

Language use is a constructive process. Writers and speakers create complete thoughts and ideas out of simple building blocks. At the most elemental level, sentences are made of morphemes[†]. Single morphemes or combinations of morphemes make up words which are then strung together to make sentences. Chapter 10 dealt with subjects and predicates in the most basic sentences. This chapter is about adding complexity to the structure of language.

SIMPLE SENTENCES

Until now, our discussion has been limited to **simple sentences**; that is, sentences which contain a single subject-predicate set.

We entered the topiary labyrinth.

Tuesday is payday.

Her ordinary dress did not detract from her natural beauty.

[†] A morpheme is the smallest meaningful unit of word formation. For example, the word **haunted** contains two morphemes: **haunt** and **-ed**.

Each of these is a simple sentence because each possesses exactly one subject and one predicate. In the first sentence, the complete subject is **we** and the complete predicate is **entered the topiary labyrinth**. In the second sentence, the complete subject is **Tuesday** and the complete predicate is **is payday**. In the third sentence, the complete subject is **her ordinary dress** and the complete predicate is **did not detract from her natural beauty**.

The fact that a simple sentence has only one subject and one predicate does not imply that either or both cannot be compound.

> Beth and Amy paddled their raft through the rapids.
>
> My friends sang, danced, and laughed till dawn.
>
> The warriors and thieves gave their battle cries and locked swords in combat.

Each of these examples contains a compound subject, a compound predicate, or both, but they are all simple sentences. The first contains a compound subject, **Beth and Amy**. The second contains a compound predicate, **sang, danced, and laughed till dawn**. The third contains a compound subject, **the warriors and thieves**, and a compound predicate, **gave their battle cries and locked swords in combat**.

INTRODUCTION TO CLAUSES

Now that we have moved on to the business of creating bigger and better sentences, we need larger building blocks. Just as we combined words and phrases to form simple sentences, so do we combine these same elements to form the larger parts of greater sentences. We call these larger elements **clauses**.

A clause is a group of words that contains both a subject and a predicate. Clauses come in two flavors: **main** and **subordinate**. A main clause can stand alone and make sense. A subordinate clause relies on the presence of a main clause to complete its meaning. It cannot stand alone as a grammatically complete thought.

> I know the restaurant that you are thinking of.

This sentence contains both a main clause and a subordinate clause. The main clause is **I know the restaurant**. It has a subject, **I**, and a predicate, **know the restaurant**. By itself on a page or in our ears, it is a complete grammatical thought. When main clauses stand alone, we call them simple sentences.

The subordinate clause in this sentence is **that you are thinking of**. It too has a subject, **you**, and a predicate, **are thinking of that**, but this clause cannot stand alone and make sense. It relies on the presence of the main clause for a complete meaning. That is why we label it "subordinate." The word **subordinate** means "of lesser rank" or "under another's control."

Clauses are tied together by connecting words. In the example above, the relative pronoun **that** is a connecting word. Notice how we moved **that** when we analyzed the predicate so that the connecting word occupied the space reserved for an object of a preposition. This word actually functions as an object of a preposition in the clause. We will talk about connecting words in greater detail as they become important to our discussion.

COMPOUND SENTENCES

As our language skills develop, we quickly discover that simple sentences are not enough. If all we used were simple sentences, our speech and writing would be devoid of easy transitions, smooth connections, and logical relationships. We need some way to join simple sentences together to make connections and establish relationships. To our rescue come the **coordinate conjunctions**.

When we link two or more main clauses together by using a coordinate conjunction, we get a **compound sentence**. A coordinate conjunction is one type of connecting word. If the writer decides that a sentence is to be a compound sentence, two factors must be present:

1. The main clauses should be related to each other.

2. The main clauses should be of approximately equal value. The writer is not emphasizing one of the clauses over the other(s).

> Lily brought a casserole, Herman made a cheese ball, and I made the hot wings.

This compound sentence consists of three equal main clauses connected by the coordinate conjunction **and**. Notice that we replaced the first occurrence of the conjunction with a lone comma. The individual clauses are **Lily brought a casserole, Herman made a cheese ball,** and **I made the hot wings**.

Now look at this compound sentence broken into three simple sentences.

> Lily brought a casserole. Herman made a cheese ball. I made the hot wings.

They don't have the same flow or rhythm as the compound version. The three sentences are like a car driven by a teenager behind the wheel for the first time. They move in jerks and starts.

PUNCTUATION OF COMPOUND SENTENCES

There are several ways to punctuate a compound sentence. The first is to use a comma before the coordinate conjunction.

> Sam wrote the lyrics, **and** I wrote the music.

> Lenora plays the saxophone, **but** she sings better.

> I will accept your offer, **or** I will decline it.

When the same coordinate conjunction connects three or more main clauses, we can replace all but the last occurrence of that conjunction with commas.

> The sky is clear, the sun is bright, **and** I'm in the mood for a game of soccer.

Notice that a lone comma divides the first main clause, **the sky is clear**, from the second, **the sun is bright**. A comma, as well as the conjunction **and**, divides the second main clause from the third, **I'm in the mood for a game of soccer**.

Another way to punctuate a compound sentence is with a semicolon. In some cases, the ideas expressed by the main clauses are so closely related that we do not need the conjunction to spell out their relationship. Instead, we place a semicolon between the clauses.

> The king is dead; long live the king.

> The summer comes; the summer goes.

The "dot" in the semicolon marks the end of a main clause. The "comma" under the dot indicates that what follows is related and equal to the preceding main clause. Isn't this a neat explanation? Whether it's based on historical fact is up for grabs, but it works!

In other cases, main clauses already contain commas. To avoid the confusion we might create by adding more commas between the main clauses, we separate the clauses with semicolons.

> Al, an architect, donated the plans; **and** Sue, a contractor, donated the materials.

> Having said his peace, Sam departed; **but** his anger lingered in the room.

We may also omit the punctuation when the compound sentence is composed of two main clauses and those two main clauses are short.

> I caught the criminal and she saved the victim.

> I'll buy a cake or I'll make one myself.

Please remember that it *is* important to use punctuation before the coordinate conjunction **but** so that it will not be mistaken for the preposition **but**.

CONJUNCTIVE ADVERBS

Coordinate conjunctions are not the only type of word that we can use to join main clauses. A class of **conjunctive adverbs**, also called **connectors**, fills this connecting role. They are not exactly coordinate conjunctions, and they are not exactly standard adverbs, but they perform similar functions. We discussed conjunctive adverbs briefly in Chapter 8 (see p. 268). Recall that the meaning implied by the conjunctive adverb affects the entire clause of which it is a part.

accordingly	eventually	in like manner	on the contrary
afterwards	finally	in short	on the other hand
again	for example	instead	otherwise
also	for instance	in the meantime	perhaps
anyhow	furthermore	later	so
as a result	hence	likewise	still
at last	however	meanwhile	subsequently
at the same time	in addition	moreover	that is
besides	in any case	namely	then
consequently	indeed	nevertheless	therefore
earlier	in fact	next	thus

The following example illustrates the linking and modifying powers of the conjunctive adverb.

The bank's computers failed; hence, millions of dollars were lost.

In this example, the conjunctive adverb **hence** joins the main clauses **the bank's computers failed** and **millions of dollars were lost**. The meaning of this connecting word affects the entire second clause. It implies a cause and effect relationship. The event of the second clause is a direct consequence of the event of the first clause.

These alternative connecting words require a different method of punctuation than the coordinate conjunctions do. Grammar grants us two methods to accomplish the task. Using the first method, we place a semicolon between the main clauses, and use a comma to set off the conjunctive adverb from the clause of which it is a part.

The castle is in ruins; **nevertheless,** the king has ordered us to hold our ground.

We all must maintain secrecy; **otherwise,** the plan will fail.

Using the second method, we place a period between the main clauses. Technically, the two clauses are separate simple sentences, but the conjunctive adverb creates a connection between them, and we may view them as parts of a compound. Again, the conjunctive adverb is set off by commas.

Batman took care of the Riddler. **Meanwhile,** Robin subdued Catwoman.

The bridge has collapsed. **Therefore,** we must swim for our lives.

Please note that many conjunctive adverbs are mobile words. They may be placed in any one of several different spots in the clauses of which they are parts. Though the conjunctive adverbs may roam, we still punctuate the main clauses with periods or semicolons and set off the conjunctive adverbs with commas.

The duke was beheaded for the crime; another man, **however,** soon confessed.

A Buick is unsuitable for mountain driving. A Jeep, **on the other hand,** is perfect.

COMPOUND SENTENCE WOES

Compound sentences are easy to explain, but not always easy to use. The **comma splice** and the **run-on sentence** are two commonly made mistakes. Here are two calls to the Hot Line that illustrate the troubles callers have with these errors:

THE COMMA SPLICE

Q. "My son wrote the sentence 'The safe is empty, the butler is missing' in a creative writing assignment at school. I know he's got a problem with the comma. What should I tell him to do to make the sentence correct?" asked a concerned father.

A. This man was correct about his son's sentence. It contains a comma splice. A comma splice occurs when a writer links, or splices, main clauses together by using only commas. This is not one of the three correct methods of punctuating compound sentences. A comma can only join main clauses with the help of a conjunction. This young man has joined two main clauses, **the safe is empty** and **the butler is missing,** with a lone comma.

I told his caring father that we have four options at our disposal with which we might correct the comma splice:

1. We can add a coordinate conjunction after the comma.

The safe is empty, **and** the butler is missing. (correct)

2. We can replace the comma with a semicolon.

The safe is empty; the butler is missing. (correct)

3. We can also replace the comma with a coordinate conjunction. Punctuation is not necessary since the two main clauses are short.

The safe is empty **and** the butler is missing. (correct)

4. We can turn the compound sentence into two separate simple sentences.

The safe is empty. The butler is missing. (correct)

Remember to use proper punctuation. Do not commit the error of a comma splice!

THE RUN-ON SENTENCE

Q. A distressed junior high school teacher called me for a bit of advice. "He asked, "How can I make my students stop writing run-on sentences?"

A. The run-on sentence is another result of incorrectly punctuating compound sentences. Such constructions arise when writers string main clauses together without placing any punctuation or coordinate conjunctions between them.

> We knew which car we wanted to buy we went to the dealer to buy it. (incorrect)

The sentence consists of two main clauses, **we knew which car to buy** and **we went to the dealer to buy it**, the first of which runs right into the other without the help of punctuation or a conjunction. The remedies that we used for the comma splice also apply to the run-on sentence. Any of the four choices below are acceptable:

1. We knew which car we wanted to buy, and we went to the dealer to buy it. (correct)

2. We knew which car we wanted to buy; we went to the dealer to buy it. (correct)

3. We knew which car we wanted to buy and we went to the dealer to buy it. (correct)

4. We knew which car we wanted to buy. We went to the dealer to buy it. (correct)

I told the teacher that all he can do is to promote proper grammar and never to stand for sloppy writing. Papers should be checked and double-checked. No amount of proofreading is too much. Errors such as the run-on sentence or the comma splice are more often the result of carelessness than of ignorance.

DIAGRAMMING COMPOUND SENTENCES

It is a simple matter to diagram a compound sentence. We diagram each clause separately and then connect them by a dotted bridge. The coordinate conjunction fills this bridge.

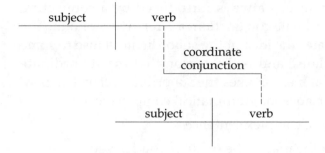

✎ The dam broke, and the waters raged through the city.

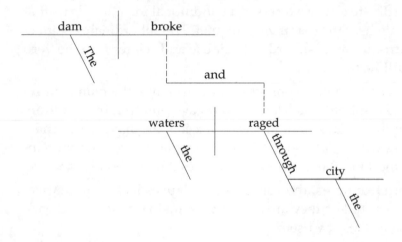

COMPLEX SENTENCES

The compound sentence is not the pinnacle of language complexity. In these, we merely join clauses of *equal* importance. Often, our thoughts and ideas demand that we link clauses that *differ* in importance. The task requires a new sort of sentence construction.

When we join a *subordinate clause* to a *main clause* by using a connecting word, we get a **complex sentence**. The main clause expresses the principal idea of the statement. The subordinate clause, on the other hand, expresses an enhancing or modifying idea; its role is to support the main clause. This is one reason why it is subordinate. Also remember that a subordinate clause *cannot* stand alone and make sense. It depends on the main clause for meaning.

A subordinate clause is always introduced by a connecting word, such as a subordinate conjunction or a relative pronoun. The connecting word relates the idea of the subordinate clause to some word in the main clause and is the reason that the subordinate clause cannot stand alone. It makes the subordinate clause dependent upon the main clause for grammatical completeness.

Take a look at these complex sentences:

You will hear the roar of the ocean if you are very quiet.

The man who gave you that information is unreliable.

The first example consists of a main clause, **you will hear the roar of the ocean**, and a subordinate clause, **if you are very quiet**. The subordinate clause expresses a conditional idea. It tells us that we will only hear the roar if we are quiet. The subordinate conjunction **if** introduces the subordinate clause and relates it to the verb phrase **will hear**.

The second example consists of a main clause, **the man is unreliable**, and a subordinate clause, **who gave you that information**. The subordinate clause modifies the subject of the main clause, **man**. It indicates which man is unreliable. The relative pronoun **who** introduces the subordinate clause and relates it to the noun **man**.

In both examples, the subordinate clauses lack grammatical completeness unless they are paired with main clauses. Read each subordinate clause by itself.

If you are very quiet

Who gave you that information

These are sentence fragments. Even an untrained ear can tell that neither of them expresses a grammatically whole idea on its own. The subordinate clauses need their partners, the main clauses, for the complete meanings to emerge.

As you may have already guessed, there are several different types of subordinate clauses in complex sentences. In fact, there are three varieties: **relative**, **adverbial**, and **nominal**.

RELATIVE CLAUSES

A standard relative clause functions just as a standard adjective does. It modifies nouns, pronoun, or other nominals[†]. Relative

---

[†] Remember that the term **nominal** applies to any noun or pronoun or any word, phrase, or clause that performs the same function as a noun.

clauses are introduced by real relative pronouns, relative adverbs, or relative determiners.

RELATIVE CLAUSES WITH REAL RELATIVE PRONOUNS

A relative pronoun is a multifaceted word. It introduces a relative clause and joins that clause to a main clause, but it also stands for a noun, as any pronoun would. Relative clauses may be introduced by any of the **relative pronouns**, including both real relative pronouns and relative adverbs, but we are limiting the immediate discussion to relative clauses introduced by the real relative pronouns **who**, **which**, and **that**.[†] As a relative pronoun, **who** may take two forms, depending on how it is used in the relative clause.

| NOMINATIVE CASE USAGE | who |
| OBJECTIVE CASE USAGE | whom |

If the real relative pronoun is a subject or a subject complement, we use the nominative case form. If the real relative pronoun is an object, we use the objective case form.

> The dinosaur exhibit **that** you have been waiting for has arrived.
>
> I covet the dress **which** she wore to the wedding.
>
> This is the man **whom** the police have been looking for.
>
> Only people **who** know computers will succeed in the modern world.

In the first example, the real relative pronoun **that** joins the relative clause **that you have been waiting for** to the main clause **the dinosaur exhibit has arrived**. The relative clause modifies the noun **exhibit**. It indicates which exhibit in particular has arrived. The antecedent of **that** is the complete subject of the sentence, **the dinosaur exhibit**.

In the second example, the real relative pronoun **which** joins the relative clause **which she wore to the wedding** to the main clause **I covet the dress**. The relative clause modifies the noun **dress**. It tells us which dress the speaker coveted. The antecedent of **which** is the direct object **dress**.

In the third example, the real relative pronoun **whom** joins the relative clause **whom the police have been looking for** to the main

---

[†] The real relative pronoun **what** does not appear in relative clauses that modify nouns, pronouns, or other nominals.

clause **this is the man**. The relative clause modifies the noun **man**. It indicates who this particular man is. The antecedent of **whom** is the subject complement **man**. In the relative clause, the relative pronoun is the object of the preposition **for**, so we use the objective case form, **whom**.

In the fourth example, the real relative pronoun **who** joins the relative clause **who know computers** to the main clause **only people will succeed in the modern world**. The relative clause modifies the noun **people**. It tells us which type of people will be successful. The antecedent of **who** is the subject of the sentence, **people**. In the relative clause, the relative pronoun is the subject of the clause, so we must use the nominative case form, **who**.

Who vs. Whom

Many people have a hard time determining which form of **who** to use in a relative clause. The key to figuring this out is to first understand what case the pronoun takes. Each relative pronoun has a function within the relative clause that it introduces, and this function determines its case.

The relative pronoun may be the **subject** of the relative clause, taking the nominative case form, **who**.

I read about the philanthropist **who** gave away his fortune.

In this example, the relative pronoun **who** introduces the relative clause **who gave away his fortune**. The clause describes the noun **philanthropist**, the antecedent of **who**. It is clear that **who** is the subject of the clause, since the philanthropist is the one giving away the fortune.

The relative pronoun may be a **subject complement** to the subject of the relative clause, again taking the nominative case form, **who**:

That is the kind of person **who** Cindy will be.

Here, the relative pronoun **who** introduces the relative clause **who Cindy will be**. The clause modifies the noun **kind** (or, more specifically, the entire noun phrase **the kind of person**), the antecedent of **who.** Within the relative clause, **who** is a subject complement, describing the subject of the relative clause, **Cindy**, and completing the meaning of the linking verb **be**.

The relative pronoun may also be a **direct object** of the verb in the relative clause, taking the objective case form:

Beth is a person **whom** I know very well.

The relative pronoun **whom** introduces the relative clause **whom I know very well**. The clause modifies the noun **person**, the antecedent of **whom**. To see that **whom** is a direct object, isolate and rearrange the clause. I know *whom* very well? I know *a person* very well. I know *Beth* very well. The pronoun **I** is the subject, and the relative pronoun **whom** is the direct object of the verb **know**.

The relative pronoun could also be the **object of a preposition**:

This is the boy **whom** the article was written about.

The relative pronoun **whom** introduces the relative clause **whom the article was written about**. The clause describes the noun **boy**, the antecedent of **whom**. The article was written about *whom*? The article was written about *the boy*. The noun **article** is the subject of the clause. The relative pronoun **whom** is the object of the preposition **about**.

THE WHO VS. WHOM DEBATE RAGES ON

Q. An administrator at a graduate school of management was writing a recommendation for a professor. He called to ask, "How is this sentence? 'He is a professor who we gladly recommend.'"

A. I advised the administrator to just say, "We gladly recommend this professor." However, if the word choice is important, then he needs to adjust his choice of a relative pronoun. **Who we gladly recommend** is a relative clause, modifying the noun **professor**. **We** is the subject of the clause, and **who**, a nominative case pronoun, is the direct object of the verb **recommend**. Should direct objects be in the nominative case form? Absolutely not. A direct object is always in the objective case form. The sentence should read, "He is a professor *whom* we gladly recommend."

RELATIVE CLAUSES WITH RELATIVE ADVERBS

The relative adverbs **when, where,** and **why** join relative clauses to main clauses in the same way that the relative pronouns do, but they also function as adverbials in those relative clauses.

Within the clause, the relative adverbs describe only verbs (see Chapter 6, p. 200 for an explanation of why we classify the relative adverbs under relative pronouns).

> The workers chose a day **when** I will be vacationing on the French Riviera.

> Uncle Murray discovered the hangar **where** the UFOs were hidden.

> Helga knows the reason **why** Jimmy Hoffa's body was never found.

In the first example, the relative adverb **when** joins the relative clause **when I will be vacationing on the French Riviera** to the main clause **the workers chose a day**. The relative clause modifies the noun **day**. It tells us what kind of day the workers chose. In the relative clause, **when** modifies the verb phrase **will be vacationing**. It indicates the time at which the vacationing will occur.

In the second example, the relative adverb **where** joins the relative clause **where the UFOs are hidden** to the main clause **Uncle Murray discovered the hangar**. The relative clause modifies the noun **hangar**. It indicates which hangar Uncle Murray discovered. In the relative clause, **where** modifies the verb phrase **were hidden**. It indicates the place at which the hiding occurred.

In the third example, the relative adverb **why** joins the relative clause **why Jimmy Hoffa's body was never found** to the main clause **Helga knows the reason**. The relative clause modifies the noun **reason**. It tells us the nature of the reason. In the relative clause, **why** modifies the verb phrase **was** *(never)* **found**. It indicates a justification for the failure to find the body.

RELATIVE CLAUSES WITH RELATIVE DETERMINERS

Relative clauses may also be introduced by **relative determiners**. The pronouns **whose** and **which** are two common examples of this type. We call them relative *determiners* because they modify the nouns that follow them in the relative clauses in the same way that articles, another type of determiner, would modify the nouns that follow them. Please note that the relative determiner **which** is always preceded by a preposition.

> That is the family **whose** dog saved our little girl.

Your reports are due by midnight at **which** time I am going to bed.

In the first example, the relative determiner **whose** joins the relative clause **whose dog saved our little girl** to the main clause **that is the family. Whose** modifies the noun **dog**. The relative clause modifies the noun **family**. It indicates which family the speaker has seen. The antecedent of **whose** is the subject complement **family**.

In the second example, the relative determiner **which** joins the relative clause **at which time I am going to bed** to the main clause **your reports are due by midnight. Which** modifies the noun **time**. The relative clause modifies the noun **midnight**. It indicates what will happen at that time. The antecedent of **which** is **midnight**.

PLACING YOUR CLAUSE

Q. A gynecologist called the Hot Line to share a silly line from a note she received. The line read, "She has two friends who just had babies who are not married."

A. To be quite honest, I have yet to meet any babies who are married. The sentence consists of two relative clauses, **who just had babies** and **who are not married**, and a main clause, **she has two friends**. The problem in this complex sentence is that the word modified by the second relative clause is unclear. As they are in the letter, the relative clause **who just had babies** modifies the noun **friends** and the relative clause **who are not married** appears to modify the noun **babies**. As we all know, babies have no interest in marriage.

The relative clauses need to swap positions, and the coordinate conjunction **and** needs to be placed between them. The sentence should read, "She has two friends who are not married and who just had babies." Now both clauses clearly modify the noun **friends**. A small change in order eliminates the confusion.

RESTRICTIVE OR NONRESTRICTIVE?

Q. "Do I put commas around relative clauses?" queried a technical writer.

A. Whether we place commas around relative clauses depends upon whether the information in the relative clause in question is restrictive or nonrestrictive. The relative clauses we have seen so far have all been restrictive. They've been essential to the complete meanings of the sentences, so we haven't set them off with commas. Other relative clauses are nonrestrictive. A nonrestrictive relative clause adds information to a sentence, but is not an essential part of the complete meaning.

> Mr. Jeffries, who is my history teacher, gave us the homework assignment.

This example contains a nonrestrictive relative clause. The relative clause **who is my history teacher** modifies the proper noun **Mr. Jeffries**. It provides information about Mr. Jeffries, but the meaning of the sentence would not suffer without the clause. The sentence "Mr. Jeffries gave us the homework assignment" communicates a nearly identical idea.

ZERO RELATIVE PRONOUNS

On occasion, we can correctly omit a relative pronoun from a relative clause. The gap left by the omitted pronoun is called a **zero relative pronoun**. If the omission does not bring a verb to the head of the relative clause, it is perfectly correct to remove the relative pronoun. The sentence will make complete sense without it.

> The car (**that**) we saw yesterday was too expensive.

> The people (**who**) we know are not very responsible.

In each example, the omitted relative pronoun is in parentheses because it is optional. In the first example, the relative clause **we saw yesterday** modifies the noun **car**. We could write the clause with the relative pronoun **that** included, but we do not have to. In the second example, the relative clause **we know** modifies the noun **people**. We could have included the relative pronoun **who** in the clause, but the sentence makes perfect sense without it.

In other sentences, removing the relative pronoun would make a verb the first word in the clause and cause the sentence to be grammatically incomplete.

> The men **who** repaired our roof did a wonderful job. (correct)

> We all saw the show **that** won the Tony Award this year. (correct)

Try leaving off the relative pronouns in each example.

> The men repaired our roof did a wonderful job. (incorrect)

> We all saw the show won the Tony Award this year. (incorrect)

These sentences do not amount to much. When appropriate, feel free to use a relative clause containing a zero relative pronoun. Just be sure that your sentence still makes sense.

DIAGRAMMING RELATIVE CLAUSES

Diagramming a complex sentence containing a relative clause is a simple process. First, diagram the main and relative clauses separately. Then use a dotted line to connect the relative pronoun, relative adverb, or relative determiner in the relative clause to the word modified in the main clause. As a modifier, the relative clause should sit below the main clause.

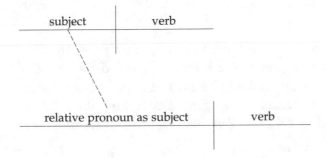

When the connecting word is a relative pronoun, it will fill some slot on the main line of the clause diagram.

☞ I do not understand people who dislike cats.

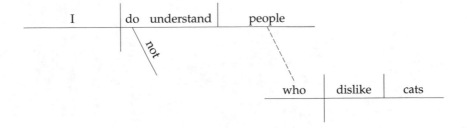

When the connecting word is a relative determiner, it will sit on a slanted line below the word it modifies. There is no neat way to draw the dotted line between the relative determiner and the word modified in the main clause, but do your best.

✏ I know the kid whose chocolate bar held the winning ticket.

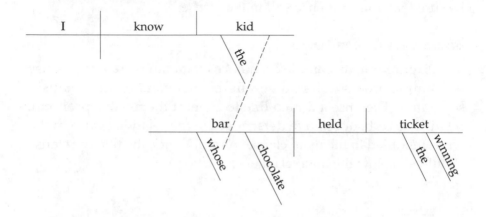

Relative adverbs present the same problem that the relative determiners did. Since a relative adverb is a modifier and a conjunction, it sits on a diagonal line below the word in the relative clause that it modifies. We may have difficulty linking the relative adverb with the word modified in the main clause, but we must try.

✏ I know a place where we can talk.

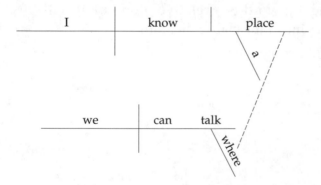

FROM MY FILES: LUNCH WITH A GREAT MASTER

Johann Sebastian Bach was sent off each day by his wife with a lunch intended to provide enough energy for him to write brilliantly; this, of course, was the origin of the "Bach's" Lunch.

ADVERBIAL CLAUSES

Adverbial clauses modify verbs, adjectives, and adverbs in the same way that standard adverbials do, but most simply modify verbs. They are always introduced by subordinate conjunctions (see Chapter 8, p. 261 for a list of subordinate conjunctions).

CLASSES OF ADVERBIAL CLAUSES

Adverbial clauses convey the meanings that standard adverbs and adverbials do in addition to a few extra: **place or location, time, manner, cause, degree or comparison**, and **possibility or conditionality**.

PLACE OR LOCATION

The adverbial clauses that indicate *place* or *location* often begin with one of these conjunctions: where, wherever.

We can eat **wherever** you want to eat.

In this example, the subordinate conjunction **wherever** joins the adverbial clause **wherever you want to eat** to the main clause **we can eat**. The adverbial clause modifies the verb phrase **can eat**. It tells us the location where the eating can occur.

TIME

The adverbial clauses that express *time* often begin with one of the following subordinate conjunctions: after, before, since, until, when, whenever, while, etc.

I watched the street **while** my partner planted the surveillance devices.

In this example, the subordinate conjunction **while** joins the adverbial clause **while my partner planted the surveillance devices** to the main clause **I watched the street**. The adverbial clause modifies the verb **watched**. It tells us when the speaker did the watching.

MANNER

Many adverbial clauses that express *manner* begin with one of these subordinate conjunctions: as, as if, etc.

She treated me **as if** I didn't exist.

In this example, the subordinate conjunction **as if** joins the adverbial clause **as if I didn't exist** to the main clause **she treated me**. The subordinate clause modifies the verb **treated**. It tells us the manner in which *she* treated *me*.

REASON

Adverbial clauses that express *reason* often begin with one of these subordinate conjunctions: as, because, in order that, since, so that, that, etc.

The sheriff skipped town **because** he had embezzled one million dollars.

Here, the subordinate conjunction **because** joins the adverbial clause **because he had embezzled one million dollars** to the main clause **the sheriff skipped town**. The adverbial clause modifies the verb **skipped**. It gives us the reason why the sheriff left.

DEGREE OR COMPARISON

These conjunctions frequently begin adverbial clauses that indicate *degree* or *comparison*: as, than, etc.

My relatives arrived earlier **than** they usually do.

In this example, the subordinate conjunction **than** connects the adverbial clause **than they usually do** to the main clause **my relatives arrived earlier**. The adverbial clause modifies the adjective **earlier**. It compares the time that the relatives usually arrive to the time that they did arrive. Adverbial clauses of comparison typically modify adjectives and adverbs and are sometimes called **comparative clauses**.

POSSIBILITY OR CONDITIONALITY

The adverbial clauses that indicate *possibility* or *conditionality* often begin with one of the following subordinate conjunctions: although, if, even if, provided, though, unless, etc.

> She will not supply the documents **unless** she is adequately reimbursed.

In this example, the subordinate conjunction **unless** connects the adverbial clause **unless she is adequately reimbursed** to the main clause **she will not supply the documents**. The adverbial clause modifies the verb phrase **will supply**. It describes the condition on which she will supply those documents. The adverbial clause indicates a possibility or condition. Her providing the documents is a possibility, but only if she is paid enough to do so.

ADVERBIAL CLAUSES MODIFYING ADJECTIVES AND ADVERBS

Most adverbial clauses modify verbs. However, adverbial clauses of comparison often modify adjectives and adverbs.

> This computer is faster **than that one is**.

> The plane landed later **than we expected it to land**.

In the first example, the subordinate conjunction **than** connects the adverbial clause **than that one is** to the main clause **this computer is faster**. The adverbial clause modifies the adjective **faster**. It compares the speed of *this computer* to the speed of *that one*. In doing so, the adverbial clause specifies the nature of the comparison made by the comparative adjective **faster**.

In the second example, the subordinate conjunction **than** connects the adverbial clause **than we expected it to land** to the main clause **the plane landed later**. The adverbial clause modifies the adverb **later**. It indicates the degree of **later** by comparing the time the speaker and his cohorts expected the plane to land to the time the plane actually did land. In doing so, the adverbial clause limits the definition of **later**. It clarifies the time that **later** is meant to indicate.

WORD ORDER AND THE ADVERBIAL CLAUSE

Q. A psychologist writing a report asked, "It's OK to put a clause at the beginning of the sentence, isn't it?"

A. Many clauses appear at the beginnings of sentences. The clauses that this psychologist was wondering about turned out to be adverbial clauses. Fortunately for her, the adverbial clause is a mobile type of clause. It is free to float about the sentence structure. Though an adverbial clause may appear at the end of a sentence in the canonical word order (see Chapter 11, p. 298), we can place the same clause at the beginning of the sentence for emphasis. In this alternative word order, we set the clause off with commas.

> Marge wouldn't be so insensitive if she knew the full story.

> If she knew the full story, Marge wouldn't be so insensitive.

In both sentences, the subordinate conjunction **if** joins the adverbial clause **if she knew the full story** to the main clause **Marge wouldn't be so insensitive**. The adverbial clause modifies the verb phrase **would**(*n't*) **be**. It indicates a possibility or condition. Marge's insensitivity could disappear on the condition that she learns the full story.

The different placements emphasize different elements of the sentence. In the first version, the placement emphasizes Marge and her insensitivity. In the second version, the placement emphasizes the fact that Marge does not know the full story. Since the adverbial clause appears first, we add a comma to separate it from the main clause. The writer or speaker must choose the placement that makes his or her point most effectively.

DIAGRAMMING ADVERBIAL CLAUSES

Adverbial clauses do not cause the diagramming conflicts that relative clauses do because the subordinate conjunctions that introduce adverbial clauses do not play nominal or modifying roles in the clauses of which they are parts. In complex sentences with adverbial clauses, we diagram the main and the adverbial clauses separately, and then connect the verbs in each with a dotted line. The subordinate conjunction resides on this line. As a modifying clause, the adverbial clause sits below the main clause.

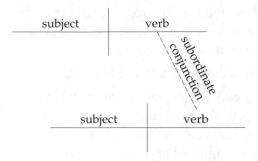

⮑ The band lingered in the club after the concert ended.

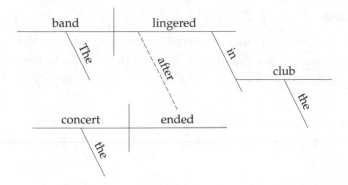

Nominal Clauses

The final type of subordinate clause is the nominal clause. Like the relative and adverbial clauses, the nominal clause plays a subordinate role in the sentence and begins with some type of connecting word. Unlike the relative and adverbial clauses, the nominal clause does not play a modifying role. As its name suggests, the nominal clause has a nominal role, filling almost any spot that a standard noun would.

A sentence containing a nominal clause is a complex sentence, but it is different from the complex sentences that we encountered in the discussions of relative and adverbial clauses. These consisted of subordinate clauses attached to main clauses by subordinate conjunctions, real relative pronouns, relative adverbs, or relative determiners. The nominal clause, a subordinate clause, completes the group of words that we once called a main clause. Therefore, this "main clause" itself is grammatically incomplete without the subordinate clause. For this reason, contemporary grammarians use the term **host clause** to describe the group of words that the nominal clause completes. Here is an example of a complex sentence containing a host clause and a nominal clause:

What I really need is three cases of cold Dr. Pepper.

In this sentence, **what I really need** is a nominal clause. With relative and adverbial clauses, we assume the remainder of the sentence to be a main clause, but anyone can see that **is three cases of cold Dr. Pepper** is a sentence fragment and cannot stand alone. We rightly label it a **host clause**. The complex sentence is only complete if the nominal clause is present.

Using Nominal Clauses

As was stated before, a nominal clause may play just about any role that a standard noun would. We see nominal clauses used as *subjects of sentences*, *subject complements*, *delayed subjects*, and *appositives*:

That they have not heard the news astounds me. (subject)

The latest news is **that the workers are still on strike**. (subject complement)

It is clear **that they do not enjoy lutefisk**. (delayed subject)

The notion **that we will never see each other again** is unbearable. (appositive)

In the first example, the nominal clause **that they had not heard the news** is the subject of the sentence. It names the thing that the writer or speaker is writing or speaking about: that which astounds the speaker.

In the second example, the nominal clause **that the workers are still on strike** is a subject complement. It completes the linking verb **is** and complements the subject **news**.

In the third example, the nominal clause **that they do not enjoy lutefisk** is a delayed subject, replaced in the true place of the subject by the dummy **it**. (To the uninitiated, lutefisk is a particularly disagreeable Scandinavian dish made of cod soaked in lye.) While the dummy element and delayed subject may create a more pleasant or readable construction, any sentence with the subject delayed has an alternative wording. This sentence could have appeared as follows:

That they do not enjoy lutefisk is clear.

We removed the delay and restored the nominal clause to the true space of the subject.

In the fourth example, the subordinate conjunction **that** introduces the nominal clause **that we will never see each other again**. The nominal clause is in apposition with the noun **notion**. As an appositive, it explains the noun, telling us what kind of notion is unbearable.

We also see nominal clauses used as *direct objects* and *objects of prepositions*:

I know **who your secret admirer is**. (direct object)

The FBI agents were interested in **why he opened a Swiss bank account**. (object of preposition)

In the first example, the nominal clause **who your secret admirer is** is the direct object of the verb **know**. It answers the question "*What* do you know?" In the second example, the nominal clause **why he opened a Swiss bank account** is the object of the preposition **in**. It names the thing that the agents were interested in.

We rarely use nominal clauses as *indirect objects*. The constructions that result from such usage are simply too awkward. However, one common but colloquial example of a nominal clause used as an indirect object comes from the expression **you know who**. **You know who** is a nominal clause with **you** as its subject and **who** as the direct object of the verb **know**. Please note that the direct object is incorrectly in the nominative case form. A sentence containing this colloquial expression used as an indirect object might read as follows:

I gave **you know who** a piece of my mind.

The nominal clause **you know who** is the indirect object of the verb **gave**. It answers the question "*To whom* did you give a piece of your mind?" The conscientious grammarian, however, would have used the correct form of the nominal relative pronoun. His or her sentence would read as follows:

I gave you know *whom* a piece of my mind.

AN ASIDE ON NOMINAL CLAUSES USED AS APPOSITIVES

Nominal clauses used as appositives are some of the hardest constructions to recognize. The problem is that such nominal clauses bear a striking resemblance to relative clauses. Let's look again at the example of a noun clause used as an appositive from our previous discussion:

> The notion **that we will never see each other again** is unbearable.

The nominal clause **that we will never see each other again** is in apposition with the noun **notion**, but some might argue that the nominal clause actually modifies **notion**. It is the connecting word that gives the true identity of the nominal clause away.

Relative clauses only begin with real relative pronouns, relative adverbs, or relative determiners. Though **that** can be a relative pronoun, its sole function in a nominal clause used as an appositive is to connect a main clause and a subordinate clause. Because it does not stand in for a noun within the subordinate clause, it cannot be a relative pronoun. It must be a subordinate conjunction. Only adverbial clauses and nominal clauses may begin with subordinate conjunctions.

Since a nominal clause used as an appositive does not modify a verb, an adjective, or an adverb, we know that it is not an adverbial clause and that it must be a nominal clause. The functions of such clauses are similar to those of modifiers, so we look for a role that a nominal can play where it enhances or explains. Our best option is to call these nominal clauses *appositives*.

What you must realize is that this distinction is somewhat arbitrary. Grammar is a model of language, and no model will ever perfectly capture its subject. There are always holes and loose ends that we try to avoid but can never eliminate. When the grammarians who developed our system of grammar encountered nominal clauses such as the ones we just saw, they too were unsure of what to do with them. To make the system whole and to tie up any loose ends, the grammarians decided to call the clauses appositives.

Thankfully, grammar is ever evolving. The inadequacies of one model are swept away as another takes its place. As you read this book, grammarians, teachers and other academics are working to create a new model of grammar that better describes our speech and writing. Who knows what methods students will be learning to model language in 2050?

WHO VS. WHOM REVISITED

The controversy over whether to use **who** or **whom** is just as perplexing with nominal clauses as it was with relative clauses. Remember, the key to solving the puzzle is to determine the role that the relative pronoun plays in the clause. If it is a subject or a subject complement, use the nominative case form of the pronoun, **who**. If it is an object, use the objective case form, **whom**.

> **Who** gave you permission to skip my physics class does not matter to me.

> The kids could not stop talking about **whom** we will see in a few hours.

In the first example, the nominal clause **who gave you permission to skip my physics class** is the subject of the sentence. The relative pronoun **who** begins the nominal clause. We use the nominative case form because the pronoun is the subject of the clause. Let's replace the pronoun with a random noun.

> **Bobby** gave you permission to skip my physics class.

The proper noun **Bobby** is clearly the subject of the sentence. The relative pronoun **who** replaces **Bobby** and turns the word group into a nominal clause.

In the second example, the nominal clause **whom we will see in a few hours** is the object of the preposition **about**. The relative pronoun **whom** introduces the clause. We use the objective case form because the pronoun is the direct object of the verb phrase **will see**. We now replace the pronoun with a random noun.

> We will see **Susan** in a few hours.

The proper noun **Susan** is the direct object of the verb **see**. It tells whom we will see. The relative pronoun **whom** replaces **Susan** and turns our temporary sentence into a nominal clause.

BE SURE ABOUT THE CASE

Q. "I'm sending our board of directors a memo, and I don't know what pronoun to use. Should I write, 'Our concern is about *who* or *whom* we should contact'?" asked the CEO of an internet firm in Silicon Valley.

A. Please use **whom**. **About who/whom we should contact** is a prepositional phrase. **Who/whom we should contact** is a nominal clause serving as the object of the preposition **about**. The relative pronoun introducing the nominal clause is the direct object of the verb **contact**. **We** is the subject of the nominal clause. We should contact whom? We should contact him. The relative pronoun needs to be in the objective case form. Since **whom** is the objective case form, the memo should read, "Our concern is about *whom* we should contact."

Also note that we have not used **whom** because the nominal clause is the object of the preposition **about**. This fact does not affect the case of the relative pronoun. We use **whom** instead of **who** because the relative pronoun is an object within the nominal clause and so must take the objective case form.

CONNECTING WORDS IN NOMINAL CLAUSES

Q. A colleague from a nearby college asked me, "When I use the word **that** in a sentence like 'That they have not found your car is all I know,' is **that** a relative pronoun or a subordinate conjunction?"

A. My colleague had hit upon a particularly sticky issue in the grammar of nominal clauses. **That** can be either a relative pronoun or a subordinate conjunction, but which is it in sentences such as this one? Fortunately, there is a clear answer.

That, when used in nominal clauses, is a subordinate conjunction. In my colleague's sentence, the only function of **that** is to join the subordinate clause **that they have not found your car** to the host clause **is all I know**. It does not stand in for a noun in the nominal clause, so it is not a relative pronoun. **That** must be a subordinate conjunction.

Please note that nominal clauses may begin with a variety of words. The subordinate conjunction **whether** often introduces nominal clauses.

I cannot tell **whether** the sweater is blue or black.

In this example, **whether** introduces the nominal clause **whether the sweater is blue or black**. The nominal clause is the direct object of the verb **tell**. It answers the question "*What* can you not tell?"

Many other nominal clauses are introduced by one of the relative pronouns (real relative pronouns and relative adverbs alike). The relative pronoun joins a nominal clause to a host clause, but it also takes the place of a noun in the clause of which it is a part. Because nominal clauses that begin with relative pronouns so closely resemble the relative clauses of which we previously spoke, grammarians sometimes refer to them as **nominal relative clauses**.

We will do **whatever** we need to do.

Did you hear **what** those goody-goodies said about us?

Home is **where** you hang your hat.

In the first example, the compound relative pronoun **whatever** (a real relative pronoun) introduces the nominal clause **whatever we need to do**. The nominal clause is the direct object of the verb **do**. It answers the question "*What* will you do?" Within the nominal clause, **whatever** is the direct object of the infinitive **to do**.

In the second example, the relative pronoun **what** (a real relative pronoun) introduces the nominal clause **what those goody-goodies said about us**. This nominal clause is the direct object of the verb **hear**. It answers the question "*What* did I hear?" Within the nominal clause, **what** is the direct object of the verb **said**. It answers the question "*What* did they say?"

In the third example, the relative pronoun **where** (a relative adverb) introduces the nominal clause **where you hang your hat**. The clause is a subject complement, completing the linking verb **is** and complementing the subject **home**. Within the nominal clause, **where** modifies the verb **hang**.

OTHER CONNECTING WORDS IN NOMINAL CLAUSES

Q. A friend who teaches English at a high school in my town said to me, "Michael, what kind of conjunction is **whatever** in the sentence 'I will perform **whatever** service you request'? One of my students came to me with some grammar questions, but I couldn't answer this one."

A. I answered that **whatever** is a connecting word, but it is not a conjunction. It is a compound relative pronoun, specifically, a compound relative determiner. **Whatever** introduces the nominal clause **whatever service you request**. In the sentence, the clause is the direct object of the verb **perform**.

I then told my friend to look closely at the role that **whatever** plays within the nominal clause **whatever service you request**. It does not simply take the place of a noun. This compound relative determiner also modifies **service**, the direct object of the verb **request**. We use relative determiners and their compound counterparts to join main and subordinate clauses and to modify nouns within the subordinate clauses (see p. 346).

Here are a couple more examples of relative determiners, modifying nouns in nominal clauses:

Take **what** money you need from my wallet.

You should wear **whichever** jacket will be warmest.

In the first example, the nominal clause **what money you need** is the direct object of the verb **take**. The relative determiner **what** introduces the nominal clause and modifies the noun **money**. In the second example, the nominal clause **whichever jacket will be warmest** is the direct object of the verb **wear**. The compound relative determiner **whichever** introduces the nominal clause and modifies the noun **jacket**.

CHOOSING THE CONNECTING WORD

Q. A mother was writing a note to her son's teacher. The boy was returning to school after a week-long illness. She asked, "Can I write, 'The reason is because Bobby had a cold'?"

A. This mother has chosen the wrong connecting word to introduce her nominal clause. In her sentence, the subordinate conjunction **because** introduces the nominal clause **because Bobby had a cold**. The clause is a subject complement of the noun **reason**.

We only use the subordinate conjunction **because** to introduce adverbial clauses. There is, however, another subordinate conjunction that is right for this job. Mom should have written, "The reason is *that* Bobby had a cold."

THE ZERO THAT IN NOMINAL CLAUSES

There is one special case in which we can correctly omit the connecting word from the nominal clause. This case arises when the subordinate conjunction **that** introduces a nominal clause that serves as a direct object in the sentence. Grammarians call such clauses **zero that-clauses**:

I knew **that** everything would turn out for the best.

In this sentence, the subordinate conjunction **that** introduces the nominal clause **that everything would turn out for the best**. The nominal clause is the direct object of the verb **knew**. It answers the question "*What* did you know?" This sentence fits the description of our special case, so we can omit **that**.

I knew everything would turn out for the best.

The sentence is clear and complete without subordinate conjunction.

A CONFUSING MATTER

Q. This caller told us of a failed dinner party where one couple stormed out after an embarrassing incident. The caller said, "Our former friends left us this note, but I guess their anger got the better of their grammar. Here's the line: 'We were so disgusted we are going home.' How would I correct this? I'm still peeved at those two."

A. The writers of the note must have been quite angry because they managed to leave a note that lacks a single clear meaning. The Hot Line wondered if there were any semicolons in the note. The caller answered, "No, there are not." Knowing this, we can look at the line from any number of viewpoints.

We may have a run-on sentence. Under this interpretation, there are two main clauses, **we were so disgusted** and **we are going home**. There is no punctuation mark or conjunction between the two, so the sentence runs on. The Hot Line suggested that the best solution for this problem be to place a semicolon between the clauses. The sentence would read, "We were so disgusted; we are going home."

We might also claim that this is a complex sentence where the subordinate conjunction has been wrongfully omitted, a misuse of **that** in a **zero that-clause**. The subordinate conjunction **that** should join the subordinate clause **that we are going home** to the main clause **we were so disgusted**. The sentence would read, "We were so disgusted *that* we are going home." Once the conjunction has been restored, we can interpret the sentence in one of two ways.

If we claim that the adverbial clause **that we are going home** modifies the past participle **disgusted**, then the couple was disgusted that they had to leave. They may have wished that they could stay. Modifying **disgusted**, the clause indicates what the couple was disgusted about. They were disgusted about having to go home.

If we claim that the adverbial clause modifies the adverb **so**, then the couple was disgusted to such an extent that their disgust caused them to leave. The clause indicates the degree of **so**. It tells us how much disgust "so disgusted" implies. I believe that this is the message that the angry couple intended to leave behind.

CAREFUL WITH THOSE CLAUSES

Q. "I've used this sentence: 'I never knew that there was so many opportunities out there,' " stated a young teacher looking for a job. "My advisor told me to call you for some advice on straightening out my grammar."

A. This young fellow has a verb error in his nominal clause. In the sentence, the nominal clause **that there was so many opportunities out there** is the direct object of the verb **knew**. This is fine.

Within the clause, **there** is a dummy element. It stands in for the delayed subject **so many opportunities**. The verb that follows the dummy element, **was**, is singular. However, the subject that the dummy element stands for is plural. For subject and verb to agree, the verb must be plural. The sentence should read, "I never knew that there *were* so many opportunities out there." Thank God that the Hot Line corrected his grammar before his bad habits wore off on any impressionable young minds.

DIAGRAMMING NOMINAL CLAUSES

Nominal clauses in diagrams of complex sentences are nothing but trouble. A nominal clause may begin with a subordinate conjunction, most likely **that** or **whether**, a real relative pronoun, a relative adverb, or a relative determiner, and the structure of the diagram changes, depending on which connecting word it is. In every case, the nominal clause perches on a stick with a forked base. The base rests in a slot on the main line of the main clause diagram. That slot represents the role filled by the nominal clause in the main clause.

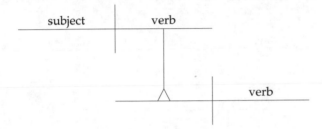

When a subordinate conjunction introduces the nominal clause, we put the conjunction on a line above the verb. This indicates that the conjunction plays only a connecting role.

☞ Whether the ship sank is another mystery.

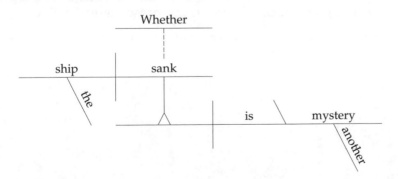

When a real relative pronoun introduces the nominal clause, it occupies a slot corresponding to its role in the nominal clause.

✎ Whoever takes the gold will receive a handsome endorsement contract.

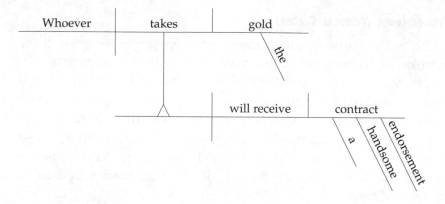

✎ We are willing to take whatever we can get.

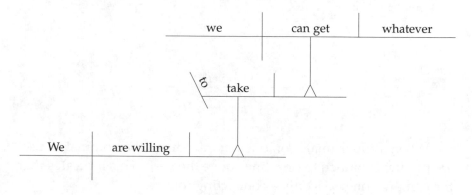

When a relative adverb introduces the nominal clause, it rests on a slanted modifying line under the word or phrase being modified.

✎ The leprechaun told us where his treasure is hidden.

When a relative determiner introduces the nominal clause, it rests on a slanted modifying line under the noun that it modifies.

☞ You may purchase whatever materials you need.

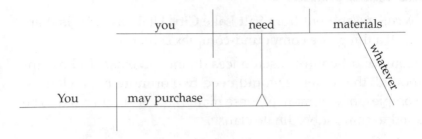

A nominal clause used as an appositive requires special notation.

☞ The idea that we might escape kept our spirits high.

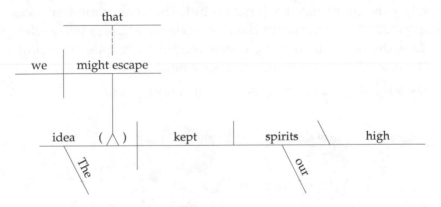

The parentheses indicate that the nominal clause is an appositive. It explains or enhances the noun in whose slot the forked base rests, but it does not play the same role as that noun.

SOME OTHER THINGS YOU SHOULD KNOW ABOUT COMPOUND & COMPLEX SENTENCES

Clauses and complex sentences are two of the most difficult topics that the determined student of grammar will encounter. Believe me, many do not make it this far. Schools do not have the time or resources to teach such tricky material, and too many students lack the determination to learn it. The following discussion should help you in some of the stickier situations that clauses and complex sentences may present.

COMPOUND-COMPLEX SENTENCES

Q. A college student from Salt Lake City, Utah, asked, "Is there such a thing as a compound-complex sentence?"

A. Compound-complex sentences do indeed exist. To be compound, the sentence would need two or more main clauses. To be complex, one or more of these main clauses would need to be connected to some subordinate clause.

> The winner may receive the trophy, but anyone who finishes the race is a champion.

The sentence consists of two main clauses, **the winner may receive the trophy** and **anyone who finishes the race is a champion**, joined by the coordinate conjunction **but**. This makes the sentence compound. The second main clause contains a relative clause **who finishes the race**. The relative clause modifies the indefinite pronoun **anyone**. This makes the sentence complex.

Here is a diagram of this compound-complex sentence:

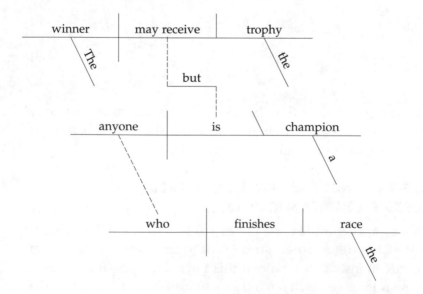

ABBREVIATED ADVERBIAL CLAUSES

Q. "Why, exactly, are we allowed to write sentences like 'My sister is smarter than I'? I mean, they sound fine, but is there some sort of justification for them?" asked a veteran English teacher.

A. Here is yet another probing question from a curious and thoughtful mind. Sentences such as the one our caller provided are ubiquitous in the English language, but why have they come into use? What is their justification for being? Well, here is the answer:

English idiom allows speakers and writers to omit words that are shared with the main clause from **adverbial clauses of comparison** (also known as **comparative clauses**). Some portion of the adverbial clause is obvious, even if unspoken or unwritten, so we omit it to avoid repetitive or clumsy sentence construction.

In sentences such as the caller's, it is the entire predicate of the adverbial clause that we omit.

> My sister is smarter **than I**. (abbreviated)

> My dog can jump **as** high **as my cat**. (abbreviated)

In the caller's sentence, the subordinate conjunction **than** introduces the abbreviated adverbial clause **than I**. In the other example, the correlative conjunction **as-as** introduces the abbreviated adverbial clause **as-as my cat**. The missing portion of each clause is a potentially awkward predicate.

Here are the sentences, unabbreviated:

> My sister is smarter than I **am smart**. (unabbreviated)

> My dog can jump as high as my cat **can jump high**.
> (unabbreviated)

In the original versions, the predicates **am smart** and **can jump high** were rightly omitted because they are nearly identical to elements in the main clauses. With the predicates restored, the sentences sound stiff and silly.

At other times, we omit the subject and the verb from the adverbial clause, leaving only a direct object behind.

> He likes ice cream better **than cake**. (abbreviated)

Thomas found more garbage in the wreck **than treasure**. (abbreviated)

In the first example, the subordinate conjunction **than** introduces the abbreviated adverbial clause **than cake**. In the second example, the subordinate conjunction **than** introduces the abbreviated adverbial clause **than treasure**. Subjects and verbs have been omitted from both clauses.

Here are the sentences with the missing subjects and verbs, **he likes** and **he found**, restored.

He likes ice cream better than **he likes** cake. (unabbreviated)

Thomas found more garbage in the wreck than **he found** treasure. (unabbreviated)

The new versions don't sound awful, but the added elements are unnecessary. The sentences are more efficient and succinct without them.

USING THE CORRECT CASE IN ABBREVIATED ADVERBIAL CLAUSES

Q. A college student called to ask, "Why did my education professor put a big, evil, red mark around **than him** in the sentence 'Angela is more lively than him'? **Than him** is a prepositional phrase, so I used **him** rather than **he**. My grammar may not be perfect, but I think I'm right here."

A. Alas, I had to inform this young lady that her professor was in the right. **Than him** is not a prepositional phrase; it is an abbreviated adverbial clause of comparison. Writers and speakers often mistake the subordinate conjunction **than** at the beginning of an abbreviated adverbial clause of comparison for a preposition and automatically place the pronoun that follows in the objective case form. However, if it is the predicate that has been omitted from the abbreviated adverbial clause, the pronoun is the subject of the clause and should be in the nominative case form. The caller has fallen into this trap. She has omitted the predicate **is lively** from her adverbial clause of comparison. With the incorrect objective case pronoun and a restored predicate, her sentence would read as follows:

Angela is more lively than him **is lively**. (unabbreviated and incorrect)

The sentence is clearly incorrect. Unabbreviated, it should appear as follows:

Angela is more lively than **he** is lively. (unabbreviated and correct)

In my opinion, the caller was right to omit the predicate **is lively**, but she does need to use a pronoun in the nominative case form. I told her that she should have written this sentence:

Angela is more lively than **he**. (abbreviated and correct)

Be careful, though! In other sentences, a pronoun in an abbreviated adverbial clause may be in the nominative or the objective case form, depending on the intended meaning of the sentence. The following two sentences contain pronouns in the objective case form because their subjects and predicates are missing:

Mr. Phillips respects you more than **me**. (abbreviated and correct)

The kids enjoy me more than **her**. (abbreviated and correct)

Me and **her** are both objective case pronouns. With the missing subjects and verbs restored, the sentences would read as follows:

Mr. Phillips respects you more than he respects **me**. (unabbreviated and correct)

The kids enjoy me more than they enjoy **her**. (unabbreviated and correct)

The pronouns are direct objects of their respective verbs. **Me** is the direct object of **respects**, and **her** is the direct object of **enjoy**.

Written with pronouns in the nominative case form, the sentences could appear as follows:

Mr. Phillips respects you more than **I**. (abbreviated and correct)

The kids enjoy me more than **she**. (abbreviated and correct)

I and **she** are both nominative case pronouns. The predicates in these two sentences are missing. This is how each would appear with its predicate restored:

Mr. Phillips respects you more than **I** respect you. (unabbreviated and correct)

The kids enjoy me more than **she** enjoys me. (unabbreviated and correct)

As you can see, the pronouns in these abbreviated adverbial clauses can be in either the nominative or the objective case form, but which case the writer uses has a great effect on the meaning of the sentence.

LOVE AND GRAMMAR

Q. A jilted lover called the Hot Line and wanted to know the meaning of what a former beloved had said. "She loves you more than me."

A. The caller's ex-girlfriend omitted a portion of an adverbial clause, but didn't put the remaining pronoun in the proper case form. What she said but didn't mean was "She loves you more than she loves me." **Me** is the objective case form of the first person, singular personal pronoun. Knowing this, we can conclude that it was a subject and a predicate that were excluded. The resulting sentence doesn't communicate the speaker's intended meaning.

His ex should have excluded the predicate, leaving behind a first person, singular pronoun in the nominative case form, **I**. The sentence should read, "She loves you more than I." With the predicate included, it would read, "She loves you more than I love you." Lovers, beware of how you phrase those love notes, and check with the Hot Line before sending them!

SUBJECT-VERB AGREEMENT IN CLAUSES

Don't be hasty with the verbs that you use in subordinate clauses. Subjects and verbs must agree no matter where they fall, but in sentences that begin with relative pronouns, this agreement can be difficult to maintain.

Relative pronouns, such as **who** or **which**, possess no inherent number. When one of these functions as the subject of a clause, the verb that follows must agree with it, but how do we decide what number our verb should take? Just look to the antecedent of the relative pronoun for the answer.

Those three boys are the ones **who** are causing trouble.

My sister is a person **who** knows many jokes.

In the first example, the relative pronoun **who** introduces the relative clause **who are causing trouble**. The plural pronoun **ones** is the antecedent of the subject of the clause, **who**. Since we have a plural antecedent, we need a plural verb. The plural verb **are** (in the relative clause) fits the bill.

In the second example, the relative pronoun **who** introduces the relative clause **who knows many jokes**. The singular noun **person** is the antecedent of the subject of the clause, **who**. Since we have a singular antecedent, we need a singular verb. The relative clause contains a singular verb, **knows**, as it should.

AN AGREEMENT ISSUE

Q. A banker from Kentucky called to ask about a photo caption printed in a nationally syndicated newspaper. She said, "Check out this sentence: 'Officers inspect motorcycle of one of the two patrolmen who were shot.' Tell me what the problem with this is. It sounds off to me."

A. The editors have printed a complex sentence with a disagreement between the subject and verb in the relative clause. The relative pronoun **who** joins the relative clause **who were shot** to the main clause **officers inspect motorcycle of one of the two patrolmen**. To the untrained eye, the antecedent of **who** appears to be the plural noun **patrolmen**, but it is actually the singular pronoun **one**. **Patrolmen** is the object of the preposition **of**.

The relative pronoun **who** is the subject of the relative clause. Since its antecedent is singular, it is also singular and demands a singular verb. **Were** is a plural verb. The sentence should read, "Officers inspect motorcycle of one of the two patrolmen who *was* shot."

The Hot Line recognizes that the sentence is still technically incomplete—the writers could add articles at a number of spots—but space limitations in newspaper captions and headlines do require the elimination of words that will not affect the clarity of the sentence. If we had to write the truly complete version, it would appear as follows: "*The* officers inspect *the* motorcycle of one of the two patrolmen who *was* shot."

ANOTHER AGREEMENT ISSUE

Q. One caller complained, "I've found another television personality with bad grammar. This one said, 'Five finalists will be selected by using the ABC criteria which includes the final four steps.' Will they never learn?"

A. Again, the subject and verb in a relative clause do not agree. The relative pronoun **which** joins the relative clause **which includes the final four steps** to the main clause **five finalists will be selected by using the ABC criteria**. The antecedent of **which** is the plural noun **criteria**.

Which is the subject of the clause. Since its antecedent is plural, it is plural as well and needs a plural verb. **Includes** is a singular verb. The sentence should read, "Five finalists will be selected by using the ABC criteria which *include* the final four steps."

Yet Another Agreement Issue

Q. An attorney was writing a speech. He called to ask, "What's up with this sentence? I know there's something amiss. 'We present this award in grateful recognition of Bob and Jim who has participated in the work of this event.' "

A. It's the same old story. There is subject-verb disagreement within the relative clause. The relative pronoun **who** joins the relative clause **who has participated in the work of this event** to the main clause **we present this award in grateful recognition of Bob and Jim**. The subject of the relative clause is **who**. The proper nouns **Bob** and **Jim** are both antecedents of this relative pronoun.

With multiple antecedents, the pronoun is a plural subject and needs a plural verb. **Has participated** is a singular verb phrase. The sentence should read, "We present this award in grateful recognition of Bob and Jim who *have* participated in the work of this event."

If the attorney were to place a comma after the first proper noun, **Bob**, then the only antecedent of the relative pronoun **who** would be the second proper noun, **Jim**. The relative clause would need a singular verb, and the sentence would appear as follows: "We present this award in grateful recognition of Bob, and Jim who *has* participated in the work of this event." The comma divides the two proper nouns, so that **who** cannot claim any noun beyond **Jim** as an antecedent.

AGREEMENT AND NOMINAL CLAUSES

Q. A director of personnel asked us to check his grammar. He said, "Here's my sentence: 'What business needs most are some good ideas.' What do you think? Sometimes I think it's right, but sometimes it sounds wrong. I just can't tell."

A. The Hot Line guessed that the caller was concerned about the agreement between the subject and the verb. Creating agreement in a complex sentence can be tricky. In this sentence, the relative pronoun **what** introduces the nominal clause **what business needs most**, the subject. **Are** is the verb in the sentence. It is plural. We need to verify that the subject and verb agree, but the number of the subject, singular or plural, is ambiguous.

For an answer to the mystery, we turn to the nominal clause **what business needs most**, the subject of the sentence. The pronoun **what** refers to the plural subject complement **some good ideas**. This might lead us to believe that the subject is plural and needs a plural verb, **are**. Unfortunately, the answer is not quite so simple.

The pronoun **what** is always singular in form when it is the subject of a sentence even though it may be plural in meaning. As we know, **what** refers to a plural subject complement. Even so, this pronoun is singular in form. For subject and verb to agree, our director needs to use a singular verb. The sentence should read as follows:

What business needs most *is* some good ideas.

PRONOUN-ANTECEDENT AGREEMENT IN CLAUSES

Equally troubling are personal pronouns found in subordinate clauses. When the antecedent of a personal pronoun is a relative pronoun, how do we know which person, number, and gender to assign it? Again, look to the antecedent of the relative pronoun for the answer.

Bill is a man **who** carries his heart on his sleeve.

Mountain climbing is a sport **which** has its share of hazards.

In the first example, the relative pronoun **who** introduces the relative clause **who carries his heart on his sleeve**. Within the relative clause, the pronoun **his** modifies the noun **heart**. The antecedent of **his** is the relative pronoun **who**. The antecedent of **who** is the masculine, third person, singular noun **man**. This noun, **man**, is the ultimate antecedent of **his**. Since **his** is masculine, singular and in the third person, the pronoun and its antecedent agree.

In the second example, the relative pronoun **which** introduces the relative clause **which has its share of hazards**. Within the relative clause, the pronoun **its** modifies the noun **share**. The antecedent of **its** is the relative pronoun **which**. The antecedent of **which** and the ultimate antecedent of **its** is the neuter, third person, singular noun **sport**. Since **its** is neuter, singular, and in the third person, the pronoun and its antecedent agree.

AGREEMENT ISN'T EASY

Q. One caller said, "Every day, on my way home from work, I hear this car dealer on the radio. His grammar is atrocious. What should he do to clean up this sentence: 'This is for anyone who don't think that they have the cash'? "

A. The relative clause in this complex sentence contains a faulty verb. The relative pronoun **who** connects the relative clause **who don't think that they have the cash** to the main clause **this is for anyone**. The relative pronoun **who** is the subject of the clause. Its antecedent is the singular indefinite pronoun **anyone**. To make a singular subject and verb agree, the dealer needs to use a singular verb, **doesn't**. As it stands, the sentence contains a plural verb, **don't**.

To make matters worse, there is a faulty nominal clause, **that they have the cash**, within the relative clause just mentioned. The subject of the nominal clause is the pronoun **they**. The ultimate antecedent of **they** is the singular indefinite pronoun **anyone**—the antecedent of **they** is **who**, and the antecedent of **who** is **anyone**. The dealer needs to use a singular personal pronoun, such as **he** or **she**, and he needs to change his plural verb, **have**, to agree with a singular subject. If the dealer has any pride, he will re-tape his spot to say, "This is for anyone who *doesn't* think that *he or she has* the cash."

A JUDGMENT CALL

Q. A writer for the AFL-CIO called about a sentence he was using in a report. He said, "I have a sentence that I want you to look at. 'I have a pool of skilled workers who are able to complete the task.' Is it acceptable?"

A. I told the writer that he had asked a question which could not be answered easily. In his sentence, the relative pronoun **who** introduces the relative clause **who are able to complete the task**. The antecedent of **who** is the collective noun **pool**. **Pool** is generally inanimate, as in "a *pool* of resources." This sort of pool is an abstract idea, rather than a concrete object. If this is how the writer views the pool to which he refers, he must use a relative pronoun, such as **that**, that may stand for an inanimate noun. Under this interpretation, his sentence would read, "I have a pool of skilled workers *that* are able to complete the task."

However, the members of this particular pool are human beings, and the argument could be made that this fact gives the pool an animate quality. It is not a pool of money or weapons or machines. This pool is composed of living, breathing people, so the collective noun must live and breathe as well. Under this very reasonable interpretation, the sentence would not require change.

Grammar, like any other complex and engaging topic, will never be cut and dry. It is interesting *because* it is arguable and *because* there are issues that lack clear solutions. The path that leads to proper grammar is a dialogue, not a dogmatic monologue. Don't ever let anyone tell you otherwise!

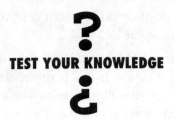

TEST YOUR KNOWLEDGE

QUESTIONS

1. What do we call a main clause that stands alone?

2. If a sentence has a compound subject, is it necessarily a compound sentence?

3. What is wrong with the following sentence: "The rain fell, the streets flooded"?

4. How does a compound sentence differ from a complex sentence?

5. What type of connecting word is the word **that** when it introduces a relative clause?

6. What meanings can adverbial clauses indicate?

7. What do we call the group of words that a nominal clause completes?

8. Which relative pronoun does this sentence need: "Who/whom we might see affects what I will wear"?

9. Is this a complex sentence: "My grip is stronger than his grip"?

10. How do we determine the number of a relative pronoun when this pronoun is the subject of a relative clause and we are concerned about subject-verb agreement?

(SEE ANSWERS ON FOLLOWING PAGE)

Answers

1. We call such a clause a simple sentence.

2. No, it is not necessarily a compound sentence. A compound sentence consists of two or more main clauses. A compound subject just consists of two or more subjects. A compound sentence may contain a compound subject, but a compound subject also can be a part of a simple sentence.

3. The sentence contains a comma splice. We could correct it to read, "The rain fell, and the streets flooded."

4. A compound sentence consists only of main clauses, while a complex sentence is a mixture of main and subordinate clauses.

5. Introducing a relative clause, the word **that** is a relative pronoun. In this role, it links clauses and replaces a noun in the relative clause. **That** can also be a subordinate conjunction in adverbial and nominal clauses, but there it only plays a connecting role.

6. Adverbial clauses can indicate place, time, manner, cause, degree or comparison, intention, and possibility or conditionality.

7. We call this group of words a host clause.

8. In the sentence, the relative pronoun functions as a direct object of the verb **see**, so we need the objective case form, **whom**. The sentence should read, "*Whom* we might see affects what I will wear."

9. This is a complex sentence, but part of the adverbial clause beginning with the conjunction **than** has been omitted.

10. We look to the antecedent to determine the number of the relative pronoun.

Part III

Spelling, Vocabulary, & Punctuation

14.

Spelling

> **Spelling** is the art of writing words with the correct sequence of letters, and, believe me, while it may not be as riveting as some, it is an art.

The academic term for spelling is **orthography**. It comes from the two Greek words **orthos**, meaning "straight," and **graphein**, meaning "to write." Together in **orthography**, they mean "to write or spell correctly."

Why is our spelling system so difficult? Why are so few of us able to become competent orthographers? It is because the spellings of English words have developed in such a haphazard manner. From the beginning, ours has been an amalgamated language, influenced by contacts with languages across the globe. English, a Germanic language, was born among three Germanic tribes, the Jutes, the Angles, and the Saxons, along the shores of the North Sea in what we now call northern Germany and southern Denmark. With the invasion of Britain by the Angles and the Saxons, English felt a Celtic influence as it spread across the English channel to a people who spoke the Celtic tongue. During its early years, English also experienced a Scandinavian influence as England was subject to frequent Viking invasion. The first major change to the English language arrived with William of Normandy and his conquering French legions in 1066 A.D.; the invaders brought the influence of Norman French with its Latin origins to the language of the Britons. Later, during the Renaissance, English would borrow great numbers of words, particularly from French and Italian, as the language acquired more scholarly functions once reserved for Latin. Although English has become a major international language, it still retains spelling irregularities, products of these many influences.

Linguists view the evolution of English in stages. The oldest form of English was spoken between 700 and 1100 A.D. and has been appropriately named Old English. A more recent but not yet modern version of English is known as Middle English. This language existed until approximately 1500 A.D. English then began its gradual evolution into the language we speak today, sometimes called Modern English.

Though speakers of Old and Modern English would certainly have trouble holding conversations with one another, many Old English spellings are quite similar to those of Modern English. For instance, the Modern **heart** was spelled **heorte** in Old English, and the Modern **breast** was spelled **breost** in Old English. The articles **a** and **an** are two of the oldest English words. In Old as in Modern English, they "marked" or modified nouns.

Somewhere along the line, English speakers realized the value of a comprehensive list and description of English words, and, in England, in 1775, Dr. Samuel Johnson published the first English dictionary. Dr. Johnson had a great love for Latin and was directly responsible for some of the strange spellings in English today. He inserted a silent **b** in **debt** because the Latin word from which **debt** is derived is **debitum**. He even inserted a silent **p** in **receipt** (from the Latin **recepta**) for the same reason but chose not to in **conceit** (from the Latin **conceptum**) and **deceit** (from the Latin **deceptus**).

In America, Noah Webster's dictionary altered many words from their original English spellings:

AMERICAN SPELLING	ENGLISH SPELLING
jail	gaol
honor	honour

AMERICAN SPELLING	ENGLISH SPELLING
wagon	waggon
jewelry	jewellry

English continues to evolve today. Spellings and pronunciations change. New words are added to the lexicon. With the infiltration of mass media into our daily lives we are bombarded with words from across the globe. If a foreign word or phrase is heard often enough, it becomes part of our everyday speech and writing. Growth and change keep the language from stagnating and dying.

SPELLING RULES

If only English words were so simple that we could spell them by a single, clear, and well-defined set of rules . . . . While it may be said that spellings follow a number of common themes, these themes are full of exceptions and contradictions. Nevertheless, there are a number of rules that can help you become a better speller. Here they are:

1. The consonant letters **f, l, s,** and **z** at the ends of one-syllable words containing short vowel sounds are written twice.

Examples: dress, drill, cuff, fuzz

Exceptions: bus, gas

2. The **/k/** sound at the end of words containing short vowel sounds is spelled with a **ck.**

Examples: back, rack, hammock, sock, cassock

Exceptions: picnic, panic, sonic, tonic, caustic

3. Since **c** and **k** can both have the same sound, it can be difficult to decide when to use which letter. The following general rules will help you to make the correct choice:

Rule 1: When a word begins with a **/k/** sound that is followed by one of the short vowels **a, o,** or **u,** the **/k/** sound is spelled with the letter **c.**

Examples: casserole, cot, culprit

Rule 2: When a word begins with a **/k/** sound that is followed by one of the short vowels **e** or **i,** the **/k/** sound is spelled with the letter **k.**

Examples: kiss, kelp, kit, kept

4. Most nouns are made plural simply by adding **-s**. In these words, the final sound blends well with the /s/ sound.

      hill → hills   cake → cakes   cereal → cereals

However, nouns ending in the letters **ch**, **sh**, **s**, **x**, or **z**, whose sounds are called the sibilant sounds, are made plural by adding **-es**. The sibilant sounds do not blend well with the sound of the pluralizing **-s**. Please note that you must double the final consonant **z** before adding **-es**.

      watch → watches   wish → wishes   kiss → kisses
      fox → foxes   whiz → whizzes   miss → misses

5. To pluralize a noun ending in a **y** preceded by a consonant, simply change the **y** to **i** and add **-es**.

      daddy → daddies   puppy → puppies   lily → lilies

If the final **y** is preceded by a vowel, simply add **-s**.

      key → keys   delay → delays   relay → relays

6. To pluralize a compound of words that serves as a single noun, like **mother-in-law**, add **-s** or **-es** to the most important word in the group.

      mother-in-law → mothers-in-law

      sergeant-at-arms → sergeants-at-arms

7. It can be difficult to pluralize nouns ending in **f**, **ff**, or **fe**. These general rules will help.

    Rule 1: Generally, with nouns that end in **f** or **fe**, change the **f** or **fe** to **v**, and add **-es** to form the plural.

      wife → wives   knife → knives   life → lives
      shelf → shelves   calf → calves   loaf → loaves

    Rule 2: To form the plurals of nouns ending in **ff**, just add **-s**.

      puff → puffs   muff → muffs   cuff → cuffs

    Exceptions to Rule 1: There are a number of words that end in **fe** or **f** to which we simply add **-s** to form their plurals.

      safe → safes   chief → chiefs   roof → roofs

8. Here are two rules that will help you form the plurals of words ending in **o**:

Rule 1: If the final **o** follows a vowel, simply add **-s**.

stereo → stereos   radio → radios

Rule 2: If the final **o** follows a consonant, add **-es**.

potato → potatoes   tomato → tomatoes

Exception 1: Many musical names end in **o** preceded by a consonant. To form the plural, simply add **-s**.

piccolo → piccolos   alto → altos   soprano → sopranos

Exception 2: There are a few other nouns ending in **o** preceded by a consonant whose plurals we form by adding **-s**.

albino → albinos   halo → halos

Exception 3: We form the plurals of some nouns with the **o** ending preceded by a consonant with either **-s** or **-es**.

hero → heros *or* heroes   tornado → tornados *or* tornadoes

9. The **/ch/** sound at the end of a word is generally spelled with a **tch**.

Examples: watch, catch, match, hatch, latch

However, if that **/ch/** sound is preceded by an **/n/** or **/r/** sound or a vowel sound spelled with more than one vowel letter, it is spelled with a **ch**.

Examples: lunch, brunch, march, arch, brooch, approach

10. If a word ends with the long **/a/** sound, it usually has an **ay** ending.

Examples: array, play, stay

However, a few words that end with the long **/a/** sound have an **ey** ending.

Examples: they, prey

11. Remember the **i** before **e** rule! **I** before **e** except after **c** or when sounded like **a** as in **neighbor** and **weigh**.

Examples: relieve, mischief, receive, conceive

There are, however, a number of exceptions to this classic rule:

caffeine	height	seize
either	neither	sheik
foreign	protein	weird

12. Words that end with a /j/ sound are spelled with a **dge** ending.

Examples: edge, bridge, nudge

13. When forming contractions, use the apostrophe to replace missing letters:

they will → they'll   you would → you'd   they have → they've
did not → didn't   would not → wouldn't

Remember that the possessive pronouns are never spelled with apostrophes. They already show possession, and there are no missing letters for the apostrophe to replace.

Examples: yours, hers, its, ours, theirs

14. It can be difficult to figure out how to spell the **/seed/** sound cluster that ends some words. Should you use **sede, ceed,** or **cede**? These general rules will help:

Rule 1: I know of only one word in English that ends in **sede**. It is **supersede**.

Rule 2: I know of only three words in English that end in **ceed**. They are **proceed, exceed,** and **succeed**.

Rule 3: All other words with the final **/seed/** sound cluster end with **cede**.

Examples: precede, recede

15. Adding a prefix does not change the spelling of the base word. If you know how to spell the base word, all you need to do is add the prefix.

dis- + similar → dissimilar   re- + enter → reenter
un- + constitutional → unconstitutional

16. When should we use the prefixes **ante-** and **anti-**? Even though they sound the same, their meanings are different. The prefix **ante-** means "before," as in **antebellum**, meaning "before the war." The prefix **anti-** means "against," as in **anti-intellectual**, meaning "against intellectuals or intellectual thought." Knowing the context in which the word is written or spoken should help you determine which prefix is appropriate.

17. When adding a suffix that begins with a vowel to a word, double the final consonant in the base word only if the following conditions are met:

Condition 1: The base ends with a single consonant.

Condition 2: The vowel sound preceding the final consonant in the base is made with a single vowel letter.

Condition 3: The final consonant of the base is in an accented syllable.

expel + -ed → expelled   submit + -ing → submitting

admit + -ed → admitted

Do not double the final consonant before adding the suffix if any one of these three conditions is not met.

prefer + -ence → preference   find + -er → finder

reap + -ing → reaping

18. Here are some notable exceptions to Rule 17:

Exception 1: Always double the final **m** of base words that end in the syllable **-gram** before adding the suffix.

diagram + -ed → diagrammed   diagram + -ing → diagramming

Exception 2: Do not double a final l before the suffix **-ize, -ism, -ist,** or **-ity.**

scandal + -ize → scandalize   plural + -ism → pluralism

final + -ist → finalist   equal + -ity → equality

Exception 3: Never double a final **x**. It is pronounced as two consonants, **/ks/**, and so violates Condition 1 of Rule 17.

tax + -ed → taxed   mix + -er → mixer   fix + -ing → fixing

19. Generally, when adding a suffix that begins with a vowel to a word ending in **e**, drop the **e** and then add the suffix.

debate + -ing → debating   relate + -ed → related

As you may have expected, there are exceptions to this rule.

dye + -ing → dyeing   be + -ing → being

20. When adding a suffix that begins with **a** or **o** to a word that ends with **ce** or **ge**, do not drop the final **e** from the base word.

change + -able → changeable   courage + -ous → courageous

If the suffix begins with **e, i,** or **y,** however, drop the final **e** from the base.

manage + -er → manager   face + -ing → facing

mange + -y → mangy

21. If words end in **ye, ee,** or **oe,** drop their final **e** before adding a suffix that starts with **e.**

>   canoe + -ed → canoed   dye + -ed → dyed

If the suffix does not begin with the letter **e,** do not drop the final **e** from the word.

>   canoe + -ing → canoeing   dye + -ing → dyeing

22. When adding a suffix that begins with a vowel to a word that ends with **ue,** drop the final **e** before adding the suffix.

>   issue + -ing → issuing   ensue + -ed → ensued

23. Do not drop the final **e** before adding a suffix that begins with a consonant.

>   strange + -ly → strangely   bare + -ly → barely

Watch out though! There are some unusual and unexplainable exceptions to this rule.

>   judge + -ment → judgment   true + -ly → truly
>   awe + -ful → awful   argue + -ment → argument
>   nine + -th → ninth   whole + -ly → wholly
>   acknowledge + -ment → acknowledgment

24. When adding the suffix **-ing** to a word that ends in **ie,** change the **ie** to **y,** and then add the suffix.

>   die + -ing → dying   belie + -ing → belying

25. If a word ends in **y,** change the **y** to **i** before adding any of the suffixes **-able, -ance,** or **-ant.**

>   apply + -ance → appliance   ply + -able → pliable
>   rely + -ant → reliant

>   **Exception:** charity + -able → charitable

26. For most words that end in **c,** insert a **k** before a suffix that begins with **i, e,** or **y.** The final **c** in these words retains the /k/ sound after the suffix has been added.

>   panic + -ing → panicking   picnic + -ed → picnicked
>   panic +- y → panicky

If the final **c** does not retain the /k/ sound, do not add a **k.**

>   caustic + -ity → causticity   electric + -ity → electricity
>   toxic + -ity → toxicity

27. It is sometimes difficult to determine when to use the suffix **-ible** and when to use the suffix **-able** at the end of a word. The following general rules will show you the way.

Rule 1: If the base word ends in a hard **c** or a hard **g,** use the suffix **-able.**

Examples: amicable, **navig**able

Rule 2: If the base itself is a complete English word, use the suffix **-able.**

Examples: changeable, **fly**able

Rule 3: If the base is not a complete English word and does not end in a hard **c** or **g** , use the suffix **-ible.**

Examples: susceptible, **vis**ible

Rule 4: If you can add the suffix **-ion** to the base to make a legitimate English word, then you should use the suffix **-ible.**

Examples: corruptible (**corrupt**ion), **perfect**ible (**perfect**ion)

28. When in doubt, look it up! Use your dictionary. It is a powerful tool and your key to becoming a perfect speller.

FROM MY FILES: THE DANGERS OF SPELL-CHECK

CAUTION: Your computer's spell-checker is stupid. Though an invaluable time-saver, spell-checking is far from infallible. Your computer may indicate that a word is spelled correctly, but it cannot tell if its choice of word is correct for the sentence. For example, look at this sentence: "The ideal candidate will *posses* a flair for the dramatic." Run the sentence through your spell-checker, and it will tell you that everything is okay, even though the fifth word is misspelled. The computer is ignorant of context. It does not know that the sentence needs a verb that means "to have" and does not realize that this word ends with a double **s: possess.** The computer only knows that the plural of **posse** is **posses** and that the sentence contains what could be a legitimate English word. The spell-checker is a fine tool for the initial round of editing, but only a sharp human mind can ensure perfect writing. The following poem illustrates just why a keen proofreading eye is a writer's most valuable asset:

Word Processing

I have a lovely spelling check
That came with my PC,
Witch plainly marks, four my revue,
Miss takes I can not sea.
I've run this poem threw the thing,
I'm sure your please too no.
It's latter perfect in every weigh.
My checker tolled me sew.

—Author unknown

HETERONYMS, HOMONYMS, HOMOPHONES, AND HOMOGRAPHS

Once you have learned the rules, you must learn the exceptions that turn the rules upside down. What do you do with words that have identical spellings or pronunciations but different meanings? There is no easy answer to that question. Only experience, persistence, and a watchful eye will help the cautious speller avoid the pitfalls that these words pose. To enhance our understanding of the lexicon, grammarians have divided such tricky words into four categories: **homophones**, **homographs**, **homonyms**, and **heteronyms**.

Homophones are words that are pronounced alike and that have different meanings but that may or may not be spelled the same. The noun **quail**, meaning "a type of game bird," and the verb **quail**, meaning "to falter," are homophones. The verb **pray**, meaning "to address a deity," and the noun **prey**, meaning "a victim," are also homophones.

Some homophones are also **homonyms**. These are words that have the same pronunciation and spelling but different meanings. The noun **quack**, meaning "the sound made by a duck," and the noun **quack**, meaning "a charlatan," are homonyms.

There is another set of tricky words called **homographs**. These words have the same spelling but different origins, meanings, or pronunciations. The noun **homer**, meaning "an ancient Hebrew unit of measure," and the noun **homer**, meaning "a home run," are homographs.

Some homographs are also **heteronyms**. These are words with the same spelling but different pronunciations and meanings. The noun **conduct** (accent on the first syllable), meaning "behavior," and the verb **conduct** (accent on the second syllable), meaning "to guide," are heteronyms. The adjective Polish (with a long /o/), meaning "originating in the land of Poland," and the verb **polish** (with a short /o/), meaning "to make smooth and shiny," are also heteronyms.

The definitions of the different categories can become confusing; the different names sound quite similar. One way to tell them apart is to learn the Greek origin of each word. The syllable **homo** comes from the Greek word **homos**, meaning "same." The syllable **hetero** comes from the Greek word **heteros**, meaning "different." The syllable **graph** comes from the Greek word **graphein**, meaning "to write." The syllable **nym** comes from the Greek word **onyma**, meaning "name." The syllable **phone** comes from the Greek word **phone**, meaning "sound." The word **homophone**, then, means "same sound." The word **homonym** means "same name." The word **homograph** means "same spelling." And the word **heteronym** means "different names."

Heteronyms, homonyms, homophones, and homographs almost defy description. The problems they present are mind-boggling, and they are quite difficult to learn. To make the process as painless as possible, the Hot Line has compiled a list of the most common. You'll simply have to learn them all in order not to make an embarrassing mistake.

ad (n)	The **ad** for new shoes interested me.
add (v)	I can **add** up the numbers that you require.
aid (n)	The Red Cross gives **aid** to people in need.
aide (n)	An **aide** is always there to give assistance.
ail (v)	What **ails** you?
ale (n)	Don't drink too much **ale**.
air (n)	The **air** was stifling.
heir (n)	He was **heir** to a fortune.
aisle (n)	He proudly escorted the bride down the **aisle**.
I'll (contraction)	**I'll** go to the movies with you.
isle (n)	Oh, what adventures they had on Gilligan's **Isle**.

altar (n)	The **altar** of the church is magnificent.
alter (v)	No one can **alter** the past.
arc (n)	The thin **arc** of the moon illuminated the night.
ark (n)	The **ark** almost foundered in the water.
ate (v)	We **ate** our dinner by candlelight.
eight (n)	The number **eight** has some strange connotations.
aught (n)	Many mathematicians say "**aught**" instead of "zero."
ought (v)	You **ought** to learn the homonyms.
bail (n)	The **bail** was set at $1,000,000.
bail (v)	The survivors must **bail** the water from their boat.
bale (n)	We counted three **bales** of hay.
band (n)	The marching **band** played wonderfully.
band (n)	Don't snap me with that rubber **band**!
band (v)	We will lose the fight unless we **band** together.
banned (v)	The authorities **banned** the film from the festival.
bare (v)	Dare you **bare** your head to the blazing sun?
bear (v)	I cannot **bear** that awful noise.
bear (n)	The grizzly **bear** was extremely menacing.
bases (n)	With two men out, the **bases** are loaded.
basis (n)	He has no **basis** for his argument.
beat (v)	Can you **beat** his score?
beat (n)	The cop walks his **beat** at night.
beet (n)	The **beet** is a nutritious red root.
beau (n)	She came to the dance with her new **beau**.
bow (n)	A red **bow** adorned the little girl's hair.
bow (n)	Robin of Locksley was master of the **bow** and arrow.
bow (v)	You must **bow** before the king.
been (v)	The tourists have **been** to The Plaza in Athens.
bin (n)	Throw the remnants into the trash **bin**.
berry (n)	A freshly picked **berry** is a fine summer treat.
bury (v)	**Bury** the evidence quickly!

berth (n)	Give that crazy man a wide **berth**.
birth (n)	The **birth** of their first child was a joyous occasion.
bid (n)	Duke Hawthorne placed the winning **bid** at the auction.
bid (v)	The gentleman **bid** the lovely lady adieu.
blew (v)	The winds **blew** ferociously
blue (n)	The color **blue** is my favorite.
board (n)	The rotting, wooden **board** split in two.
board (v)	All passengers may now **board** the airliner.
bored (adj)	The **bored** child turned the television off and went outside.
bolder (adj)	The child grew **bolder** with each success.
boulder (n)	A large, granite **boulder** blocked the trail.
born (v)	Eileen was **born** on a glorious day.
borne (v)	You have **borne** your troubles majestically.
brake (n)	My car needs new **brakes**.
break (v)	Don't **break** anything in the china shop.
bread (n)	There are few foods so satisfying as freshly baked **bread**.
bred (v)	My uncle **bred** horses for a living.
bridal (adj)	We attended the **bridal** shower.
bridle (n)	The groom adjusted the horse's **bridle**.
borough (n)	The Bronx is a **borough** of New York City.
burrow (v)	The mole **burrowed** under the house.
burrow (n)	The rabbits retreated into their **burrow**.
buy (v)	How much can you **buy** with so little money?
by (prep)	The tired runner fell **by** the roadside.
bye (int)	**Bye**! Have a nice day!
cache (n)	The burglar's **cache** held all the loot from the robbery.
cash (n)	I don't have enough **cash** to pay for dinner.
canvas (n)	As an artist, my dad always had a large stock of **canvas**.
canvass (v)	Senator Bigs **canvassed** the neighborhood for support.

capital (adj)	The murderer was given **capital** punishment.
capital (n)	The **capital** of California is Sacramento.
capitol (n)	The United States Congress meets in the **Capitol**.
carat (n)	That diamond is one **carat**.
carrot (n)	Everyone knows about beta carotene in **carrots**.
karat (n)	The purity of gold is measured in **karats**.
cede (v)	In 1899 Great Britain **ceded** Hong Kong from China.
seed (n)	Every mighty oak grew from a tiny **seed**.
ceiling (n)	The **ceiling** must be painted as well.
sealing (v)	She is **sealing** the envelope with wax.
cell (n)	Let the villain rot in his **cell**.
sell (v)	He will **sell** his car through the classifieds.
cellar (n)	Rudy kept his fine wine in the **cellar**.
seller (n)	The watch **seller** got a fair price for his wares.
census (n)	The bureau conducted a population **census** last year.
senses (n)	Taste is one of the five **senses**.
cent (n)	One **cent** used to buy a stick of gum.
scent (n)	The dog's keen nose picked up the **scent**.
sent (v)	The teacher **sent** the upstart to the principal.
cereal (n)	Cold **cereal** with bananas sounds like a fine breakfast.
serial (adj)	These murders appear to be the work of a **serial** killer.
cession (n)	England's **cession** of Hong Kong created controversy.
session (n)	I missed my **session** with the therapist.
chased (v)	The police **chased** the suspect.
chaste (adj)	He is virtuous and **chaste**.
chews (v)	The cow **chews** contentedly on her cud.
choose (v)	You must **choose** between the two sweaters.
choir (n)	I appreciate the sweet sounds of a fine **choir**.
quire (n)	One needs many **quires** of paper to write a book.

chord (n)	The strange musical **chord** made me shiver.
cord (n)	They tied the **cord** around the box.
chute (n)	Dispose of the papers in the garbage **chute**.
shoot (v)	"Stop or I'll **shoot**!" yelled the policeman.
cite (v)	Always **cite** your sources when writing essays.
sight (n)	Is the Statue of Liberty in **sight**?
site (n)	The mayor chose this **site** for the new building.
climb (v)	The courageous defy death and **climb** mountains.
clime (n)	The birds flew south toward gentler **climes**.
colonel (n)	She attained the rank of army **colonel**.
kernel (n)	How many **kernels** are there on an ear of corn?
complement (v)	The debutante's hat **complemented** her outfit.
compliment (n)	She gave me a flattering **compliment**.
conduct (n)	Benny's **conduct** in class has been less than admirable.
conduct (v)	Reginald will **conduct** the tour of the museum.
core (n)	Some people enjoy eating the **core** of the apple.
corps (n)	The Marine **Corps** is a force to be reckoned with.
council (n)	The city **council** met in special session.
counsel (n)	His **counsel** gave him good advice.
coarse (adj)	The **coarse** fabric was uncomfortable to wear.
course (n)	The runners followed the **course** through the forest.
course (n)	She enrolled in a Medieval English **course**.
coward (n)	He was labeled a **coward** after he ran from a challenge.
cowered (v)	During the storm, the kitten **cowered** under the bed.
creak (v)	The stairs **creak** at night.
creek (n)	The waters of the **creek** babbled outside my window.
cue (n)	The **cue** to begin the race was the sound of a gunshot.
cue (n)	She struck the ball with the pool **cue**.
queue (n)	Standing in a **queue** requires patience.

currant (n)	The black **currant** is a delicious berry.
current (n)	The **current** of the river was swift.
current (adj)	It is good to be knowledgeable about **current** events.
cymbal (n)	The sound of clashing **cymbals** is thrilling.
symbol (n)	The American flag is a **symbol** of freedom.
dear (adj)	**Dear** reader, you should learn these homonyms.
deer (n)	New Zealanders raise **deer** as Americans raise cows.
desert (v)	The frightened soldier **deserted** his platoon.
desert (n)	Only the hardiest of plants survives in the **desert**.
dessert (n)	Crème brûlé is a special **dessert**.
dew (n)	The pearly **dew** glistened on the lawn.
do (v)	Please **do** the work immediately.
due (adv)	The assignment is **due** next week.
die (v)	Water the plant or it will **die**.
dye (n)	The **dye** made the white shirt green.
discreet (adj)	The diplomat handled the affair in a **discreet** fashion.
discrete (adj)	Ours was a **discrete** department, separate from the rest.
doe (n)	A female deer is a **doe**.
dough (n)	The baker kneaded the **dough**.
done (v)	The job is **done**.
dun (n)	The smog turns the color of the sky to **dun**.
dun (v)	Don't **dun** me for what I owe.
dual (adj)	The coupe had **dual** exhausts.
duel (n)	The adversaries fought a fearsome **duel**.
earn (v)	The more you **earn**, the more you spend.
urn (n)	We keep Grandpa's ashes in an **urn**.
elicit (v)	I **elicit** thoughtful responses from my pupils.
illicit (adj)	The politician's **illicit** affair caused quite a scandal.
ewe (n)	**Ewes** roam the pastures in Scotland.
you (pro)	**You** are very special.

exercise (n)	My lack of **exercise** contributes to this unsightly bulge.
exorcise (v)	The priest will **exorcise** the demon.
faint (adj)	**Faint** sounds caught our attention.
feint (n)	With a quick **feint**, the fencer won the match.
fair (n)	We journeyed to the county **fair**.
fair (adj)	Children are taught to be **fair** with each other.
fare (n)	Rapid transit **fares** seem to go up and up.
fated (adj)	To be **fated** is to be destined by fate.
feted (v)	For his accomplishment, we **feted** him.
faze (v)	Such behavior does not **faze** me.
phase (n)	She is going through a difficult **phase** in her life.
feat (n)	The stuntman began another absurd **feat** of daring.
feet (n)	After a long day, the **feet** are tired.
feet (n)	There are three **feet** in a yard.
find (v)	What did you **find** in the shipwreck?
fined (v)	The scoundrel was **fined** $1,000.
fir (n)	The Douglas **fir** is a magnificent tree.
fur (n)	It's all right to wear imitation **fur**.
fisher (n)	The **fishers** caught their limit at the lake.
fissure (n)	The quake opened several **fissures** in the ground.
flair (n)	My sister has a **flair** for baking.
flare (v)	Why do you **flare** up in anger?
flea (n)	That **flea** is driving my dog crazy.
flee (v)	The town's inhabitants must **flee** the volcano's wrath.
flew (v)	The young birds **flew** from their nest.
flu (n)	Each winter I catch a nasty case of the **flu**.
flue (n)	We found it necessary to clean the **flue** of the chimney.
flour (n)	I always use unbleached **flour** in my bread.
flower (n)	Place the **flower** in the vase.
flower (v)	When she turned thirteen, her musical abilities **flowered**.

for (prep)	These flowers are **for** you.
fore (adj)	The **fore** three seats are empty.
four (n)	The number **four** is a perfect square.
forbear (v)	**Forbear** from speaking when I am perturbed.
forebear (n)	My **forebear** gave me some good genes.
foreword (n)	Many readers ignore the **foreword** of a book.
forward (adv)	We marched straight **forward**.
fort (n)	The children gleefully played in their tree **fort**.
forte (n)	Mathematics has never been my **forte**.
forth (adv)	It is time to go **forth** and seek your fortune.
fourth (adj)	April is the **fourth** month of the year.
foul (n)	Wilt didn't like the **foul** called against him.
fowl (n)	I enjoy eating **fowl**, especially chicken.
freeze (v)	The butcher will **freeze** the meat.
frieze (n)	The artist did a fine job with the **frieze**.
gamble (v)	Many people **gamble** away their money for pleasure.
gambol (v)	The children **gambol** about the playground with joy.
gibe (v)	Do not **gibe** me for I resent sarcasm.
jibe (v)	The sail **jibed** from one side to the other.
jibe (v)	Does my observation **jibe** with yours?
gilt (n)	The **gilt** on the balcony glistened brightly.
guilt (n)	Carrying **guilt** is a burden that devours the guilty.
gnu (n)	The **gnu** is a graceful beast.
knew (v)	All of us **knew** the truth.
new (adj)	I just bought a **new** car.
grate (v)	The sound of my neighbor's singing **grates** on my nerves.
grate (n)	The ashes rested on the fireplace **grate**.
great (adj)	Thomas told me a **great** joke.
groan (v)	I **groan** at bad jokes.
grown (v)	The sapling has **grown** into a mature tree.

groom (n)	I fear that the **groom** has developed cold feet.
groom (n)	The **groom** takes excellent care of the horses.
guessed (v)	We **guessed** that this book was needed.
guest (n)	Being a gracious **guest** is easier than being a gracious host.
hail (n)	In Illinois we have **hail** the size of golf balls.
hail (v)	My friend **hailed** a cab.
hale (adj)	The President looks **hale** and hearty.
hair (n)	She has beautiful, thick, dark **hair**.
hare (n)	The **hare** lost a famous race with a tortoise.
hall (n)	The **hall** in the Sheraton Palace is magnificent.
haul (v)	After the quake, trucks **hauled** away the debris.
hangar (n)	The plane is kept in the **hangar**.
hanger (n)	My **hangers** always seem to be on the closet floor.
hart (n)	The **hart**, a mighty stag, leapt over the rock.
heart (n)	I beg you not to break my **heart**.
heal (v)	Time **heals** all wounds.
heel (n)	Achilles' **heel** proved to be his downfall.
heel (v)	In the strong wind, the boat **heeled** leeward.
hear (v)	Can you **hear** the whispering of the forest nymphs?
here (adv)	We came **here** on our honeymoon.
heard (v)	They obviously haven't **heard** the news.
herd (n)	A **herd** of bison raced just ahead of our train.
higher (adv)	The plane flew **higher** than ever before.
hire (v)	They will **hire** you if you are literate.
him (pro)	His teacher gave **him** an "A."
hymn (n)	The choir sang a lovely **hymn**.
hoard (n)	We discovered a **hoard** of fine books.
horde (n)	A **horde** of students awaited me.

hoarse (adj)	One's voice becomes **hoarse** after a day of lecturing.
horse (n)	My one experience riding a **horse** was not pleasant.
hole (n)	Alice fell down a very deep **hole**.
whole (adj)	Our research required a **whole** set of encyclopedias.
holey (adj)	The moth-eaten sweater was quite **holey**.
holy (adj)	In Judaism, Saturday is a **holy** day.
wholly (adv)	Having cavities filled is a **wholly** unpleasant experience.
homer (n)	Timmy hit a **homer** at the top of the fifth inning.
homer (n)	The ancient Hebrews measured volume in **homers**.
hour (n)	My watch shows one minute before the **hour**.
our (pro)	This is **our** greatest triumph.
idle (adj)	I like to read in my **idle** time.
idol (n)	My boyhood **idol** was Joe DiMaggio.
idyll (n)	An **idyll** is a short poem describing a pleasant, rural scene.
in (prep)	Did you go **in** the room?
inn (n)	I frequent a certain **inn** in Greenwich.
indict (v)	The drug lord was **indicted** by a grand jury.
indite (v)	Shelly **indited** many wonderful poems.
its (pro)	The dragon returned to **its** cave.
it's (contraction)	**It's** going to be a fine, sunny day.
jam (n)	It's difficult to find fresh gooseberry **jam**.
jamb (n)	The door was stuck because the **jamb** was warped.
key (n)	Education is the **key** to unlocking closed doors.
quay (n)	The four-masted schooners unloaded at the **quay**.
knight (n)	Sir Lancelot was a brave **knight**.
night (n)	Only marauders and spirits walk at **night**.
know (v)	I now **know** what his motives were.
no (adv)	**No**, I haven't seen Elvis in the mall lately.

lead (n)	The walls of this building are lined with **lead**.
lead (v)	Our guide will **lead** us out of the jungle.
led (v)	Why is he **led** about so easily?
lean (v)	**Lean** on me for support.
lien (n)	The bank has a **lien** on her property.
lessen (v)	Antibiotics will **lessen** the infection.
lesson (n)	The first **lesson** is to pay close attention.
lie (v)	Why don't you **lie** down and take a nap?
lie (v)	Do not **lie**. A falsehood is always discovered.
lye (n)	**Lye** is a poison used in making soap and lutefisk.
load (n)	We all carry a heavy **load** in life.
lode (n)	The mother **lode** was rich in gold.
made (v)	Her successes **made** her happy.
maid (n)	She works as a **maid** at the Ritz.
main (adj)	What is your **main** goal in life?
mane (n)	The horse's **mane** was long and burnished.
manner (n)	She has a pleasant **manner**.
manor (n)	A tree-lined road leads to the Duke's country **manor**.
marshal (n)	A **marshal** carries out court orders.
marshal (v)	The colonists **marshaled** their defenses against the British.
martial (adj)	She studies the **martial** arts.
meat (n)	Being a vegetarian, he didn't eat **meat**.
meet (v)	Please **meet** us at noon.
mete (v)	My teacher **metes** out "A's" as if they were made of gold.
mean (adj)	That was a **mean**, wicked act.
mien (n)	He has a noble **mien**.
might (v)	Things **might** have been different between us.
might (n)	Her **might** was expressed in her mind and her muscles.
mite (n)	The **mite** is a minuscule creature.
mite (n)	This farthing, only a **mite**, is hardly worth anything.

miner (n)   **Miners** often develop black lung disease.

minor (adj)   The petty theft was only a **minor** infraction.

missed (v)   We **missed** you at dinner tonight.

mist (n)   The **mist** hovered over the tranquil lake.

morn (n)   On Christmas Day, the children awoke in early **morn**.

mourn (v)   At funerals, we **mourn** the death of a loved one.

morning (n)   The **morning** of the twelfth, I took the train to Tulsa.

mourning (v)   Some never stop **mourning** the loss of a loved one.

naval (adj)   The **naval** battle was fought at Trafalgar.

navel (n)   Your **navel** is your belly button.

one (n)   **One** comes just before two.

one (pro)   **One** can do anything **one** sets **one's** mind to.

won (v)   These knights have **won** many battles.

overdo (v)   Do not **overdo** it.

overdue (adj)   This is your seventh **overdue** library book this year.

paced (v)   He **paced** about the room nervously.

paste (n)   Only **paste** held the costume together.

packed (v)   She **packed** her bags and left.

pact (n)   The countries signed a **pact** to codify the peace agreement.

pail (n)   The **pail** was filled with fresh, warm milk.

pale (adj)   His **pale** color after surgery was quite shocking.

pain (n)   My tolerance for **pain** is high.

pane (n)   The stone broke the **pane** of glass.

pair (n)   What a lovely **pair** of vases.

pare (v)   Please **pare** the fruit.

pear (n)   There is no fruit better than a ripe, juicy **pear**.

passed (v)   The time **passed** so quickly.

past (prep)   She ran **past** the lake.

peace (n)	The enemies ceased fighting and declared **peace**.
piece (n)	That **piece** of strudel is fattening.
peak (n)	The adventurers climbed to the mountain's **peak**.
peek (v)	**Peek** behind the curtain and see if he's there.
pique (v)	The discovery **piqued** my curiosity.
peal (n)	The **peal** of the bells rang through the town.
peel (n)	The **peel** on the avocado is thick.
peer (n)	Don't give into pressure from your **peers**.
pier (n)	Fishermen cast their lines from the end of the **pier**.
plain (n)	A great, barren **plain** stretched before us in every direction.
plain (adj)	I prefer **plain** colors to busy patterns.
plane (n)	The **plane** began a sharp decent through the clouds.
pleas (n)	We can still hear their **pleas** for help.
please (v)	A firm back rub will always **please** me.
polish (v)	We must **polish** the silver before the company arrives.
Polish (adj)	I love the flavor of a **Polish** sausage with mustard and kraut.
pole (n)	The barber's **pole** is an ancient symbol.
poll (n)	The latest election **poll** bodes ill for the incumbent.
poor (adj)	The **poor** farmers do not need another summer of floods.
pore (n)	Sweat passes through the **pores** in your skin.
pour (v)	**Pour** the milk, please.
populace (n)	The **populace** rallied to overthrow the monarchy.
populous (adj)	A **populous** city has a large population.
port (n)	The ship returned to its **port** of call.
port (n)	Father has a number of fine bottles of **port** in his wine cellar.
praise (n)	The book has received nothing but high **praise**.
prays (v)	He **prays** for humankind's well being.
preys (v)	The tiger **preys** on smaller, weaker animals.

present (n)	I bought her a birthday **present**.
present (n)	Many of us think of the future, while ignoring the **present**.
present (v)	I will **present** my findings to the committee.
principal (adj)	The **principal** ideas are the main ones.
principal (n)	The **principal** of the school was my pal.
principle (n)	The Golden Rule is my guiding **principle**.
profit (n)	He failed to make any **profit** on the risky investment.
prophet (n)	The **prophet** foretold a time of peace and prosperity.
quack (n)	I heard the **quack** of a duck close by our shelter.
quack (n)	Do not put your faith in the medical miracles of that **quack**.
quail (n)	The **quail** warbled merrily in its nest.
quail (v)	The explorers **quailed** at the sound of the raging rapids.
rack (n)	I have no need for a gun **rack**.
wrack (n)	The storm brought to the town **wrack** and ruin.
rain (n)	We seldom see **rain** in Southern California.
reign (n)	The **reign** of the last czar proved to be tragic.
rein (n)	It is sometimes difficult to hold on to the **reins** of the horse.
raise (v)	Please **raise** your hand if you have a question.
raze (v)	This demolition team can **raze** a city block in one afternoon.
rays (n)	The **rays** of the sun can be harmful.
rap (n)	A loud **rap** at the door woke us.
rap (n)	The patsy took the **rap** for a crime he didn't commit.
rap (v)	You can **rap** with your friends when the lecture is over.
wrap (v)	The salesman will **wrap** the package in festive paper.
read (v)	He **read** the poem beautifully.
red (n)	**Red** is the color of passion.
read (v)	Please **read** me a story.
reed (n)	Oboes and clarinets are both fitted with **reeds**.
real (adj)	**Real** life is often stranger than fiction.
reel (n)	The fisherman used a fine **reel** to land the marlin.

rest (n)	A long **rest** after this hike will do us good.
wrest (v)	The thief could not **wrest** the briefcase from my hands.
rhyme (n)	The poem has a pleasing, melodic **rhyme**.
rime (n)	The freezing temperatures coated the windows with **rime**.
right (adj)	The contestant failed to provide the **right** answer.
right (n)	The **right** to privacy should be guaranteed to everyone.
rite (n)	They must pass an initiation **rite** when they turn thirteen.
wright (n)	A **wright** is a worker.
write (v)	Please **write** a letter to her soon.
ring (n)	The **ring** on her finger glittered with diamonds.
ring (v)	Please **ring** the bell before entering.
wring (v)	I **wring** my hands as a nervous habit.
road (n)	Few cars travel this desolate, desert **road**.
rode (v)	They **rode** in the car.
role (n)	The politician vehemently denied his **role** in the scandal.
roll (n)	I'll have a salami sandwich on an onion **roll**.
roll (v)	**Roll** out the red carpet.
root (n)	The police discovered the **root** of the problem.
route (n)	A paper **route** is a good way to make some money.
rose (n)	She received a dozen **roses** for Valentine's Day.
rose (v)	At the shrill sound of the alarm, I **rose** from my slumber.
rows (n)	There are **rows** and **rows** of seats at The Hollywood Bowl.
rows (v)	He **rows** the boat.
rote (n)	My brother learned the names of the presidents by **rote**.
wrote (v)	I **wrote** to my friend today.
sail (n)	The wind ripped the **sail** from the mast.
sale (n)	They're having a **sale** on velvet paintings.
scene (n)	The next **scene** in the movie is dreadful.
seen (v)	None of us had ever **seen** a sunset so beautiful.
sea (n)	The gentle **sea** has a salubrious effect on most viewers.
see (v)	Did you **see** that car racing down the highway?

seam (n)	The **seam** in my pants came undone.
seem (v)	It may **seem** silly at first, but his plan has merit.
serf (n)	A **serf** is little more than a slave.
surf (n)	The sand and **surf** give me a peaceful feeling.
serge (n)	**Serge** is a heavy material suitable for winter wear.
surge (v)	When the show starts, the crowd will **surge** forward.
sew (v)	I will **sew** the button onto your shirt.
so (adv)	Those basketball players are **so** tall.
shear (v)	Some farmers **shear** their sheep.
sheer (adj)	The face of the cliff was **sheer** granite.
shone (v)	The midnight moon **shone** on the lake.
shown (v)	Our daughter's teacher has **shown** us her fine grades.
slay (v)	The prince will **slay** any who dare to challenge his power.
sleigh (n)	We rode in a one-horse, open **sleigh**.
sleight (n)	The magician's **sleight** of hand is unbelievable.
slight (adj)	The rescue team has only a **slight** chance of success.
sloe (n)	The blackthorn fruit **sloe** is often used to flavor gin.
slow (adj)	The journey was a **slow** one.
soar (v)	Airplanes **soar** above the clouds.
sore (n)	The physician examined the **sore**.
soared (v)	The toy rocket **soared** into the sky.
sword (n)	Excalibur was the name of King Arthur's **sword**.
sole (n)	My favorite dish, Dover **sole**, was listed on the menu.
sole (n)	I have a corn on the **sole** of my left foot.
soul (n)	Blues music speaks to my **soul**.
some (pro)	**Some** of them are actually angry.
sum (n)	She embezzled a substantial **sum** of money.
son (n)	His **son** has made him very proud.
sun (n)	The **sun** is bright today.

sow (v)	In the spring, I will **sow** the seeds into the fertile earth.
sow (n)	A **sow** is an adult, female hog.
spade (n)	He dug in the earth with his **spade**.
spayed (v)	My dog Gertie was **spayed** after her first litter was born.
stair (n)	The third **stair** from the top always creaks.
stare (v)	Don't **stare** at others.
stake (n)	To destroy a vampire, pound a **stake** through its heart.
steak (n)	Barbecued **steak** is my favorite summer meal.
stationary (adj)	She rides a **stationary** bike at the gym after work.
stationery (n)	Our new **stationery** is printed on recycled paper.
steal (v)	Many workers **steal** office supplies.
steel (n)	**Steel** now fortifies the infrastructures of most buildings.
steel (v)	**Steel** yourself against the temptation of chocolate.
staid (adj)	His **staid** character prevents him from overreacting.
stayed (v)	They **stayed** on in London until their fortune was spent.
steer (n)	We raised a **steer** for slaughter, but it became a household pet.
steer (v)	**Steer** the car to the right.
straight (adj)	The arrow flew in a **straight** line.
strait (n)	It was a rocky journey through the **strait** to Morocco.
suite (n)	Most travelers rent a single room rather than a **suite**.
sweet (adj)	Every day can be as **sweet** as candy or as bitter as vitriol.
tail (n)	The puppy's **tail** wagged happily.
tale (n)	I love to spin a **tale** of adventure.
tare (n)	A **tare** is a seed of a herbaceous plant.
tear (n)	I have a **tear** in my shirt.
tear (n)	Her first **tear** signaled an onslaught of weeping.
tier (n)	I love sitting in the highest **tier** at the Met.
taught (v)	My teachers **taught** me well.
taut (adj)	His **taut** nerves have been stretched to their breaking point.

team (n)	The basketball **team** is out of town.
teem (v)	In summer, the air will **teem** with flying insects.
their (pro)	**Their** gifts sat under the Christmas tree.
there (adv)	**There** she goes again.
they're (contraction)	**They're** my friends.
threw (v)	She **threw** the bouquet to her bridesmaids.
through (prep)	We ran **through** the woods.
throes (n)	He was in the **throes** of a special passion.
throws (v)	Buddy **throws** a mean curve ball.
throne (n)	The queen sits on the **throne**.
thrown (v)	Someone had **thrown** a snowball at the car.
tide (n)	The motion of the **tide** is as certain as death and taxes.
tied (v)	We **tied** the burglar to a chair.
to (prep)	The hikers walked **to** the falls.
too (adv)	You study **too** much.
two (n)	One plus one is **two**.
troop (n)	He led a Boy Scout **troop**.
troupe (n)	Many adventurers would love to join a circus **troupe**.
undo (v)	Sometimes you cannot **undo** what has already been done.
undue (adj)	Your actions caused **undue** commotion.
vain (adj)	He is **vain** and egotistical.
vane (n)	The weather **vane** swung slowly in the breeze.
vein (n)	The miners stumbled upon a rich **vein** of gold.
wade (v)	Let's **wade** into the cool, shallow water.
weighed (v)	They **weighed** the apples on the grocery scale.
waist (n)	This old belt no longer fits around my **waist**.
waste (n)	His death is a terrible **waste**.
wait (v)	Please **wait** here.
weight (n)	The **weight** of a car is related to its performance.

waive (v)	Don't **waive** your voting rights.
wave (v)	She **waved** to me.
want (v)	If you **want** it, you must work for it.
wont (adj)	You are **wont** to eat too much; it is a bad habit.
ware (n)	He tried to sell us his cheap **wares**.
wear (v)	**Wear** your jacket.
where (adv)	**Where** in the world have you been?
way (n)	Do you know the **way** to Lodi?
weigh (v)	I **weigh** myself on a digital scale.
weak (adj)	She makes my knees feel **weak**.
week (n)	The **week** flew by.
weather (n)	The **weather** is cloudy and cool.
whether (conj)	**Whether** or not you may go has yet to be decided.
which (pro)	**Which** purse will go best with your outfit?
witch (n)	Glinda, the good **witch**, charms me still.
whine (v)	No one enjoys a child who **whines**.
wine (n)	A merlot is a fine **wine** for any occasion.
whose (pro)	**Whose** book is this?
who's (contraction)	**Who's** coming to your party?
wood (n)	These floors are of polished **wood**.
would (v)	We all wish that peace **would** prevail.

From My Files: It's Fun to Share

Caller: "I don't have a question. I just called to share something amusing," chuckled a junior high English teacher. "I assigned words for a spelling test in my seventh grade class, and one of the words was **fascinate**. On the test, the words had to be used in sentences, and one of my pranksters wrote, 'I had nine buttons on my jacket but could only **fasten eight**.' "

My Reply: I told the teacher to give the kid an "A" for his sense of humor but to make sure that he could spell the word correctly. Even spelling can be good for a laugh.

OTHER CONFUSING WORD PAIRS

Casual speech is one of the most fiendish culprits behind confused spellings. English is full of words that sound quite similar when spoken but whose pronunciations are technically different. These sets of words are not homophones or homographs, but they can be confusing for the same reasons.

ONE OR TWO WORDS?

Some sets consist of one single word and one pair of words. Casual conversation slurs the word pair together so that each becomes indistinct and the pair has the same sound as the single word. Though the single word and the word pair may sound the same, their spellings and usages are quite different. Careful writers should recognize the distinction.

allot (v)	The judge will **allot** us twenty minutes for our presentation.
a lot (article + n)	There is **a lot** of material to scrutinize.
all ways (adj + n)	In **all ways**, life is a splendid adventure.
always (adv)	My best friend is **always** kind to me.
anyone (pro)	Is **anyone** here dissatisfied?
any one (adj + num)	Pick **any one** number and bet on it.
anyway (adv)	**Anyway**, we wouldn't have had fun if we had gone.
any way (adj + n)	I will help in **any way** possible.
everyday (adj)	We all have certain **everyday** tasks to perform.
every day (adj + n)	We perform these tasks **every day**.
everyone (pro)	**Everyone** we loved was present.
every one (adj + pro)	**Every one** of the watches is fine.
nobody (pro)	**Nobody** knows the trouble I've seen.
no body (adj + n)	Despite the solid clues, **no body** was ever found.

CONFUSING SPELLINGS

The following pairs of words defy categorization. For your edification, I have included clarifying commentary.

boy (n)   Her young **boy** is quite precocious.

buoy (n)   Many had trouble spotting the **buoy** in the channel.

Clarifying Commentary: We all know how to pronounce **boy**. It rhymes with **joy, toy,** and **Roy**. That tricky word **buoy**, on the other hand, has two pronunciations. Some pronounce the word as if it rhymes with **suey**, as in **chop suey**: /bōō´ē/. Others say it as if it ends with a single /oi/ sound. In this second case, the words **boy** and **buoy** have identical sounds. Make sure that you know which is which.

breadth (n)   They measured the length and **breadth** of the field.

breath (n)   In polluted air, a **breath** is sometimes agony.

Clarifying Commentary: Sloppy speakers often forget the /d/ sound in **breadth**, and the result sounds just like **breath**. Try not to include yourself among their legions.

decent (adj)   Most people are good and **decent**.

descent (n)   After the climb, they began their **descent**.

Clarifying Commentary: The words look similar, but they are accented on different syllables. The adjective **decent** is accented on the first syllable. The noun **descent** is accented on the second syllable. Make sure that your pronunciation puts the emphasis in the right place.

latter (n)   The **latter** is closer than the former.

ladder (n)   The technician climbed the **ladder** onto our roof.

Clarifying Commentary: Reckless speakers often turn the voiceless /t/ sound and the voiced /d/ sound into the flap sound[†], /D/. As a result, the difference in pronunciation between /t/ and /d/ is lost, and it can be difficult to distinguish **latter** from **ladder**.

[†] The flap sound /D/ is produced when the tip of the tongue rapidly touches the alveolar ridge (the inner ridge of the gums behind the upper front teeth).

SPELLING SHORTCUTS

Q. A caller asked, "Are there any shortcuts to spelling words correctly? Are there tricks by which I can remember the words more easily?"

A. Many master spellers have made up their own mnemonics to help them learn the spellings of words. A mnemonic is a trick or shortcut, such as a formula or a rhyme, that helps to strengthen your memory. The best spellers have created mnemonics with which they memorize the most difficult words and clarify the most difficult distinctions.

For instance, one of my students has a short sentence that he uses to remember to spell **calendar** with an **e** rather than another **a** (cal**a**ndar). He says, "I never **lend** my cal**end**ar." Another student never forgets that there are two **t**'s in **attendance** because he has coined the sentence "At ten, dance." A friend of mine knows to spell the word **accommodate** with two **m**'s because he is an m&m's® junkie. He has trained himself to say, "I always accommodate myself with at least two m&m's®." Do you get it? Two **m**'s in **accommodate**. Two m&m's®. These tricks may seem silly, but they do work. Here are some other mnemonics that friends and students have used successfully:

all right	It's the opposite of all wrong, *not* **alwrong**.
candidate	A good **candid**ate is **candid**.
complement	**Comple**ments **comple**te.
embarrass	When I'm embar**r**assed, my face gets **r**ed, **r**ed.
grammar	**Ma** taught me gram**ma**r.
lose vs. loose	To **lose**, you must lose an **o** from lo**o**se.
miner vs. minor	The **mine**r is in a **mine**.
moral vs. morale	Too much **ale** pulls down mor**ale**.
peace vs. piece	There's **pie** in a **pie**ce.
precede vs. proceed	A **pro** team **pro**ceeds down the field.
principal vs. principle	My **pal** is the princi**pal**.
stationary	Remember the **a** in "stand still."
stationery	Remember the **e** in "envelope." Stationery goes in an envelope.

superintendent	The superintend**ent** collects the **rent**.
their	There's an **heir** in **their** for ownership.
there	There's a **here** in **there**.

A SPELLING QUESTION

Q. This caller said, "I read an ad that went like this: 'If you're loosing hair, call us immediately.' With **loosing** spelled this way, what does it mean?"

A. If one is "loosing hair," one is hurling it at others, much as a porcupine shoots its quills. What follicles those are! The ad should read, "If you're *losing* hair, call us immediately."

ANOTHER SPELLING QUESTION

Q. A college student called the Hot Line to ask about the spelling in a sentence from her school's newspaper. The offending sentence read, "We will spend money on censor devices." The student asked, " Is **censor** correct?"

A. The word for devices that sense is **sensor**. The sentence should have read, "We will spend money on *sensor* devices."

STILL ANOTHER SPELLING QUESTION

Q. A restaurateur called to ask, "Should I write **Lofat**, **Lo Fat**, **Lo-fat**, **Low-fat**, or **Low fat** on our dessert menu?"

A. Desserts with lower quantities of fat could be described as **low fat** or **low-fat**. The other options compromise the purity of written English. They are unacceptable.

YET ANOTHER SPELLING QUESTION

Q. "I see the word **sic** quite a bit in newspapers and magazines. Is it spelled correctly and what does it mean?" asked a caller.

A. The word **sic** is Latin and means "thus." One uses **sic** after a word or phrase that is obviously incorrect but that has been reproduced purposefully in its flawed form despite the error. The word is generally bracketed and italicized.

The drunken senator yelled, "I ain't never [*sic*] going to get reelected."

The quote in this sentence contains a double negative, "ain't never," but it has been reproduced in its original form. We place **sic** afterwards to say, "I know the error exists. I have placed it there on purpose."

MY GOODNESS! ANOTHER SPELLING QUESTION

Q. "A car advertisement in the paper offers 'easy-to-use gages.' I always thought the word was spelled **gauges**. Which is correct?" wondered a caller.

A. Either spelling is correct, although **gauge** is the original form of the word. **Gage** is a variant. Check your dictionary. It's true.

NUMBERS AND SPELLING

Q. A caller queried, "When should I spell out numbers, and when should they just be written as numbers?"

A. Always spell out numbers (including years) at the beginnings of sentences. Within a sentence, spell the numbers zero through ninety-nine, and write the numbers 100 and higher by using digits.

A SPELLING CHALLENGE

Q. A colleague issued me a challenge one afternoon. He said, "I have this sentence, and I've never met anyone who can spell every word in it. Do you think you have what it takes to beat the odds?" The sentence he then spoke went as follows: "Outside a minuscule cemetery, an embarrassed peddler and a harassed cobbler gnawed on a desiccated bone while gazing on a lady's ankle with unparalleled ecstasy."

A. Oh, I was so close. In my haste to win, I dropped an **r** from **embarrassed**. The sentence does indeed contain some tough words. Try it on your friends!

WORD HISTORY

Q. One caller asked, "If a word has two accepted spellings, one old and one new, which one should I choose?"

A. The caller was thinking of word pairs such as **draught** and **draft**, **theatre** and **theater**, or **cheque** and **check**. Since both spellings are correct, consider the preferences of the readers. This was a smart question from a sophisticated caller. Always consider the audience!

FROM MY FILES: MISSPELLED NAMES AND WORDS

These commonly misspelled names and words were faxed to the Hot Line one night by a language lover who was tired of seeing them written incorrectly:

accordion	fascist	mannequin
aficionados	fettuccine	Muhammad Ali
Allen Ginsberg	forgo	Soho
anointed	Gandhi	Philip Morris
convalescent	Guinness	pizzeria
cypress	guttural	Raquel Welch
daiquiri	Harley Davidson	S. J. Perelman
discernible	julep	Schick Shavers
Edgar Allan Poe	likable	subtly
Evel Knievel	Madam Tussaud	unmistakable

READING

The flip side of spelling is reading. While we must know which string of letters comprises a word when we hear it spoken, we must also recognize the word represented by a string of letters when we see such a string written. Over the years, educators have tried many methods to teach adults and children to read, but the only one worthy of our attention is the **phonics** method.

The word **phonics** comes from the Greek **phonetikos**, meaning "to sound with the voice." One who learns to read phonetically learns to identify the sounds represented by single letters, which are called **phonemes**, and combinations of letters and then to blend those sounds into a whole word. Phonemic awareness leads to word identification, an essential component of reading comprehension.

Many readers who were fortunate enough to learn to read in phonics programs may be thinking, "Of course this is the correct way to learn to read. What else is there?" But believe me, not every-one is as enlightened as you are. In the 1950s and 1960s, a few powerful but misguided school administrators began to emphasize the **look-say** method, which essentially asked students to memorize words and their corresponding strings of letters. The memorization approach was a total failure. The brain cannot retain and utilize that much information, and adults taught by the look-say method have found their reading and spelling skills to be lacking.

The competent reader must know the mechanics of reading, and phonics is a phenomenal tool for teaching the basics. As one's grasp of English strengthens, however, one begins to encounter words that do not always follow the rules of phonics. For those in-stances, the reader and speller must rely on a combination of decoding skills, context clues, and memory. But for the basics, phonics is still a superior method. After all, how many first-graders would say, "Oh Mommy, you're so *bourgeois*!"

The following chart, definitions, and rules appear courtesy of *The CodeBreakers*™ *Phonics Workbook Series*.

SPELLINGS AND SOUNDS

Though the English spelling system has a close association with its sound system, such a correspondence is not very accurate or exact. For many English words, there is a discrepancy between their written representations and their actual pronunciations. Thus, a variety of sounds can be represented by the same letter in differ-ent words and the same sound can also be represented by different letters. For example, the letter **c** stands for two sounds in English: a **k**-like sound, as in **scout**, and an **s**-like sound, as in **piece**. On the other hand, the sound /**j**/ is shared by two letters: the letter **g**, as in **gym**, and the letter **j**, as in **jet**. The following spelling-sound chart illustrates the pronunciation of English letters in actual words. Some of the sound symbols used in this chart may look strange, but please place your skepticism aside. These symbols are true charac-ters in the International Phonetic Alphabet (IPA).

The chart is certainly not an exhaustive list of the sounds that comprise words in the English language. Such a list is far too com-plex for a simple chart to accommodate. It is, however, a fine guide to the most basic of those sounds and an excellent place for those with a budding interest in phonetics[†] to start.

CONSONANTS

LETTER		SOUND			KEY WORD		
		Common Dictionary Symbol	IPA Symbol		Initial	Medial	Final
B	→	/b/	/b/	→	bat	labor	tab
C	→	/k/	/k/	→	cat	scat	critic
C	→	/s/	/s/	→	city	deceive	peace
D	→	/d/	/d/	→	dog	seduce	pad
F	→	/f/	/f/	→	fat	beefy	chief
G	→	/g/	/g/	→	gift	longer	bag
G	→	/j/	/dʒ/	→	gym	region	change
H	→	/h/	/h/	→	house	ahead	—
J	→	/j/	/dʒ/	→	jet	misjudge	—
K	→	/k/	/k/	→	kite	skin	milk
L	→	/l/	/l/	→	lamb	silk	feel
M	→	/m/	/m/	→	mouse	smack	broom
N	→	/n/	/n/	→	nest	snow	spoon
P	→	/p/	/p/	→	pig	ample	tip
Q	→	/kw/	/kw/	→	queen	inquisition	—
R	→	/r/	/ɹ/	→	ring	great	deer
S	→	/s/	/s/	→	sun	mason	pats
S	→	/sh/	/ʃ/	→	sugar	ensure	rush
S	→	/z/	/z/	→	—	design	his
S	→	/zh/	/ʒ/	→	—	leisure	—
T	→	/t/	/t/	→	telephone	stick	pit
V	→	/v/	/v/	→	van	saving	grave
W	→	/w/	/w/	→	watch	swim	cow
X	→	/ks/	/ks/	→	—	oxygen	box
X	→	/gz/	/gz/	→	—	example	—
X	→	/z/	/z/	→	xylophone	—	—
Y	→	/y/	/j/	→	yarn	beyond	joy
Y	→	/ī/	/aɪ/	→	—	dynamite	by
Y	→	/ē/	/i/	→	—	—	puppy
Y	→	/ĭ/	/ɪ/	→	—	lynch	—

[†] Phonetics is the study of speech sounds.

| Z | → | /z/ | /z/ | → | zebra | razor | jazz |
| Z | → | /zh/ | /ʒ/ | → | — | azure | — |

VOWELS

| LETTER | | SOUND | | | KEY WORD | | |
		Common Dictionary Symbol	IPA Symbol		Initial	Medial	Final
A	→	/ă/	/æ/	→	apple	pan	—
A	→	/ā/	/e/	→	ape	cake	bay
A	→	/ä/	/a:/, /a/	→	art	father	aha
A	→	/ə/	/ə/	→	around	lament	pizza
E	→	/ĕ/	/ɛ/	→	egg	bet	—
E	→	/ē/	/i/	→	eager	recede	be
E	→	/ə/	/ə/	→	—	item	—
I	→	/ĭ/	/ɪ/	→	injury	pit	—
I	→	/ī/	/aɪ/	→	island	like	tie
I	→	/ə/	/ə/	→	—	gullible	—
O	→	/ŏ/	/ɑ/	→	octopus	top	—
O	→	/ō/	/o/	→	over	rope	go
O	→	/ô/	/ɔ/	→	order	for	—
O	→	/ə/	/ə/	→	—	nation	—
U	→	/ŭ/	/ʌ/	→	umbrella	cut	—
U	→	/yo͞o/	/ju/	→	use	huge	—
U	→	/ə/	/ə/	→	upon	success	—

COMMON LETTER COMBINATIONS

| LETTER | | SOUND | | | KEY WORD |
		Common Dictionary Symbol	IPA Symbol		
AW	→	/ô/	/ɔ/	→	straw
AY	→	/a/	/e/	→	stay
CH	→	/ch/	/tʃ/	→	challenge
CK	→	/k/	/k/	→	thick
DGE	→	/j/	/dʒ/	→	edge
ED	→	/d/	/d/	→	tried
ED	→	/t/	/t/	→	mopped

GH	→	/f/	/f/	→	rough
IE	→	/ī/	/aɪ/	→	die
NG	→	/ng/	/ŋ/	→	wing
OE	→	/ō/	/o/	→	doe
OI	→	/oi/	/ɔɪ/	→	hoist
OO	→	/o͝o/	/u/	→	cook
OO	→	/o͞o/	/u/	→	shoot
OU	→	/ou/	/au/	→	cloud
OW	→	/ō/	/o/	→	blow
OW	→	/ou/	/au/	→	wow
OY	→	/oi/	/ɔɪ/	→	boy
PH	→	/f/	/f/	→	phone
SH	→	/sh/	/ʃ/	→	shop
TH	→	/th/	/θ/	→	think
TH	→	/th/	/ð/	→	then
WH	→	/hw/	/ʍ/	→	where

SOME USEFUL PHONIC TERMS

Here are some phonic terms you should know:

- **Long** vowel sounds, except for the /o͞o/ sound of long vowel **u**, are identical with the sounds of their own letter names, such as /ā/ in **cake**.

- **Short** vowel sounds do not have the same sounds as their own letter names, such as /ĕ/ in **wet**. A short vowel sound has a shorter duration than a long vowel sound.

- **Hard** and **soft** sounds are made by the letters **c** and **g**. A **hard c** makes the /k/ sound, as in **cat**, and a **soft c** makes the /s/ sound, as in **city**. A **hard g** makes the /g/ sound, as in **gut**, and a **soft g** makes the /j/ sound, as in **gym**.

- A **digraph** is a grouping of two letters, vowels, or consonants that makes a single sound, like **ai** in **fairy** or **ch** in **lunch**.

- A **trigraph** is a grouping of three letters, vowels, or consonants that makes a single sound, like **tch** in **scratch** or **ght** in **bright**.

BASIC RULES OF PHONICS

1. A single vowel letter between two single consonant letters almost always stands for a short vowel sound.

>   **Examples:** cot, hat, fat, mat

2. An **e** at the end of a word gives a single vowel before the final consonant the long vowel sound or gives the first vowel in a vowel combination before the final consonant the long vowel sound. The second vowel in a vowel combination is silent.

> **Examples:** race, wise, dive, grease, please

> **Exceptions:** live, give

3. When two vowel letters are together, the first says its own letter name and the second is silent.

> **Examples:** peace, fair, receipt

> **Exceptions:** meant, said

4. If a word contains only one vowel and that vowel is situated at the end of the word, it has a long vowel sound.

> **Examples:** me, he, so, be, I, we, no, she

5. If a word contains no vowels, and a **y** is present at the end of the word, the **y** usually has the long /i/ sound.

> **Examples:** by, my, sly, fly

Also, if you see an **e** preceded by a **y** at the end of a word, the **y** makes the long /i/ sound and the **e** is silent.

> **Examples:** bye, dye

6. If a word ends in a **y** that is preceded by a consonant, but a vowel has appeared previously in the word, the **y** usually has a long /e/ sound. If the previous vowel appears two letters to the left of **y**, that vowel makes the long sound.

> **Examples:** navy, shady, ivy

If the previous vowel appears more than two letters to the left of **y**, it makes the short vowel sound.

> **Examples:** daddy, ugly, candy

If the final **y** is preceded by two or more vowels, use Rules 1 and 2 to determine what sounds those vowels make. The final **y** will still have the long /e/ sound.

> **Examples:** likely, fairy

7.   We hear the name of the letter **r** in a number of vowel-consonant combinations.

> • The **ar** combination sounds like the name of the letter **r**.

Examples: car, bar, star

Exception: war

Please note that a /k/ sound following the **ar** combination is spelled with a single **k**.

Examples: spark, mark, dark

- The **or** combination has the same sound as the sound you hear in the word **horn**.

Examples: torn, corn, worn

- The **er**, **ir**, and **ur** combinations have the same sound you hear in the word **girl**.

Examples: fern, fir, burn

8. The **ew** digraph makes the long /u/ sound. We usually see this letter combination at the end of a word.

Examples: dew, stew, flew, newt

9. The **ow** digraph can make two sounds.

- It can make the sound you hear in the word **cow**, the sound you make when you hurt yourself.

Examples: brown, town

- It can also make the long /o/ sound you hear in **blow**.

Examples: crow, mow

10. How do you know if **c** or **g** makes a hard or soft sound?

- When the letter **c** or **g** is followed by **a**, **o**, or **u**, that **c** or **g** makes a hard sound.

Examples: camp, gape, coffee, go, cup, gully

- When the letter **c** or **g** is followed by **e**, **i**, or **y**, that **c** or **g** has a soft sound.

Examples: ice, image, city, magic, fancy, gym

11. In most cases, the **gh** letter combination is silent.

Examples: through, thought, though

But often, when **gh** at the end of a word is preceded by the letter **u**, the **ugh** combination makes a /f/ sound.

Examples: cough, enough, rough, tough, trough

12. The **t** before **ch** in the **tch** trigraph is silent, since all three letters of a trigraph make a single **/ch/** sound.

Examples: catch, latch, watch

13. When the letter **a** is followed by the letter **u** or **w**, together they make the sound we hear in the words **caught** and **crawl**. It is that **aw** sound you make when you see a cute baby . . . or even an ugly baby if the parents are nearby.

14. In one-syllable words that end with two consecutive vowels, the first of the two vowels is long and the second is silent.

Examples: lie, sea

15. The letter x can make several sounds, depending on its position in a word.

- At the beginning of a word, x can make a **/z/** sound or an **/ĕks/** sound.

  Examples: xylophone, x-ray

- Within a word, the letter x makes a **/ks/** sound or a **/gz/** sound.

  Examples: fixes, excommunicate, examine, exile, example

- An x at the end of a word makes the **/ks/** sound.

  Examples: fix, mix, tax, wax

16. The **ph** digraph makes the **/f/** sound.

Examples: dolphin, graph, telephone

17. A single **s** or **z** before **ure** in a word is pronounced **/zh/**, the same sound that begins the first two syllables of the name Zsa Zsa Gabor.

Examples: azure, leisure, measure

18. If a word contains consecutive double consonants, the vowel before the double consonants is usually short.

Examples: doll, fuzz, mull

19. A single consonant before a suffix beginning with a vowel usually indicates that the vowel preceding that single consonant makes a long sound. The final **e** that would let us know that the vowel is long has been dropped to make room for the suffix. Despite the absence of the **e**, we still pronounce the vowel with a long vowel sound.

- care + -ing → caring → long **a**

- flute + -d → fluted → long **u**

20. Some consonants become silent in certain consonant combinations.

- The letter **p** is silent when directly followed by an **s** at the beginning of a word.

  Examples: psalm, pseudonym

- The letter **w** is silent when directly followed by an **r**.

  Examples: write, writhe, wrong

- The letter **h** is silent when directly preceded by an **r**.

  Examples: rhino, rhyme, rhapsody

- The letter **b** is silent when preceded by an **m**.

  Examples: climb, dumb, plumb

- The letter **c** is sometimes silent when preceded by an **s**.

  Examples: scene, science, scent

21. When a double **c** appears in a word, the first **c** usually makes the /k/ sound and the second **c** makes the /s/ sound.

  Examples: accident, accent

  Exception: occur

22. The letter **i** usually has a long sound when it is followed by **nd** or **mb**.

  Examples: climb, find, rind

  Exceptions: limb, wind

23. The consonant digraph **ch** can make two different sounds.

- It most often makes the sound we hear in the word **chair**.

  Examples: cheese, choose, lunch

- It can also make the /k/ sound. In fact, any time **ch** is followed by **r**, it will make the /k/ sound.

  Examples: machinations, chrome, chronometer, chronic

24. There is no word too difficult to pronounce. With a little practice and the right know-how, you can wrap your tongue around the worst the English language has to offer. Try this one for starters: **opthalmodynamometer**.

25. If you aren't sure of the pronunciation, look it up. The dictionary is just as valuable to readers as it is to spellers.

PHONICS PHUN

Q. The same colleague who challenged me with that ridiculous sentence a number of pages back asked, "Under the phonics rules of pronunciation, what does **ghoti** spell?"

A. He was obviously using that old teachers' trick to twist the rules of phonics and turn this nonsensical string into a real word. The **gh** should be pronounced with a /f/ sound, as in **rough**. The **o** should be pronounced with a short /i/ sound, as in **women**. The **ti** should be pronounced with a /sh/ sound, as in **notion**. Put those sounds together, and we get the word **fish**.

FROM MY FILES: A DRIVING LESSON

Much of my spare time is spent in my office at the college, grading papers. Sometimes they pile up, and many an early evening has turned into a late night before I know it. One night, after four tedious hours of reading essays, I once again found myself speeding down that familiar stretch of freeway between school and home. About a mile from my exit, I became aware of red and blue lights flashing in my rearview mirror. I pulled my car into the right-hand lane and hoped that the cruiser would pass. It didn't. He was stuck to my bumper.

A siren wailed in the darkness; a bullhorn voice commanded, "Pull your vehicle to the side of the road and remain in your car." I did as I was told.

In my side view mirror, a shadow emerged from the police cruiser. I listened to the sound of his approach; my stomach churned. I practiced what I would say. "What seems to be the trouble, Officer? No. I wasn't aware of how fast I was going."

I turned toward the torso that had filled my half-open window. It leaned down and a familiar head barked, "Hey, Professor Strumpf, when's that paper due?" A student in police officer's clothing. He just wanted to say "Hi." I swallowed my bile as he cracked up.

He still waves when we pass on the freeway. And I always wave back. Out of respect? Out of fear? Or maybe now it's just out of habit.

And, by the way, he did get an "A" in the class. Yes, I desperately wanted to give him that other grade (the big "F"), but to be perfectly honest, I don't always observe the speed limit.

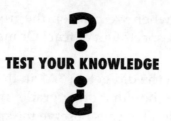

TEST YOUR KNOWLEDGE

QUESTIONS

1. Why is English spelling so tricky?

2. How do you pluralize a noun that ends in a sibilant sound?

3. How do you spell the /j/ sound at the end of a word?

4. If I am opposed to society's conventions, should I describe myself as being *ante-establishment* or *anti-establishment*?

5. What do we call words with the same spelling but different pronunciations and meanings?

6. Give an example of words that are heteronyms.

7. What is a mnemonic?

8. Why is the phonics method superior to the look say method for learning to read?

9. When is the letter **p** silent?

10. If you can't figure out the pronunciation or spelling of a word, what should you do?

(SEE ANSWERS ON FOLLOWING PAGE)

Answers

1. English spelling is tricky because the language developed in such a haphazard manner from so many different sources.

2. Such nouns are pluralized with an **-es** ending.

3. The /**j**/ sound at the end of a word is spelled with the letters **dge**, as in **ledge**.

4. I am *anti-establishment*.

5. We call these words **heteronyms**.

6. The words **present** (accented on the first syllable), meaning "a gift," and **present** (accented on the second syllable), meaning "to give," are heteronyms. There are many other acceptable answers to this question.

7. A mnemonic is a memorization device that has helped many people learn the spellings of difficult words.

8. The look-say method is too unwieldy. No one can memorize and utilize the huge number of words that a healthy vocabulary requires. The phonics method teaches the necessary skills to read almost any word. We then use memorization to fill in the gaps.

9. The letter **p** is silent when it is followed by the letter **s** at the beginning of a word, as in **psalm**.

10. Grab your dictionary. Look it up!

15.

Vocabulary

> **Vocabulary** is the complete collection of the words in a language.

The true mark of an educated person is a well-developed vocabulary. An extensive understanding of language indicates a thirst for knowledge, and the closer to unquenchable this thirst becomes, the more interesting and intelligent a person will be. This is not to say that one must be snobbish to be smart but that a smart person is one who listens, reads, comprehends, and remembers. Such individuals cannot help but cultivate a robust vocabulary.

The dictionary is the word-enthusiast's best friend. After all, anyone who seeks to enhance his or her vocabulary needs a tool with which he or she can discover the meanings of new words. The dictionary is the best and only tool for the job. One could use one of those little pocket dictionaries, a helpful companion for the word sleuth on-the-go but insufficient for more than a cursory glance at the lexicon.

One could also purchase a dictionary of the portable, hardbound variety. These are too large to fit in your pocket, but, at three or four pounds in weight, they are small enough to sit on a desk or a bookshelf for casual perusal. These larger guides to the lexicon are complete enough to satisfy an average curiosity but still unsatisfactory for the most serious students of language. Such dictionaries only cover ten to fifteen percent of the total selection of words in English.

The word lover's best option is the unabridged dictionary. These will cover most, if not all, of the one million two hundred thousand English words. The primary drawback to these language titans is that lifting one can result in a hernia. The reward for the pain of manipulating an unabridged dictionary is possession of a comprehensive listing of words and an ever-reliable source of new vocabulary.

Of course, a dictionary is much more than just a list of words and basic definitions. Any good dictionary will provide information on pronunciation, origin, and subtleties of meaning. An entry for a word will probably list several definitions. The first is not necessarily the best one. It is merely the one which the authors of the dictionary decided to place in the first position. Similarly, the dictionary may list several pronunciations for a single word. The first isn't the best. It merely indicates the most common way that people pronounce the word.

Another piece of information that a dictionary will provide is the origin or etymology of a word. English is composed of words from many different languages, so it can be interesting to find out where a particular word came from. A good dictionary will indicate the language of origin of a word. Looking in my dictionary at home, I discovered that the English word **church** comes from a Dutch word, **kerk**. I love random tidbits of information!

Dictionaries may also provide information about the usage of a word, whether it is slang, colloquial, or nonstandard English. Dictionaries should provide information about parts of speech and other grammatical issues, too. They will indicate what part of speech a word is, when it is used in a particular way, or whether a verb is transitive or intransitive. Most of this information comes in the form of abbreviations, and the dictionary should include an abbreviation key. This is a chapter about vocabulary, however, and we need to re-route the discussion back to the meanings of words.

DEFINITION DISTINCTIONS

Since its inception, The National Grammar Hot Line has received thousands of calls concerning misused, mispronounced, or misunderstood words. The words about which people call most often have changed over the years. The following is a list of the most common and most interesting word distinctions that callers have asked the Hot Line to make:

KEY: adj = adjective   v = verb   adv = adverb   n = noun
con = conjunction   pro = pronoun   prep = preposition

accept (v), **except** (prep): The verb **accept** means "to receive with approval" or "to agree with."

> The school board **accepts** the generous donation.

> I **accept** your terms.

The word **except** is most often used as a preposition, meaning "excluding" or "but."

> My friend Bud does nothing **except** play the guitar.

At times, we see **except** used as a verb. There, it means "to exclude."

> The defense **excepted** crucial evidence from its arguments.

administer (v), **administrate** (v): In most cases these words both mean "to manage."

> The teacher **administered** the test.

> The new officials **administrated** the season poorly.

However, **administer** has an additional meaning, "to give aid," that **administrate** does not.

> The relief workers **administer** food and medicine to the poor.

admit (v), **allow** (v): These words are close in meaning. **Admit** can mean "to permit entrance," "to grant a privilege," or "to confess or acknowledge."

> The tickets **admitted** us to the fair.

> The lawyer was **admitted** to the bar.

> He **admits** that he committed the crime.

The verb **allow** also involves permission but in a more general sense.

> We were **allowed** to enter the castle.

> The judge **allowed** the attorney's remarks.

One can *allow* someone to exit while one can only *admit* someone in entrance.

adverse (adj), **averse** (adj): Both words have negative connotations. **Adverse** is an adjective, meaning "antagonistic, opposing, or negative."

> The experimental treatments had **adverse** effects on the patients.

> Benny does not hold up well under **adverse** circumstances.

The adjective **averse** means "strongly opposed or repulsed." One usually describes a person as being *averse*.

> He is **averse** to eating meat.

> The council is **averse** to any change in the budget.

advice (n), **advise** (v): The verb **advise** means "to offer opinion or counsel."

> The old sage **advises** the community.

The noun **advice** names the wisdom received when another offers this counsel.

> The community ignored the **advice** of the elders.

One *advises* others and receives *advice*.

affect (n, v), **effect** (n, v): **Affect** (accented on the second syllable) is usually a verb. It means "to influence."

> The cast on my arm **affects** my ability to drive.

Psychologists do use **affect** (accented on the first syllable) as a noun, meaning "one's feelings or emotions."

> The patient exhibits a flat **affect**.

Effect is usually a noun. It means "a result or consequence."

> The **effects** of the plague were devastating.

In some cases, **effect** can also be a verb, meaning "to bring about or accomplish."

Jerry Garcia **effected** a change in the world of rock and roll.

The confusion between **affect** and **effect** is not only quite common but has a long history. **Effect** was used in place of **affect** as early as 1494. If you are unsure of which word to use, check the dictionary.

all right (adv + adj), **alright** (adv): Both constructions mean the same thing: "everything is correct."

We kids were **all right**.

However, **alright** is an example of poor English. The expression should always be written as two separate words.

The confusion exists because of the word **already**. If we can change **all ready** into a single word, why can we not do this to **all right**? Some dictionaries even state that there is no difference between the two. These authors and many other experts agree that there is only one spelling: **all right**. This is not a point worth resisting. Those dictionaries are wrong. It is simply a fact of life.

alumnus (n), **alumna** (n): Most of the callers for this distinction wonder if the noun **alumni** covers both men and women. In fact, **alumni** is the plural form of the word **alumnus**. An *alumnus* is a male graduate. The word for "female graduate" is **alumna**. Its plural form is **alumnae**. In modern usage, the word **alumni** often refers to both male and female graduates even though its origins are masculine.

among (prep), **between** (prep): The words **between** and **among** are both prepositions. **Between** refers to just two individuals.

This information must stay **between** the two of us.

The sailors were caught **between** a rock and a hard place.

Among refers to more than two individuals.

The feeling **among** the crew members was that mutiny was in the wind.

Dr. Hastings lived **among** the people of the Sahara for several years.

anxious (adj), **eager** (adj): One who is *anxious* may be worried or strained about some issue or event.

The struggling medical student was **anxious** for his board exams to be over.

My younger brother is **anxious** about starting kindergarten.

One who is *eager* is excited or gleeful in anticipation.

My sister is **eager** for Christmas Day to arrive.

We are all **eager** to see our cousins again.

Anxious can also be a synonym for **eager**.

My sister is **anxious** for Christmas Day to arrive.

We are all **anxious** to see our cousins again.

apprise (v), **appraise** (v): When you give notice or inform, you *apprise*.

Please **apprise** me of any change in her condition.

When you judge, estimate, or rate, you *appraise*.

The mechanic **appraised** the vintage sports car.

The words sound alike, but their meanings are different.

attorney (n), **lawyer** (n): Believe it or not, these nouns are not synonyms. A *lawyer*, as we all know, is a person who conducts lawsuits for clients or who advises on legal matters.

Schultz's **lawyer** successfully argued his innocence.

An *attorney*, as distinguished from an attorney at law, is a person who has been legally appointed to carry out business for another person. An attorney may be a lawyer, but he or she may also fill any one of a number of business-related roles.

My **attorney** will be the executor of my estate.

bathos (n), **pathos** (n): The word **pathos** names some element of art or experience that arouses sympathy or compassion.

The plight of the orphaned kittens aroused feelings of **pathos**.

The word **bathos**, on the other hand, means "insincere or phony pathos." It names an element of art or experience that indicates gross insincerity or maudlinism.

The hero's empty rhetoric was a perfect example of **bathos**.

biannual (adj), **biennial** (n, adj): An event that occurs twice a year is *biannual*.

> The town council holds **biannual** referendums in April and August.

An event that occurs every two years is *biennial*.

> Our **biennial** celebration of the sun will not come around for another two years.

Horticulturists also use the noun **biennial** to name plants that take two years to reach maturity.

> I planted a few **biennials** in the garden.

bring (v), **take** (v): Many people use the word **bring** when they really need **take**. The verb **bring** means "to deliver toward the speaker."

> **Bring** the newspaper to me.

> I asked Mother to **bring** us breakfast.

The verb **take** means "to deliver away from the speaker.

> Please **take** this message to my family.

> The ferryman would not **take** us across the river.

burglary (n), **robbery** (n): Burglaries and robberies are different sorts of crimes. One who commits a *burglary* breaks into a house and removes items of value.

> We lost our television and some jewelry in the **burglary**.

One who commits a *robbery* takes property directly from another person.

> The person who committed the **robbery** took my wallet and my wits.

capital (adj, n), **capitol** (n): These two words sound alike but have very different meanings. The noun **capitol** names the building or buildings where the state or federal government meets.

> My class visited the nation's **capitol** last November.

The adjective **capital** indicates that something is of the utmost seriousness. When it describes punishment, this adjective indicates punishment by death.

Murder is a **capital** offense.

Many Americans oppose **capital** punishment.

Capital can also be a noun. In this role, it names stock, resources, or worth.

The small company did not possess enough **capital** to stay in business.

A sense of humor can be valuable **capital**.

climactic (adj), **climatic** (adj): We derive the adjective **climactic** from the noun **climax**. This adjective describes the point of highest tension in a drama or an event.

We missed the **climactic** ending of the disaster movie.

We derive the adjective **climatic** from the noun **climate**. This adjective describes a weather-related condition or event.

The **climatic** conditions are very poor for sailing at this time of the year.

These two words sound similar, but their meanings are different.

colloquy (n), **soliloquy** (n): Both nouns involve different types of speeches. A *colloquy* is a formal conversation or discussion.

The dean engaged us in an interesting **colloquy**.

A *soliloquy* is a monologue. These are especially common in dramas where a character reveals his or her thoughts in a speech to himself or herself.

Romeo's **soliloquy** moves me to tears.

complement (n, v), **compliment** (n, v): The verb **complement** means "to complete or make perfect."

Your eyes **complement** your dress quite nicely.

We can also use **complement** as a noun with a related meaning.

The full moon is a perfect **complement** to this beautiful evening.

The noun **compliment** names an expression of praise or admiration.

My friend Bill does not take **compliments** well.

We can also use **compliment** as a verb with a related meaning.

I must **compliment** you on your fine choice of attire.

compose (v), **comprise** (v): The verb **comprise** is a verb of condition. It means "to consist of or include."

The whole of my savings **comprise** these four dollars.

The bomb **comprises** four hidden pieces.

The verb **compose** is often a verb of action. It means "to create from parts."

The maestro **composed** a great symphony.

The disgruntled tenants **composed** a lengthy letter of complaint to the landlord.

We can also use the verb **compose** as a verb of condition, meaning "to make up the whole."

The fossilized remains **compose** this layer of rock.

The ingredients that **compose** this cake are very unhealthy.

The condition of **comprise** travels from the whole to the parts, whereas the condition of **compose** travels from the parts to the whole.

connote (v), **denote** (v): Both verbs are words of identification, but theirs are different types of identification. To *connote* something is to suggest it. The verb creates a figurative identification.

Memories of his illness **connote** sadness and loss.

My stuffed bear **connotes** security and well-being.

To *denote* something is to mark or indicate it. This verb creates a literal identification.

The distant thunder **denotes** a heavy storm on its way.

His actions **denote** bravery and loyalty.

continual (adj), **continuous** (adj): These words are close in meaning but not quite synonyms. The adjective **continual** describes a constant but occasionally interrupted series of events, while the adjective **continuous** describes a constant and uninterrupted series of events.

> The **continual** flow of traffic was broken every few minutes by the family of geese who waddled back and forth across the busy road.

> The **continuous** racket from downstairs is threatening my sanity.

deprecate (v), **depreciate** (v): Both verbs involve some kind of loss. To *deprecate* is to express disapproval or to belittle. It involves a loss of respect.

> The teacher **deprecated** her students for their atrocious behavior.

To *depreciate* is to lower in value.

> After the scandal broke, the value of the once-stable stock **depreciated** rapidly.

disinterested (adj), **uninterested** (adj): Now here is a subtle distinction. The prefix **dis-** means "apart from." One who is *disinterested* is indifferent, impartial, or unconcerned. The word denotes a lack of feeling for an issue.

> The **disinterested** children ignored their teacher's stern reprimands.

The prefix **un-** means "not." One who is *uninterested* lacks interest in a particular matter. It is not that the individual is unconcerned. In fact, he or she wishes to actively avoid the matter.

> We were **uninterested** in the ambassador's dull speech.

discreet (adj), **discrete** (adj): These words are pronounced the same but have entirely different meanings and spellings. The adjective **discreet** means "tactful, prudent, careful, or cautious."

> The surveillance car maintained a **discreet** distance.

> The clumsy spy's questions were anything but **discreet**.

The adjective **discrete** means "separate."

> Light travels in **discrete** packets.

> The four warring powers divided the country into four **discrete** territories.

empathy (n), **sympathy** (n): Both words involve a sharing of emotion. *Empathy* is an understanding of another's emotions or thoughts so complete that one actually feels physical manifestations of those emotions and thoughts.

> The **empathy** I felt toward my ailing twin made my insides ache.

Sympathy is a weaker degree of empathy. It is the ability to share and understand the feelings and thoughts of another, but that understanding does not involve the same physical symptoms that the understanding in empathy does.

> All I saw in the eyes of the people at the funeral were **sympathy** and tears.

entrée (n), **entry** (n): The noun **entrée** has two meanings. It can name the freedom to enter or the main course at a meal.

> The immigration services granted us **entrée** into the country.

> We enjoyed the **entrée** at Bonaparte's.

The noun **entry** merely names the act of entering or the right to enter.

> The police allowed us **entry** into the crumbling apartment building.

> The explorers' **entry** into the fifth dimension was marked by a moment of panic.

envelop (v), **envelope** (n): We mail letters in an *envelope* and *envelop* our packages in brightly colored paper. The noun **envelope** names a wrapper or package. The most common sort is the flat paper kind that we send through the mail, but we can also say that a layer of air forms an envelope around the earth.

> The **envelope** had been torn by the time that it arrived in the mail.

The verb **envelop** means "to enfold, enclose, or cover." It is the action that an envelope performs.

> The thick fog **enveloped** the road.

epitaph (n), **epithet** (n), **epaulette** (n): An *epitaph* is a memorializing phrase written on a gravestone.

> I want my **epitaph** to read, "He was a man of many hats."

An *epithet* is an insulting or disparaging word or phrase.

> The crowd hurled **epithets** at the shocked politician.

An *epaulette* is a decorative patch worn on either shoulder of a uniform.

> The **epaulettes** on the dusty old uniform were falling off.

especial (adj), **special** (adj): These two words differ in the degree of the quality that they express. Something that is *special* is distinctive or unique.

> This picture is **special** to me.

Something that is *especial* is also distinctive or unique but outstandingly so.

> The moment my daughter was born was an **especial** day in my life.

extant (adj), **extent** (n): The adjective **extant** describes something that is still in existence.

> There are only two **extant** practitioners of the ancient art of alchemy.

The noun **extent** names a range or scope.

> It is difficult to judge the extent of the hurricane's damage.

The words sound alike but have very different meanings.

fated (adj), **feted** (v), **fetid** (adj): The adjective **fated** describes something that is predetermined or destined to be.

> My brother feels that he is **fated** to become a millionaire.

The verb **feted** means "to be honored with a large party."

> The Academy **feted** the winners with an extravagant banquet.

The adjective **fetid** describes something that smells bad.

> That cheese has a **fetid** smell.

figurative (adj), **literal** (adj): Things that are *figurative* possess metaphorical similarity but not factual similarity.

> My remarks about his shark fins and sharp teeth were **figurative**.

Things that are *literal* are true in fact.

The **literal** meaning of that saying is silly, but the **figurative** one makes sense.

The words are opposites.

flammable (adj), **inflammable** (adj): Both words mean "easily ignited." **Inflammable** seems as if it should mean "not easily ignited," but its origins are in the verb **inflame**, meaning "to set on fire."

The costume should not be made of **flammable** material.

The fire spread quickly because of the **inflammable** material.

Inflammable can also mean "easily angered or provoked."

His quick temper made him an **inflammable** opponent.

Think of the adjective **inflammable** as "able to be inflamed."

founder (n, v), **flounder** (n, v): As a noun, a *founder* is one who founds.

The **founders** of our country were brave men.

As a verb, to *founder* is to collapse or become disabled.

The ship **foundered** on the reef.

As a noun, a *flounder* is a flat, bottom-dwelling, and quite tasty fish.

We will have the **flounder** with mango salsa, please.

As a verb, to *flounder* is to act or proceed clumsily.

The nervous dancers **floundered** on the stage.

gastronome (n), **gourmet** (n), **gourmand** (n): *Gastronomes, gourmets,* and *gourmands* are all lovers and connoisseurs of fine food and drink, but gourmands express this interest in a gluttonous manner. If you invite any one of these three to dinner, be sure the food is well presented and well prepared, and, in the case of the gourmand, be sure there is plenty of it.

guaranty (n, v), **guarantee** (n, v): These words are synonyms. As verbs, they both mean "to assure another of the quality of goods or the completion of services." As nouns, both name an assurance of this quality or completion. **Guaranty**, however, is most commonly used as a noun.

> I **guarantee** that you will be satisfied with your lama-hair jacket.

> The **guaranty** states that we can return the vacuum for a full refund.

hardy (adj), **hearty** (adj): Someone who is stalwart, rugged, strong, courageous, stouthearted, intrepid, capable of surviving unfavorable conditions, brazenly daring, and audacious is *hardy*. The word refers to people or animals.

> They had to be a **hardy** people to survive these brutal winters.

> Only the **hardiest** of the explorers survived the ordeal.

However, more things than just people and animals can be *hearty*. Someone or something that is hearty is supportive, enthusiastic, and joyful.

> He gave me a **hearty** handshake.

> The **hearty** troop members picked up their instruments and played a polka.

We also use the adjective **hearty** to describe things that are nourishing or invigorating.

> After the long walk home, the weary wanderers downed a **hearty** meal.

> A **hearty** kiss in the morning starts my day off right.

hanged (v), **hung** (v): Both **hanged** and **hung** are past indicative forms and past participle forms of **hang**, but the types of hanging that they imply are different. Use **hanged** when the verb carries the sense of capital punishment.

> The sheriff **hanged** the cattle rustlers for their crimes.

Use **hung** when the verb carries the sense of everyday suspension of objects.

> The kids **hung** their coats in the closet.

hurdle (n, v), **hurtle** (v): To *hurdle* is to leap over an obstacle.

> The horse **hurdled** the barrier with ease.

A *hurdle* can also be a barrier over which one leaps.

The runner leaped over the highest set of **hurdles**.

To *hurtle* is to move with great speed.

The car **hurtled** down the Autobahn.

illicit (adj), **elicit** (v), **licit** (adj): The adjective **illicit** describes something that is illegal.

The men were caught bringing **illicit** drugs into the country.

The verb **elicit** means "to bring out" or "to draw forth."

My vicious attack failed to **elicit** a response from my stoic opponent.

The adjective **licit** means "legal."

Our business here is **licit**.

insure (v), **ensure** (v), **assure** (v): All three words mean "to make certain, sure, or secure." They are interchangeable in some contexts but can have subtle differences in meaning. The act of *insuring* involves taking steps to create security before an event happens.

Your careful planning **insures** our safety.

The act of *assuring* involves removing doubt or worry from another person's mind or one's own mind.

I **assure** you that we are perfectly safe.

The act of *ensuring* can take either meaning but is closer to **insuring**.

My promise should **ensure** your complete satisfaction.

irregardless (adv), **disregardless** (adv), **regardless** (adv): The first two adverbs, **irregardless** and **disregardless**, are not real words. If you are using them, drop them from your vocabulary *at once*! When you want to say "in spite of," the only word to use is **regardless**.

I am going to the dance **regardless** of what you say.

later (adj, adv), **latter** (n, adj): The word **later** refers to some point in time that comes after another reference point. We can use it as an adjective or an adverb.

We will attend the **later** show of the two.

The concert began **later** than we expected it to.

The word **latter** refers to the second of two items. We can use it as a noun or an adjective.

> He offered me money or happiness, and I chose the **latter**.

> The **latter** option was the only sensible one to pick.

lectern (n), **podium** (n): The *lectern* is the stand that holds the speaker's books and notes. The *podium* is the elevated platform on which the speaker stands, but it is the lectern that he or she approaches. Delivering a speech, one does not walk up to a podium unless one is only a foot high.

lend (v), **loan** (n, v): Both words involve the giving and taking of money. **Lend** is a verb. It means "to give money with the expectation that the money will one day be returned."

> I agreed to **lend** my buddy two thousand dollars.

The word **loan** is usually a noun. It names the sum of money that is lent.

> The bank would not give me a **loan**.

However, **loan** has acquired verb characteristics through common usage. English allows us to use it as we would the true verb **lend**.

> Will you **loan** me a few dollars for lunch?

libel (n, v), **slander** (n, v): *Libel* is a defamation of character in writing.

> The author's remarks in the unauthorized autobiography constitute **libel**.

> I cannot believe that a close friend would **libel** me as he did in his book.

Slander is a spoken defamatory statement.

> Her statement to the media is nothing short of **slander**.

> Be careful that you do not **slander** your opponent in a fit of rage.

lightening (n, adj), **lightning** (n): The word **lightening** indicates a decrease in weight. The weight can be physical, emotional, or psychological.

The **lightening** of my pack as the trip progressed made hiking so much easier.

Anticipating her full exoneration is **lightening** my mental load.

The word **lightning** names the magnificent electrical discharges that occur in the clouds during thunderstorms.

The fierce bolt of **lightning** snapped the great oak in two.

memoriam (n), **memorial** (n, adj): Many callers have been torn between holding a *memorial* or a *memoriam*. Unless you speak Latin, the correct choice is **memorial**. This word can be a noun, naming some event or item that preserves a memory, or an adjective, describing some event or item that preserves a memory.

The **memorial** stands at the crest of a high hill.

The **memorial** service will begin at noon.

Memoriam is a Latin word that most English speakers have seen at the heads of plaques and monuments bearing the text "in memoriam." We take it to mean "in memory of," but the strict Latin means "into memory."

misogynist (n), **misanthrope** (n), **misogamist** (n): The prefix **miso-** comes from the Greek word **misos**, meaning "hatred." A *misogynist* is a person who hates women.

My boss, a piggish **misogynist**, refused to give any of the women raises.

A *misanthrope* is a person who hates and distrusts mankind.

The terrorist, a pathetic **misanthrope**, turned his rage against innocent people.

A *misogamist* is a person who hates marriage.

My brother, once an ardent **misogamist**, is tying the knot next month.

The spelling of the prefix changes when it is placed before a base word that begins with a vowel, as it did in **misanthrope**. For the sake of easy pronunciation, we dropped the **o**.

moot (adj), **mute** (adj): The adjective **moot** describes something that is debatable, doubtful, or of no importance.

> The question is **moot**.

The adjective **mute** describes someone or something that cannot produce sound. We often use it to describe people who cannot speak.

> Since the accident, her husband has been **mute**.

moral (n, adj), **morale** (n): The word **moral**, as a noun or an adjective, concerns humankind's distinction between right and wrong. When we say that something is *moral*, we mean that it falls on the side of good.

> His **morals** are suspect.

> That was not a terribly **moral** decision.

The noun **morale** names a person's or group's spirit or enthusiasm.

> Following the crushing defeat at Bangor, my platoon's **morale** plummeted.

motive (n), **motif** (n): The noun **motive** names the force that drives one to act toward a certain end.

> We will never know what his **motives** for robbing the bank were.

The noun **motif** names a recurring theme. The word is common in descriptions of art and literature.

> The critic sensed a cyclical **motif** in the painter's work.

naked (adj), **nude** (adj, n): As adjectives, both words mean "without clothes," but nakedness is somehow barer or starker than nudeness is. Someone who is *nude* is unclothed in an almost artistic sense. Artists paint *nudes*, not *nakeds*.

> The **naked** figures shivered in the morning sun.

> The **nude** model strolled onto the stage.

> My artist friend paints only **nudes**.

We can also use **naked** to mean "exposed or unprotected."

> The soldiers felt **naked**, marching across the barren plain.

> Losing one's house in a fire leaves one feeling **naked**.

nauseous (adj), **nauseated** (adj): Very few people use these words correctly. When you're feeling queasy, you're feeling *nauseated*, not *nauseous*. Something that is *nauseous* causes you to feel *nauseated*. The adjective **nauseated** means "feeling sick." The adjective **nauseous** means "causing sickness."

The details of the accident left me feeling **nauseated**.

The **nauseous** smell drove even the rats from the building.

nuance (n), **subtlety** (n): A *nuance* is a kind of *subtlety*. The noun **subtlety** names a fine or delicate quality.

Any great work of literature contains **subtleties** in meaning.

The noun **nuance** names a slight variation in meaning, quality, or expression.

Mastering the **nuances** of international politics takes a lifetime.

ordinance (n), **ordnance** (n): An *ordinance* is a rule or regulation.

The Mayor wants to pass a new **ordinance** regarding garbage collection.

The noun **ordnance** names military weapons or the branch of the military that manages the weapons.

The squadron leader demanded that her **ordnance** be replenished before the next strike.

parameter (n), **perimeter** (n): These two words are constantly confused and misused. A *parameter* is a limit or boundary. We often hear mathematicians use the word **parameter** to mean "a constant or variable in an equation."

The young scientist struggled to define the **parameters** of his startling equation.

The team leader clarified the **parameters** of the mission.

A *perimeter* is the boundary of a closed figure or body.

The guards watched the **perimeter** of the military compound.

The **perimeter** of a square equals the length of any side times four.

pendant (n), **pedant** (n), **pendent** (adj): A *pendant* is a hanging object such as an ornament or an electrical fixture.

> My mother wears an ornate **pendant** on a chain around her neck.

A *pedant* is one who pays undue attention to book learning and formal rules without understanding them.

> I grant no weight to the rantings of a **pedant** like Frances.

The adjective **pendent** describes something that is overhanging, suspended, or undetermined.

> The tree leaned **pendent** over the edge of the cliff.

> The resolution to this investigation remains **pendent**.

penultimate (adj), **ultimate** (adj, n): The adjective **penultimate** describes the next to the last item in a series.

> This is the **penultimate** step in our journey.

The word **ultimate**, as a noun or an adjective, refers to the last item in a series or to something that is the most extreme of its type.

> We have reached the **ultimate** stage of our development.

> Skydiving is the **ultimate** thrill.

persecute (v), **prosecute** (v): To *persecute* is to harass or oppress.

> The villagers **persecuted** the mysterious scientists.

To *prosecute* is to bring legal action against someone.

> The district attorney decided to **prosecute** the accused arsonists.

practical (adj), **practicable** (adj): Something that is *practical* is realistic, sensible, or efficient.

> The station wagon was a **practical** purchase.

Something that is *practicable* is something that can be accomplished.

> His plan to climb the Matterhorn was not **practicable**.

principal (n, adj), **principle** (n): The word **principal** refers to the person or thing that is the most important or influential.

> Our lack of capital is the **principal** issue.

The **principal** suspended the recalcitrant students.

The noun **principle** names a fundamental rule, belief, or truth.

His actions are not consistent with his **principles**.

qualitative (adj), **quantitative** (adj): The adjective **qualitative** involves the quality or kind of things or people.

The researchers conducted a **qualitative** analysis of their patients.

The adjective **quantitative** involves measurements of quantity or amount.

A **quantitative** approach to economics is fundamentally flawed.

quiet (adj), **quiescent** (adj): To be *quiet* is to make little or no noise.

Quiet children are a rare treat.

To be *quiescent* is to be inactive, still, or dormant.

The virus has become **quiescent** for the time being.

rational (adj), **rationale** (n): To be *rational* is to be logical, reasonable, or understandable.

She is grief-stricken and not forming **rational** thoughts.

A *rationale* is a fundamental reasoning or explanation.

Please share your **rationale** for running away from home.

rebound (v), **redound** (v): The verb **rebound** means "to spring back."

Sarah **rebounded** quickly after the painful breakup.

The verb **redound** means "to have an effect."

The President's actions **redounded** to his reputation.

recur (v), **reoccur** (v): There's no such word as **reoccur**. If you want to use a verb that means "to occur again," you must use **recur**.

The damaging floods of springs past are bound to **recur** this season.

regime (n), **regimen** (n): The noun **regime** names a system of rule or government.

> The rebels vowed to overthrow the fascist **regime**.

The noun **regimen** names any systematic procedure whether it be one of government, of therapy, or of natural phenomena.

> My wife began a **regimen** of daily exercise.

> The **regimen** of spring renews life.

regretful (adj), **regrettable** (adj): The adjective **regretful** describes someone who is filled with sorrow and regret.

> The children felt **regretful** about their behavior at the movies.

The adjective **regrettable** describes a situation that deserves regret.

> The current circumstances are **regrettable**, but there is nothing we can do.

respectfully (adv), **respectably** (adv), **respectively** (adv): The adverb **respectfully** means "with respect."

> **Respectfully**, I send my condolences.

The adverb **respectably** means "in a manner worthy of esteem or respect."

> Samuel is dressed quite **respectably** tonight.

The adverb **respectively** refers to items in a series and means "in the order named."

> Fred, Daphne, and Velma, **respectively**, will give their presentations.

spit (n, v), **spat** (n, v): The word **spit** refers to saliva. As a noun, it can refer to the stuff itself, and as a verb, it can refer to the act of turning the stuff into an airborne projectile.

> A thin line of **spit** dribbled down the baby's chin.

> I **spit** the spoiled cheese into the garbage.

The word **spat** is sometimes the past indicative form of **spit**.

> The cowboy **spat** tobacco into the urn.

At other times, **spat** is a verb, meaning "to strike with the sound of falling rain."

The popcorn **spats** against the edge of the pan.

At still other times, **spat** is a noun that names a small quarrel, a young mollusk, or a cloth or leather gaiter which covers the upper part of the shoe.

The dog and cat engaged in a **spat** over the chicken bone.

The octopus ate the unfortunate **spat**.

The members of the marching band wore bright red **spats** over their shoes.

splutter (v), **sputter** (v): One who makes a spitting noise or who speaks incoherently *splutters*.

The embarrassed gourmet **spluttered** as he spat the hot pepper into his napkin.

One talks so excitedly or confusedly that one *sputters*.

The distraught mother could do nothing but **sputter**.

stationary (adj), **stationery** (n): The adjective **stationary** means "immobile."

The prowler remained **stationary** in the bushes until the police had gone.

The noun **stationery** means "writing or typing materials."

Doesn't my résumé look professional on this **stationery**?

statute (n), **statue** (n): A *statute* is a law.

The legislature enacted a number of new **statutes**.

A *statue* is a form or likeness sculpted, modeled, carved, or cast in material such as stone, clay, wood, or bronze.

I have always wanted a **statue** sculpted in my likeness.

temblor (n), **trembler** (n), **tremor** (n): A *temblor* is an earthquake.

The last **temblor** struck in the dead of night.

A *trembler* is one who shakes and trembles.

My tiny cousin is a **trembler** when lightning strikes.

A *tremor* is a shaking or trembling motion. We can use the word in several contexts. A tremor can be the result of physical or emotional weakness.

> As the jury read the verdict, the accused murderer felt a **tremor** of anxiety.

A *tremor* can be a small trembling of the land that precedes or follows a major seismic disturbance.

> Several **tremors** followed the large jolt of the earthquake.

A *tremor* can also be a feeling of doubt.

> Agnes felt a **tremor** of uncertainty over her decision.

than (con), **then** (adv): The conjunction **than** joins main and subordinate clauses and makes a comparison of inequality.

> Pie is richer **than** cake.

> I like to swim more **than** I like to run.

The adverb **then** means "next in space, time, or order."

> **Then** we went to the movies.

> The soldiers came first, and **then** came the queen's entourage.

tortuous (adj), **torturous** (adj): The adjective **tortuous** describes something that is winding and twisty or something that is devious and crooked.

> The **tortuous** road brought the daring driver to his knees.

> The thieves hatched a **tortuous** plan to steal all the water in the world.

The adjective **torturous** describes something that causes torture or pain.

> The dull ceremony became **torturous** after just an hour.

> My neighbor's singing voice is **torturous**.

toward (prep), **towards** (prep): These words are interchangeable. They both mean "in the direction of," "for the purpose of," "near," or "with regard to."

> The foot soldiers marched **toward** the enemy encampment.

> Tommy is saving money **towards** buying a new bike.

The church was built **toward** the crest of the hill.

His attitude **towards** the death penalty disturbs me.

wench (n), **wrench** (n, v), **wince** (n, v), **wretch** (n): The noun **wench** is a rude name for a young girl. We also use it to name an unsavory woman.

The king ordered the **wench** to bring him his dinner.

The word **wrench** involves a twisting motion. As a noun, it names a sudden, violent jerk or twist or a tool used to hold or twist an object. As a verb, wrench means "to twist suddenly."

The repairmen loosened the bolts with a **wrench**.

Montgomery **wrenched** his knee in the game last Sunday.

As a noun, a *wince* is a flinch. As a verb, it is the act of flinching.

Tom gave a **wince** as the doctor set his broken leg.

The child only **winced** when the doctor inserted the needle.

A *wretch* can be either a terribly unhappy person or an odious and hateful person.

We gave the poor **wretch** what money we could spare.

The soldiers tossed the **wretch** into the deepest prison cell.

while (n, v, con), **wile** (n): The word **while** is multifunctional. We most often see it as a conjunction meaning "for the time that," "whereas," or "although."

Be good **while** I am away.

While the solution was clear to the teacher, the pupils were stymied.

While we located the missing explorers, we could not find the lost artifact.

As a verb, **while** means "to cause to pass."

She and I **whiled** away the hours in pleasant conversation.

As a noun, **while** names a period of time.

We decided to remain in Maine for a **while**.

A *wile*, on the other hand, is a deceitful stratagem or a trick. We usually see this noun in plural form.

> The princess used her feminine **wiles** to outwit the dim palace guards.

> Her **wiles** alone have kept them alive in the wilderness.

wont (adj, n), **won't** (contraction): The word **wont** involves habit or practice. As an adjective, it means "accustomed to or used to." As a noun, it names a habit.

> He is **wont** to complete the crossword puzzle each day.

> His **wont** to exercise borders on the fanatical.

The word **won't** is a contraction of the auxiliary verb **will** and the adverb **not**.

> The council **won't** listen to my warning.

> The kids **won't** go to bed.

 FROM MY FILES: POSITIONS

Would a body lie *prone* at the murderer's feet? Or would it be *supine*? Or perhaps it lay *prostrate*? Or *recumbent*? Or was that *procumbent*? No one seems to know the difference between these position words. Fortunately, the Hot Line is here to help.

One who is *prone* is lying face down, while one who is *supine* is lying face up. One who is *recumbent* has lain down in any position appropriate for rest or sleep, while one who is *procumbent* is simply lying face down. Finally, one who is *prostrate* has thrown himself or herself into a prone position in adoration, praise, humility, or submission.

The victim may have been recumbent at the time of his or her death or he or she may have made himself or herself prostrate in a final plea for mercy (if this sentence isn't a cry for a gender neutral pronoun, I don't know what is), but it is more likely that the body was prone/procumbent or supine. Whichever position you pick, be sure that it is not "prostate." The prostate is a gland that surrounds the mammalian male urethra where it meets the bladder.

ROOTS, PREFIXES, AND SUFFIXES

Q. One desperate caller asked, "What can I do to improve my vocabulary? There are too many words that I don't know."

A. The only surefire method for cultivating a refined vocabulary is to read, READ, **READ**. Only the avid reader truly knows his or her words. He or she will encounter new words daily and, because of a love for reading, will look up these new words in a dictionary and add them to his or her ever-growing vocabulary arsenal.

One might also become the master of several of the languages from which English is derived, but this requires more time than most Americans care to spare. My other recommendation is that those concerned about their vocabularies learn the Greek and Latin roots, suffixes, and prefixes that are so common in English words. The following list will aid those who decide to embark upon this endeavor:

ROOTS

Root	Meaning	Examples
acer, acr	sharp, bitter	acerbic, acrid, acrimonious
am	love	amateur, amiable, amorous, paramour
anthrop	man	anthropology, anthropomorphic, misanthrope
aud	hear	audience, audition, auditorium, auditory
bene	good, well	beneficent, beneficial, benign, benevolent
cap	head	decapitate, capital, capitulate
cap, cept, cip	take, hold	captive, perceptible, receptacle, incipient
ced (ceed), cess	move, yield	antecedent, precedent, recede, succeed, procession
chron	time	anachronism, chronic, chronology
cid, cis	to cut	decide, homicide, exorcise, incision
cred	believe	credibility, credit, creed, incredulous
fac, fact, fect, fic, fict	make, do	facility, fact, factory, faction, perfection, infectious, efficiency, proficient, fiction

Root	Meaning	Examples
fer, lat	carry, bring, bear	defer, infer, reference, vociferous, relate, translation
fin	end, limit	affinity, definite, infinitesimal
gen	race, stock, decent	eugenics, geneology, heterogeneous, homogenous, indigenous
geo	earth	geography, geology
graph	write	autograph, epigraph, graphic, telegraph
greg	flock, group, herd	congregation, egregious, segregation
hydr	water	hydrant, hydraulic, hydrometer, hydroplane
log	speak, speech, word	apology, dialogue, epilogue, eulogy, ideology
meter	measure	centimeter, kilometer, metric, metronome
path	feeling, disease, experience, suffering	apathy, empathy, pathetic, telepathy, pathology
phil	love	philanthropy, philodendron, philosophy
spec, spect, spic	look at	speculum, speculate, inspection, retrospect, conspicuous, perspicacious
ten (tain), tent	hold	countenance, tenacious, abstain, obtain, intent
tend (tens, tent)	stretch	contentious, extend, ostensible, ostentatious, pretend, tendon
therm	heat	thermal, thermometer, thermostat
tom	to cut	appendectomy, atom, dichotomy, epitome

PREFIXES

PREFIX	MEANING	EXAMPLES
a-, ab-, abs-	from , away from, without, not	agnostic, amoral, atheist, atonal, atypical, avert, abnormal, abolish, aboriginal, abstain
ambi-	both, around	ambidextrous, ambivalent, ambiance
ana-	against, back, opposite	anachronism, anathema
anti-	opposed	antifreeze, antipathy, antithesis
auto-	self, same	autocratic, automation, automobile
bi-	two, twice	bicentennial, bicuspid, bicycle, biped
circum-	around	circumcision, circumference, circumstantial
co-, col-, com-	together, with	coherent, cooperative, correspond, collective, committee, complement
de-	down from, away, off	decaffeinated, declare, deductive, defer, delusion,demeanor, deprecate, derogatory, descend
dem-	the people, citizens	democratic, demagogue
di-	two, double	dichotomy, dichromatic, dilemma
dia-	across, through	diacritical, diagram, dialogue, diatribe
di(s)-	apart	diffident, different, divergent, disconnect, dissociate, dissolve
em-, en-, im-, in-	in, on, onto	embrace, entomb, immigrate, induce
eu-	well, good	eugenics, euphemism, eulogy, euphoric, euthanasia
hetero	different	heterogeneous, heteronym, heterosexual
homo	same	homogeneous, homogenize, homonym, homosexual
in-	not	inaudible, incapable, incomplete
inter-	between, among	international, intercede, interdict, interstate
intra-, intro-	within, inside	intramural, intravenous, introduce, introvert
micro-	small	microbe, micrometer, microscope
mis-	wrong, wrongly improper, improperly	mismanage, misjudge, misdeed

Prefix	Meaning	Examples
miso-	hatred	misanthropy, misogamy, misogyny
para-	beyond, contrary to	paradox, paramedic, paranormal
per-	through, completely	percentile, perfect, permeate, persevere, perpetual, perspicacious
peri-	about, around, near	perimeter, peripatetic, peripheral
post-	after	posthumous, postgraduate, postbellum
re-	back	recalcitrant, reciprocate, refute, retrieve, revert
retro-	back	retroactive, retrogress, retrospective
se-	apart, aside	segregation, seduce
sub-	below	submarine, subversive, subway
super-	above, beyond, over	supercilious, superconductor, supervision
syn-	with	synagogue, synonymous, syntax, synthesis
trans-	across, through	transcontinental, transfer, transient, transitory, transparent

SUFFIXES[†]

Suffix	Meaning	Examples
-able, -ible	capable of, fit, for	arable, adaptable, credible, possible
-al, -ic, -ical	of, relating to	nocturnal, maternal, anthropomorphic, fantastic, magical, musical, paradoxical
-ar, -ary, -ory	like, providing, connected with	circular, judiciary, satisfactory
-ar, -er, -or	one who	liar, farmer, trader, actor, doctor, tractor, traitor
-ate	to make	aggravate, ameliorate, gravitate
-ation, -ition	state of, act of	aspiration, inundation, invitation, admonition
-crat	power, strength	autocratic, aristocrat, theocracy
-cy	condition, act of	clemency, democracy, tendency
-ive	connected with, like	native, restive, protective

[†] Some of the suffixes have even more meanings not listed here, depending on the parts of speech they are added to. There is only so much information one can place in a simple table.

SUFFIX	MEANING	EXAMPLES
-ine	pertaining to, resembling, made of	equine, marine, sanguine
-ism	state of, act of, quality of	anachronism, baptism, communism
-ist	one who	capitalist, lyricist, pharmacist, satirist
-logy	study of	anthropology, astrology, biology, ecology
-mania	great enthusiasm or madness for	egomania, kleptomania, megalomania
-ment	state of being, action of	atonement, government, judgment
-ose, -ous, -ious	possessing, full of	verbose, nervous, ridiculous, fictitious, glorious
-phobia	fear, dread	agoraphobia, claustrophobia
-ty	quality of	affinity, dignity, heredity

A PREFIX QUESTION

Q. One caller asked, "How is something that is *atypical* different from something that is *typical*?"

A. The words are opposites. The prefix **a-** means "not," so something that is atypical is *not* typical.

ANOTHER PREFIX QUESTION

Q. Another caller wondered, "What's the difference between an *interoffice* and an *intraoffice* memo?"

A. The prefix **inter-** means "between or among," so an interoffice memo moves between two or more offices. The prefix **intra-** means "within," so an intraoffice memo remains within a single office.

ONE THOUSAND WORDS YOU SHOULD KNOW

While I wish that I could reasonably say that there are twenty thousand words that any proud English speaker should command, I know that such a request is absurd and unfair. Therefore, I give you this list of one thousand words that every one of us should master:

A

abase
abate
abdicate
abet
aborigine
abscond
absolve
abstemious
abstract
abstruse
abut
accredit
accrue
acerbic
acquiesce
acrimony
adjudge
adjunct
admonish
adroit
adulation
aesthetic
affable
affinity
affluence
aggrandize
aggregate
agnostic
agrarian
alacrity

alibi
alimentary
allay
allegory
allocate
allude
ally
aloof
amalgamation
amass
ambiguous
ambush
ameliorate
amiable
amnesty
amuck
anachronism
anarchy
animate
animosity
annals
anneal
anomaly
anthology
antipathy
antipodes
apathy
aphorism
apoplexy
apostasy
apostle

apothecary
appall
appease
apportion
apposite
appropriation
arabesque
arable
arcane
archaic
archipelago
archives
arduous
armament
armoire
array
arrears
articulate
artifice
ascendancy
ascertain
aspect
assay
assent
assert
assessment
assiduous
assumption
astral
astute
atheism

athwart
atoll
atrophy
attenuate
attest
attire
audacious
audible
auspicious
austerity
autocratic
autonomy
auxiliary
avarice
avatar
avow
awry

B

badger
balm
bandy
bastion
beatitude
bellicose
benediction
benefactor
beset
bestial
bestow
bestride
bewitch

bicker
bide
biennial
bigot
binary
blasphemy
blazon
blithe
bluster
bombastic
bondage
bounty
bourgeois
brandish
breech
brigand
broach
brocade
brooch
browbeat
browse
bruit
brusque
buffoon
bullion
bureaucracy
burlesque
burnish
butte

C

cachet

cad
cadence
caliber
caliph
calumny
candid
canvass
capitulate
capricious
captivate
careen
carnage
carnivorous
carp
carrion
cartel
cassock
cataclysm
cathartic
caustic
censure
centrifugal
chaff
chamberlain
chamois
chancery
chaste
chattel
chide
chilblain
chronic

chronicle

circumspect

citadel

civility

clack

claret

clime

coffer

cogent

cogitation

cognate

cognizant

collate

collation

colloquial

colloquy

collusion

commensurate

commissary

commodious

complaisance

compulsory

concave

conclave

concur

condescend

condolence

congeal

congenital

congruent

conifer

conjecture

connote

connubial

conscience

conscript

conservative

consign

consort

constellation

consternation

constrict

consul

contagion

contemn

contemplate

contiguity

contingent

contumely

conundrum

convex

conveyance

convivial

convoke

convolution

copious

corollary

corona

corporeal

correlate

corroborate

couplet

covert

cower

cozen

crag

credible

credulity

creed

cretin

crimp

crony

crusade

crux

cudgel

cult

currency

curry

cursory

curtail

D

dank

dearth

debase

debit

debunk

decadence

decant

declaim

decorum

decrease

decrepit

defection

deference

defile

definitive

degrade

delta

demeanor

denomination

denote

denude

deplore

deposition

deprecate

descent

desecrate

desist

despondent

despot

destitute

desultory

devoid

dictum

digress

dilate

diligent

diocese

discompose

disconsolate

discountenance

discredit

discursive

disdain

disingenuous

disparage

disparity

disseminate

dissenter

dissertation

dissipate

dissonant

diurnal

diverge

diversion

divest

docile

doggerel

dogmatic

dollop

dolor

dolt

domineer

dormant

dowager

droll

drone

dross

dubious

ductile

dulcet

dupe

duplicity

duress

dynasty

dystrophy

E

ebullient

eccentric

ecclesiastical

echelon

ecumenical

edifice

educe

efficacy

effigy

effluence

effrontery

egregious

elegy

elixir

elocution

emanate

embellish

emboss

emendation

emulate

encomium

enfranchise

engender

enmity

ennui

ensconce

ensign

entity

entropy

enunciate

ephemeral

epic

epithet

epoch

eponymous

equestrian

equinox

erudite

escarpment

eschew

esculent

esoteric

ethereal

etymology

eulogy

euphony

evangelist

evince

evoke

evolve

exchequer

exhume

excise

exodus

exorcist

expatiate

expectorate

expedient

expound

expunge

extant

extol

extradite

extricate

extrinsic

exuberant

F

facade

facetious

facile

facsimile

fallacy

fastidious

feasible

felicity

fervent

fetid

fettle

fief

fiend

filial

fjord

flaccid

flagrant

flail

flaunt

fledged

florid

flout

foible

font

forensic

foreshadow

forgo

formidable

fortitude

fortnight

fortuitous

fraudulent

fray

freeholder

frizzle

frugal

furor

fustian

G

gaffe

gallant

garble

garrulous

gauntlet

gentrification

germane

gerrymander

gesticulate

gibe

girt

glib

goad

gradient

grandee

gratuitous

gregarious

gripe

grist

grueling

guild

gyrate

H

hackneyed

hale

hallow

hallucination

harbinger

harry

hearth

heathen

heckle

hegemony

hegira

heinous

heresy

heritage

heyday

histrionics

hoax

homily

horticulture

huggermugger

humbug

humdrum

hurtle

husbandry

hydraulic

hyperbole

hypocrite

I

idiom

idyll

ignoble

ignominious

ignoramus

illicit

imbecile

imbibe

imbroglio

imbue

immaculate

impartial

impede

impel

imperative

impertinent

implicit

importune

impudent

impugn

inaugurate

incendiary

incidence

increment

incursion

indenture

indigent

indignant

inimitable

induct

induction

indulgence

ineffable

inert

inevitable

infernal

infidel

infirm

inherent

initiate

injunction

innate

insinuate

insolvent

instantaneous

insular

insurrection

intangible

interdict

interim

interminable

interpolate

interregnum

intrepid

intrigue

intrinsic

intuition

inveigle

investiture
investment
inveterate
invidious
irony —
isthmus
italics
iterate
itinerant

J

jaded
jargon
jaundice
jejune
jetty
journeyman
jubilee
juggernaut

K

kaleidoscope
kestrel
kibbutz
kudos

L

labile
laity
lampoon
lancet
languid
latent

laud
laureate
leech
legerdemain
levy
lexicon
liability
libretto
liege
lieu
litany
lithe
litigation
liturgy
livid
longevity
lucid
lucrative
lucre
luminary
lurid
lymph

M

macabre
madrigal
malcontent
malfeasance
manifest
maw
maxim
mellifluous

menial
meniscus
metaphor
mete
method
mettle
microcosm
mien
milquetoast
minion
missal
miter
montage
mosque
mummery
myopia
myriad

N

nadir
naiad
naiveté
narcissism
natal
nativity
nemesis
neologism
nescience
node
nonplus
nosegay
noxious

nugatory

numinous

nurture

O

obdurate

obeisance

obelisk

oblation

obscure

obsolescence

obstinate

obtrude

odious

officious

ogre

oligarchy

omen

ominous

omniscient

omnivorous

onerous

onomatopoeia

oppress

opulence

oracle

oration

orbit

organic

orifice

ornate

osmosis

ossify

ostracize

overt

overture

P

pacify

paddock

paean

pagan

palatable

palatial

pall

palpable

palsy

panacea

parable

paradox

parallel

paramour

parapet

paraphernalia

parody

parsimony

partisan

pastoral

patent

patriarch

patrician

patrimony

patron

pectoral

pecuniary

pedant

pejorative

penal

pendant

perdition

peremptory

perennial

perforce

periphery

pernicious

perpetrate

perquisite

personification

perspicuous

pert

pertinent

peruse

pervade

perverse

pestilence

pestle

petition

petulance

pewter

phalanx

phantom

philander

philanthropy

philology

piety

pilaster

pillory

pious

pittance

plagiarism

plait

plumb

plutocracy

poach

poignant

politic

political

portend

posit

posse

posterity

potentate

pottage

prate

precise

preclude

precursor

predator

predicament

predicate

predilection

predispose

preempt

preen

prefect

premier

premise

prerogative

presbyter

prescience

presentiment

presidio

presume

pretentious

preternatural

pretext

primogeniture

primordial

procrastinate

prodigious

profane

proffer

profuse

progeny

proletarian

prolific

promontory

promptitude

prone

propitious

prorate

prosaic

prose

proselytize

prosody

protégé

prude

prudent

pseudonym

psyche

pungent

purge

purloin

purport

putrid

Q

quaff

qualm

query

queue

quietus

quintessential

quirk

quittance

quorum

R

raconteur

raillery

raiment

rambunctious

rancor

rankle

rant

rapacity

rapt

rapture

rasp

ravish

reactionary

rebuke

reciprocal

reconnaissance

reconnoiter

recriminate

rectitude

refute

regale

regent

regicide

regimen

rejuvenate

relegate

relevant

remission

remonstrate

remuneration

renegade

renounce

reparation

repartee

repast

repertory

replete

reprehend

reprisal

reproach

reproof

repudiate

repugnant

repute

requisite

resound

respite

restitution

résumé

resuscitate

reticence

retribution

revile

rift

robust

rote

rotundity

rudiment

S_____

sable

saboteur

saccharine

sacrament

sacrilege

sagacity

salacious

salient

saline

saltation

salubrious

salutary

salutatory

sanguine

satire

savant

scant

scathing

schism

schmaltz

scintillation

scoff

scope

scrutinize

scurrilous

secede

seclude

secrete

sect

sector

secular

sedentary

sedition

sedulous

seethe

segment

segue

semblance

sentient

servitude

shamble

sheepish

shrew

shunt

signify

simile

simper

skeptic

slake

sloth

sluice

sojourn

soliloquy

somber

sophist

sophomoric

sordid

sovereignty

specious

specter

speculate

sporadic

steppe

stilted

stint

stoicism

strait

stratagem

strategy

strident

stygian

subjugate

sublimate

submission

subservient

subsidiary

subsidy

subterfuge

succinct

succor

succulence

sully

superfluous

supernal

supersede

supervene

supplant

supple

surfeit

surmount

surveillance

sustenance

swathe

syllogism

symposium

synonymous

syntax

T

tableau

tacit

taciturn

tack

tactic

tangent

tangible

tankard

tantamount

tariff

tawny

telltale

temerity

tempest

temporal

tenacity

tenuous

tenure

terminus

terse

testimonial

thesis

thrall

tiara

tirade

tithe

tome

tonic

torpid

torque

tort

tortuous

totalitarian

traduce

trait

transient

transitory

transpire

transpose

transubstantiate

transverse

trappings

travail

travesty

treacle

tremulous

trencher

tribulation

tribute

truant

truncheon

trundle

trust

tureen

turnkey

tutelage

twain

twit

U

ubiquitous

ulterior

umbrage

unanimity

unctuous

undercurrent

undulate

unison

untold

upbraid

uproarious

usurp

usury

utilitarian

utmost

V

vacillate

vacuous

vagary

valiant

valorous

vanguard

vaunt

vellum

veneer

venerate

verisimilitude

verity

vermilion

vernacular

verve

vestige

vicissitude

vigilant

vindicate

vintage

virtual

virtuoso

visage

vivacious

vociferous

volatile

volition

W

waif

wainscoting

wan

weal

wheedle

willful

windfall

woolgather

wraith

wrangle

wroth

wrought

wry

X

xenophobia

xylophone

Y

yeoman

Z

zealot

zephyr

zodiac

WORD ORIGINS

As was mentioned earlier, one way to enhance your vocabulary is to understand the etymologies or origins of words. While many words have their origins in the classical languages, others have emerged from more obscure places and cultures in our world. Several callers have contacted the Hot Line with questions about word origins. The following calls are the most interesting and informative of the bunch.

WORDS FROM LITERATURE

Q. "Is **lilliputian** a real English word?" asked a researcher from Nova Scotia.

A. The curious researcher has exposed one of the more interesting origins that a word can have, that is, literature. **Lilliputian** is a real English word. It comes from Jonathan Swift's satirical novel *Gulliver's Travels*. In the book, Gulliver visited a land called Lilliput that was populated by tiny people. We now call something or someone who is very small *lilliputian*. Gulliver also visited a land called Brobdignag that was filled with giants. The English adjective **Brobdignagian** describes people or things that are very large.

The contemporary English word **malapropism** comes from the name of a character in the Richard Brinsley Sheridan play *A School for Scandal*. The character's name is Mrs. Malaprop, and she has become famous for using words in ridiculous contexts. A malapropism is an intentional and often amusing misuse of a word. One who utters a malapropism might speak of "polo bears" and "hermit's nests," rather than "polar bears" and "hornet's nests."

We have even created words from the names of authors.[†] Literature that is written in the style that Charles Dickens used is described as being *Dickensian*. And a bleak, hopeless, and oppressive situation similar to that devised by George Orwell for his novel *1984* is described as being *Orwellian*. This has been a small sample of words with literary origins. Doubtless there are others, but you will need a book on etymologies to complete the study.

[†] Words that come from proper names are called **eponyms**. We will discuss these shortly (see p. 476).

THE SHAKESPEAREAN CONNECTION

Q. A caller asked, "What does the expression "hoisted by one's own petard" mean? It's Shakespearean, isn't it?"

A. The contemporary noun **petard** names a type of firecracker or a case for an explosive device used to blow a hole in a wall or door. The word comes from the French **péter**, meaning "to break wind." Those firecrackers and engines of destruction make a noise similar to that of a person loudly passing gas.

One who has been hoisted by his or her own petard has been caught in his or her own trap or deceived by his or her own trickery. Perhaps this sad individual has been caught, figuratively, in the blast from his or her own explosive device. Or maybe he or she has been humiliated by the release of his or her own hot and noxious air.

In any case, the phrase is indeed Shakespearean. It comes from *Hamlet* (III, iv, 206). The original text reads:

> For 'tis sport to have the engineer
> Hoist with his own petar.

PORTMANTEAU WORDS

Q. "I heard a game show host talking about portmanteau words yesterday. What are they?" one caller asked.

A. A portmanteau is a large leather suitcase that opens on hinges into two halves. A portmanteau word is a word with the meanings and sounds of two words packed into it. Lewis Carroll, author of *Alice in Wonderland*, was a skilled user of these clever little words. He had creatures which he described as *slithy*. They were *lithe* and *slimy*. You see, the word is like a portmanteau. It has two parts and two meanings and sounds packed into one word.

Many of us use portmanteau words each day without realizing it. *Smog* is both *smoke* and *fog*. When we go to *brunch*, we are attending a meal somewhere between *breakfast* and *lunch*. A *motel* is a combination of **motor** and **hotel**. Someone who is *prissy* is *prim* and a *sissy*. A *simulcast* is a *simultaneous broadcast*. *Smoke* and *haze* make *smaze*, and the amalgamation of *agriculture* and *business* gives us *agribusiness*.

EPONYMS

Q. "I know what synonyms and antonyms are, but I read the word **eponym** in a book the other day, and I don't know what those are. Could you give me a definition and a few examples?" the caller asked.

A. The Hot Line is always happy to oblige a curious caller. An eponym is a word which has come into the language from a person's proper name. Often, the person has gained fame from some outstanding event or utterance. For instance, when we *dun* someone, we repeatedly insist that the person repay a debt. We are using the last name of Joe Dun, a popular London bailiff during the 1820s, who was exceedingly efficient in catching defaulting debtors.

A more famous example of an eponym comes from the name of a Texan, Samuel August Maverick (1803-1870). The mayor of San Antonio and, later, a member of the Texas Congress, Maverick refused to have his cattle branded as the law required him to do. Initially, the word **maverick** was a name for an unbranded range animal. Later, it came to name or describe an individual who refuses to go along with the group.

Other eponyms you will recognize are the noun **leotard** from the name of Jules Leotard, a 19th century trapeze artist who designed and popularized the tight-fitting body suits, and the noun **nicotine** from the name of Jean Nicol who introduced tobacco into France in 1560. The noun **silhouette** comes from the name of another Frenchman, Etienne de Silhouette (1709-1767). To ridicule this despised finance minister, his enemies gave his name to a mere outline, indicating that, as a man, he was something less than substantial. Finally, Ambrose E. Burnside (1824-1881) lent his name to those famous bits of facial hair, *sideburns*.

Perhaps these few examples have fueled your desire to learn more about the origins of words. There are many more eponyms in the English language, and it is worth a trip to the library to check out a book on these fascinating words and their stories. Our own Auriel Douglas has written an excellent book on this very topic entitled *Webster's New World Dictionary of Eponyms: Common Words from Proper Names.*

EPIPHANY

Q. A curious teenager asked, "Where does the word **epiphany** come from? It's become the cool word to use, and all my girlfriends are saying it."

A. In contemporary usage, the noun **epiphany** names a moment of revelation or insight. Originally, Epiphany was a Christian holiday celebrated on January 6 to commemorate the divine manifestation of Christ. The day of Epiphany is sometimes called Twelfth Day, and the eve of Epiphany is sometimes called Twelfth Night. The realization of Christ's divine nature was a profound spiritual revelation for Christians, but the resulting holiday spawned a word that encompasses revelations in general, spiritual and otherwise.

COMMONLY USED FOREIGN WORDS AND PHRASES

Q. A caller commented, "I'm often unsure about foreign words and phrases that my friends and teachers use from time to time. I'm never sure that they mean what I think they mean. Do you have some list that I could look at?"

A. I bet many readers share our caller's insecurity. See if this list of foreign words and phrases commonly used in English helps.

KEY:	F = French	G = German	Gk = Greek	Heb = Hebrew
	Hw = Hawaiian	I = Italian	L = Latin	R = Russian
	S = Spanish	Y = Yiddish		

a bas (F)	down with
a capella (I)	without instrumental accompaniment (literally, "in the chapel style")
ad hoc (L)	for a particular purpose (literally, "for this")
ad infinitum (L)	forever; without limit or end
aficionado (S)	enthusiast; fan
alfresco (I)	in the open air
alma mater (L)	the school, college, or university that one has attended or from which one has graduated; the song or hymn of a school, college, or university (literally, "fostering mother.")
aloha (Hw)	greeting or farewell (literally, "love")

ancien régime (F)	the old regime
anno Domini (A.D.) (L)	in the year of the Lord
a priori (L)	deductive (literally, "from what comes before" or "from the former")
ars longa, vita brevis (L)	art is long, life is short
au contraire (F)	on the contrary
au naturel (F)	nude; plain; in a natural style or condition
avant-garde (F)	forward; advanced; vanguard
beau geste (F)	noble gesture
beau idéal (F)	highest ideal; ideal or perfect beauty
bête noire (F)	pet peeve (literally, "black beast")
billet doux (F)	love letter
bon marché (F)	inexpensive (literally, "good market")
bon mot (F)	clever saying
bonne chance (F)	good luck
bon voyage (F)	good journey
carpe diem (L)	seize the day
carte blanche (F)	unrestricted delegated authority; full power (literally, "white card")
cause célèbre (F)	scandal; notorious incident
caveat emptor (L)	let the buyer beware
c'est la vie (F)	that's life
cherchez la femme (F)	look for the woman
chutzpah (Y)	gall; daring
cogito ergo sum (L)	I think, therefore I am
cognoscenti (I)	those in the know; a person knowledgeable in fine arts and fashion
comme il faut (F)	proper; appropriate
con mucho gusto (S)	with pleasure
corpus delicti (L)	evidence (literally, "body of the crime")
coup de grâce (F)	a mortal or final blow
coup d'état (F)	overthrow of government
da capo (I)	from the beginning
de facto (L)	in fact; in reality
de jure (L)	in law; by right, legal

demimonde (F)	underworld; the other side of the tracks; the social class of prostitutes
dernier cri (F)	the last word
déshabillé (F)	disheveled; slovenly
deus ex machina (L)	contrived solution (literally, "God from a machine")
enfant terrible (F)	a child or adult who behaves in an infantile manner; in English, usually applied to artists or celebrities who behave this way (literally, "terrible child")
entre nous (F)	between us; privately
et cetera (etc.) (L)	and others of the same class; and so forth (literally, "and other [things]")
eureka (Gk)	I've found it!
ex cathedra (L)	with high authority (literally, "from the chair")
exempli gratia (e.g.) (L)	for example; by way of example (literally, "for the sake of an example")
ex post facto (L)	after the fact; afterward
fait accompli (F)	accomplished fact
faux pas (F)	social error (literally, "false step")
femme fatale (F)	an alluring, dangerous woman
fin de siècle (F)	characteristic of the end of the nineteenth century, especially that which references the decadence of the period (literally, "end of the century")
flagrante delicto (L)	in the very act of committing a misdeed
glasnost (R)	openness
gonif (Y)	thief
goy (Y)	gentile
habeas corpus (L)	writ requiring a court appearance (literally, "you should have the body)
haute couture (F)	high fashion
haute cuisine (F)	fine cooking
haut monde (F)	high society
hoi polloi (Gk)	common people
honi soit qui mal y pense (F)	evil to him who thinks evil
hubris (Gk)	overwhelming pride, arrogance

ibidem (ibid.) (L)	in the same book or chapter (literally, "in the same place")
idée fixe (F)	fixed idea; obsession
in medias res (L)	in the middle of things
in vino veritas (L)	in wine (there is) truth
joie de vivre (F)	keen enjoyment of life
magnum opus (L)	the greatest achievement of an artist or writer; masterpiece (literally, "great work")
manqué (F)	failed; unsuccessful
maven (Y)	expert; authority
mazel tov (Heb)	congratulations
mea culpa (L)	I am guilty (literally, "my fault")
mens sans in corpore sano (L)	a sound mind in a sound body
meshuggah (Y)	crazy
mirabile dictu (L)	amazing (literally, "wonderful to tell")
modus operandi (M.O.) (L)	method of operation
ne plus ultra (L)	the height of achievement or excellence (literally, "no more beyond")
nobless obligé (F)	noble obligation
nom de plume (F)	pen name
non sequitur (L)	a response that does not follow from anything previously said (literally, "it does not follow")
nota bene (N.B., n.b.) (L)	note well
par excellence (F)	above all; preeminently
par exemple (F)	for example
parvenu (F)	newcomer; upstart
per diem (L)	daily
per favore (I)	please
por favor (S)	please
prima facie (L)	on the face of it; at first sight
qué será será (S)	what will be, will be
raison d'être (F)	reason for being
rara avis (L)	rarity (literally, "rare bird")
reductio ad absurdum (L)	reduction to absurdity (in logical argument)
sang-froid (F)	aplomb; composure

santa sanctorum (L)	the holy of holies; inner circle
semper fidelis (L)	always faithful
sic (L)	thus or so—used after a printed passage or word to indicate that it exactly reproduces the original, including errors
sic transit gloria mundi (L)	thus passes the glory of the world
sine qua non (L)	an essential element, condition, or thing (literally, "without which not")
status quo (L)	current state of affairs (literally, "the state in which")
Sturm und Drang (G)	name for a late eighteenth century German romantic literary movement (literally, "storm and stress")
sub rosa (L)	secretly
sui generis (L)	one of a kind; unique (literally, "of his, her, or its own kind")
tabula rasa (L)	the mind before it is developed and changed by experience (literally, "an erased [wax] tablet")
tempus fugit (L)	time flies
terra firma (L)	solid ground
terra incognita (L)	unknown territory
tout de suite (F)	immediately
trompe l'oeil (F)	illusionary (literally, "fool the eye")
vade mecum (L)	handbook; guide (literally, "go with me")
vox populi, vox Dei (L)	the voice of the people (is) the voice of God
Wunderkind (G)	prodigy
yenta (Y)	busybody; gossip
Zeitgeist (G)	spirit of the times

FROM MY FILES: GRAMMAR IS GLAMOROUS

Through the ages, there has been a sense of mystery and wonder attached to words. Ancient Egyptian priests, anxious to maintain their power, kept the art of reading and writing a secret of the temple, and common people looked upon these skills with superstitious awe.

Even in sixteenth century England, the ability to read and write was regarded suspiciously, and this special knowledge was associated with black magic. The illiterate masses, wary of the literati and frustrated with their own lot in life, accredited occult and devilish powers to those who were fluent in Latin, the language of the cultured few. Books were written in Latin, and intellectuals conversed in it.[†] To the masses, the mere word **grammar** implied magic or sorcery.

That intriguing word **glamour** was born out of the magic and fear associated with knowledge of grammar. As the years went by, the letter **r** in the mysterious word **grammar** changed to **l**, as **r** often does when language mutates. Other modifications crept in, and a new word **glamor** was born that originally carried the cabalistic undertones once attached to **grammar**. It meant "magic or enchantment." Over the years, that old, mystical **glamor** has undergone more changes, so that, in modern English, it has become **glamour** and means "compelling charm, romance, and excitement."

SYNONYMS FOR SAID

Q. A caller queried, "What are the synonyms for **said**? I'm writing a story, and I need a few alternatives for the times I'm writing dialog."

A. Our budding author was wise to bring novelty and variety to his work. The past indicative verb **said** is so dull. It implies a very generic form of saying. Often, moments in a story need a special type of communication and require a word with a more complex meaning. I faxed the author the following list of synonyms for **said**:

accused	answered	charged
acknowledged	approved	cited
added	argued	claimed
advanced	asserted	commented
advised	avowed	complained
affirmed	believed	conceded
agreed	called	concluded
alleged	cautioned	confessed
announced	certified	confided

[†] One professor was actually defrocked for daring to deliver a lecture in English.

confirmed	insisted	recited
contended	intimated	recounted
continued	iterated	reiterated
countered	jested	related
decided	lashed	remarked
declaimed	lauded	reminded
declared	maintained	repeated
demanded	mentioned	replied
denied	murmured	reported
denoted	named	responded
described	narrated	retorted
designed	noted	returned
disclosed	notified	revealed
discussed	observed	reviewed
divulged	opined	shouted
elucidated	orated	sighed
emphasized	ordered	signified
ended	pleaded	specified
exclaimed	pointed out	spoke
explained	posted	stated
exploded	praised	stressed
exposed	predicated	submitted
expostulated	predicted	suggested
expounded	proclaimed	summarized
expressed	professed	swore
felt	prompted	talked
foretold	pronounced	testified
found	proposed	thought
held	propounded	told
hinted	protested	trumpeted
imparted	put forward	turned
implied	questioned	uncovered
indicated	quoted	urged
informed	recalled	uttered
insinuated	recapitulated	

MISUSED VOCABULARY

Our world is in a sad state of affairs. Overwhelming social and environmental crises aside, I turn to the trauma that is being inflicted on our language. Mrs. Malaprop and her cousins run rampant through our streets, speaking with no regard for proper context or rules of usage. Their mistakes are not always amusing. Many of our callers have caught this devilish family at its worst, and these are the best of those calls.

CALENDARS AND VERBS

Q. "My boss always wants me to do the 'calendarizing.' Is there such a word?" asked a caller.

A. This sort of misuse makes me want to wear earplugs. There is no such word as **calendarize**. I assume the caller's boss was asking him to make an entry in a calendar or planner. Why did the boss not ask his employee "to enter these into the calendar"? Is our need for brevity so intense that it blinds us to the righteous standards of the language?

This type of mistake is not a limited phenomena. Many lazy speakers and writers add **-ize** to a noun base in the hopes of creating a legitimate verb, but their efforts are in vain. They see words such as **categorize**, from **category**, and **stigmatize**, from **stigma**, and assume that the procedure is valid for any noun. We must not forget that brevity isn't everything. It is better to use a few extra words than to pull nonsense out of thin air.

REDUNDANT PREFIXES

Q. "I question the use of the prefix **co-** in the word **co-conspirator**. What do you think?" queried an attorney with the Justice Department in the state of Virginia.

A. The attorney has raised an excellent point. The prefix in **co-conspirator** is redundant. It is meant to indicate that the *conspirator* named was conspiring with others. However, a conspiracy, by definition, is a plot hatched among a group of conspirators. If one is a conspirator, then one automatically has fellow conspirators. The prefix provides no useful information.

Common English is full of nonsensical constructions. Have you ever been offered a "free gift" or been asked to "reserve ahead?" Well, what kind of a gift isn't free, and how can anyone reserve *behind*? Such usage is thoughtless and sloppy. I'm tempted to believe that there exists a group of *co-conspirators* bent on destroying proper English.

ESOTERIC ENGLISH

Q. "Do terms like **deplaning, offloading**, and **preboarding** annoy you as much as they annoy me?" asked a professional travel agent.

A. Personally, I live in constant fear of ever having to *preboard*. I have no idea what I would do. To me, preboarding activity seems like the fidgeting I do in the waiting area while I wait for the airline attendants to call my flight. I'm certain that the airlines have something else in mind, but I can't imagine what it is. If these commercial flight conglomerates feel the need to justify their own existence by adding words to the language, they should at least choose a few that make sense.

To be honest, some of the airport lingo has a history. The word **deplane** has been used in print since 1923, long before the commercial airline service was established, and **offload** dates back to 1851. It probably was used in the shipping or railroad industry, since the Wright Brothers didn't take flight at Kittyhawk until 1903. Just how these words came into being is lost to history.

What I say to you now is that our language has no use for ill-conceived and esoteric words such as these. Instead of asking passengers to *preboard*, why not call for *early boarding*. Instead of instructing us to *deplane*, couldn't the flight attendants request that we *exit the aircraft*? And rather than *offloading* the baggage, the ground crew should *remove* the baggage from the plane. The alternative words and phrases are equally clear and so much more agreeable.

LEGAL JARGON

Q. A disturbed caller asked, "How can lawyers and judges get away with the kind of writing and speech that they use? All the **whereas's, not pursuant's**, and **not withstanding's** are absurd."

A. Legal jargon is a double-edged sword. In one sense, reading a brief makes me want to scream. The language is archaic and murky, and its only purpose seems to be to create confusion. Conversing with an attorney, one sometimes gets the feeling that one is speaking with a creature from another universe. The truth of the matter is, however, that legal jargon serves a purpose.

If any one of us were to enter a standard English sentence into a book of law, we would be introducing the legal system to a world of trouble. Everyday language is full of assumptions. Shared contexts and meanings abound, and we are not obliged to put every detail of an expression into words.

Lawyers and judges do not share this luxury. Their job is to make a law in impeccable and incontestable language. To make a clear and lasting point, there can be few assumptions and little room for interpretation. The language, in and of itself, must be enough to define the law, and the unfortunate side effect is legal jargon. A law in normal language would be argued and contested from Portland to the steps of the Supreme Court until the end of time.

This is, of course, a simplified explanation. Many say that the founding fathers wrote the Constitution in a vague manner, so that it would be a robust document, applicable across a wide expanse of time and in varying contexts. Even so, the language of law must be confining. Legal jargon is an unavoidable consequence of this fact.

Unique Overuse

Q. "The people in my office, myself included, have fallen into the bad habit of using **unique** in every letter or report or memo that we write. We need some alternatives. Can you make any suggestions?" asked a concerned manager.

A. How sad that **unique** has fallen into overuse. I suggested that they try using several of the following words and phrases and then pull **unique** off the shelf when it feels fresh again.

absolute	one of a kind	supreme	unprecedented
critical	perfect	ultimate	unusual
essential	rare	unequaled	vital
extreme	singular	unparalleled	zenith

PHOBIAS

Q. "My younger sister claims to be terrified of the number 13. I told her there was a word for just about every kind of phobia in the world, and I bet her there was one for this one, too. Is there a name for a fear of the number 13?" asked a teenage caller from the Los Angeles area.

A. We call a fear of the number 13 triskaidekaphobia. Other callers have contacted the Hot Line with phobia questions, so I prepared this list of fears and their names.

The *Diagnostic and Statistical Manual*, the definitive guide to psychological disorders, divides the phobias into three basic types: agoraphobia, social phobia, and simple phobia. Agoraphobia is a fear of "being alone or in public places from which escape might be difficult or help not available in case of sudden incapacitation . . . ." A social phobia is "a persistent, irrational fear of, and compelling desire to avoid, situations in which the individual may be exposed to scrutiny by others." A simple phobia is "a persistent, irrational fear of, and compelling desire to avoid, an object or a situation other than being alone or in public places away from home (Agoraphobia), or of humiliation or embarrassment in certain social situations (Social Phobia)." It is under this last category of social phobias that psychologists would place most of the specific phobias we list below.

You can find the following phobias in any dictionary:

PHOBIA:	FEAR OF/AVERSION TO:
acrophobia	heights
agoraphobia	open or public places
claustrophobia	narrow or enclosed spaces
homophobia	homosexuality
hydrophobia	water
triskaidekaphobia	the number 13
xenophobia	strangers or foreigners

The authors created these next phobias by adding the suffix
-phobia to base words, all of which have Greek or Latin origins:

PHOBIA:	FEAR OF/AVERSION TO:
algophobia	pain
apiphobia	bees
bathophobia	deep water
batrachophobia	frogs and toads
brontophobia	thunder
coprophobia	feces
cryophobia	cold
dendrophobia	trees
entomophobia	insects
eruthrophobia	the color red
gamophobia	marriage
gymnophobia	nudity
gynophobia	women
hedonophobia	pleasure
hippophobia	horses
hypsophobia	heights
koniphobia	dust
necrophobia	corpses
ophiophobia	snakes
ornithophobia	birds
peccatophobia	sin
selaphobia	sharks
thanatophobia	death
tocophobia	childbirth

PECULIAR WORDS AND PHRASES

English, like any other interesting language, has its share of
peculiar words and phrases. The next two calls will give you a
taste of these.

OXYMORONS AND PALINDROMES

Q. "I love the words **oxymoron** and **palindrome**, but what are they exactly?" asked a caller.

A. Those are wonderful-sounding words, aren't they? There is just something fun and engaging about them. To answer the caller's question, an oxymoron is a figure of speech that combines contradictory terms. For instance, the phrase **mournful optimist** is an oxymoron. One who is mourning has a sad or negative outlook while one who is optimistic has a happy or positive outlook. The meanings of the words are contradictory, yet they are used in the same phrase. Here are some more oxymorons:

bad health	intense uninterest
genuine imitation	idiot savant
free gift	friendly invasion
exact estimate	good war
extensive briefing	definite maybe
old news	cold as hell
friendly fire	

A palindrome is a word, phrase, or sentence that reads the same forwards and backwards. People have been creating palindromes since the third century B.C. The word comes from the Greek words **palin**, meaning "back or again," and **dramein**, meaning "to run." Together these words form the Greek **palindromos**, which means "to run back again." Here's a great palindrome: A man, a plan, a canal: Panama. Now read it backwards. I guarantee that you'll get the same thing.

Read the following palindromes carefully. Do you see how cleverly their authors have constructed them?

Able was I ere I saw Elba.	Draw, O Caesar, erase a coward.
Madam, I'm Adam.	He lived as a devil, eh?
Enid and Edna dine.	Niagara, O roar again!
Ma is a nun, as I am.	Dennis Krats and Edna Stark sinned.

SPOONERISMS

Q. "My mother transposes syllables constantly. The other day, she said, 'Here comes Mr. Clown with his brass,'" instead of

"Here comes Mr. Brown with his class." There's a word for this, isn't there?" queried a caller.

A. We call these transpositions **spoonerisms**. The word is an eponym, derived from the name of Reverend William A. Spooner (1844-1930), Dean and later Warden of New College at Oxford. Spooner's penchant for transposing bits of words endeared him to his students. In chapel one day, he announced the next hymn as "Kinguering Congs," instead of "Conquering Kings," and he once reprimanded a student by telling him, "You have deliberately tasted two worms," instead of "You have deliberately wasted two terms."

SOME OTHER THINGS YOU SHOULD KNOW ABOUT VOCABULARY

If only there were time and space enough in this book to delve deeply into the issue of vocabulary. The origins of our language and the nature of current word use are truly fascinating topics, but the issues involved are too vast for a single book on grammar to make significant headway. I hope that the preceding information was helpful and that these last few pointers will strengthen your grasp on vocabulary.

A VOCABULARY QUANDARY

Q. "Which is correct: 'We reached a happy median' or 'We reached a happy media'?" asked a caller.

A. At first, her question was unclear. Did she mean members of the press, the media, or a statistical midpoint, the median? A few moments of discussion unraveled the puzzle. She was trying to describe the situation where two individuals agree upon a middle ground. The word she needed was **medium**. "We reached a happy medium."

A VOCABULARY DISTINCTION: *ADVISOR* AND *ADVISER*

Q. "What is the difference between the nouns **advisor** and **adviser**?" asked a market research analyst.

A. The caller had been told, somewhere, sometime, that an *adviser* is a group or a company that gives advice and that an *advisor* was an individual who gives advice. NO! NO! NO! Both words mean "one who gives advice." They are synonyms.

ANOTHER VOCABULARY DISTINCTION: *USING* AND *UTILIZING*

Q. "What's the difference between *using* and *utilizing* resources?" wondered the president of a college as he wrote a commencement address.

A. To *utilize* is to put to use for a specific purpose or to make practical, productive, or worthwhile use of something not obviously intended for the job.

The teachers **utilized** the materials available to them.

To *use*, on the other hand, is to put into action or service.

The teachers **used** the display to teach long division.

The words are similar and somewhat interchangeable, but **use** is preferred to the more pretentious **utilize** where there is no particular sense of urgency.

ANOTHER VOCABULARY DISTINCTION: *ALLUDE, ELUDE,* AND *ILLUDE*

Q. "These words have always confused me: **allude, elude**, and **illude**. Can you clarify them?" asked a political cartoonist.

A. **Allude** means "to refer to." **Elude** means "to avoid," and, to the best of our knowledge, there is no such word as **illude**. However, the first two are verbs, as is **delude**, which means "to mislead."

ANOTHER VOCABULARY DISTINCTION: *FLOUT* AND *FLAUNT*

Q. "Does one *flout* or *flaunt* one's assets?" asked a disgruntled marital partner, contemplating divorce.

A. To *flout* is to treat contemptuously. To *flaunt* is to display ostentatiously. One would *flaunt* one's assets or *flout* the rules. I hope her husband wasn't doing either.

ANOTHER VOCABULARY DISTINCTION: *DISSEMINATE* AND *DECIMATE*

Q. In an interview, a football quarterback was asked if he "disseminated" his opposition. A journalist called to ask if **disseminate** was the right word.

A. The interviewer was actually looking for the word **decimate**, meaning "to demolish or destroy." **Decimate** is based on the prefix **deci-**, meaning "ten," so technically it means "to destroy a tenth of the whole." That's quite a large portion of the opposing team for one player to handle.

Disseminate means "to spread or share." Activists *disseminate* information. Newspapers *disseminate* news.

ANOTHER VOCABULARY DISTINCTION: *DECRY* AND *DESCRY*

Q. A tour operator inquired about the use of the word **decry**. In a travel article, she had written, "I could barely *decry* the Golden Gate Bridge through the fog."

A. **Decry** is a verb, meaning "to belittle or blame." It is not the word that the tour operator was looking for.

We **decry** their hostile actions.

She needed the word **descry**, meaning "to discern or detect." This portion of her article should have read, "I could barely *descry* the Golden Gate Bridge through the fog."

ANOTHER VOCABULARY DISTINCTION: *IMMIGRATE* AND *EMIGRATE*

Q. A history teacher asked, "Can you help me with the difference between *immigrate* and *emigrate*?"

A. One *emigrates* when one leaves a country. One *immigrates* when one enters a country. I am moving from North America to South America. More specifically, I *emigrate* from the United States, and I *immigrate* into Brazil.

ANOTHER VOCABULARY DISTINCTION: *IMPLY* AND *INFER*

Q. During a recent, highly publicized trial in Los Angeles, we received a call from a bailiff on his lunch break. He said, "I think the defense attorney is misusing words. I've heard him begin a sentence with 'He inferred that . . . .' I'm thinking that he meant to say 'implied' rather than 'inferred.' What do you think?"

A. The Hot Line replied that we would need to read the session transcripts to be sure, but that we would take her word for it that the attorney was misusing the word. To **imply** an idea is to suggest it without expressly stating it.

Her remarks **implied** that she was guilty.

To **infer** an idea is to conclude it without having heard it expressly stated.

The jury **inferred** from her remarks that she was guilty.

The distinction is a crucial one. I hope someone sends this attorney a dictionary.

ANOTHER VOCABULARY DISTINCTION: *ITERATE* AND *REITERATE*

Q. A concerned teacher called to say, "In class, one of my students asked, 'Do you have to reiterate it again? I got it right the first time.' Something is wrong here, but I'm not sure what."

A. To *iterate* is to repeat once. To *reiterate* it is to repeat it again. Since the teacher has only made one repetition, her student should have said, "Do you have to *iterate* it?" Notice that I have dropped the adverb **again**. Iterating a statement again is the same thing as reiterating it.

ANOTHER VOCABULARY DISTINCTION: *FLUTIST* AND *FLAUTIST*

Q. "Do *flutists* or *flautists* play flutes?" asked a music-lover who had long been perplexed by these two words.

A. Both do. People who play flutes can be called *flutists* or *flautists*. Either word is acceptable, although I prefer the ring of elegance that I hear in **flautist**.

VOCABULARY MISUSE

Q. The president of an association of pathologists wanted to know if the noun phrase "such egregiously good service" contained an oxymoron.

A. An oxymoron is a combination of two contradictory words. We've all heard of "old news" and "cruel kindness." In the president's sentence, the adjective **good** describes the noun **service**. The adverb **egregiously** describes **good**. Grammatically, it's perfect. It just doesn't make any sense. **Egregiously** means "outstandingly bad." The Hot Line believes that the president was commenting on outstandingly good service. Unless she intends to utter an oxymoron, we suggest a different choice of adverb. Any of the adverbs **amazingly**, **shockingly**, or **phenomenally** would work.

WINE TERMINOLOGY

Q. "Wine terminology cracks me up. It's snooty and silly but strangely engaging. I'd like to be in the know, so that I'll sound like I know what I'm talking about when I have dinner with friends and we order wine. Can you give me a few pointers?"

A. I was glad to be of service to a fellow wine lover, and I know that many readers are probably hungry, or should I say thirsty, for similar information. A knowledge of some of the basic terminology can only increase your ability to order the right wine at the right time. The task of defining all of the terms that apply to wine is worthy of its own book, but these few samples should start you on your way to becoming a connoisseur.

There are a number of terms that we use to describe the general character of the wine. The **acidity** of a wine describes the natural tartness that provides it with *body* and *structure*. **Body** is the feel of the wine in your mouth, and is frequently described in terms of **weight** (*light*, *medium*, and *heavy*). The general term **structure** describes the body of wine and is based on acidity, alcohol, and tannins. The **attack** of wine is the initial impression it gives as the liquid flows over your taste buds, and **bouquet** is the aroma that fine wine develops as it ages. The **aftertaste** of wine is the flavor that remains in your mouth after you have swallowed the liquid.

Any connoisseur will also know the terms that we use to describe the components of wine. The **tannins** are the natural component in red wine that makes your mouth pucker, and **alcohol** is that social lubricant that also adds to the body and texture of wine.

The most fun wine terms are those that we use to describe the flavor, scent, or appearance of wine or the feel of wine in the mouth. Connoisseurs use the term **cat spray** to describe the sharp and musky flavor of some Sauvignon Blancs. Wine that is **cheesy**, due to unsanitary wine-making conditions, possesses an undesirable cheese-like aroma. We describe the color of deep red wines as **dark**, and a **chewy** wine has such a full body that it almost seems as if one could chew the liquid.

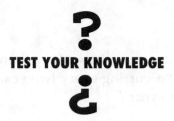

TEST YOUR KNOWLEDGE

Questions

1. Does a *biennial* event occur more or less often than a *biannual* event?

2. A gastronome, a gourmet, and a gourmand come to your house for dinner. Who has the worst manners?

3. Pick ten words from the list of one thousand that you should know. Look them up and write their definitions down.

4. What's an eponym?

5. What's an *enfant terrible*, and what is the country of origin of the phrase?

6. What's wrong with the word **co-conspirator**?

7. What do the psychologists call a fear of bees?

8. Is the description "cold as hell" a palindrome or an oxymoron?

9. If I repeat something, have I *iterated* it or *reiterated* it?

10. Does one *immigrate* or *emigrate* from Texas to Idaho?

(SEE ANSWERS ON FOLLOWING PAGE)

ANSWERS

1. A biennial event occurs less often than a biannual event. **Biennial** means "occurring every two years." **Biannual** means "occurring twice a year."

2. The gourmand will probably have the worst manners, since he or she expresses his or her love of food in a piggish or gluttonous manner.

3. This is a do-it-yourself question.

4. An eponym is a word, such as **maverick,** that has come into the language from a person's proper name.

5. An enfant terrible is, literally, a terrible child. We often use it to describe artists or celebrities who behave in an infantile manner. The phrase comes from French.

6. The prefix **co-** is redundant. The simple noun **conspirator** provides all the information we need.

7. They call this fear apiphobia.

8. It's an oxymoron, a figure of speech that combines contradictory terms. Since hell is hot, how can it be cold? A palindrome is a word, phrase, or sentence that reads the same forwards and backwards.

9. I have only *iterated* it. I must repeat it again to *reiterate* it.

10. One *emigrates* from Texas and *immigrates* into Idaho.

16.

Punctuation

> **Punctuation** is the system of symbols that writers use to make their writing clear and to add emphasis, intonation, and pause to a work.

Our discussion of grammar is close to completion. With parts of speech, clauses and sentences, and a bit of spelling and vocabulary under our belts, we are almost ready to re-enter the world as expert writers and speakers. However, no discussion of grammar is complete without mention of **punctuation**. Marks of punctuation are traffic signs for readers. They guide us through the maze of words and ideas that any piece of writing presents.

Writers punctuate sentences for two reasons. The first and most common is to provide order and structure to an otherwise dark and disorganized stream of words. Without punctuation marks to indicate starting and stopping points, pauses, and other breaks, most readers would drown in a sea of undifferentiated thoughts, facts, and ideas.

The second reason that writers punctuate their sentences is to add style to writing. Speech is punctuated with hand gestures, pauses, tone changes, breathing, and facial expressions. Each of these adds a subtle meaning to the spoken sentence that it accompanies, but all of them disappear when words are put to the page. Writers sometimes use punctuation in place of the natural stylings. A comma adds a dramatic pause. An exclamation mark emphasizes a crucial moment. A mark of punctuation can serve the same purpose as frantically waving hands or a pair of crooked eyes.

Examine this incomprehensible set of words. Without punctuation, we have no idea what it means:

That that is is that that is not is not is that it it is

Watch the magic of punctuation work on this murky stream of words:

That that is, is. That that is not, is not. Is that it? It is.

Punctuation is powerful enough to change the meaning of an entire sentence. In this next example, a simple apostrophe turns a rude butler into a master of decorum:

> RUDE: The butler stood at the door and called the guests names.

> MASTERFUL: The butler stood at the door and called the guests' names.

HISTORY OF PUNCTUATION

Punctuation is a vital tool in clear, precise communication. The word itself is expressively lucid, derived as it is from the Latin **punctus**, meaning "a point." The first use of punctuation appears on the Moonbite Stone, dating from 850 B.C., on which each word is separated from the others by a vertical line.

Most scholars attribute the invention of punctuation to Aristophanes of Byzantium (not to be confused with Aristophanes, the Athenian playwright, 450-388 B.C.) who was in charge of the great library of Alexandria around 194 B.C. He created a system of points that correspond roughly to our period, comma, and semi-colon. Aristophanes is also credited with inventing other marks of punctuation, such as the virgule, hyphen, apostrophe, and question mark.

Manuscripts dating back to the fourth century B.C. contain rudimentary marks of "pointing," and, in the earliest stone inscriptions, a dot is sometimes placed between each word to separate it from its predecessor. The modern uses of the period evolved around the eighth century A.D. The comma at first looked just like the number seven, then slowly evolved into a slash mark or virgule, and, eventually, was altered into its present form.

Charlemagne, King of the Franks from 768 to 814 A.D. and Holy Roman Emperor for the latter part of this period, and Alcuin, the English director of Charlemagne's palace school, led an educational revival which produced superior spelling and punctuation. Lowercase letters came into use (formerly, the use of all uppercase letters was the custom), but the ascenders and descenders of these letters made it difficult to read a manuscript without punctuation. The men adopted a simplified version of Aristophanes's system to clarify the writing. The punctuation set consisted of a full stop, or period, and an intermediate stop, written with what we know today as a colon.

By the eleventh century, writers had adopted Aristophanes's full system which included the *punctus interrogatives*, an ancestor of today's question mark. Modern punctuation can be loosely traced back to Aldus Manutius, a sixteenth century Venetian printer, who is generally given the credit for systematizing punctuation.

RULES OF PUNCTUATION

Today, questions about punctuation range from where to put a comma to whether or not the period goes inside or outside of the quotation marks. Much of our punctuation can be explained as part of our grammatical structure, so, when discussing certain marks, one often refers to the grammatical structures that the marks support.

The modern system of English punctuation is by no means simple and straightforward. A book that covers all the bases would need to be of considerable breadth and weight, and anyone interested in such a resource is advised to consult *The Chicago Manual of Style*. However, these authors will do what we can to enhance your knowledge of the subject in one meager chapter. The following rules and guidelines should illuminate the basic structure of contemporary punctuation.

THE PERIOD

The purpose of the period, as any first-grader knows, is to represent a strong pause or a break. This pause or break may be a physical pause, as occurs between sentences, or a pause in meaning, as occurs between the different letters in an abbreviation. There, the period indicates that each letter represents a word separate from the words represented by the other letters in the abbreviation. Here are a few rules that govern the use of the period:

WITH IMPERATIVE AND DECLARATIVE SENTENCES

The period ends imperative and declarative sentences that are not written or spoken with the force of an exclamation.

> Pass the salt.

> The postman always rings twice.

WITH REQUESTS AND QUESTIONS

The period may end a request, an indirect question, a rhetorical question, or an imperative sentence phrased as a question.

> Would you please turn your stereo down. (request)

> He wonders who she is. (indirect question)

> May I make a suggestion. (rhetorical question)

> Would you stop tapping your foot. (imperative sentence phrased as question)

WITH ABBREVIATIONS

The period appears after some abbreviations and between certain initials.

A.D.	E.J.E.	Mrs.
A.M.	Feb.	Ms.
B.C.	i.e.	P.M.
D.W.G.	Mr.	Ph.D.

Please note that abbreviations and initials are a tricky bunch. Some take the period, while others do not, and there does not seem to be much rhyme or reason to the system. If in doubt, contact the organization or individual named or consult a more complete punctuation resource for the correct answer.

Also note that a sentence that ends with an abbreviation or set of initials does not require an additional period to mark its end.

The relics date back to 800 B.C.

However, if the sentence is a question or an exclamation, add the appropriate punctuation after the period that ends the abbreviation or set of initials.

Did he earn a B.S.?

Meet me at nine A.M.!

I asked him to meet me at seven P.M., but he didn't arrive till eight.

WITH ELLIPSES

A series of periods, known as an ellipsis, indicates missing words in a quote. Three periods indicate words missing at the beginning of the quote or within the quote.

"Unless we can surmount the crises . . . all the plans for the rebuilding of backward countries in other continents will all be put on the shelf, because war interrupts everything like that." —Walter Lippmann

We place an ellipsis of four periods at the end of a quote where words are missing. This series of periods includes the period that ends the sentence.

"Give me a dozen healthy infants . . . and I'll guarantee to take any one at random and train him to become any type of specialist I might select . . . . " —J. B. Watson

IN PLACE OF PARENTHESES

The period often appears in place of a parenthesis after a letter or number that marks an item in a series.

a. Chop the carrots.   1. Set the modifier switch to seven.
b. Cook the rice.   2. Turn the modulating dial to fourteen.

ELLIPSES, QUESTION MARKS, AND EXCLAMATION MARKS

Q. "Can question marks and exclamation marks follow ellipses?" wondered a caller.

A. Of course ellipses can be used with question marks and exclamation marks. Simply place the appropriate punctuation
after an ellipsis of three periods.

> She cried, "How can that be . . . ?"

> I exclaimed, "You're leaving me . . . !"

ABBREVIATIONS

Q. "When do I put a period after an abbreviation?" A hospital
administrator explained that his secretary put them in, and
he kept taking them out. "Is there a list available?" he asked.

A. Here are some abbreviations which require periods: **Dr., Jr.,
pp., etc., e.g., i.e.** On the other hand, well-known organizations, such as government agencies, radio and TV stations, and
large corporations do not require periods: **AT&T, UNICEF, CBS,
ASCAP, IBM**. Abbreviated chess terms (**Bk 5**) and chemical symbols (**Fe**) do not receive periods either. One abbreviation which
most get wrong is TV; it doesn't take periods. The following is a list
of common abbreviations that should help out:

ABBREVIATIONS

A

AA	Administrative Assistant, Alcoholics Anonymous, American Airlines
aa	author's alterations
AAA	American Accounting Association, American Automobile Association
AAAL	American Academy of Arts and Letters
AAF	Army Air Force
AARP	American Association of Retired Persons
ab.	about
AB	able bodied (seaman)
ABA	American Bar Association, American Basketball Association, American Booksellers Association
abbr., abbrev.	abbreviation
ABC	American Broadcasting Company
ab init.	ab initio (Latin for "from the beginning")
ABS	American Bureau of Shipping, Antilock Braking System

abt.	about
AC	alternating current, air conditioner, Athletic Club, ante Christum (Latin for "before Christ"), ante cibum (Latin for "before meals")
acct.	account
actg.	acting
ACLU	American Civil Liberties Union
A.D.	anno Domini (Latin for "in the year of our Lord")
ad lib.	ad libitrum (Latin for "at pleasure")
AEC	Atomic Energy Commission
AFL-CIO	American Federation of Labor and Congress of Industrial Organizations
AFTRA	American Federation of Television and Radio Artists
agitprop	agitation and propaganda
AIDS	Acquired Immune Deficiency Syndrome
ALA	American Library Association
A.M.	ante meridiem (Latin for "before noon")
AMA	American Medical Association
Amex	American Stock Exchange
AMPAS	Academy of Motion Picture Arts and Sciences
ANPA	American Newspaper Publishers Association
appt.	appoint, appointed
APR	American Public Radio, Annual Percentage Rate
ARC	AIDS-Related Complex, American Red Cross
ASAP	as soon as possible
ASCAP	American Society of Composers, Authors, and Publishers
ASCII	American Standard Code for Information Interchange
ASL	American Sign Language
ASPCA	American Society for the Prevention of Cruelty to Animals
AT&T	American Telephone & Telegraph
atty.	attorney
AU	angstrom unit, astronomical unit
Au	the chemical symbol for gold (from the Latin word "aurium")
AV	audiovisual
Av.	Avenue
av.	average

AWACS	Airborne Warnings and Control Systems
AWOL	absent without leave
AZT	azidothymidine

B

bach	bachelor
BART	Bay Area Rapid Transit System
BBB	Better Business Bureau
BBC	British Broadcasting Corporation
bbl, bbl.	barrel
B.C.	before Christ
bet.	between
Bib.	Bible, Biblical
bibliog.	bibliographer, bibliography
BIP	Books in Print
bkpt.	bankrupt
BLT	bacon, lettuce, and tomato
BPOE	Benevolent and Protective Order of Elks
bro.	brother
BSA	Boy Scouts of America
Bt.	baronet
bus.	business
B.W.I.	British West Indies
bx.	box

C

C	Celsius
CAB	Civil Aeronautics Board
CAD	Computer-Aided Design, Control Alternate Delete
CAP	Civil Air Patrol
CAT scan	computerized axial tomography scan
CB	citizens' band (radio)
CBS	Columbia Broadcasting System
C.C., c.c.	carbon copy
CD	Certificate of Deposit, compact disc
CD-ROM	compact disc-read only memory

CEO	chief executive officer
CIA	Central Intelligence Agency
cm.	centimeter, centimeters
C.O.	commanding officer, conscientious objector
co.	company, county
Co.	company
c/o	care of
COD, C.O.D.	cash on delivery, collect on delivery
COLA	cost-of-living allowance/adjustment
COMEX	New York Commodity Exchange
comp.	companion, compensation, compilation, composer
C.P.	Communist Party

D

DAV	Disabled American Veterans
D.D.S.	Doctor of Dental Science, Doctor of Dental Surgery
DEA	Drug Enforcement Agency
DJ	disk jockey
DLO	dead letter office
DMV	Department of Motor Vehicles
D.O.A.	dead on arrival
DOS	disk operating system
Dr.	Doctor
DST, D.S.T.	Daylight Savings Time

E

ECG	electrocardiogram
ecol.	ecological, ecology
econ.	economics, economist, economy
ed.	edition, editor, education
EDT	Eastern Daylight Time
e.g.	exempli gratia (Latin for "for the sake of an example")
Ens.	ensign
E.N.T.	ears, nose, and throat
EOB	end of block, end of buffer
EOF	end of file

EPA	Environmental Protection Agency
ESL	English as a second language
ESP	extrasensory perception
etc.	et cetera (Latin for "and other [things]")
ex.	example, except, exception, exchange, executive, extra

F

FAA	Federal Aviation Administration
FAQ	frequently asked question(s), frequently answered question(s)
fax	facsimile (as in "fax machine")
FCC	Federal Communications Commission
FDIC	Federal Deposit Insurance Corporation
FEMA	Federal Emergency Management Agency
fict.	fiction
FORTRAN	formula translator (computer programming language)
FPC	Federal Power Commission
frt.	freight
ft.	foot, feet
FTC	Federal Trade Commission
FTD	Florists Transworld Delivery

G

gal.	gallon
GAO	General Accounting Office
gds.	goods
GED	General Education Diploma
G.O.P.	Grand Old Party
GQ	general quarters
gtd.	guaranteed

H

H-bomb	hydrogen bomb
hdqrs.	headquarters
HEW	Department of Health, Education, and Welfare
H-hour	the hour at which a military operation is set to begin.
HIV	human immunodeficiency virus

HMO	health maintenance organization
H.M.S.	His or Her Majesty's Ship
HQ	headquarters

I

ibid.	ibidem (Latin for "in the same place")
IBM	Independent Business Machines
ICBM	intercontinental ballistic missile
id.	idem (Latin for "the same")
I.D.	identification, intelligence department
ILA	International Longshoremen's Association
ILGWU	International Ladies Garment Workers Union
INS	Immigration and Naturalization Service
INTELSAT	International Telecommunications Satellite Consortium
Interpol	International Police
IPA	International Phonetic Alphabet
IQ	Intelligence Quotient
IRS	Internal Revenue Service

J

JAMA	Journal of the American Medical Association
JD	Justice Department, juvenile delinquent
jg	junior grade
Jr.	Junior

K

K-12	kindergarten through twelfth grade
KGB	Komitet Gosudarstvennoi Bezopaznosti (Soviet Secret Police)
kilo	kilogram, kilometer
km.	kilometer, kilometers
KO	knock out

L

LA	Los Angeles, low altitude
L.A.	Legislative Assembly, local agent
L.C.	Library of Congress

legis.	legislation, legislative, legislature
LSD	lysergic acid diethylamide
lv	leave, livre

M

m.	meter, meters
MASH	mobile army surgical hospital
MAYDAY	international distress signal, meaning "Help me!" (from the French "m'aider")
M.D.	Medicinae Doctor (Latin for "Doctor of Medicine")
mgr.	manager
Mgr.	Manager, Monseigneur, Monsignor
mi.	mile, miles
mm.	millimeter, millimeters
M.O.	modus operandi (Latin for "method of operation")
MODEM	modulator-demodulator
MOMA	Museum of Modern Art (New York City)
Mr.	mister—title of courtesy used before a man's surname
Mrs.	mistress—title of courtesy used before a married woman's surname
Ms.	title of courtesy placed before a woman's surname that does not indicate marital status—a combination of **Mrs.** and **Miss**

N

NAFTA	North American Free Trade Agreement
NA	Narcotics Anonymous, North America
NASA	National Aeronautics and Space Administration
NASDAQ	National Association of Securities Dealers Automated Quotations
nat.	national, native, natural
NATO	North Atlantic Treaty Organization
N.B., n.b.	nota bene (Latin for "note well")
NBA	National Basketball Association, National Braille Association
NBC	National Broadcasting Company
NCTE	National Council of Teachers of English
NOW	National Organization for Women

| NPR | National Public Radio |
| NYSE | New York Stock Exchange |

O

OA	Overeaters Anonymous
ob.	obiter (Latin for "incidentally"), obstetric
OCS	Officer Candidate School, Outer Continental Shelf
O.D.	officer of the day, overdrawn
OP, op, o.p.	out of print
Op., op.	operation, opus
OPEC	Organization of Petroleum Exporting Countries
oz	ounce

P

p.	page, part, pawn, penny, per, pint, population
P.A., P/A	power of attorney
PAC	Pan African Congress, political action committee
PBS	Public Broadcasting Service
PDQ	pretty damn quick
P.M.	post meridiem (Latin for "after noon")
P.O., p.o.	petty officer, post office
pp.	pages, pianissimo, privately printed
pro tem.	pro tempore (Latin for "temporarily")
PTA	Parents-Teacher Association

Q

| qb | quarterback |
| Q.E.D. | quod erat demonstrandum (Latin for "which was to be demonstrated") |

R

radar	radio detecting and ranging
RAM	random access memory
R&B	rhythm and blues
R.C.	Red Cross, Roman Catholic
R&D	research and development
recap	recapitulate

ROM	read only memory
RR	railroad
R.R.	railroad, rural route
R.S.V.P.	répondez s'il vous plait (French for "please reply")

S

SAG	Screen Actors Guild
sase	self-addressed, stamped envelope
scuba	self-contained underwater breathing apparatus
SEC	Securities and Exchange Commission
SIDS	sudden infant death syndrome
snafu	situation normal, all fouled up
SOP	standard operating procedure
SPCA	Society for the Prevention of Cruelty to Animals
S.R.O.	standing room only
SWAT	special weapons and tactics

T

TA	teaching assistant, transfer allowed
TB	tuberculosis, terabyte
TGIF	Thank God it's Friday!
theol.	theologian, theological, theology
TKO	technical knock-out
TM	trademark, transcendental meditation
TTFW	Ta ta for now.

U

UAW	United Auto Workers
U-boat	a German submarine (from the German word **untersee-boot**, meaning "undersea boat")
UMWA	United Mine Workers of America
UNESCO	United Nations Educational, Scientific, and Cultural Organization
UNICEF	United Nations International Children's Emergency Fund
UNIVAC	universal automatic computer
UPC	universal product code
UPI	United Press International

USAF	United States Air Force
USM	United States Mail
USMC	United States Marine Corps
USN	United States Navy

V

VA	Veterans' Administration
VD	venereal disease
vi.	intransitive verb
VIP	very important person
vl.	linking verb
VSOP	very special, old product (French cognac)
vt.	transitive verb

W

WCTU	Women's Christian Temperance Union
WWI	World War I
WWII	World War II

X

| XL | extra large |
| Xmas | Christmas |

Y

yd.	yard, yards
YMCA	Young Men's Christian Association
YMHA	Young Men's Hebrew Association
yuppie	young urban professional
YWCA	Young Women's Christian Association
YWHA	Young Women's Hebrew Association

Z

ZIP Code	zone improvement plan code
zoo	zoological garden
ZPG	zero population growth

U.S. Postal Service Abbreviations

Alabama	AL	North Dakota	ND
Alaska	AK	Ohio	OH
Arizona	AZ	Oklahoma	OK
Arkansas	AR	Oregon	OR
California	CA	Pennsylvania	PA
Colorado	CO	Rhode Island	RI
Connecticut	CT	South Carolina	SC
Delaware	DE	South Dakota	SD
District of Columbia	DC	Tennessee	TN
Florida	FL	Texas	TX
Georgia	GA	Utah	UT
Hawaii	HI	Vermont	VT
Idaho	ID	Virginia	VA
Illinois	IL	Washington	WA
Indiana	IN	West Virginia	WV
Iowa	IA	Wisconsin	WI
Kansas	KS	Wyoming	WY
Kentucky	KY		
Louisiana	LA		
Maine	ME		
Maryland	MD		
Massachusetts	MA		
Michigan	MI		
Minnesota	MN		
Mississippi	MS		
Missouri	MO		
Montana	MT		
Nebraska	NE		
Nevada	NV		
New Hampshire	NH		
New Jersey	NJ		
New Mexico	NM		
New York	NY		
North Carolina	NC		

FROM MY FILES: PANDEMONIUM

My office is at the end of a hall in the college library. Downstairs are the stacks where students browse and sometimes study. There is a stairway from my floor to the first floor, but it is only meant to be ornamental, and it is not to be used. There is a door leading to the staircase, however, and a sign on the door. At least ten times a week, someone will open the door to traipse down the stairs. The moment the door is ajar, a loud, piercing alarm begins to wail. It's no wonder that, despite the sign on the door, innocents continue to open it and to create pandemonium. The foolish sign-makers hung these words on the door:

NO ENTRANCE
ALARM WILL SOUND

The sign makes it sound as if there is no alarm that will sound. It should read:

NO ENTRANCE.
ALARM WILL SOUND.

Punctuation makes all the difference.

THE COMMA

The comma is a mark of separation. It may divide items in a series, distinguish subordinate from main clauses, and insert stylistic pauses, among other things. The comma is a useful tool, but it is all too often misused. Please pay close attention to the dos and don'ts that follow. They will start you on your way to becoming the master of the comma.

WITH ADVERBIAL CLAUSES

Do place a comma after an adverbial clause that begins a sentence.

> Until we have your final report, we cannot make a decision.
>
> Because we are such great friends, I am asking you for this favor.

When the adverbial clause ends the sentence, the comma is optional. Use a comma if you feel that it clarifies the meaning of the sentence or makes the sentence easier to read.

> We cannot make a decision until we have your final report.

or   We cannot make a decision, until we have your final report.

> I am asking you for this favor because we are such great friends.

or   I am asking you for this favor, because we are such great friends.

WITH VERBALS

Do place a comma after a participle phrase, a simple infinitive, or an infinitive phrase (see Chapter 5) that introduces a sentence.

> Seeing her again, I felt my heart go pitter-patter.

> To fly, one needs a strong pair of wings.

> To win this competition, we must trust each other completely.

Please **do not** place a comma after an infinitive that functions as the subject of the sentence.

> To drive a Porsche would be an exhilarating experience.

> To sail the high seas was a childhood fantasy of mine.

WITH PREPOSITIONAL PHRASES

Do place a comma after a prepositional phrase that begins a sentence if you feel that the comma clarifies the meaning or makes the sentence easier to read. This comma is optional.

> After the concert, we stopped for a cup of coffee.

or   After the concert we stopped for a cup of coffee.

> In Sweden, we toured the royal palace.

or   In Sweden we toured the royal palace.

WITH CONJUNCTIVE ADVERBS

Do use commas to set off a conjunctive adverb from the sentence of which it is a part. If a conjunctive adverb begins the sentence, place a single comma after it. If a conjunctive adverb appears amidst the other words in the sentence, place a comma before and after it.

> Consequently, the freighter sank just three miles from its home port.

> Sherman said, however, that he could not let these mistakes go unreported.

WITH NEGATIVE AND AFFIRMATIVE ADVERBS

Do place a comma after a negative or affirmative adverb (**no** or **yes**) that begins a sentence.

> Yes, that is Merv Griffin.

> No, I will not buy you a velvet Elvis.

WITH NOUNS IN DIRECT ADDRESS

Do use commas to set off nouns in direct address.

> Mr. Grennan, assume the push-up position.

> I told you, Ms. Stevens, that we no longer sell garlic shakes.

WITH INTERJECTIONS

Do place a comma after an interjection at the beginning of a sentence.

> Oh, I didn't expect to see you here.

> Well, that was certainly an unusual movie.

WITH APPOSITIVES

Do place commas before and after appositives in the midst of the words in a sentence.

> Jennifer, the consummate hostess, put together another staggering dinner party.

> I sent my complaint to Herb Lornthorpe, the head of employee relations, but haven't received a response.

If an appositive ends the sentence, a comma need only precede it.

> I met my best friend, Susan.

> That's Herbie, my dog.

WITH THREE OR MORE ITEMS IN A SERIES

Do use commas to separate the items in a series of three or more words, phrases, or clauses.

> I need you to buy olive oil, sun dried tomatoes, and paprika for me.

> We looked around the yard, by the pond, in the cave, and along the tracks.

> I sheared the wool, Beth spun the yarn, and Agnes knit the sweater.

> A dank, oily, and gray cloud of smoke bellowed out from the machine's innards.

WITH ADJECTIVES

Do place a comma between two adjectives that describe the same noun and that precede the noun they describe when no coordinate conjunction is present.

> A damp, gray day greeted us this morning.

> Our chicken dinner benefited from those large, aromatic cloves of garlic.

Do not place a comma between two adjectives that modify the same noun when the first adjective modifies the entire idea created by the second adjective and the noun modified.

> The brave young man rode into battle without fear.

In this example, the adjective **brave** describes the noun phrase **young man**. He is a young man who is brave. The braveness affects the youngness.

Adding a comma would imply that we could have written the sentence with the conjunction **and** between the two adjectives without changing the meaning. However, we would never write the sentence in this way:

> The brave *and* young man rode into battle without fear.

We are writing of a young man who is brave, not a man who is brave and young.

WITH COORDINATE CONJUNCTIONS

Do place a comma before a coordinate conjunction that separates two main clauses of a compound sentence.

> I saw the game, but I don't remember the final score.

> She drove us to the market, and I bought another pack of cream soda.

Do not place a comma before a coordinate conjunction that connects two subordinate clauses.

> Because time is short, and because the matter is so urgent, we must act now. (incorrect)

The first comma in this sentence, the one that appears before the conjunction **and**, is unnecessary. The sentence should read as follows:

> Because time is short and because the matter is so urgent, we must act now. (correct)

That first comma is gone, and all is well.

TO INDICATE OMISSIONS

Do use a comma to indicate the omission of a word.

> Frank is a strong man, and Hank, a clever man.

In this example, the second comma marks the omission of the main verb **is**. We could have written the sentence as follows:

> Frank is a strong man, and Hank is a clever man.

TO SET OFF PHRASES OF CONTRAST

Do use a comma to set off a phrase of contrast at the end of a sentence.

> Jeff told her to chop the onion, not dice it.

> Bev ordered the shrimp salad, not the chicken salad.

> The concert was loud, yet dull.

TO SET OFF INTERROGATIVE CLAUSES

Do use a comma to separate a declarative clause from an interrogative clause that follows it.

> She has beautiful eyes, doesn't she?

> This is the place, isn't it?

WITH QUOTED MATERIAL

Do use commas to set off quoted material from the main body of the sentence in sentences that contain quotes. If the main body precedes the quote, one comma appears between the end of the main body and the start of the quote.

> Terry said, "Bring me the flashlight."

> The speaker wondered, "Do any of you understand what I am talking about?"

In these cases the commas appear outside of the quotation marks.

If the main body follows the quote, one comma appears between the end of the quote and the beginning of the main body.

> "I am overjoyed," my mother cried.

> "I think that music is going to drive me crazy," John said.

In these cases the commas appear inside the quotation marks.

If the main body comes between the pieces of a broken quote, two commas separate the quote from the body, one before and one after the body.

> "What," she asked, "is the point of this display?"

The comma between the first piece of quote and the main body appears inside the quotation marks. The comma between the second piece of quote and the main body appears outside the quotation marks.

WITH SALUTATIONS

Do place a comma after the salutation in an informal letter and after the complimentary close in an informal or formal letter.

> Dear Wendy,
>
>   Thank you so much . . . .

> Your friend,
> Stephen

WITH DATES

Do place a comma between the day and year in a date.

January 8, 1702   August 14, 1998   May 1, 1004

Some authorities also feel that a writer must *always* place a comma after the year in a date used in a sentence. The authors and editors of this book, however, recommend that such commas be excluded when the date is used as the subject of a sentence.

On November 4, 1972, a miracle occurred. (date used as *object* of preposition)

March 17, 1948 is her birthday. (date used as *subject* of sentence)

WITH ADDRESSES AND LOCATIONS

Do place a comma between the elements of an address or geographic location.

His address is Vern Nutley, 57 Hawthorne Way, Rockford, IL 61114.

Bentley visited Greenwich, CT, over the break.

The comma after **CT** in the second example is correct. You need to place a comma after the final element in an address or geographic location when that element falls before the end of the sentence.

WITH TITLES

Do use a comma to separate a name from titles that may follow. If multiple titles follow, place a comma between each title and the next.

John Addison, Ph.D., M.D. has agreed to consult on the research project.

William Ray Bedford, Sr. called his family together for an emergency meeting.

WITH NUMBERS

Do use commas to separate sets of three digits in numbers one thousand and greater.

1,927   50, 876   1,408, 863

WITH NAMES

Do place a comma after the last name in a list where the first and last names have been inverted.

> Frampton, Peter
>
> Lightfoot, Gordon
>
> Willis, Bruce

TO ELIMINATE AMBIGUITY

Do place commas in sentences when the placement eliminates ambiguity. Read the following ambiguous sentences without commas.

> Before Mary Lou was our accountant.
>
> The finer the silk the higher the price.

As they stand, these sentences are a bit confusing. They need commas for their meanings to become clear.

> Before Mary, Lou was our accountant.
>
> The finer the silk, the higher the price.

WITH NONRESTRICTIVE AND RESTRICTIVE INFORMATION

Do use commas to set off nonrestrictive words, phrases, and clauses.

> My only sister, Bernie, is coming for a visit next month.
>
> Many dogs, such as poodles and dachshunds, do not contribute to home security.
>
> The particulars of the game, which I have never learned, are terribly confusing.

In each sentence, the word, phrase, or clause set off by commas is nonrestrictive because it does not change the meaning of the sentence. These words, phrases, and clauses describe an antecedent rather than limit or define it.

Do not use commas to set off restrictive words, phrases, or clauses. Such items define or limit the meanings of their antecedents. The use of commas would indicate that the meanings they provide are not essential.

My brother Timmy graduated at the top of his class.

Times like these test the strength of familial ties.

The man who gave you that information cannot be trusted.

The information that the word, phrase, or clause provides in each example is essential and restrictive, so we do not set it off with commas. In the first example, the proper noun **Timmy** identifies which brother graduated at the top of his class. The speaker must have more than one. In the second example, the phrase **like these** limits the definition of the noun **times**. It tells us just what kind of times we are discussing. In the third example, the clause **who gave you that information** tells us which man the speaker is mentioning. Without the noun **Timmy**, the phrase **like these**, and the clause **who gave you that information**, the meanings of the sentences would be quite different.

AVOID COMMA SPLICES

Do not place a comma between main clauses unless it is accompanied by a coordinate conjunction.

Harry robbed the bank, Billy drove the escape car. (incorrect)

This sentence contains a comma splice. We need to change the comma to a period or a semicolon, replace the comma with a conjunction, or add a conjunction.

Harry robbed the bank. Billy drove the escape car. (correct)

Harry robbed the bank; Billy drove the escape car. (correct)

Harry robbed the bank and Billy drove the escape car. (correct)

Harry robbed the bank, and Billy drove the escape car. (correct)

Each of these sentences is acceptable. Remember that a comma is not required when a compound sentence is composed of two main clauses and those two main clauses are short.

A COMMA QUESTION

Q. "Please tell me what this sentence means?" asked a piano teacher. "It goes, 'Those who can practice ten hours a day.' "

A. As it stands, the sentence has a problem with its verb. There seems to be a verb phrase, **can practice**, in a relative clause beginning with the pronoun **who**—**who can practice**—but the resulting sentence doesn't make any sense. We need a comma to help us eliminate the ambiguity.

> Those who can, practice ten hours a day.

Now, the purposes of the two verbs become clear. The former, **can**, is part of the relative clause **who can**. The latter, **practice**, is the verb in the main clause **those practice ten hours a day**. The sentence is informing us that those who are able to practice ten hours a day do so.

COMMAS WITHIN A SERIES OF ITEMS

Q. "When you have items in a series, do you put commas after each one?" asked a secretary for a large shipping firm. "Here is my sentence. 'The company needs notification of what is important relevant or new for the new season.'"

A. If there are three or more items in a series and a coordinate conjunction between the last two, expert grammarians will recommend placing a comma after each item in the series (including the item before the coordinate conjunction) except the last. The secretary's sentence contains a series of three adjectives: **important**, **relevant**, and **new**. The coordinate conjunction **or** connects the final two. This fellow must place commas between his items.

> The company needs notification of what is important, relevant, or new for the new season.

BACON AND EGGS AND COMMAS

Q. A nurse, transcribing the description of a patient's meal, asked, "Where should I put commas in this sentence: 'The patient had coffee bacon and eggs and orange juice.'?"

A. The sentence contains a series of three or four items, the last two of which are connected by the coordinate conjunction **and**. Whether the series is of three or four items depends upon whether we consider bacon and eggs to be a single unit or two separate items. With bacon and eggs as a single unit, the sentence reads as follows:

> The patient had coffee, bacon and eggs, and orange juice.

With bacon and eggs as two separate items, we must remove the conjunction **and** between them before we insert the commas. The sentence would appear as follows:

The patient had coffee, bacon, eggs, and orange juice.

However, most people, through common usage, have come to regard bacon and eggs as a single unit. Colloquial speech, therefore, would dictate that the former interpretation is correct. The rule is certainly not hard and fast, and, if the latter option suits you, that is fine. It is just that most people would naturally pick the former.

A Judgment Call

Q. "Should I place a comma between **rough** and **wood** in the phrase **rough, wood fence**?" asked a newly retired lady who was building a new house.

A. The adjectives **rough** and **wood** both describe the noun **fence**. Our comma rules recommend that the writer place a comma between two adjectives in a series if both describe the same noun and no coordinate conjunction separates them. Without the commas, we might be talking about wood that is rough, rather than a fence that is rough.

To determine whether or not a comma should be placed between the two adjectives, insert the word **and** between them. If the presence of the conjunction does not change the meaning of the sentence, the comma is appropriate. Otherwise, no comma is necessary. Just don't forget to remove the **and** which you inserted.

Purified Punctuation

Q. A forest ranger asked, "Do I need the commas in this sentence: 'Water, which is boiled, is safe to drink'?"

A. Whether we place commas around the subordinate clause **which is boiled** depends upon whether we feel that it is restrictive or nonrestrictive information. Nonrestrictive information requires commas. Restrictive information does not.

It seems to the Hot Line that the clause **which is boiled** is absolutely necessary to the meaning of the sentence. I think we can assume that only *boiled* water is safe to drink. The modifying effect of the clause is essential. Therefore, the commas are unnecessary.

Water which is boiled is safe to drink.

The ranger could also pick a better phrasing for his sentence.

Boiled water is safe to drink.

A COMMA SPLICE

Q. A writer with an active word processing business wrote this sentence and wanted to know if the commas were necessary. Her sentence read, "We don't know if he took his medicine, however, we hope he did."

A. The writer has placed a comma between two complete thoughts (main clauses) and created a comma splice, a mistake that writers and grammarians consider quite serious. The first complete thought is **we don't know if he took his medicine**. The second is **however, we hope he did**. This writer needs to separate the two thoughts with a semicolon or a period.

We don't know if he took his medicine; however, we hope he did.

We don't know if he took his medicine. However, we hope he did.

The comma after the conjunctive adverb **however** is fine.

FOR CLARIFICATION

Q. "Is a subordinate clause ever separated from a main clause by a comma?" a typesetter asked.

A. Of the three varieties of subordinate clause, only the adverbial clause requires a comma to separate it from the main clause. Remember that the adverbial clause often answers one of the adverb questions: when?, where?, how?, or how often?

If the adverbial clause starts the complex sentence, we must place a comma after it:

As you might have guessed, I'm not feeling too well.

As you might have guessed is an adverbial clause. It begins the sentence, so we place a comma between it and the main clause **I'm not feeling too well**.

If the adverbial clause had ended the complex sentence, the comma would have been optional:

I'm not feeling too well, as you might have guessed.

or   I'm not feeling too well as you might have guessed.

A MATURE QUESTION

Q. This caller asked, "Do I need a comma before the **and** in this sentence: 'As a person gets older and as she becomes more mature she begins to look at things differently.' "

A. Well, a comma definitely belongs after the word **mature** since the word ends an adverbial clause that begins the sentence. The caller, however, thought that she might need a comma before the coordinate conjunction **and**. I told her that a comma in that spot was unnecessary. **As a person gets older** and **as she becomes more mature** are both adverbial clauses in a series. Since the series consists of just two items, the conjunction **and** is sufficient to connect them. No comma is necessary. This is how the sentence should read:

As a person gets older and as she becomes more mature, she begins to look at things differently.

APPOSITIVE PUNCTUATION

Q. "How do I punctuate appositives?" asked a caller who was helping her daughter finish her homework.

A. Remember that an appositive is a word or phrase that is placed beside another word to rename, explain, or enhance it. How one should punctuate the appositive depends on whether it is nonrestrictive or restrictive. Nonrestrictive appositives are set off from the rest of the sentence by commas, while restrictive appositives require no punctuation.

She lives in a beautiful city, Santa Monica. (nonrestrictive)

Shakespeare's play *As You Like It* is one of my favorites. (restrictive)

In the first example, the appositive **Santa Monica** is nonrestrictive, so we set it off from the rest of the sentence with a comma. Since the appositive ends the sentence, we need use only one comma. In the second example, the appositive *As You Like It* is restrictive, so we do not use any punctuation.

FROM MY FILES: ON THE IMPORTANCE OF COMMAS

A Russian nobleman had been sentenced to hard labor in Siberia for opposing the Czar. The night before the nobleman was to be sentenced, a friend sneaked into the imperial palace and found the order that would send the poor man to a life of misery. The order read, "Pardon impossible, to be sent to Siberia." With a few quick strokes of his quill and some clever embellishment of letters to hide the previous punctuation, the friend was able to move the comma one word back in the sentence so that it then read, "Pardon, impossible to be sent to Siberia." The fortunate nobleman was set free.

THE COLON

Those two little dots we know as the colon often indicate a strong break in a sentence and mean "as follows." In fact, the colon often follows the words **following** and **as follows**.

WITH APPOSITIVES

The colon can emphasize an appositive at the end of a sentence.

> There is only one word that can describe the President's decision: ridiculous.

> I have only one thing to say to you: "Get a life."

WITH LISTS

Use a colon to introduce a list that appears at the end of a sentence.

> Mom asked us to get these things from the grocer's: bread, milk, and cheese.

WITH QUOTED MATERIAL

Use a colon to introduce a long quote.

> The first page of the novel reads as follows:

> > "It was a dark and stormy night . . . ."

WITH PAGE SPECIFICATIONS

Use a colon to separate the pieces of a page specification.

John 3:16

The New Republic 22:72

Chapter 8: Section 7

WITH RATIOS

Use a colon to separate the numbers in a ratio.

Combine the three chemicals in a 3:5:1 ratio.

WITH TIME

Use a colon to separate the elements in written time.

By Greenwich mean time, it is 22:34:56:05.

WITH TITLES AND SUBTITLES

Use a colon to separate the title and subtitle of a book.

I just read a book called *Too Many Hats: A Man and His Compulsions.*

WITH SALUTATIONS

Place a colon after the salutation in a formal letter.

Dear Ms. Flatchet:

I am writing to express my displeasure . . . .

QUESTION: COMMA OR COLON?

Q. A fledgling writer asked, "Before I quote someone's words, should I use a comma or a colon?"

A. Unless it is a long quote, use a comma to separate the main body of the sentence from the quoted material.

Mary said, "I'm ready to quit today; let's go home."

Ali said, "I'm still the champ."

Writers often use colons to introduce long quotes.

> This tedious book began with a twelve line description of her shoes:
>
>> "The color of her shoes matched the color of the sky that afternoon . . . ."

THE SEMICOLON

The semicolon indicates a stronger pause than the comma but a weaker pause than the period. Though a useful tool, the semicolon must be employed cautiously. Misused, this mark of punctuation can result in overly wordy and convoluted sentences. These are the rules governing the use of the semicolon:

WITH COMPOUND SENTENCES

The semicolon may separate main clauses in a compound sentence when no coordinate conjunction is used. The meanings of the two clauses should be closely related for the semicolon to be appropriate punctuation.

> I woke up; I got out of bed.

> Their house is a mess; their yard is a disgrace.

The semicolon may also separate main clauses in a compound sentence when a conjunctive adverb introduces the second clause.

> Your plan is insane; nevertheless, it is our only hope.

> Santa didn't bring the toys we expected; instead, he left socks and underwear.

The semicolon may separate main clauses linked by a coordinate conjunction in a compound sentence when one or both of the clauses contain internal punctuation and additional commas would create a muddled sentence.

> Mr. Stafford, president of this corporation and corporate genius, has predicted a banner year; but his reasoning is not beyond reproach.

> The chef at this restaurant, which I have never liked, makes terrible bouillabaisse; but we will eat wherever you like on your birthday.

WITH ITEMS IN A SERIES

The semicolon may separate items in a series when one or more of the items contain internal punctuation. The use of commas as separators in this situation would result in confusion.

> The guest list includes Bill, my cousin; Susan, my best friend; and Arnold, my annoying brother.

> Tommy Gissard, the movie star; Harry Tupins, the publisher; and Blue Eisen, the model, donated their time to this charity event.

THE APOSTROPHE

The apostrophe is used to indicate plural and possessive forms of words or to indicate missing letters and digits. We will take a brief look at each use now.

WITH POSSESSIVE NOUNS

The apostrophe is used to create the possessive forms of nouns. With singular and plural nouns that do not end in **s**, place apostrophe **s** ('s) at the end of the word to create the possessive form.

SINGULAR:	dog → dog's	chef → chef's	William → William's
PLURAL:	geese → geese's	men → men's	feet → feet's

With singular nouns that do end in **s**, add apostrophe **s** ('s). We should stick to the general rule when we can.

boss → boss's	Jones → Jones's	bus → bus's
lass → lass's	class → class's	Charles → Charles's

Please note that there are several exceptions to this rule:

1. The possessive forms of the names **Jesus** and **Moses** take a simple apostrophe.

> Jesus → Jesus'   Moses → Moses'

2. The possessive forms of names of more than one syllable that end in **s** and whose final syllable has an /ēz/ sound take only an apostrophe.

> Euripides → Euripides'   Socrates → Socrates'
> Ramses → Ramses'

Please remember, however, that most of these are names of long-deceased Greek philosophers or Egyptian pharaohs and of little concern to the general populace.

3. When the object of the preposition in the expression **for** *something's* **sake** ends in **s**, that object takes only an apostrophe.

for goodness' sake   for Jones' sake

To add apostrophe **s** ('s) would give us three **s** sounds in a row and that is too many for an articulate speaker to make.

With plural nouns that end in **s**, just add an apostrophe.

tigers → tigers'	boys → boys'	hearts → hearts'
rats → rats'	beasts → beasts'	militias → militias'

WITH PLURALS OF LETTERS AND ABBREVIATIONS

The apostrophe is used to create the plural forms of letters and abbreviations.

1. To form the plurals of single letters, add apostrophe **s** ('s): R's, t's.

2. To form the plurals of abbreviations with internal periods, add apostrophe **s** ('s): Ph.D.'s, M.D.'s.

For more information on pluralizing letters and abbreviations, please refer to Chapter 1, p. 15.

WITH CONTRACTIONS

The apostrophe is used in contractions to indicate missing letters.

is not → isn't   he is → he's   could not → couldn't

WITH MISSING LETTERS

We often pronounce words in a colloquial manner, leaving off a letter or two. When these colloquially spoken words are written, we use apostrophes to indicate the missing letters.

That ol' car has served me well.

In this example, the adjective **old** has been shortened into **ol'**. The apostrophe stands in for the missing **d**.

WITH MISSING DIGITS

The apostrophe appears in numbers to indicate missing digits.

$1981 \rightarrow '81$ $1917 \rightarrow '17$ $1941 \rightarrow '41$

THE POSSESSIVE DICKENS

Q. "I collect first editions. My favorites are by Charles Dickens. Do I write that they are *Dicken's*, *Dickens'*, or *Dickens's* novels?" asked a book collector.

A. The apostrophe rules advise that you add apostrophe **s** (**'s**) to show possession with singular nouns that end in **s**. The phrase **Dickens's novels** is the correct choice.

This is a difficult and controversial issue. There are two schools of thought regarding the use of the apostrophe with singular nouns: the pro-apostrophe **s** camp and the apostrophe only camp. The latter camp suggests that we add only the apostrophe and eliminate the **s**. Some books say to do it one way; some say to do it the other; some say that both ways are all right, depending upon the writer's preference. This writer is of the apostrophe **s** (**'s**) camp, but you should choose the method that you feel communicates the idea of possession most effectively.

THE FOLLOW-UP CALL

Q. That same book collector phoned the Hot Line a few nights later with another question. He said, "I've been thinking about this whole **Dickens's** thing, and it's got me wondering. How do I pronounce **Dickens's**?' Do I say the word with two **s** sounds at the end—to be honest, that way sounds awful—or do I pronounce it with one **s**?"

A. Our inquisitive book collector had raised an important point. The way we spell a word does not always match the way that we pronounce it. In this caller's case, we pronounce the word **Dickens's** in the same way that we would the word **Dickens**, as if the former ended in a single **s** sound.

Possessive pronunciation becomes an issue with singular nouns that end in **s**. Since we add apostrophe **s** (**'s**) to these words to create their possessive forms, they appear to end with two **s** sounds. Such pronunciations may seem awkward, but, in practice, are not. The rules to follow are these:

1. If the word ends in **s's** and is of only one syllable, it is pronounced as if it ended with **es** in the place of the apostrophe **s** ('s). The word **bus's** is pronounced in the same manner as the word **buses**, the word **class's** is pronounced in the same manner as the word **classes**, the word **Gus's** is pronounced in the same manner as the word **Guses**, and so on.

2. If the word ends in **s's** and is of two or more syllables, it is pronounced as if the apostrophe **s** ('s) had never been added. The word **Charles's** is pronounced in the same manner as the word **Charles**, the word **Williams's** is pronounced in the same manner as the word **Williams**, and so on.

The Program for Proper Punctuation

Q. "How do you write the possessive form of **Mr. Powers** in the phrase 'Mr. Powers program'?" asked a systems analyst who readily admitted that his high-tech education had not included much of what he now finds mandatory for survival.

A. As with all other singular nouns, just add apostrophe **s** ('s): Mr. Powers's program. Remember that the pronunciations of the words **Powers** and **Powers's** are the same.

Sports Writers and Apostrophes

Q. A sports writer asked, "Do I need apostrophes in this headline: 'Clippers loss is Hornets win'?"

A. The loss belongs to the Clippers and the win belongs to the Hornets. Both team names need to be in their possessive forms. Since the words **Clippers** and **Hornets** are singular collective nouns, we add apostrophe **s** ('s) after each.

Clippers's loss is Hornets's win.

This Stuff Isn't Easy

Q. "Where do I put apostrophes in this sentence: 'They met with the railways divisions counsel'?" asked a vice president of public relations who was puzzled by a press release he had written.

A. First, we needed to determine which words were possessive. The VP indicated that the divisions belonged to the railway and that the counsel belonged to the divisions.

Second, we needed to know whether the noun **railway** was singular or plural. The VP said that he was writing only of the railway that he worked for, so we put an apostrophe between the **y** and the **s** in railway. One would add apostrophe **s** ('s) to create the possessive form of the singular noun **railway**.

That left the word **divisions** to be dealt with. Since something divided always has at least two divisions, I assumed it to be plural. To make this noun possessive, we added an apostrophe after the **s**. Simply add an apostrophe to create the possessive forms of plural nouns that end in **s**. The VP's amended sentence read:

They met with the railway's divisions' counsel.

APOSTROPHIED DEGRESS

Q. A caller from the Dean of Instruction's office at an Eastern university asked, "Should the titles **Bachelors Degree** and **Masters Degree** contain apostrophes since the degrees belong to the master or the bachelor?"

A. There are two approaches. For sheer elegance, The National Grammar Hot Line recommends not using the apostrophe. Grammatically, however, an apostrophe does belong in each word: **Bachelor's Degree** and **Master's degree**. In the battle between grammatical correctness and aesthetics, I side with the former.

POSSESSIVE YEARS

Q. A legal researcher at the District Attorney's office was composing a document regarding an individual previously incarcerated. He asked, "Do I need to put an apostrophe somewhere in the word **years** in this sentence: 'The board gave him three years probation'?"

A. Since the probation belongs to the years, we need to put the word **years** in its possessive form. The apostrophe rules mandate that we add a lone apostrophe to this plural noun.

The board gave him three years' probation.

Wasn't that easy?

SETTLING A DISPUTE

Q. A call came from the president of the student council at a local high school with an interesting question regarding apostrophes. She and the editor of the school's paper were arguing about the plural of the phrase **student body**. The president felt that the plural of **student body** should be **student bodies**. The editor felt that the plural of **student body** should be **student body's**. The sentence under dispute was this:

> The student bodies/body's from several high schools came together at the tournament.

A. The matter was easily solved. The editor had confused his plurals and his possessives. The plural of the noun **body** is **bodies**. The word **body's** indicates possession or ownership.

> The student body's mascot was a large green rabbit.

The president of the student council won this battle. Her sentence was correctly printed in the school paper.

> The student bodies from several high schools came together at the tournament.

EVENTFUL APOSTROPHES

Q. "Do we need an apostrophe in this statement: 'Mayors Office of Special Events Music Alive Nights'?" asked a caller from the Chicago mayor's office.

A. The sentence contains two apostrophe issues, the first of which is easily solved. Since the office belongs to the mayor, we need to insert an apostrophe between the **r** and the **s** in the word **mayors**.

The second issue requires a more complex resolution. Since the "Music Alive Nights" belong to the Office of Special Events, we must somehow make the noun phrase **Office of Special Events** possessive. To do so, we make the last word in the noun phrase possessive. **Events** is a plural noun that ends in **s**, so we add a lone apostrophe (') after the **s**. The amended statement would read as follows:

> Mayor's Office of Special Events' Music Alive Nights

The Hot Line then asked the caller to consider rewriting her sentence into a more understandable form. We suggested a statement such as this one:

Mayor's Office of Special Events Hosts Music Alive Nights

The caller concurred, and the deed was done.

THE QUESTION MARK

Some say that the shape of the question mark is based on the curving tail of that enigmatic and beloved creature, the cat. This is only a rumor and should be taken as all rumors should: with a grain of salt. These are the rules that govern the use of the question mark:

WITH DIRECT INTERROGATIVE SENTENCES

The question mark ends all direct interrogative sentences.

What did you order?

Can I have another cookie?

WITH IMPERATIVE SENTENCES WRITTEN AS QUESTIONS

Either a question mark or a period may end an imperative sentence written as a question.

Will you please stop that infernal racket?

or   Will you please stop that infernal racket.

Would you fetch the paper, Deary?

or   Would you fetch the paper, Deary.

WITH INTERROGATIVE SENTENCE ELEMENTS

We can place question marks after each interrogative element in a sentence that contains multiple questions.

Are you sure of her loyalty? her skill? her determination?

TO INDICATE UNCERTAINTY

Question marks often appear in parentheses in a sentence to indicate uncertainty about some piece of information given.

King Monty ruled between 1015 (?) and 1030 A.D.

The divers discovered twelve (?) bronze statues among the undersea ruins.

RHETORICAL QUESTIONS

Q. "If a question is rhetorical, does it deserve a question mark?" wondered a teacher of English.

A. No question mark is required with a rhetorical question. In fact, neither indirect nor rhetorical questions require question marks since they are more commands or statements than questions.

A rhetorical question is defined as one which is asked for effect rather than in expectation of an answer. The answer is usually very obvious, and the speaker already knows the answer.

How many times do I have to tell you to shut the door.

What is the meaning of this.

The indirect question asks a question in a declarative manner. The difference between the direct and indirect questions will be subtle.

DIRECT: What kind of pasta is that?

INDIRECT: She asked what kind of pasta that is.

The direct question always ends with a question mark.

THE EXCLAMATION MARK

The exclamation mark indicates strong emotion, surprise, or urgency. These are the situations in which its use is appropriate:

WITH DECLARATIVE SENTENCES

The exclamation mark ends any declarative sentence that is written with the force of an exclamation.

I have never been so disgusted!

This is the most awful concoction I have ever had the displeasure of consuming!

WITH IMPERATIVE SENTENCES

The exclamation mark ends any imperative sentence that is made with the force of an exclamation.

Watch out for that tree!

Come back here!

WITH INTERJECTIONS

We sometimes place exclamation marks after interjections. Often, the sentence that follows is made with the force of an exclamation.

Ouch! That stings!

Pshaw! I don't believe that for a second!

WITH INTERROGATIVE SENTENCES

The exclamation mark sometimes ends interrogative sentences that are written as exclamations.

Do you realize what this will do to our company!

How can you think that!

WITH EXCLAMATORY SENTENCES

The exclamation mark always ends exclamatory sentences.

How big your teeth are!

What a weekend we had!

PARENTHESES

WITH EXPLANATIONS OR COMMENTARY

Parentheses enclose words, phrases, clauses, and sentences that are included in a sentence as explanations or commentary but that are main constructions unto themselves. The punctuation for parenthetical items remains within the parentheses. Punctuate the primary portion of the sentence as if the parenthetical portion were not there.

Jack acted surprised (as if he didn't know) when Rachel told him the news.

She promised (she has never kept a promise in her life) to pass on the information.

Those boys (Bob, Harry, and Andy) will cause no end of trouble.

WITH NUMBERS, LETTERS, AND SYMBOLS

Parentheses often enclose numbers, letters, and symbols that are used as appositives in sentences.

The price of this meal ($200.00) is outrageous.

We will use the ampersand (&) in place of the word **and** in the title.

I disagree with the third item (C) on the agenda.

WITH DIVIDERS AND SUBDIVIDERS

Parentheses enclose numbers and letters that divide and subdivide items in a sentence.

The rebels' plan is to (1) take over the television station, (2) urge the citizens to revolution through hourly freedom broadcasts, and (3) topple the communist regime.

The items on the shopping list include (a) motor oil, (b) tissue paper, (c) ground beef, and (d) turnips.

BRACKETS

WITH INFORMATION INSERTED INTO QUOTED MATERIAL

Brackets enclose information that an editor inserts into a quote.

The story read, "When it [the Crystal Park Hotel and Casino] opened last fall, it was a gambler's dream."[†]

WITH PARENTHETICAL MATERIAL WITHIN PARENTHESES

Brackets also enclose parenthetical material within parentheses.

He (the driver of the car [a Ferrarri]) had the car going over one hundred miles per hour when he was stopped.

THE HYPHEN

WITH WORDS IN A COMPOUND

The hyphen links multiple words into a single expression.

Don't look at me with that holier-than-thou expression.

This town is full of has-beens and wanna-bes.

[†] Leeds, Jeff. "Tough Times at Compton Casino," *Los Angeles Times*, October 6, 1997.

WITH PREFIXES

The hyphen is often placed between the root word and a prefix when the alternative (no hyphen) can be easily misread.

> Despite his record, the company decided to re-employ Mr. David Jones.

> The city officials are taking a pro-orthodoxy standpoint.

WITH WORDS BROKEN OVER TWO LINES

When a word is broken between the end of one line and the beginning of the next, place the hyphen after the first piece to indicate that the remainder will follow on the next line.

> Marjorie and Her Singing Spaniels are to perform their **rendition** of Handel's Messiah this Thursday. It is an event not to be missed.

MORE FUN WITH HYPHENS

Q. "Please tell me about hyphens. I feel like I never know where to put them," despaired a fledgling copywriter.

A. Hyphens are really very simple. And, they have a few uses in addition to those mentioned above.

1. Hyphens are used to separate syllables in words.

> in-te-ri-or
>
> plan-e-tar-y
>
> rhyth-mi-cal

Please remember that each syllable in an English word must contain at least one vowel. If none of the five regular vowels (**a**, **e**, **i**, **o**, and **u**) are present, count **y** as a vowel.

2. Hyphens are also used to separate the words in the written form of a fraction.

> The vote passed by a two-thirds majority.

3. Hyphens are used in compound adjectives. A compound adjective consists of two or more words that are read as one and function as a single adjective. Since the two words cannot be joined into a single word, we place a hyphen between them.

> Those are sweet-smelling gardenias.

Thankfully, it was a well-planned meeting.

We live in an eighth-floor apartment.

4. Here's a short list to help you remember other words that need hyphens and a few that do not. *Always* hyphenate

- all forms of in-law: **brother-in-law, father-in-law**.
- all **great** compounds: **great-aunt, great-grandfather**.
- all **vice** compounds: **vice-consul, vice-chairperson**.
- all **elect** compounds: **mayor-elect, president-elect**.
- all **self** compounds: **self-taught, self-assured**.

Do not hyphenate

- any **ache** compound: **toothache, backache** (unless forced to at the end of a line).
- any **book** compound: **textbook, notebook** (unless forced to at the end of a line).

DOWNSIZING

Q. "Everyone at our company uses the word **downsizing**. Is it spelled as one word or two?" wondered a consultant from San Francisco.

A. There's an informal guideline that will tell you whether such constructions as **downsizing** are written as one word or two. When two words mean something different separately but, when joined together, take on a third meaning that is widely accepted, they can be written as one word. Therefore, it would be appropriate to squeeze **down** and **sizing** into one word: **downsizing**. If in doubt, check your dictionary.

THE IMPORTANCE OF HYPHENS

Q. A hospital administrator, baffled by the words given to him by a colleague, called for clarification. He asked, "How should this headline read: 'Lessons Learned from Multi Disciplinary Patient Focused Care Will Aid Future Patients at the Hospital'?"

A. Someone went mad with the lexicon here. I advised the caller to add hyphens for clarification. The headline should appear as follows:

Lessons Learned from Multi-Disciplinary Patient-Focused Care Will Aid Future Patients at the Hospital

The headline looks much better with the hyphens.

PREFIXES AND HYPHENS

Q. "When do I place a hyphen between a prefix and the rest of the word?" asked an accountant.

A. We place hyphens between root words and prefixes when the unhyphenated alternatives can be easily misread or misinterpreted. For instance, the noun meaning "to form again" is spelled **re-formation** while a similar noun meaning "a change" is spelled **reformation**. Similarly, the verb meaning "to form again" is spelled **re-form** while the verb meaning "to change" is spelled **reform**.

We also place hyphens between prefixes and root words that are proper nouns or proper adjectives: **non-Jewish**, **anti-American**, **pro-Israel**. The proper noun or adjective must begin with a capital letter. Without the hyphen, the small letter at the end of the prefix would sit next to the capital letter at the start of the noun or adjective: nonJewish, antiAmerican, proIsrael. This result is too strange, so we add the hyphen to separate them.

THE DASH

An extended hyphen, the dash (—), is primarily a stylistic mark. It usually sets off words that represent an abrupt change of thought or shift of flow in a sentence. Though it does have its place, the dash is a mark of punctuation that the conscientious author should use sparingly. There is often another mark that is more appropriate.

WITH PARENTHETICAL MATERIAL

The dash may set off parenthetical material. With the dash present, the parentheses are excluded. The use of the dash puts more emphasis on the word, phrase, or clause than a set of parentheses would.

> I am sure that the Wizard's force—and the other forces of Evil—will be waiting for our attack.

> From beneath his jacket he drew forth a device that turned our blood to ice—a nuclear detonator.

With Afterthoughts

The dash may set off and emphasize an afterthought at the end of a sentence.

> It is possible that we will not see each other for a long while—maybe never again.

With Dialogue

In dialogue, the dash may indicate hesitant or stumbling speech.

> His—his face was—it was covered with—with worms.

With Numbers and Dates

The dash is often placed between inclusive numbers and dates to replace one of the words **to** or **and**.

> Charlemagne ruled the Franks from 768–814.

> Ms. Creeper asked us to read pages 5–85 over the weekend.

A Dash Question

Q. "Can the dash replace a comma?" asked a studious printer's apprentice.

A. Yes, it is perfectly acceptable to replace a comma with a dash when the comma precedes a direct quote.

> Sherman said, "War is hell."

> Sherman said—"War is hell."

However, the version with the comma is preferable.

Here is a note for the curious. In print shop lingo, dashes are referred to as **em dashes** or **en dashes**, depending on their sizes. The em dash was formerly the width of the letter **M** of any given font and is now the width of a square of any type body used as a unit of measure. The em pica, for instance, is about one-sixth of an inch in width. The mark — is an em dash. The en dash is one-half the width of an em dash. The en dash,–, looks much like a hyphen and is mainly used between inclusive numbers and dates, as seen above.

ANOTHER DASH QUESTION

Q. "Do dashes ever belong with appositives?" asked an English tutor whose pupils were working on punctuation.

A. We often see dashes before such expressions as **namely** and **for instance**, expressions that introduce appositives.

Some kids—namely, the twins—are incorrigible.

This usage is perfectly acceptable.

STILL ANOTHER DASH QUESTION

Q. "Can I use a dash to introduce a list?" asked a writer of history textbooks.

A. Dashes may be used to introduce lists and also to introduce each item in a list as a bullet would.

These are the items that we need—

— chocolate

— flour

— sugar

— eggs

QUOTATION MARKS

Quotation marks come in two varieties: single and double. The more common of the two is the double quotation mark. We will tackle this variety first.

DOUBLE QUOTATION MARKS WITH QUOTED MATERIAL

Quotation marks enclose quoted material.

Then, the pig said, "But, we already have a chicken."

"Who," she asked, "is responsible for this debacle?"

Notice that each piece of the broken quote in the second example is surrounded by quotation marks and that only the first word in the quote is capitalized.

DOUBLE QUOTATION MARKS WITH TITLES

Quotation marks may enclose the titles of short works and portions of larger works, such as magazine articles, newspaper articles,
essays, short stories, songs, poems, chapters of books, short films,
sculptures, and paintings.

> Have you read the story "The Illustrated Man" by Ray
> Bradbury?

> I call this short film "T for Trombone."

DOUBLE QUOTATION MARKS WITH WORDS CALLED TO THE READER'S ATTENTION

Writers often enclose words in quotation marks to which they
wish to call the reader's attention. These include nicknames, slang,
and coined words or phrases, among others.

> John "Big Boy" Samuels has been a loyal friend of mine
> since we were kids.

> My son told me that my new hairstyle looks "fat," whatever
> that means.

> I suffer from "9021ophobia," the fear of the cast and charac-
> ters of the hit television series *Beverly Hills 90210*.

DOUBLE QUOTATION MARKS WITH REFERENCED WORDS, PHRASES, CLAUSES, AND SENTENCES

Quotation marks often enclose words, phrases, clauses, and
sentences that are referred to within a sentence.

> The origins of the word "grammar" are quite fascinating.

> I think the description "a few sandwiches short of a picnic"
> fits her well.

> The sentence "He took the time to take my temperature"
> contains alliteration.

Please note that the writers of *The Grammar Bible* have chosen to
place most of the words, phrases, and clauses referred to within
our sentences in bold-face rather than within quotation marks. We
refer to so many words, phrases, and clauses that quotation marks
would clog the pages of the book. This is a stylistic issue, and, for
the sake of our readers, we opted for the clarity and visual aesthetic of bold-faced print.

SINGLE QUOTATION MARKS

Single quotation marks enclose material that the standard double quotation marks would when that material is enclosed within a sentence already enclosed in double quotation marks.

> Bobby said, "Did you bother to consult Morty 'Bookworm' Morrison?"

> I said, "Jennifer said, 'You haven't heard the last of the Cromwells!' "

> The president commented, "Sadly, we are all victims of 'Reaganomics'!"

ANOTHER USE OF QUOTATION MARKS

Q. "Are quotation marks used to indicate irony?" asked a college student.

A. Quotation marks can be used to indicate irony, but only as a last resort, when the irony might otherwise be lost. A skillfully prepared ironic meaning should not elude the reader. Quotation marks should not be necessary.

QUOTATION MARKS AND OTHER MARKS OF PUNCTUATION

Punctuation can become most troublesome when the quotation marks come into play. It is usually obvious when and where the quotation marks are necessary, but what is not quite so obvious is how the other marks of punctuation should be placed in relation to those quotation marks. Many callers have phoned the Hot Line with questions on this issue, so we will let their calls show us the Way.

COMMAS, PERIODS, AND QUOTATION MARKS

Q. "Where do periods and commas go in relation to closing quotation marks?" asked an English teacher.

A. The comma and the period go inside the closing quotation marks at all times. There are no exceptions to this rule.

> My advisor told me, "You better pick another project."

> "That," she said, "is a large steak."

QUESTION MARKS AND QUOTATION MARKS

Q. "If a sentence ends with a quoted word or phrase, does the question mark belong inside or outside of the closing quote?" asked a state department researcher.

A. If the entire sentence, including the material within the closing quotes, is a question, place the question mark outside the quote.

> Did you see "La Bohème"?

Since the sentence itself is interrogative (it asks a question), the question mark affects more than just the quoted material and belongs outside the quote.

If only the quoted material is a question, place the question mark inside the closing quote.

> I heard you say, "When is the play over?"

Here, only the quoted material is interrogative. The sentence as a whole is declarative. Therefore, we place the question mark inside the closing quote.

EXCLAMATION MARKS AND QUOTATION MARKS

Q. Moments later, the same caller was back on the line. He asked, "What should I do with exclamation marks and closing quotes?"

A. I told him, "The very same rules apply. If the entire sentence, including the quoted material, is an exclamation, place the exclamation mark outside the quote.

> How awful it was to hear him say, 'I won't work'!

If only the quoted material is an exclamation, place the exclamation mark inside the closing quote.

> I heard him say, "I hate you!"

COLONS, SEMICOLONS, AND QUOTATION MARKS

Q. "Do any punctuation marks *always* go outside closing quotes?" a graduate student wondered.

A. There are only two marks of punctuation that are almost always placed outside closing quotes: the colon and the semicolon. Unless it is a part of the quoted material, you will never find one of these within the quotation marks.

> My teacher feels that these books are "highbrow reading": *Catcher in the Rye* by J.D. Salinger, *Remembrance of Things Past* by Marcel Proust, and *Ulysses* by James Joyce.

> My mother said, "You may not attend the dance!"; therefore, I know that I must attend.

SINGLE QUOTATION MARKS AND OTHER MARKS OF PUNCTUATION

Q. "What do I do with the punctuation next to single quotes within double quotes?" asked an assistant copy editor.

A. Among contemporary linguists, this is a controversial matter. The most important thing to remember in choosing a method of punctuation is that your marks should clarify, not confuse, the meaning of the sentence. In general, American-style punctuation suggests that we follow these three rules:

A GENERAL RULE

Place any mark of punctuation that belongs to the quoted material enclosed in single quotes within those single quotes.

> Bob said, "She asked me, 'Where should we go to eat?' "

> He said, "Then the policeman yelled, 'Stop!' "

SINGLE QUOTATION MARKS WITH PERIODS AND COMMAS

Place commas and periods that do not belong to the quoted material enclosed in single quotes within those single quotes unless you feel that such placement is confusing.

> I said, "Barry complained that he 'doesn't get any respect.' "

> Randy stated, "They call me Randy 'The Shrimp,' but I don't mind."

SINGLE QUOTATION MARKS WITH EXCLAMATION MARKS, QUESTION MARKS, SEMICOLONS, AND COLONS

Do not place exclamation marks, question marks, semicolons, and colons within single quotation marks unless they belong to the quotation within those single quotation marks.

He exclaimed, "I don't know the meaning of the word 'palatalize'!"

She asked, "What did he mean when he said, 'I'm never coming back'?"

SOME OTHER THINGS YOU SHOULD KNOW ABOUT PUNCTUATION

Here are a few more points to consider before our discussion of punctuation comes to an end:

PUNCTUATION OF BUSINESS LETTERS

Q. "I'm writing a business letter. Can I put a comma after the opening salutation, or is it a colon or a semicolon?" asked a bank manager.

A. The opening salutation of a formal letter is followed by a colon, never a comma or a semicolon. However, use a comma after the salutation in an informal letter. Commas are also appropriate in business letters written to friends.

SLASHES

Q. "What are the proper grammatical uses of the slash mark?" asked a post office clerk.

A. The slash mark, also known as the virgule, is used to mark the divisions between words, lines, and numbers. The word **virgule** comes from the Latin **virgula**, meaning "little rod." We often see the slash mark in the expression **and/or** and in the informal writing of a date between the day and the month and between the month and the year: **9/22/95**. The expression **in care of** is frequently abbreviated **c/o**.

ASTERISKS

Q. "Where did the asterisk come from?" asked a caller who had just finished formatting footnotes in a research papter.

A. This starlike sign (*) is used in print to refer the reader to footnotes, references, omissions, and the like. The word comes from the Greek word **asteriskos**, meaning "little star." You may have seen the flower, the aster. It resembles a star.

BULLETS

Q. "How do I use bullets?" asked a toy company representative. "I always list the virtues of our toys when I write letters to clients."

A. As the representative's remarks suggest, bullets (•) mark items in a list. If a sentence follows the bullet, place a period at its end. Words and phrases that follow bullets need no ending punctuation. It is never necessary to place the conjunction **and** before the list item in a bulleted list.

> Birthday Wish List:
>
> • Dynamo with Explosive Action Arm
>
> • Ballerina Bobby
>
> • Monkey Madness Playset

OTHER FORMATTING

Q. One caller commented, "I remember from my school days that we were told to underline titles of books in our papers. I'm writing a memo at work and it has a title in it. Does it need underlining or quotes or italics or what?"

A. There are very few rules to guide us when we need to set off a word or a group of words, such as a title, in our writing. Some people use quotation marks. Others insist on underlining. Still others use italics for the job. The issue is primarily stylistic. Whatever method offsets your word or words the most effectively is the one that you should use. In my opinion, underlining is overkill. Italics are more subtle and equally effective.

Despite the fuzzy nature of the issue, I would suggest some special formatting of a word or words that need to be offset from the main text in the following situations:

1. Foreign words and phrases should be placed in italics.

> The governor's steamy affair quickly became a *cause celebre*.

2. Words used as words should be set off in bold-faced or italicized type.

> The word **sinister** has interesting Latin origins.

or   The word *sinister* has interesting Latin origins.

3. The titles of books, newspapers, magazines, movies, plays, television shows, and works of art should be italicized.

> I've read *Watership Down* eight times.

> I laughed so hard during *The Foreigner* that my stomach hurt.

> *Seinfeld* is a brilliant television program.

Writing Dialogue

Q. A novelist, tired of writing **he said** or **she said** before each line of dialogue, asked if I knew of a simpler way to create conversation in writing.

A. I advised him to just start a new paragraph every time the speaker changes. The careful reader will easily follow the change and will appreciate the simplicity and brevity that the elimination of those **he saids** and **she saids** creates.

> "Are we going out tonight?"

> "No, I've decided that we should stay home."

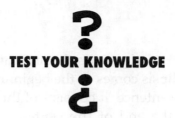

TEST YOUR KNOWLEDGE

QUESTIONS

1. What is an ellipsis?

2. What type of information do nonrestrictive commas set off?

3. What does the colon often mean?

4. When does a semicolon separate items in a series?

5. Which two punctuation marks almost always go outside the closing quotes?

6. How do we create the possessive form of the noun **classes**?

7. Does parenthetical material affect the punctuation of the primary portion of the sentence?

8. Why is there a hyphen in the word **re-formation**?

9. Do periods ever appear outside of closing quotes?

10. How does one punctuate an item in a bulleted list?

(SEE ANSWERS ON FOLLOWING PAGE)

ANSWERS

1. An ellipsis is a series of periods that indicates missing words in a quote. If the ellipsis comes at the beginning or somewhere in the midst of the sentence, it consists of three periods. If the ellipsis comes at the end of the sentence, it consists of four periods, one of which closes the sentence.

2. Nonrestrictive commas set off information that is not vital to the meaning of the sentence.

3. The colon often means "following" or "as follows."

4. The semicolon separates items in a series when one or more of those items contain internal punctuation.

5. The colon and the semicolon will go outside the closing quotes unless they are part of the quoted material.

6. Add a lone apostrophe: **classes'**.

7. No, the primary portion of the sentence should be punctuated as if the parenthetical material were not there.

8. There is a hyphen in the word **re-formation**, meaning "to form again," to distinguish it from the word **reformation**, meaning "a change."

9. No, periods always appear inside the closing quotes.

10. If the item is a sentence, it requires a period, question mark, or exclamation mark. If the item is a word or a phrase, it requires no punctuation.

Glossary

abstract noun: a noun that cannot be touched or held, existing only as a thought or a feeling, such as **hatred** or **loyalty**; see p. 5

action verb: a verb which expresses action; see p. 40

active voice: the stronger form of voice in which the subject performs the action of the verb; see p. 43

adjective: a type of word that modifies nouns or pronouns; see p. 97

adverbial clause: a clause that modifies a verb, an adjective, or an adverb in the same way that a standard adverbial would; see p. 351

adverbial complement: a special adverbial without which the sentence is incomplete or ungrammatical; see p. 147

adverbial: a sentence element that performs the same function as a normal adverb and is optional; see p. 146

adverb: a type of word that modifies verbs, adjectives, or other adverbs; see p. 125

affirmative adverb: the adverb **yes**, which answers questions; see p. 144

antecedent: the word for which a pronoun stands (see p. 182)

apostrophe: a mark of punctuation that is used to indicate plural and possessive forms of words or to indicate missing letters and digits; see p. 529

appositive: a word, phrase, or clause that is placed beside another word to rename, explain, or enhance it; see p. 33

article: a word, either **a**, **an**, or **the**, used to determine the references of a noun; see p. 117

auxiliary verb: the verb in a verb phrase that precedes the principal or main verb (also known as **helping verbs**); see p. 41

base: the base of a verb is its present indicative form; see p. 59

bare infinitive: an infinitive written without the infinitive marker **to**; see p. 173

canonical order: the word order used with a declarative sentence in which the subject of the sentence appears first, followed by the predicate; see p. 298

cardinal number: a number that expresses absolute number without any implication of position or order—the counting numbers (**one, two, three**, etc.); see p. 116

case: describes the relationship of a noun or pronoun to the other words in the sentence; see p. 26

clause: a group of words that contains both a subject and a predicate; see p. 334

collective noun: a noun that names a group of people or objects, see p. 18

colon: a mark of punctuation that is used to indicate a strong break within a sentence and that means "as follows"; see p. 526

comma: a mark of punctuation that may divide items in a series, distinguish subordinate from main clauses, and insert stylistic pauses, among other things; see p. 513

comma splice: a common mistake that occurs when a writer links, or splices, main clauses together by using only commas; see p. 339

common noun: a general noun, such as **goat** or **knife**; see p. 5

comparative clause: an adverbial clause of comparison that typically modifies adjectives and adverbs; see pp. 352 and 369

comparative degree: the degree of comparison that indicates that one object, verb, adjective, or adverbial holds a greater or lesser degree of a quality or quantity than the object(s),verb(s), adjective(s), or adverbial(s) with which it is compared; see pp. 101 and 130

comparison: the characteristic of an adjective or adverb that indicates the degree of a quality expressed by that adjective or adverb; see pp. 101 and 130

complete predicate: the head predicate along with its modifiers and any objects and complements; see p. 285

complete subject: the head subject along with its attendant modifiers; see p. 284

complex preposition: a combination of two or three words, such as **across from** or **in addition to**, that function together as a single preposition; see p. 228

complex sentence: a sentence consisting of a subordinate clause linked to a main clause by some connecting word; see p. 341

compound predicate: two or more predicates connected by a coordinate conjunction in the complete predicate of the sentence; see p. 286

compound sentence: a sentence consisting of two or more main clauses linked together by a coordinate conjunction; see p. 335

compound subject: two or more subjects connected by a coordinate conjunction in the complete subject of the sentence; see p. 286

concrete noun: a noun that can be touched or held, such as **brick** or **street**; see p. 5

conjugation: the complete set of forms for a particular verb inflected across tense, mood, voice, person, and number; see p. 56

conjunction: a word that creates a connection between words or groups of words; see p. 261

conjunctive adverb: a connecting word, such as **again** or **otherwise**, that is similar to a standard adverb because of the meaning that it conveys, but that is also similar to a coordinate conjunction because it connects main clauses—more often referred to as a **connector**; see pp. 268 and 337

conjunctive conjunction: a coordinate conjunction, such as **and**, that has an additive function; see p. 262

connector: a connecting word, such as **again** or **otherwise**, that is similar to a standard adverb because of the meaning that it conveys, but that is also similar to a coordinate conjunction because it connects main clauses—sometimes referred to as a **conjunctive adverb**; see pp. 268 and 337

contraction: an abbreviated version of a subject and a verb (i.e., he is → he's) or of a verb and the negative adverb **not** (i.e., is not → isn't); see pp. 90 and 217

coordinate conjunction: a conjunction that connects sentence elements of equal importance; see p. 262

dangling participle: a participle or participle phrase that does not clearly modify a particular word or phrase in a sentence; see p. 160

dash: a mark of punctuation that is used to indicate an abrupt change of thought or shift of flow in a sentence; see p. 541

declarative sentence: a sentence that is used to make a statement of fact or possibility; see p. 295

definite article: the article **the**, which points to particular people, places, things, and ideas; see p. 118

delayed subject: a subject that is pushed to the end of the sentence and replaced in the true place of the subject by some dummy element, such as **it** or **there**; see p. 172

demonstrative pronoun: a pronoun that points to the noun that it is replacing; see p. 194

descriptive adjective: an adjective that describes the noun or pronoun that it modifies by indicating color, shape, texture, scent or any other quality that entities named by nouns and pronouns can possess; see p. 98

determiner: a word that determines the reference of a noun phrase; see p. 115

diagramming: the process of creating a pictorial representation of a sentence; see p. 288

digraph: a grouping of two letters, vowels, or consonants that makes a single sound, like **ay** in **stay**; see p. 421

direct object: a noun, pronoun, or other nominal that receives the action of the verb; see p. 76

disjunctive conjunction: a coordinate conjunctive, such as **but**, that ties words and groups of words together, and that also implies an opposition or separation; see p. 262

double negative: a grammatical construction in which two negative words are used to make a positive; see p. 145

dummy element: a word, such as **it** or **there**, that takes the place of some word(s) in a sentence; see p. 172

eponym: a word which has come into the language from a person's proper name, such as **maverick** from the name of the famous Texan, Samuel August Maverick; see p. 476

exclamation mark: a mark of punctuation that is placed at the end of a sentence to indicate strong emotion, surprise, or urgency; see p. 536

exclamatory sentence: a sentence that expresses a thought with strong emotion; see p. 295

first person (with nouns and pronouns): a noun or pronoun in the first person names the person or persons speaking; first person nouns are always used in apposition with first person pronouns; see p. 24

first person (with verbs): with a first person verb, the speaker includes himself or herself as one who takes the action of the verb or whose condition is described by the verb; see p. 42

form (of a sentence): the appearance or shape of a sentence, determined by the order in which the elements that make up the sentence appear and the end punctuation; see p. 296

fronting: the act of moving some element of the complete predicate to the beginning of the sentence, especially in front of the subject; see p. 299

function: the intended purpose of a sentence, determined by the way the sentence is spoken or read (placement of emphasis and changes of intonation), its intended meaning, and the end punctuation; see p. 296

future tense: encompasses all actions or states of being we might encounter in a verb between the briefest of moments after the present and the end of time; see p. 48

gender: the classification of nouns according to sex; see p. 8

gerund: a type of verbal that takes the place of a noun in a sentence; see p. 164

gerund phrase: a gerund together with its modifiers, objects, and complements; see p. 165

hard sound: the /k/ sound made by the letter **c** in words such as **cut** and **cake** or the /g/ sound made by the letter **g** in words such as **gap** and **gut**; see p. 421

head predicate: the one word in the complete predicate that unlocks the central meaning of the predicate; see p. 285

head subject: the one word in the complete subject that names the entity spoken of; see p. 284

helping verb: the verb in a verb phrase that precedes the principal or main verb (better known as an **auxiliary verb**); see p. 41

heteronyms: words which have identical spellings but different pronunciations and meanings, such as the noun **conduct** (accent on the first syllable), meaning "behavior," and the verb **conduct** (accent on the second syllable), meaning "to guide"; see p. 392

homonyms: words which have the same sound and spelling but different meanings, such as the noun **quack**, meaning "the sound made by a duck," and the noun **quack**, meaning "a charlatan"; see p. 392

homographs: words which have the same spelling but different origins, meanings, or pronunciations, such as the noun **homer**, meaning "an ancient Hebrew unit of measure," and the noun **homer**, meaning "a home run"; see p. 392

homophones: words that are pronounced alike and that have different meanings, but that may or may not be spelled the same, such as the noun **quail**, meaning "a type of game bird," and the verb **quail**, meaning "to falter"; see p. 392

host clause: the group of words that the nominal clause completes in a sentence containing a nominal clause; see p. 356

imperative mood: a mood or property of the verb that characterizes commands, orders, or requests; see p. 46

imperative sentence: a sentence that makes a request or gives a command; see p. 295

indefinite article: the article **a** or **an**, both of which do not point to any noun in particular; see p. 118

indefinite pronoun: a pronoun, such as **anyone** and **everybody**, that has no specific antecedents; see p. 203

independent clause: a clause that has a subject and predicate and may stand on its own as a complete thought—more often referred to as a **main clause**; see p. 334

indicative mood: a mood or property of the verb that characterizes statements, questions, or exclamations; see p. 45

indirect object: a noun, pronoun, or other nominal that receives and precedes the direct object in the sentence; see p. 76

infinitive: a type of verbal that can function as a nominal, an adjective, or an adverbial and that usually begins with its marker **to**; see p. 169

infinitive phrase: an infinitive together with its objects, complements, and modifiers; see p. 171

interjection: a word, such as **alas** or **mercy**, used to grab attention, create interest, or highlight the speaker's strong emotions; see p. 275

interrogative adverb: an adverb usually used at the beginning of a sentence to ask a question (i.e., **how, when, where**, and **why**); see p. 143

interrogative pronoun: a pronoun, such as **who, which** and **what**, that asks a question; see p. 195

interrogative sentence: a sentence that asks a question; see p. 295

intransitive verb: a verb that does not take a direct object; see p. 78

irregular verb: a verb whose past indicative and past participle forms are generated in an irregular way; see p. 58

lexicon: a catalog of words, often those defined in the dictionary, but also those appropriate to more specialized contexts, such as professions or pasttimes

limiting adjective: an adjective which restricts the definition of the noun or pronoun that it modifies; see p. 99

linking verb: a verb that joins the subject of the sentence to some word or words in the predicate; see p. 40

long vowel sound: a vowel sound which is identical with the sound of its own letter name, such as the /i/ sound in **ride**; see p. 421

main clause: a clause that may stand on its own as a complete thought—sometimes referred to as an **independent clause**; see p. 334

main verb: the head of the verb phrase that can express action, existence, or condition by itself and that always appears at the end of the verb phrase—also known as the **principal verb**; see p. 41

mnemonic: a trick or shortcut, such as a formula or a rhyme, that helps to strengthen your memory and that you can use to remember those hard-to-spell words; see p. 414

modal auxiliary verb: an auxiliary verb that indicates the attitude of the subject toward the action of the verb; see p. 86

modifier: any word that acts to describe or qualify another word in such a way that it changes the meaning of that other word; see p. 97

mood: the form or property of the verb that indicates the speaker's attitude toward what is communicated in the sentence; see p. 45

negative adverb: the adverbs **no** or **not**; **no** answers questions or modifies nouns; **not** modifies verbs; see p. 144

nominal: any noun or pronoun or any word, phrase, or clause that performs the same function as a noun; see p. 32

nominal clause: a subordinate clause that functions as a nominal within a sentence; see p. 355

nominal relative clause: a nominal clause that begins with a relative pronoun; see p. 361

nominative case: nouns and pronouns in the nominative case name the words that statements are made about; see p. 26

nonrestrictive: descriptive information in a sentence that can be eliminated without changing the meaning of the sentence; see p. 34

noun: a naming word that gives a title to a person, place, thing, or idea; see p. 3

noun phrase: a group of words that is composed of a noun and a number of optional modifiers and that lacks a subject or a predicate; see p. 32

number: indicates how many people or objects a noun, pronoun, or verb refers to; see pp. 9 and 42

objective case: nouns and pronouns in the objective case are objects, such as direct objects, indirect objects, and objects of prepositions; see p. 26

object complement: a noun, pronoun, other nominal or adjective which renames or describes a direct object; see p. 80

object of preposition: one of the partners of the preposition—it is usually a noun or a pronoun and always follows the preposition; see p. 229

ordinal number: a numbers that indicates position or order in relation to other numbers (**first, second, third,** etc.); see p. 116

orthography: the academic term for **spelling**; see p. 383

oxymoron: a figure of speech that combines contradictory terms, such as "exact estimate"; see p. 489

palindrome: a word, phrase, or sentence that reads the same forwards and backwards, such as "Madam, I'm Adam," see p. 489

participle: a verb form that may be used as an adjective or an adverbial (when it is a verbal) or as the main verb in a verb phrase; see pp. 152 and 158

participle phrase: a participle together with its objects, complements, and modifiers; see p. 155

passive voice: the weaker form of voice in which the subject is acted upon; see p. 43

past participle: the **-ed** participle form (i.e., **baked**)—when used as a verbal, it implies action now completed but that may have been ongoing at the time of the main verb; see pp. 59 and 152

past tense: includes any action or state of being that we could find in a verb between the dawn of time and a split second before the present; see p. 48

perfect form (of verb tense): a characteristic of verb tense that indicates that the action of the verb ends; see p. 50

period: a mark of punctuation that represents a strong pause or break and that is often seen between sentences and between the letters in abbreviations; see p. 500

person: the characteristic of a noun, pronoun, or verb that describes the relationship of that noun, pronoun, or verb to the speaker; see pp. 24 and 42

personal pronoun: a pronoun that represents a specific person speaking, spoken to, or spoken of; see p. 182

personification: the act of treating an inanimate object or an idea as if it had human qualities; see p. 31

phonics: a method of teaching reading in which students learn to identify the sounds made by single letters and combinations of letters and then to blend the individual sounds into a whole word; see p. 417

phrase: a group of words that lacks both a subject and a predicate and that functions as a single part of speech, see pp. 32, 233

plural: the number of a noun, pronoun, or verb that refers to more than one of anything; see pp. 9 and 42

portmanteau word: a word with the meanings and sounds of two words packed into it, such as **smog** from **smoke** and **fog**; see p. 475

positive degree: the degree of comparison that indicates a lack of comparison; see pp. 101 and 130

possessive pronoun: a pronoun that shows possession; see p. 189

predicate: the sentence element that indicates action performed or existence expressed by the subject; see p. 282

prepositional phrase: a phrase that consists of a preposition, the object of the preposition, and any modifiers of that object; see p. 230

preposition: a word that shows the relationship between two words or phrases in a sentence; see p. 227

present participle: the **-ing** participle form of a verb (i.e., **baking**); when used as a verbal, it implies action that is ongoing at the time of the action of the main verb in the sentence; see pp. 61 and 152

present tense: includes only those actions or states of being that exist in the immediate moment; see p. 48

principal verb: the head of the verb phrase that can express action, existence, or condition by itself and that always appears at the end of the verb phrase— more often referred to as the **main verb**; see p. 41

pronoun: a word takes the place of a noun in a sentence; see p. 181

proper noun: a noun that refers to a specific person, place, or thing, such as **Eric** and **Springfield**; see p. 5

possessive case: nouns in the possessive case show ownership; see p. 29

progressive form (of verb tense): a characteristic of verb tense that implies that the action or condition of the verb is specifically ongoing; see p. 51

punctuation: the system of symbols that writers use to make their writing clear and to add emphasis, intonation, and pause to a work; see p. 497

question mark: a mark of punctuation that is placed at the end of a sentence to indicate that a question is being asked; see p. 535

real relative pronoun: one of the relative pronouns, **who, which that**, or **what**, each of which plays a nominal role, such as s ject, object, or subject complement, within the clause to which it belongs; see p. 200

reciprocal pronoun: the pronoun phrase **each other** or **one another** in which the action of each member of the group that the pronoun phrase stands for affects all the other members of that group; see p. 191

reflexive pronoun: a pronoun, such as **myself** or **ourselves**, that refers or reflects back to the subject of the sentence or places emphasis on another noun or pronoun in the sentence; see p. 191

regular verb: a verb whose past indicative and past participle forms are generated in a regular or standard way; see p. 58

relative adverb: one of the relative pronouns, **when**, **where**, and **why**, each of which functions as an adverbial within the clause to which it belongs; see p. 200

relative clause: a subordinate clause that modifies a noun, pronoun, or other nominal; see p. 342

relative determiner: a pronoun, such as **whose** or **which**, that introduces a relative clause but that also modifies the noun that follows it in the relative clause in the same way that an article, another type of determiner, would modify the noun that follows it; see pp. 346 and 362

relative pronoun: a pronoun that takes the place of a noun as a normal pronoun would but that also connects the replaced noun to a subordinate clause; see p. 197

restrictive: descriptive information in a sentence that cannot be eliminated without changing the meaning of the sentence; see p. 34

run-on sentence: a mistake that occurs when writers string main clauses together without placing any punctuation or coordinate conjunctions between them; see p. 340

second person (with nouns and pronouns): a noun or pronoun in the second person names the person or persons spoken to; second person nouns are always appositives or nouns in direct address; see p. 25

second person (with verbs): the speaker uses a verb in the second person to address the person or people around him or her; see p. 43

semicolon: a mark of punctuation that indicates a stronger pause than the comma but a weaker pause than the period; see p. 528

sentence diagramming: the process of creating a pictorial representation of a sentence; see p. 288

sentence structure: the formula used to build a sentence; see p. 304

sentence type: a category used to classify a sentence according to function; see p. 295

short vowel sound: a vowel sound which does not have the same sound as its own letter name, such as /e/ in **wet**; see p. 421

simple form (of verb tense): characteristic of verb tense that indicates action that merely occurs at its respective place in time; see p. 50

simple predicate: a predicate consisting of just one predicate element; see p. 286

simple sentence: a sentence which contains a single subject-predicate set; see p. 333

simple subject: s subject consisting of just one subject element; see p. 286

singular: the number of a noun, pronoun, or verb that refers to just one of anything; see pp. 9 and 42

soft sound: the /s/ sound made by the letter **c** in **city** and **peace** or the /j/ sound made by the letter **g** in words such as **gym** and **village**; see p. 421

spelling: the art of writing words with the correct sequence of letters; see p. 383

split infinitive: any infinitive phrase construction that separates the infinitive marker **to** from the verb; see p. 174

spoonerism: a word or phrase in which syllables have been transposed, such "Mr. Clown's Brass" instead of "Mr. Brown's Class"; the term **spoonerism** is an eponym, derived from the name of Reverend William A. Spooner (1844-1930), Dean and later Warden of New College at Oxford; see p. 489

subject: the sentence element that names whom or what a sentence is about; see p. 284

subject complement: a noun, pronoun, other nominal, or adjective that renames or describes the subject of a sentence; see p. 81

subject-verb inversion: placement of the verb in front of the subject in some declarative sentences and in many interrogative sentences; see p. 299

subjunctive mood: a mood or property of the verb that characterizes wishes or contradictions of fact; see p. 46

subordinate clause: a clause that cannot stand alone and make sense; see p. 334

subordinate conjunction: a conjunction that connects sentence elements of differing importance; see p. 264

substantive: a dated term for any noun or pronoun or any word, phrase, or clause that performs the same function as a noun—modern grammarians use the term **nominal**; see p. 32

superlative degree: the highest degree of comparison—no object, verb, adjective, or adverbial can possess a quality to a degree higher than the superlative; see pp. 103 and 130

tense: the placement of a verb in time; see p. 48

third person (with nouns and pronouns): a noun or pronoun in the third person names the person or persons spoken of; see p. 25

third person (with verbs): to speak in the **third person** is to use the verb to speak or write about those around you; see p. 43

transitive verb: any verb that requires an object; see p. 78

trigraph: a grouping of three letters, vowels, or consonants that makes a single sound, like **tch** in **witch**; see p. 421

verbal: a form of a verb that is used as another part of speech; see p. 151

verb phrase: a complete verb composed of more than one word; see p. 40

verb: a type of word which expresses action, existence, or condition; see p. 39

vocabulary: the complete collection of the words in a language; see p. 431

voice: the characteristic of a verb that indicates the strength of the subject in a sentence; see p. 43

zero relative pronoun: the gap left by an omitted relative pronoun in a relative clause; see p. 348

zero that-clause: a nominal clause from which the subordinate conjunction **that** has been omitted; see p. 363

Bibliography

Appel, William R. "Letters to the Editor," *Smithsonian*, March 1995.

Chalker, Sylvia. *The Little Oxford English Dictionary*. New York: Oxford University Press, 1995.

Cousin, Pierre-Henri, Lorna Sinclair, Jean-Francois Allain, and Catherine E. Love, eds. *Harper Collins French Dictionary*. New York: HarperCollins, 1990.

Douglas, Auriel. *Webster's New World Dictionary of Eponyms: Common Words from Proper Names*. New York: MacMillan General Reference, 1990.

Ehrlich, Eugene, and Marshall De Bruhl, compilers. *The International Thesaurus of Quotations*. rev. ed. New York: HarperCollins, 1996.

Fargis, Paul, ed. *The New York Public Library Writer's Guide to Style and Usage*. New York: HarperCollins, 1987.

Flexner, Stuart Berg, ed. *Random House Unabridged Dictionary Second Edition*. New York: Random House, 1993

Fortsch, Dagmar, Hildegard Pesch, Lorna Sinclair, and Elspeth Anderson, eds. *Harper Collins German Dictionary*. New York: HarperCollins, 1990.

Grafton, Sue. *L is for Lawless*. New York: Henry Holt, 1995.

Greenbaum, Sidney. *The Oxford English Grammar*. New York: Oxford University Press, 1996.

Grossman, John, ed. *The Chicago Manual of Style*. 14th ed. Chicago: The University of Chicago Press, 1993.

Hemingway, Ernest. *A Farewell to Arms*. New York: Simon & Schuster, 1995.

Kilpatrick, James J. "Mrs. Malaprop's Prose Set a Precedent," *Smithsonian*, January 1995.

Leeds, Jeff. "Tough Times at Compton Casino," *Los Angeles Times*, October 6, 1997.

Lerner, Alan J., lyricist, Frederick Loewe, composer, George Cukor, director. *My Fair Lady*. Burbank, Calif.: Warner Bros., 1964.

McShane, Frank, ed. *Selected Letters of Raymond Chandler*. New York: Columbia University Press, 1981.

Sisson, A.F. *Sisson's Synonyms: An Unabridged Synonym and Related-Term Locator*. West Nyack, NY: Parker Publishing Company, 1969.

Soukhanov, Anne H., ed. *Roget's II The New Thesaurus*. rev. ed. Boston: Houghton Mifflin, 1988.

Thurber, James. *The Years with Ross*. Boston: Little, Brown and Company, 1959.

Traupman, John C., Ph.D. *The New College Latin & English Dictionary*: rev. ed. New York: Bantam Books, 1995.

Williams, Janet B.W. *Diagnostic and Statistical Manual of Mental Disorders III-R*. Washington, DC: American Psychiatric Association, 1987.

Index

A

a vs. an, 118
abbreviations
  list of, 502–512
  plurals of, 15, 530
  postal service, 512
  with articles, 121
  with periods, 500–501, 502–512
abstract nouns, 5
action verbs, 40
adjectives
  defined, 97
  articles, 117–121
    a vs. an, 118
    determiners, 117
    definite article, 118–119
    diagrammed, 289
    indefinite articles, 118
    positions of, 117–118
    turning adjectives into nouns,
      120–121
    with abbreviations, 119–120
  comparison of, 100–110
    adjectives not compared, 109
    by adverb, 104–105
    by suffix, 104
    comparative degree, 101–102
    irregular comparison, 107–108
    positive degree, 101
    superlative degree, 103
  compound adjectives, 539–540
  demonstrative pronouns used as, 194
  descriptive adjectives, 98
  diagrammed, 289
  distinguished from adverbs, 137–143
    bad vs. badly, 141
    good vs. well, 141–142
    real vs. very, 142–143
  indefinite pronouns used as, 205
  infinitives used as, 169–170
  interrogative pronouns used as, 196
  limiting adjectives, 99–100
  modifying gerunds, 166

adjectives (continued)
  nominal adjectives
    articles with, 120–121
    used as objects of prepositions, 231
  nouns used as, 112
  numbers, 116–117
    cardinal numbers, 116–117
    ordinal numbers, 116–117
  overuse of, 114–115
  participles used as, 152–154
  possessive pronouns used as, 189,
    221–223
  position of, 110–112
  prepositional phrases used as, 233
    diagrammed, 316
  proper adjectives, 98
    capitalization of,
      see capitalization of proper nouns
    with prefixes and hyphens, 541
  punctuation with, 516
adverbial clauses, 351–355
  abbreviated, of comparison, 369–372
    case with, 370–372
  classes of, 351–353
  comparative clauses, 352, 353,
    369–372
  diagrammed, 354–355
  placement of, in sentence, 353–354
  punctuation of, 513–514, 517, 524–525
adverbial complements, 147
adverbials
  defined, 146–147
  adverbial clauses, 351–355
  adverbial complements, 147
  infinitives used as, 170
  modifying gerunds, 165–166
  modifying infinitives, 171
  modifying participles, 155–156
  participles used as, 152, 154
  prepositional phrases used as,
    233–234
    diagrammed, 316–317
  relative adverbs functioning as, 202,
    345–346

adverb phrases, 146
    used as adverbials, 146–147
adverbs
    defined, 125
    -ly ending, 127–128
    adverbial complements, 147
    adverbials, 146–147
        adverbial clauses, 351–355
        infinitives used as, 169–170
        modifying gerunds, 165–166
        modifying infinitives, 171
        modifying participles, 155–156
        participles used as, 152, 154
        prepositional phrases used as,
            233–234
            diagrammed, 316–317
        relative adverbs functioning as,
            200–201, 345–346
    adverb phrases, 146
        used as adverbials, 146–147
    affirmative adverb, 144, 515
    comparison of, 130–133
        adverbs not compared, 133
        by adverb, 131
        by suffix, 131
        comparative degree, 130
        positive degree, 130
        superlative degree, 130
        irregular comparison, 132
    conjunctive adverbs, 268–270, 337–338
        list of, 269, 337
        meanings of, 269
        punctuation with, 338, 514–515
    diagrammed, 289
    distinguished from adjectives,
        137–143
        bad vs. **badly**, 141
        good vs. **well**, 141–142
        real vs. **very**, 142–143
    distinguished from prepositions,
        236–237
    hard vs. **hardly**, 128–129
    double negatives, 145–146
    interrogative adverbs, 143
    meanings of, 129–130
    modifying gerunds, 165–166
    modifying infinitives, 171
    modifying participles, 156
    negative adverbs, 144, 515

adverbs (continued)
    nominal adverbs
        used as objects of prepositions, 231
        positioning of, in sentences, 134–136
    affirmative adverb, 144, 515
agreement
    between indefinite pronoun and verb,
        220–221
    between pronoun and antecedent,
        206–217
        in gender, 211–213
            with compound antecedents, 213
        in number, 207–211
            with collective nouns, 209
            with compound antecedents,
                207–208
            with indefinite pronouns, 207
        in person, 207
        in subordinate clauses, 375–377
            nominal clauses, 376
            relative clauses, 375–377
    between subject and verb, 53–56
        in subordinate clauses, 372–375
            nominal clauses, 364–365, 375
            relative clauses, 372–374
        in number, 53–55
            with compound subjects, 53–54
            with collective nouns, 55
        in person, 53
airline lingo, 485
antecedents
    of pronouns, 182
        agreement with pronouns, 206–217
            compound antecedents, 208
            in gender, 211–213
                with compound antecedents,
                    213
            in number, 207–211
                with collective nouns, 209
                with compound antecedents,
                    207–208
                with indefinite pronouns, 207
            in person, 207
            in subordinate clauses, 375–377
                nominal clauses, 376
                relative clauses, 375–377

antecedents
  of pronouns (continued)
    unnecessary with
      indefinite pronouns, 217
      interrogative pronouns, 216
      personal pronouns, 216
      relative pronoun **what**, 216–217
    vague antecedents, 213–214
ante- vs. **anti-**, 388
apostrophes, 529–535
  with contractions, 530
  with missing digits, 531
  with missing letters, 530
  with plurals of letters and abbreviations, 16, 530
  with possessive nouns, 28–30, 529–530
appositives, 33–34
  colons with, 526
  dashes with, 543
  diagrammed, 326
  nominal clauses used as, 356–357, 358–359
  parentheses with, 538
articles, 117–121
  a vs. **an**, 118
  determiners, 117
  definite article, 118–119
  indefinite articles, 118
  positions of, 117–118
  turning adjectives into nouns, 120–121
  with abbreviations, 119–120
asterisks, 548
auxiliary verbs, 41
  shall vs. **will**, 84, 85
  can, use of, 85–86
  contracted with **have**, 91, 93
  could, use of, 86–89
  may, use of 85–86
  might, use of, 86–89
  modal auxiliary verbs, 86–89
  must, use of, 86
  should, use of, 86–89
  would, use of, 86–89

B

bad vs. **badly**, 141
bare infinitives, 173–174
bare vs. **bear**, 92–93

base form of the verb, 59
  in infinitives, 168–169
be, conjugation table for, 72–73
bold text, 549–550
brackets, 538
  with information inserted in quoted material, 538
  with parenthetical material within parentheses, 538
Brodignagian, 474
Brown, James, 275
bullets, 549

C

can, use of, 85–86
canonical word order, 298
capitalization
  of proper nouns, 5–6
  of proper adjectives,
    see rules for proper nouns
cardinal numbers, 116–117
Carroll, Lewis, 475
case
  of nouns, 26–30
    nominative case, 26
    objective case, 26–27
    possessive case, 30
      creating possessive forms, 28–30
      punctuation with, 529–530
      with inanimate nouns, 29–30
  of objects of prepositions, 230–231, 235
  of pronouns
    see definitions for nouns
    indefinite pronouns, 205
    personal pronouns, 183–185
      nominative case forms of, 183
      objective case forms of, 183
    relative pronouns, 343–345
  with comparative clauses, 370–372
clauses
  defined, 333
  adverbial clauses, 351–355
    abbreviated, of comparison, 369–372
    case with, 370–372
    classes of, 351–353
    comparative clauses, 352, 353, 369–372
    diagrammed, 354–355

clauses
  adverbial clauses (continued)
    placement of, 353–354
    punctuation of, 513–514, 517,
      524–525
  host clauses, 355–356
  in compound–complex sentences, 368
  main clauses, 264, 334–335
    in complex sentences, 341–342
    in compound sentences, 335–341
  nominal clauses, 355–367
    agreement of pronoun and an-
      tecedent, 376
    agreement of subject and verb in,
      364–365, 375
    diagrammed, 365–367
    host clauses, 355–356
    nominal relative clauses, 361
    uses of, 356–357
      as appositives, 356–357, 358–359
      as delayed subject, 356–357
      as direct object, 357
      as indirect object, 357
      as object of preposition, 357
      as subject, 356
      as subject complement, 356
    who vs. whom, 359–360
    with subordinate conjunctions,
      360–361
    with relative determiners, 362
    with relative pronouns, 361, 362
    zero that, 363
  relative clauses, 342–350
    agreement between pronouns and
      antecedents, 375–377
    agreement between subject and
      verb in, 372–374
    diagrammed, 349–350
    nominal relative clauses, 202
    relative pronouns in, 203
      real relative pronouns, 343–345
      relative adverbs, 345–346
      relative determiners, 346–347
      zero relative pronouns, 348–349
    who vs. whom, 344–345
    restrictive vs. nonrestrictive,
      347–348

clauses (continued)
  subordinate clauses, 264, 334–335
    agreement between pronoun and
      antecedent in, 375–377
      nominal clauses, 376
      relative clauses, 375–377
    agreement between subject and
      verb in, 372–375
      nominal clauses, 364–365, 375
      relative clauses, 372–374
    and the subjunctive mood, 47
    in complex sentences, 341–342
    relative pronouns in, 197–203
    zero that–clauses, 363
collective nouns, 18–20
  agreement with pronouns, 213
  agreement with verbs, 55
  number of, 18–19
collocations
  with prepositions, 248–257
colons, 526–528
  with appositives, 526
  with lists, 526
  with page specifications, 527
  with double quotation marks,
    546–547
  with quoted material, 526, 527–528
  with ratios, 527
  with salutations, 527, 548
  with single quotation marks, 547–548
  with time, 527
  with titles and subtitles, 527
commas, 513–526
  altering a nominal clause, 374
  comma splice, 339, 521, 524
  in compound sentences, 336–337, 338
  in relative clauses, 347–348
  run–on sentences, 340
  to eliminate ambiguity, 520
  to indicate omissions, 517
  to set off interrogative clauses, 517,
  to set off phrases of contrast, 517
  with addresses and locations, 519
  with adjectives, 516
  with adverbial clauses, 513–514
  with affirmative adverb, 515
  with appositives, 515
  with conjunctive adverbs, 514–515
  with coordinate conjunctions, 270, 517
  with dates, 519

commas (continued)
with double quotation marks, 545
with interjections, 277, 515
with items in a series, 516, 522–523
with names, 520
with negative adverb, 515
with nonrestrictive information, 35, 347–348, 520–521, 523–524
with nouns in direct address, 515
with numbers, 519
with prepositional phrases, 514
with quoted material, 518, 527–528
with restrictive information, 35, 347–348, 520–521, 523–524
with salutations, 518, 548
with single quotation marks, 547
with titles, 519
with verbals, 514
comma splice, 339, 521, 524
common nouns, 5
comparative clauses, 352, 353
omitting portions of, 369–372
comparative degree of comparison
of adjectives, 101–102
forms of adjectives in, 104–108
irregular comparison, 107–108
with adverbs, 104–105
with suffixes, 104
of adverbs, 130
forms of adjectives in, 130–132
irregular comparison, 132
with adverbs, 131
with suffixes, 131
comparison
of adjectives, 100–110
adjectives not compared, 109
by adverb, 104–105
by suffix, 104
comparative degree, 101–102
irregular comparison, 107–108
positive degree, 101
superlative degree, 103
of adverbs, 130–133
adverbs not compared, 133
by adverb, 131
by suffix, 131
comparative degree, 130
irregular comparison, 132
positive degree, 130
superlative degree, 130

complete predicates, 285
complete subjects, 284–285
complex prepositions, 228
complex sentences, 341–367
adverbial clauses, 351–355
classes of, 249–353
commas with, 513–514, 517, 524–525
comparative clauses, 352, 353
diagrammed, 354–355
placement of, 353–354
punctuation of, 513–514, 517, 524–525
compound–complex sentences, 368
main clauses in, 341–342
nominal clauses, 355–367
agreement of pronoun and antecedent, 376
agreement of subject and verb in, 364–365, 375
diagrammed, 365–367
host clauses, 355–356
nominal relative clauses, 361
uses of, 356–357
as appositives, 356–357, 358–359
as delayed subject, 356–357
as direct object, 357
as indirect object, 357
as object of preposition, 357
as subject, 356
as subject complement, 356
who vs. whom, 359–360
with subordinate conjunctions, 360–361
with relative determiners, 362
with relative pronouns, 361, 362
zero that, 363
relative clauses, 342–350
agreement between pronouns and antecedents, 375–377
agreement between subject and verb in, 372–374
diagrammed, 349–350
restrictive vs. nonrestrictive, 347–348
who vs. whom, 344–345
with real relative pronouns, 343–345
with relative adverbs, 345–346
with relative determiners, 346–347

complex sentences
  relative clauses (continued)
    with zero relative pronouns,
      348–349
  subordinate clauses in, 341–342
compound adjectives, 539–540
compound antecedents, 208
compound–complex sentences, 368
compound indefinite pronouns, 203
compound predicates, 286–288
  diagrammed, 289–290
compound relative pronouns, 199–200,
  361, 362
compound sentences, 335–341
  comma splice, 339, 521, 524
  compound–complex sentences, 368
  conjunctive adverbs in, 337–338
  coordinate conjunctions in, 335
  diagrammed, 340–341
  punctuation of, 336–337, 338, 517, 521,
    528
  run–on sentences, 340
compound subject, 286–287
  agreement with verb, 53–54
  diagrammed, 289–290
concrete nouns, 5
conjugation, 56–75
  base form of the verb, 59
  conjugation tables, 62–73
    be, 72–73
    do, 70–71
    grow, 62–63
    have, 68–69
    look, 64–65
    run, 66–67
  future indicative forms, 60
  future perfect indicative forms, 60
  imperative forms, 60
  of irregular verbs, 59
  of regular verbs, 58–59
  past participle, 61
  past perfect indicative forms, 60
  past perfect subjunctive forms, 61
  past subjunctive forms, 61
  present perfect indicative forms, 60
  present perfect subjunctive forms, 61
  present subjunctive forms, 60
  principal parts, 56–59
    table of, 56–58
    past indicative forms, 59

conjugation
  principal parts (continued)
    past participle forms, 59
    present indicative forms, 59
conjunctions
  defined, 261
  commas with, 270, 517
  conjunctive adverbs, 268–270
    list of, 269
    meanings of, 269
  coordinate conjunctions, 262–264
    conjunctive, 262–263
    disjunctive, 263
    with items in a series, 268
  correlative conjunctions, 266–267
  like, 271–272
  list of, 261–262
  only, use of, 270–271
  subordinate conjunctions, 264–267
    list of, 264–265
    meanings of, 265–266
conjunctive adverbs, 268–270, 337–338
  list of, 269, 337
  meanings of, 269
  punctuation with, 338, 514–515
conjunctive conjunctions, 262–263
consonants
  hard sounds, 421
  soft sounds, 421
  sounds of, 419–421
contractions, 90–91
  diagrammed, 318–319
  of verbs and not, 90
  of verbs with pronouns, 90, 217–219
  of auxiliary verbs and have, 91, 93
  punctuation of, 530
coordinate conjunctions, 262–264
  conjunctive, 262–263
  commas with, 270–517
  disjunctive, 263
correlative conjunctions, 266–267
could, 86–89

D

dangling participles, 160–164
dashes, 541–543
  em vs. en dashes, 542
  with afterthoughts, 542

dashes (continued)
  with appositives, 543
  with dates, 542
  with dialogue, 542
  with lists, 543
  with numbers, 542
  with parenthetical material, 541
declarative sentences, 296
  diagrams of, 299–301
  punctuation of, 296, 500, 536
  word orders in, 298–301
    canonical order, 298
    fronting, 299
    subject–verb inversions, 299
definite article, 118–119
delayed subjects
  and dummy **it**, 187–188
  diagrammed, 310–311
  infinitives used as, 172–173
  nominal clauses used as, 356–357
demonstrative pronouns, 194–195
  used as modifiers, 194
dependent clauses
  see subordinate clauses
determiners
  defined, 115–117
  articles, 117–121
    a vs. **an**, 118
    definite article, 118–119
    diagrammed, 289
    indefinite articles, 118
    positions of, 117–118
    turning adjectives into nouns, 120
    with abbreviations, 119–120
  demonstrative pronouns used as, 194
  correlative conjunctions, 266
  indefinite pronouns used as, 205
  interrogative pronouns used as, 196
  possessive pronouns used as, 189,
    221–223
  relative determiners
    in nominal clauses, 362
    in relative clauses, 346–347
diagramming
  see sentence diagramming
dictionary symbols, 419–421
digraphs, 421
direct address
  nouns in, 309–310
    diagrammed, 309

direct address (continued)
  punctuation with, 515
direct objects, 76–80
  and intransitive verbs, 78–79
  and transitive verbs, 78–79
  identification of, 77
  in gerund phrases, 166
  in infinitive phrases, 171
  in participle phrases, 156
  nominal clauses used as, 202, 357
  object complements of, 80–81
  omission of **that** used as, in nominal
    clauses, 363
  relative pronouns used as, 345, 359
  with main verbs, 78
disjunctive conjunctions, 263
do
  as transitive or intransitive verb, 79
  conjugation table for, 70–71
  in emphatic forms of verbs, 83–84
  used to ask questions, 84
  used to express completion, 84
  used to negate verb action, 84
double negatives, 145–146
double possessives, 190
double quotation marks, 543–544
  with irony, 545
  with other marks of punctuation,
    545–547
    colons, 546–547
    commas, 545
    exclamation marks, 546
    periods, 545
    question marks, 546
    semicolons, 546–547
  with quoted material, 543
  with referenced words, phrases,
    clauses, and sentences, 544
  with titles, 544
  with words called to reader's atten-
    tion, 544
dummy elements, 172–173
  diagrammed, 310–311
  it, 187–188
  with nominal clauses used as delayed
    subjects, 356
dummy **it**
  see dummy elements

E

each other, 192
editorial **we**, 187
ellipses, 501–502
epiphany, 477
eponyms, 476, 490
etymologies
  defined, 432
  eponyms, 476
  foreign words and phrases used in
    English, 477–481
  portmanteau words, 475
  words from literature, 474–475
    Carroll, Lewis, 475
    Shakespeare, William, 475
    Sheridan, Richard Brinsley, 474
    Swift, Jonathan, 474
exclamation marks, 536–537
  with declarative sentences, 536
  with double quotation marks, 546
  with ellipses, 501–502
  with exclamatory sentences, 537
  with imperative sentences, 536
  with interjections, 277, 537
  with interrogative sentences, 537
  with single quotation marks, 547–548
exclamatory sentences, 296
  diagram of, 304
  punctuation of, 296, 537
  word order in, 303–304

F

first person
  with nouns, 24–25
  with pronouns
    see definitions for nouns
  with verbs, 43
flap sound, 413
foreign words and phrases used in
  English, 477–481
form vs. function
  of sentence types, 296–297
French
  gender in, 8
  words and phrases used in English,
    477–481
fronting, 299

future tense, 48
  perfect form, 50–51
  progressive form, 51
  shall vs. **will**, 84–85
  simple future, 50

G

gender
  of nouns, 8–9
    natural gender, 8
  of pronouns
    see definitions for nouns
    agreement between pronouns and
      antecedent in, 211–213
      with compound antecedents, 213
    of personal pronouns, 185–186
      gender neutral pronouns, need
        for, 185–186
      third person personal pronouns,
        183
German
  gender in, 8
  words and phrases used in English,
    481
gerund phrases
  see gerunds
gerunds, 164–168
  diagrammed, 321–323
  gerund phrases, 165–167
    modifiers in, 165–166
      adjectives, 166
      adverbials, 165–166
      adverbs, 165
      possessive case nouns, 166
      possessive pronouns, 166
    objects in, 166
      direct objects, 166
      indirect objects, 166
    complements in, 166–167
      subject complements, 166–167
  possessive case nouns with, 168
  used as nominals, 164–165
  used as objects of prepositions, 231
glamour
  origin of the word, 481–482
good vs. **well**, 141–142
googolplex, 117

Greek
    roots, prefixes, and suffixes, 457–461
    words and phrases used in English,
       479
grow
    conjugation table for, 62–63

H

Hamlet, 475
hard consonant sounds, 421
hard vs. **hardly**, 128–129
have
    conjugation table for, 68–69
Hawaiian
    words and phrases used in English,
       477
head predicates, 285
head subjects, 284–285
Hebrew
    words and phrases used in English,
       480
he-him in indeterminate masculine, 185
helping verbs
    see auxiliary verbs
heteronyms, 31–32, 392–411
homographs, 392–411
homophones, 392–411
homonyms, 31–32, 392–411
host clauses, 355–356
hyphens, 538–541
    with compound adjectives, 539–540
    with fractions, 539
    with prefixes, 539, 541
    with syllables, 539
    with words broken over two lines,
       539
    with words in a compound, 538

I

imperative mood, 46
imperative sentences, 296
    diagrams of, 303
    punctuation of, 296, 500, 535, 536
    understood subject **you**, 302–303
    with nouns in direct address, 309–310
indefinite articles, 118

indefinite pronouns, 203–206
    agreement with antecedent in num-
       ber, 207
    agreement with verbs in number,
       220–221
    antecedents of, 207, 217
    case of, 205
    compound indefinite pronouns, 203
    indefinite pronoun phrases, 205–206
    list of, 203
    used as modifiers, 205
    number with, 203–204
independent clauses
    see main clauses
independent elements
    interjections, 276
        diagrammed, 310
    nouns in direct address, 309–310
        diagrammed, 309
indicative mood, 45–46
indirect objects, 76–78
    identification of, 77–78
    in gerund phrases, 166
    in infinitive phrases, 171
    in participle phrases, 156
    nominal clauses used as, 357
indirect questions, 500, 536
infinitive phrases
    see infinitives
infinitives, 169–176
    bare infinitives, 173–174
    diagrammed, 323–325
    distinguished from prepositional
       phrases, 169, 231
    infinitive phrases, 171–173
        complements in, 171–172
            subject complements, 171–172
        modifiers in, 171
            adverbials, 171
            adverbs, 171
        objects in, 171
            direct objects, 171
            indirect objects, 171
    marker of, 169
    perfect forms of, 176–177
    split infinitives, 174–176
    used as adjectives, 169–170
    used as adverbials, 170
    used as delayed subjects, 172–173
    used as nominals, 169

infinitives (continued)
    without marker, 173–174
interjections
    defined, 275
    curses, 276–277
    diagrammed, 310
    independent elements, 276
    list of, 275–276
    punctuation with, 277
        commas, 277, 515
        exclamation marks, 277, 537
International Phonetic Alphabet,
    418–421
interrogative adverbs, 143
    in interrogative sentences, 301
interrogative pronouns, 195–196
    and antecedents, 196, 216
    list of, 195
    in interrogative sentences, 301
    used as modifiers, 196
    use of **what**, 196
    use of **which**, 196
    use of **who/whom/whose**, 195
interrogative sentences, 296
    diagrams of, 301–302
    identification of predicate in, 286
    punctuation of, 296, 535, 537
    word orders in, 301–302
        with interrogative adverbs, 301
        with interrogative pronouns, 301
        with subject–verb inversions, 301
intransitive verbs, 78–79
    dictionary abbreviation for, 80
irregular comparison
    of adjectives, 107–108
    of adverbs, 132
irregular verbs, 59
it
    dummy element, 172–173, 189
    in indeterminate neuter, 186
Italian
    words and phrases used in English,
        477–478, 480
italicized text, 549–550

J

Johnson, Samuel, 384

K

Kirk, James T., 175

L

Latin
    plurals used in English, 13–14
    roots, prefixes, and suffixes, 457–461
    words and phrases used in English,
        477–481
legal jargon, 485–486
leotard, 476
lie vs. **lay**, 91
like, 271–272
lilliputian, 474
linking verbs, 40
    dictionary abbreviation for, 80
    gerund forms of, with subject comple-
        ments, 166–167
    infinitive forms of, with subject com-
        plements, 171
    participle forms of, with subject com-
        plements, 157
    subject complements of, 81–82
literature
    words from, 474–475
        Carroll, Lewis, 475
        Shakespeare, William, 475
        Sheridan, Richard Brinsley, 474
        Swift, Jonathan, 474
look
    conjugation table for, 64–65
look–say method, 418
lutefisk, 356

M

main clauses, 264
    and complex sentences, 341–342
    and compound sentences, 335–341
        punctuation of, 517, 521, 528
main verbs, 41
    participles used as, 159
    with direct and indirect objects, 78
malapropism, 474
maverick, 476
may, use of, 85–86
might, as modal auxiliary verb, 86–89
Middle English, 384
mnemonics for spelling, 414–415
Modern English, 384

modifiers
defined, 97
diagrammed, 289
also see adjectives, adverbs, infinitives,
participles, prepositional phrases, rela-
tive clauses, and verbals
mood, 45–47
imperative mood, 46
indicative mood, 45–46
subjunctive mood, 46–47
and past tense verbs, 49–50
morphemes, 333
must, use of 86

N

negative adverbs, 144, 515
nice
history of the word, 121–122
overuse of, 114–115
nicotine, 476
no
in the double negative, 145
negative adverb, 144
used as a determiner, 207
nominal clauses, 355–367
agreement of pronoun and antecedent, 376
agreement of subject and verb in,
364–365, 375
diagrammed, 365–367
host clauses, 355–356
nominal relative clauses, 361
uses of, 356–357
as appositives, 356–357, 358–359
as delayed subject, 356–357
as direct object, 357
as indirect object, 357
as object of preposition, 357
as subject, 356
as subject complement, 356
who vs. **whom**, 359–360
with subordinate conjunctions,
360–361
with relative determiners, 362
with relative pronouns, 361, 362
zero **that**, 363
nominals
defined, 32
gerunds use as, 164–165
infinitives used as, 169

nominals (continued)
nominal clauses, 202, 355–367
prepositional phrases used as,
234–235
diagrammed, 318
used as objects of prepositions, 231
nominative case
with nouns, 26
with pronouns
see definitions for nouns
personal pronouns, forms of, 183
nominal relative clauses, 202, 361
nonrestrictive vs. restrictive
nouns, 34–35
punctuation of, 35, 520–521, 523–524
relative clauses, 347–348
not
contracted with verbs, 90
in the double negative, 145
negative adverb, 144
position of in sentence, 134
noun phrases, 32–33
used as adverbials, 146–147
nouns
defined, 3
abstract nouns, 5
appositives, 33–34
diagrammed, 326
case of, 26–30
nominative case, 26
objective case, 26–27
possessive case, 28–30
creating possessive forms, 28–30
punctuation with, 529–530
with inanimate nouns, 29–30
common nouns, 5
concrete nouns, 5
collective nouns, 18–20
agreement with pronouns, 213
agreement with verbs, 55
number with, 18–19
gender of, 8–9
natural gender, 8
in direct address, 309–310
diagrammed, 309
punctuation with, 515
nominals, 32
gerunds used as, 164
infinitives used as, 169
nominal clauses, 202, 355–367

nouns
  nominals (continued)
    prepositional phrases used as,
        234–235
      diagrammed, 318
    used as objects of prepositions, 231
  noun phrases, 32–33
    used as adverbials, 146–147
  number of
    Latin influence on, 13–14
    plural, 9
    pluralizing rules, 9–17, 386–387
      see number
    plural nouns treated singularly, 18
    plural only, 18
    singular, 9
    troublesome plurals, list of, 20–21
  person of, 24–25
    first person, 24–25
    second person, 25
    third person, 26
  personification of, 31
  proper nouns, 5
    capitalization of, 5–6
    with prefixes and hyphens, 541
  substantives
    see nominals
  used as adjectives, 112
number
  with nouns, 9–23
    Latin influence on, 13–14
    of collective nouns, 18–19
    pluralizing rules for, 9–17, 386–387
      for compound words, 14, 386
      for Ms., 16
      for nouns ending in f or fe,
          10–11, 386
      for nouns ending in o, 11–12,
          386–387
      for nouns ending in y, 10, 386
      for numbers, letters, and abbre-
          viations, 15, 530
      for proper names, 17
      for words not normally plural-
          ized, 16
      general rule, 9–10, 386
      irregular plurals, 12–13
    plural nouns treated singularly, 18
    plural only, 18
    troublesome plurals, list of, 20–21

number (continued)
  with pronouns
    see definitions for nouns
    agreement in, between pronoun
        and antecedent, 207–211
      with collective nouns, 209
      with compound antecedents,
          207–208
      with indefinite pronouns, 207
    indefinite pronouns, 203–204
    personal pronouns, 186–187
      editorial we, 187
      royal we, 187
      you, 186
  with verbs, 42
    agreement in, between subject and
        verb, 53–55
numbers, 116–117
  cardinal numbers, 116–117
  ordinal numbers, 116–117
  punctuation with, 519, 542
  spelling vs. writing of, 416

O

objective case
  with nouns, 26–27
  with pronouns
    see definitions for nouns
    personal pronouns, forms of, 183
objects
  direct objects, 76–80
    identification of, 77
    in gerund phrases, 166
    in infinitive phrases, 171
    in participle phrases, 156
    nominal clauses used as, 202, 357
    object complements of, 80–81
    omission of that used as, in nomi-
        nal clauses, 363
    relative pronouns used as, 345, 359
    transitive vs. intransitive verbs,
        78–79
    with main verbs, 78
  indirect objects, 76–78
    identification of, 77–78
    in gerund phrases, 166
    in infinitive phrases, 171
    in participle phrases, 156
    nominal clauses used as, 357

objects (continued)
  of prepositions, 229, 230–232
    case of, 230–231, 235
    nominals used as, 231
      gerunds, 231
      nominal adjectives, 231
      nominal adverbs, 231
      nominal clauses used as, 202,
        357
    relative pronouns used as, 345, 359
Old English, 384
one another, 192
only, use of, 270–271
ordinal numbers, 116–117
orthography, 383
oxymorons, 487

P

palindromes, 487
parentheses, 537–538
  periods used in place of, 501
  with appositives, 538
  with dividers and subdividers, 538
  with explanations or commentary, 537
  with numbers, letters, and symbols,
    538
participle phrases
  see participles
participles
  as parts of verb phrases
    distinguished from verbal partici-
      ples, 158–159
    past participles, 50–51, 59
    present participles, 51, 61
      in progressive forms of tense, 51
  as verbals
    defined, 152
    dangling participles, 160–164
    diagrammed, 319–321
    distinguished from participles in
      verb phrases, 158–159
    past participles, 152
    present participles, 152
    participle phrases, 155–157
      complements in, 156–157
        subject complements, 156–157
      implied subjects in, 157, 158
      modifiers in, 155–156
        adverbials, 155–156
        adverbs, 155

participles
  as verbals
    participle phrases (continued)
      objects in, 156
        direct objects, 156
        indirect objects, 156
      used as adverbials of reason, 154
    used as adjectives, 152–154
    used as subject complements,
      153–154
  resemblance of prepositions to, 229
past tense, 48
  perfect form, 50
  progressive form, 51
  simple form, 50
perfect forms of verb tense, 50–51
  with verbals, 176–177
    gerunds, 176
    infinitives, 176–177
    participles, 176
periods, 500–512
  and conjunctive adverbs, 338
  in place of parentheses, 501
  with abbreviations, 500–501, 502–512
  with declarative sentences, 500
  with double quotation marks, 545
  with ellipses, 501
  with imperative sentences, 500, 535
  with indirect questions, 500
  with requests, 500
  with rhetorical questions, 500
  with single quotation marks, 547
person
  with nouns, 24–25
    first person, 24–25
    second person, 25
    third person, 26
  with pronouns
    see definitions for nouns
    agreement between pronoun and
      antecedent in, 207
    gender of personal pronouns in,
      183
  with verbs, 42–43
    first person, 42–43
    second person, 43
      imperative mood, 46
    third person, 43

personal pronouns, 182–188
    antecedents of, 216
    case of, 183–185
    dummy **it**, 187–188
    gender of, 185–186
        gender neutral pronouns, need for,
            185–186
        third person personal pronouns,
            183
    list of, 183
    nominative case forms, 183
    number with, 186–187
        editorial **we**, 187
        royal **we**, 187
        you, 186–187
    objective case forms, 183

personification of nouns, 31
petard (hoisted by one's own), 475
phobias, 487–488
phonemes, 417
phonetics, 419
phonics, 417–418
    digraphs, 421
    hard consonant sounds, 421
    soft consonant sounds, 421
    rules of, 421–426
    trigraphs, 421
    vowels
        long, 421
        short, 421
phrases, 32, 233
    adverb phrases, 146
    gerund phrases, 165–167
    infinitive phrases, 171–173
    noun phrases, 32–33
    participle phrases, 155–157
    verb phrases, 40–41
pluralizing rules for nouns, 9–17
    386–387
    see number
portmanteau words, 475
positive degree of comparison
    of adjectives, 101
        forms of adverbs in, 104–108
            irregular comparison, 107–108
            with adverbs, 104–105
            with suffixes, 104

positive degree of comparison (cont.)
    of adverbs, 130
        forms of adjectives in, 130–132
            irregular comparison, 132
            with adverbs, 131
            with suffixes, 131
possessive case
    nouns, 28–30
        creating possessive forms, 28–30
        modifying gerunds, 166, 167–168
        punctuation with, 529–530
        with inanimate nouns, 29–30
possessive pronouns, 189–190
    and apostrophes, 190
    double possessives, 190
    list of, 189
    modifying gerunds, 166
    used as modifiers, 189
predicate adjectives
    see subject complements
predicate nominatives
    see subject complements
predicate nouns
    see subject complements
predicate pronouns
    see subject complements
predicates
    defined, 283–284
    complete predicates, 285
    compound predicates, 286–288
    diagrammed, 288–289
    head predicates, 285
    omitted in comparative clauses, 369
    simple predicates, 286
prefixes
    hyphens, 539, 541
    list of, 459–460
    questions about, 461
    redundancy of, 484–485
    spelling words with, 388
prepositional phrases
    see prepositions
prepositions
    defined, 227
    collocations with, 248–257
    complex prepositions, 228
    dangling prepositional phrases,
        241–242
    definitions of, 244–247
    errors made with, 238–241

list of, 228
objects of prepositions, 229, 230–232
  case of, 230–231, 235
  nominals used as, 231
    gerunds, 231
    nominal adjectives, 231
    nominal adverbs, 231
    nominal clauses used as, 204, 357
  relative pronouns used as, 345, 359
position of, 235–236
prepositional phrases, 230–235
  diagrammed, 315–318
  distinguished from infinitives, 169, 231
  placement of, in sentences, 241–242
  uses of, 233–235
    as modifiers, 233–234
      adjective roles, 233
      adverbial roles, 146–147, 233–234
    as nominals, 234–235
  resemblance to participles, 229
present tense, 48
  perfect form, 50
  progressive form, 51
  simple form, 50
Presley, Elvis
  All Shook Up, 160
principal parts of verbs, 56–59
  table of, 56–58
  past indicative forms, 59
  past participle forms, 59
  present indicative forms, 59
principal verbs
  see main verbs
progressive forms of verb tense, 51
pronouns
  defined, 181
  agreement between indefinite pro-
    nouns and verbs, 220–221
  agreement with antecedents, 206–217
    in gender, 211–213
      with compound antecedents, 213
    in number, 207–211
      with collective nouns, 209
      with compound antecedents, 207–208
      with indefinite pronouns, 207

pronouns
  agreement with antecedents (cont.)
    in person, 207
    in subordinate clauses, 375–377
      nominal clauses, 376
      relative clauses, 375–377
  antecedents of, 182
    agreement with pronoun, 206–217
    antecedents unnecessary with
      indefinite pronouns, 217
      interrogative pronouns, 216
      personal pronouns, 216
      relative pronoun **what**, 216–217
    vague antecedent, 213–214
  case of
    see case of nouns
    of indefinite pronouns, 205
    of personal pronouns, 183–185
  contracted with verbs, 90, 217–219
    diagrammed, 318–319
  compound antecedents, 208
  demonstrative pronouns, 194–195
    used as modifiers, 194
  gender
    see gender of nouns
    agreement between pronoun and
      antecedent in, 211–213
  indefinite pronouns, 203–206
    agreement with antecedents in
      number, 207
    agreement with verbs in number, 220–221
    and antecedents, 207, 217
    case of, 205
    compound indefinite pronouns, 203
    indefinite pronoun phrases, 205–206
    list of, 203
    used as modifiers, 205
    number with, 203–204
  interrogative pronouns, 195–196
    and antecedents, 196, 216
    list of, 195
    used as modifiers, 196
    use of **what**, 196
    use of **which**, 196
    use of **who/whom/whose**, 195

pronouns (continued)
number
see number with nouns
of indefinite pronouns, 207
of personal pronouns, 186–187
person
see person of nouns
agreement between pronoun and
antecedent in, 207
personal pronouns, 188
antecedents of, 216
case of, 183–185
dummy **it**, 187–188
gender of, 185–186
gender neutral pronouns, need
for, 185–186
third person personal pronouns,
183
list of, 183
nominative case forms, 183
number with, 186–187
editorial **we**, 187
royal **we**, 187
you, 186–187
objective case forms, 183
possessive pronouns, 189–190
and apostrophes, 190
double possessives, 190
list of, 189
used as modifiers, 189
reciprocal pronouns, 191
reflexive pronouns, 191–193
in emphatic roles, 191–192
in reflexive roles, 192
relative pronouns, 197–203
antecedents of, 199, 216–217
compound relative pronouns, 198,
361–362
in nominal (relative) clauses, 202,
361–362
in relative clauses, 203
list of, 198
real relative pronouns, 200–201
relative adverbs, 200–201
use of **that**, 199
use of **what**, 199
implied antecedent of, 199,
216–217
use of **when**, 199
use of **where**, 199

pronouns
relative pronouns (continued)
use of **which**, 198–199
use of **who/whom/whose**, 198
use of **why**, 200
whose as replacement for **which**,
199
zero relative pronouns, 348–349
proper adjectives, 98
capitalization of,
see *capitalization of proper nouns*
with prefixes and hyphens, 541
proper nouns, 5
capitalization of, 5–6
with prefixes and hyphens, 541
punctuation
abbreviations, 502–512
apostrophes, 529–535
with contractions, 530
with missing digits, 531
with missing letters, 530
with plurals of letters and abbreviations, 16, 530
with possessive nouns, 28–30,
529–530
asterisks, 548
bold text, 549–550
brackets, 538
with information inserted in quoted material, 538
with parenthetical material within
parentheses, 538
bullets, 549
colons, 526–528
with appositives, 526
with lists, 526
with page specifications, 527
with quoted material, 526, 527–528
with ratios, 527
with salutations, 527, 548
with time, 527
with titles and subtitles, 527
commas, 513–526
altering a nominal clause, 374
in compound sentences, 336–337,
338, 517, 521
to eliminate ambiguity, 520
to indicate omissions, 517
to set off interrogative clauses, 517,
to set off phrases of contrast, 517

punctuation
commas (continued)
with addresses and locations, 519
with adjectives, 516
with adverbial clauses, 513–514
with affirmative adverb, 515
with appositives, 515
with conjunctive adverbs, 514–515
with coordinate conjunctions, 270,
517
with dates, 519
with interjections, 277, 515
with items in a series, 516, 522–523
with names, 520
with negative adverb, 515
with nonrestrictive information,
520–521, 523–524
with nouns in direct address, 515
with numbers, 519
with prepositional phrases, 514
with quoted material, 518, 527–528
with restrictive information,
520–521, 523–524
with salutations, 518, 548
with titles, 519
with verbals, 514
comma splice, 339, 521, 524
dashes, 541–543
em vs. en dashes, 542
with afterthoughts, 542
with appositives, 543
with dates, 542
with dialogue, 542
with lists, 543
with numbers, 542
with parenthetical material, 541
ellipses, 501–502
exclamation marks, 536–537
with declarative sentences, 536
with ellipses, 501–502
with exclamatory sentences, 296,
537
with imperative sentences, 296, 536
with interjections, 277, 537
with interrogative sentences, 537
history of, 498–499
hyphens, 538–541
with compound adjectives, 539–540
with fractions, 539
with prefixes, 539, 541

punctuation
hyphens (continued)
with syllables, 539
with words broken over two lines,
539
with words in a compound, 538
italicized text, 549–550
of business letters, 548
of compound sentences, 336–337, 338
of dialogue, 550
parentheses, 537–538
periods used in place of, 501
with appositives, 538
with dividers and subdividers, 538
with explanations or commentary,
537
with numbers, letters, and symbols, 538
periods, 500–512
and conjunctive adverbs, 338
in place of parentheses, 501
with abbreviations, 500–501,
502–512
with declarative sentences, 296, 500
with ellipses, 501–502
with imperative sentences, 296,
500, 535
with indirect questions, 500
with requests, 500
with rhetorical questions, 500
question marks, 535–536
to indicate uncertainty, 535–536
with ellipses, 501–502
with indirect questions, 536
with interrogative elements, 535
with interrogative sentences, 296,
535
with rhetorical questions, 536
quotation marks, 543–548
double, 543–544
with irony, 545
with other marks of punctuation, 545–547
colons, 546–547
commas, 545
exclamation marks, 546
periods, 545
question marks, 546
semicolons, 546–547

punctuation
  quotation marks
    double (continued)
      with quoted material, 543
      with referenced words, phrases,
        clauses, and sentences, 544
      with titles, 544
      with words called to reader's at-
        tention, 544
    single, 545
      with other marks of punctua-
        tion, 547–548
        colons, 547–548
        commas, 547
        exclamation marks, 547–548
        periods, 547
        question marks, 547–548
        semicolons, 547–548
  run–on sentences, 340
  semicolons, 528–529
    in compound sentences, 336–337,
      338, 528
    with items in a series, 529
  slashes, 548
  underlined text, 549–550

Q

question marks, 535–536
  to indicate uncertainty, 535–536
  with double quotation marks, 546
  with ellipses, 501
  with indirect questions, 536
  with interrogative elements, 535
  with interrogative sentences, 535
  with rhetorical questions, 536
  with single quotation marks, 547–548
quotation marks, 543–548
  double, 543–544
    with irony, 545
    with other marks of punctuation,
      545–547
      colons, 546–547
      commas, 545
      exclamation marks, 546
      periods, 545
      question marks, 546
      semicolons, 546–547
    with quoted material, 543
    with referenced words, phrases,
      clauses, and sentences, 544

quotation marks
  double (continued)
    with titles, 544
    with words called to reader's atten-
      tion, 544
  single, 545
    with other marks of punctuation,
      547–548
      colons, 547–548
      commas, 547
      exclamation marks, 547–548
      periods, 547
      question marks, 547–548
      semicolons, 547–548

R

raise vs. rise, 91–92
real vs. very, 142–143
reading, 417–427
  phonetics, 419
  phonics, 417–418
    digraphs, 421
    hard consonant sounds, 421
    soft consonant sounds, 421
    rules of, 421–426
    trigraphs, 421
    vowels
      long, 421
      short, 421
  look–say, 418
  spelling and sounds, 418–421
    dictionary symbols, 419–421
    International Phonetic Alphabet,
      418–421
real relative pronouns, 200–201, 343–345
reciprocal pronouns, 191
reflexive pronouns, 191–193
  in emphatic roles, 191–192
  in reflexive roles, 192
regular verbs, 58–59
relative adverbs, 200–201, 345–346
relative clauses, 342–350
  agreement between pronouns and an-
    tecedents, 375–377
  agreement between subject and verb
    in, 372–374
  diagrammed, 349–350
  nominal relative clauses, 202

relative clauses (continued)
   relative pronouns in, 197–198, 200
      real relative pronouns, 343–345
      relative adverbs, 345–346
      relative determiners, 346–347
      zero relative pronouns, 348–349
      who vs. **whom**, 344–345
   restrictive vs. nonrestrictive, 347–348
relative determiners
   in nominal clauses, 362
   in relative clauses, 346–347
relative pronouns, 197–203
   antecedents of, 199, 216–217
   case of, 344–345
   compound relative pronouns, 198,
      361–362
   in nominal (relative) clauses, 202,
      361–362
      diagrammed, 366–367
   in relative clauses, 200, 342–350
      diagrammed, 349–350
   list of, 198
   real relative pronouns, 200–201,
      343–345
   relative adverbs, 200–201
   relative determiners
      in nominal clauses, 362
      in relative clauses, 346–347
   use of **that**, 199
   use of **what**, 199
      implied antecedent of, 199,
         216–217
   use of **when**, 199
   use of **where**, 199
   use of **which**, 198–199
   use of **who/whom/whose**, 198,
      344–345
   use of **why**, 201
   whose as replacement for **which**, 199
   zero relative pronouns, 348–349
restrictive vs. nonrestrictive
   nouns, 34–35
   punctuation of, 35, 520–521, 523–524
   relative clauses, 347–348
rhetorical questions, 500, 536
roots, 457–458
royal **we**, 187
run
   conjugation table for, 66–67
run–on sentences, 340

Russian
   words and phrases used in English,
      479

S

said, synonyms for, 482–483
second person
   with nouns, 25
   with pronouns
      see definitions for nouns
   with verbs, 43
      in the imperative mood, 46
semicolons, 528–529
   in compound sentences, 336–337, 338,
      528
   with double quotation marks,
      546–547
   with items in a series, 529
   with single quotation marks, 547–548
sentence diagramming, 288–291
   appositives, 326, 367
   complex sentences
      with adverbial clauses, 354–355
      with nominal clauses, 365–367
      with relative clauses, 349–350
   compound–complex sentences, 368
   compound predicates, 289–290
   compound sentences, 340–341
   compound subjects, 289–290
   declarative sentences, 299–301
   delayed subjects, 310–311
   dummy elements, 310–311
   exclamatory sentences, 304
   gerunds, 321–323
   imperative sentences, 303
   infinitives, 323–325
   interjections, 310
   interrogative sentences, 301–302
   modifiers in, 289
   nouns in direct address, 309
   participles, 319–321
   predicates in, 288–289
   prepositional phrases, 315–318
      used as modifiers, 316–317
      used as nominals, 318
   subjects of sentences, 288–289
   verbals, 319–325

sentence structures, 304–309
  defined, 295
  nouns in direct address, 309–310
    diagrammed, 309
  subject–verb, 305
  subject–verb–adverbial complement, 305
  subject–verb–direct object, 306–307
  subject–verb–direct object–adverbial complement, 307–308
  subject–verb–direct object–object complement, 308
  subject–verb–indirect object–direct object, 307
  subject–verb–subject complement, 306
sentence types, 295–304
  defined, 295
  declarative sentences, 296
    diagrams of, 299–301
    punctuation of, 296, 500, 536
    word orders in, 298–301
      canonical order, 298
      fronting, 299
      subject–verb inversions, 299
  exclamatory sentences, 296
    diagram of, 304
    punctuation of, 296, 537
    word order in, 303–304
  form of vs. function of, 297–297
  imperative sentences, 296
    diagrams of, 303
    punctuation of, 296, 500, 535, 536
    understood subject **you**, 302–303
    with nouns in direct address, 309–310
  interrogative sentences, 296
    diagrams of, 301–302
    identification of predicate in, 286
    punctuation of, 296, 535, 537
    word orders in, 301–302
      interrogative adverbs, 301
      interrogative pronouns, 301
      subject–verb inversions, 301
  word order in, 298–304
set vs. **sit**, 92
Shakespeare, William, 475
shall vs. **will**, 84–85
Sheridan, Richard Brinsley, 474
should, 86–89

sibilant sounds, 11, 386
sic, 415–416
sideburns, 476
silhouette, 476
simple forms of verb tense, 50
simple predicates, 286
simple sentences, 333–334
simple subjects, 286
single quotation marks, 545
  with other marks of punctuation, 547–548
    colons, 547–548
    commas, 547
    exclamation marks, 547–548
    periods, 547
    question marks, 547–548
    semicolons, 547–548
sit vs. **set**, 92
slashes, 548
soft consonant sounds, 421
Spanish
  words and phrases used in English, 477–478, 480
spelling, 383–417
  and sounds, 418–421
  ante- vs. **anti-**, 388
  heteronyms, homonyms, homophones, and homographs, 392–411
  history of, 383–386
  Johnson, Samuel, 384
  Middle English, 384
  mnemonics, 414–415
  Modern English, 384
  numbers, 416
  Old English, 384
  orthography, 383
  rules for, 385–391
  shortcuts, 414–415
  spell–checkers, 391–392
  Webster, Noah, 384–385
split infinitives, 174–176
Spoonerisms, 490
Start Trek, 175
structures
  see sentence structures
subject complements, 81–82
  in gerund phrases, 166–167
  in infinitive phrases, 171–172
  in participles phrases, 156–157
  participles used as, 153–154, 159

subject complements (continued)
  nominal clauses used as, 202, 356
  relative pronouns used as, 344, 359
subjects
  defined, 283–284
  agreement with verb, 53–56
    in nominal clauses, 364–365
    in number, 53–55
      with compound subjects, 53–54
      with collective nouns, 55
    in person, 53
    in relative clauses, 372–374
  complete subjects, 284–285
  compound subjects, 286–287
  delayed subjects
    infinitives used as, 172–173
  diagrammed, 288–289
  dummy **it**, 187–188
  head subjects, 284–285
  implied in participle phrases, 157, 158
  nominal clauses used as, 202, 356
  omitted in comparative clauses,
    369–370
  relative pronouns used as, 343–344,
    359
  simple subjects, 286
subject–verb inversions
  in declarative sentences, 299
  in interrogative sentences, 301
subjunctive mood, 46–47
  and past tense verbs, 49–50
subordinate clauses, 264, 334–335
  adverbial clauses, 351–355
    abbreviated, of comparison,
      369–372
      case with, 370–372
    classes of, 249–353
    commas with, 513–514, 517,
      524–525
    comparative clauses, 352, 353,
      369–372
    diagrammed, 354–355
    placement of, 353–354
  agreement between pronoun and an-
    tecedent in, 375–377
    nominal clauses, 376
    relative clauses, 375–377

subordinate clauses (continued)
  agreement between subject and verb
    in, 372–375
    nominal clauses, 364–365, 375
    relative clauses, 372–374
  and complex sentences, 341–342
  and the subjunctive mood, 47
  nominal clauses, 355–367
    agreement of pronoun and an-
      tecedent, 376
    agreement of subject and verb,
      364–365, 375
    diagrammed, 365–367
    host clauses, 355–356
    nominal relative clauses, 361
    uses of, 356–357
      as appositives, 356–357, 358–359
      as delayed subject, 356–357
      as direct object, 357
      as indirect object, 357
      as object of preposition, 357
      as subject, 356
      as subject complement, 356
    who vs. **whom**, 359–360
    with subordinate conjunctions,
      360–361
    with relative determiners, 362
    with relative pronouns, 361, 362
    zero **that** in, 363
  relative clauses, 342–350
    agreement between pronouns and
      antecedents, 375–377
    agreement between subject and
      verb, 372–374
    diagrammed, 349–350
    nominal relative clauses, 199, 202
    relative pronouns in, 197–298, 202
      real relative pronouns, 343–345
      relative adverbs, 345–346
      relative determiners, 346–347
      zero relative pronouns, 348–349
      who vs. **whom**, 344–345
    restrictive vs. nonrestrictive,
      347–348
  zero **that**–clauses, 363
subordinate conjunctions, 264–267
  in adverbial clauses, 351–353
  in nominal clauses, 360–361
  like, 271–272
  list of, 264–265

subordinate conjunctions (continued)
    meanings of, 265–266
    than, 370–372
substantives
    see nominals
suffixes
    list of, 460–461
    spelling of words with, 388–391
superlative degree of comparison
    of adjectives, 103
        forms of adjectives in, 104–108
            irregular comparison, 107–108
            with adverbs, 104–105
            with suffixes, 104
    of adverbs, 130
        forms of adjectives in, 130–132
            irregular comparison, 132
            with adverbs, 131
            with suffixes, 131
Swift, Jonathan, 474

T

tense
    future tense, 48
        shall vs. **will**, 84–85
    past tense, 48
    perfect forms, 50–51
    perfect and progressive forms, 51
    present tense, 48
    progressive forms, 51
    simple forms, 50
    with auxiliary verbs, 41
that
    used as relative pronoun, 199
    zero **that**, 363
than, 370–372
third person
    with nouns, 26
    with pronouns
        see definitions for nouns
        gender of personal pronouns in,
            183
    with verbs, 43
transitive verbs, 78–79
    dictionary abbreviation for, 80
trigraphs, 421
types
    see sentence types

U

underlined text, 549–550
unique, synonyms for, 486

V

vague antecedents of pronouns, 215–218
verbals
    defined, 151
    diagrammed, 319–325
    gerunds, 164–168
        diagrammed, 321–323
        gerund phrases, 165–167
            modifiers in, 165–166
                adjectives, 166
                adverbials, 165–166
                adverbs, 165
                possessive case nouns, 166,
                    167–168
                possessive pronouns, 166
            objects in, 166
                direct objects, 166
                indirect objects, 166
            complements in, 166–167
                subject complements, 166–167
        perfect forms of, 176
        possessive case nouns with,
            167–168
        used as nominals, 164–165
        used as objects of prepositions, 231
    infinitives, 169–176
        bare infinitives, 173–174
        diagrammed, 323–325
        distinguished from prepositional
            phrases, 169, 231
        infinitive phrases, 171–173
            complements in, 171–172
                subject complements, 171–172
            modifiers in, 171
                adverbials, 171
                adverbs, 171
            objects in, 171
                direct objects, 171
                indirect objects, 171
        marker of, 169
        perfect forms of, 176–177
        split infinitives, 174–176
        used as adjectives, 169–170

verbals
    infinitives (continued)
        used as adverbials, 170
        used as delayed subjects, 172–173
        used as nominals, 169
        without marker, 173–174
    participles, 152–164
        dangling participles, 160–164
        diagrammed, 319–321
        distinguished from participles in
           verb phrases, 158–159
        past participles, 152
        present participles, 152
        used as adjectives, 152–154
        used as subject complements,
           153–154
        participle phrases, 155–157
           complements in, 156–157
               subject complements, 156–157
           implied subjects in, 157, 158
           modifiers in, 155–156
               adverbials, 155–156
               adverbs, 155
           objects in, 156
               direct objects, 156
               indirect objects, 156
        perfect forms of, 176
           used as adverbials of reason, 154
    perfect forms of, 176
    resemblance of prepositions to, 229
verb phrases, 40–41
    and the future tense, 48
    participles in,
        distinguished from verbal partici-
           ples, 158–159
    with predicates of sentences, 285–286
verbs
    defined, 39
    action verbs, 40
    agreement with indefinite pronouns,
        221–222
    agreement with subject, 53–56
        in nominal clauses, 364–365, 375
        in number, 53–55
           with compound subjects, 53–54
           with collective nouns, 55
        in person, 53
        in relative clauses, 372–374

verbs (continued)
    auxiliary verbs, 41
        can, use of, 85–86
        contracted with **have**, 91, 93
        may, use of, 85–86
        modal auxiliary verbs, 86–89
           could, use of, 86–89
           might, use of, 86–89
           should, use of, 86–89
           would, use of, 86–89
        must, use of, 86
    bare vs. **bear**, 92–93
    conjugation, 56–75
        base form of the verb, 59
        conjugation tables, 62–73
           be, 72–73
           do, 70–71
           grow, 62–63
           have, 68–69
           look, 64–65
           run, 66–67
        future indicative forms, 60
        future perfect indicative forms, 60
        imperative forms, 60
        of irregular verbs, 59
        of regular verbs, 58–59
        past participle, 61
        past perfect indicative forms, 60
        past perfect subjunctive forms, 61
        past subjunctive forms, 61
        present perfect indicative forms, 60
        present perfect subjunctive forms,
           61
        present subjunctive forms, 60
        principal parts, 56–59
           chart of, 56–58
           past indicative forms, 59
           past participle forms, 59
           present indicative forms, 59
    contractions, 90–91
        diagrammed, 318–319
        of verbs and **not**, 90
        of verbs with pronouns, 90
        of auxiliary verbs and **have**, 91, 93
        punctuation of, 530
    direct objects, 76–80
        and intransitive verbs, 78–79
        and transitive verbs, 78–79
        identification of, 77
        object complements of, 80–81

verbs
  direct objects (continued)
    with main verbs, 78
  emphatic forms of, 83–84
  indirect objects, 76–78
    identification of, 77–78
  intransitive verbs, 78–79
  irregular verbs, 59
  lie vs. **lay**, 91
  linking verbs, 40
    subject complements of, 81–82
  main verbs, 41
  mood, 45–47
    imperative mood, 46
    indicative mood, 45–46
    subjunctive mood, 46–47
      and past tense verbs, 49–50
  number of, 42
    plural, 42
    singular, 42
  person, 42–43
    first person, 42–43
    second person, 43
      and the imperative mood, 46
    third person, 43
  principal verbs, 41
  omitted in comparative clauses,
    369–370
  raise vs. **rise**, 91–92
  regular verbs, 58–59
  shall vs. will, 84–85
  sit vs. **set**, 92
  subject complements, 81–82
  tense, 48–51
    future tense, 48
      shall vs. **will**, 84–85
    past tense, 48
    perfect forms, 50–51
    perfect and progressive forms, 51
    present tense, 48
    progressive forms, 51
    simple forms, 50
    with auxiliary verbs, 41
  transitive verbs, 78–79
  verbals
    see verbals
  verb phrases, 40–41
    and the future tense, 48
    participles in, distinguished from
      verbal participles, 158–159

verbs (continued)
  voice, 43–45
    active voice, 43–44
    passive voice, 44
  verb tense
    see tense
  very vs. **real**, 142–143
  vocabulary
    airline lingo, 485
    definition distinctions, 456
    definitions of prepositions, 243–247
    etymologies
      defined, 432
      eponyms, 476, 490
      foreign words and phrases used in
        English, 477–481
      glamour, 481–482
      portmanteau words, 475
      words from literature, 474–475
        Carroll, Lewis, 475
        Shakespeare, William, 475
        Sheridan, Richard Brinsley, 474
        Swift, Jonathan, 474
    legal jargon, 485–486
    one thousands words you should
      know, 461–473
    oxymorons, 487
    palindromes, 487
    phobias, 487–488
    prefixes, 459–460, 461
      redundancy of, 484–485
    roots, 457–458
    said, synonyms for, 482–483
    Spoonerisms, 490
    suffixes, 460–461
    unique, synonyms for, 486
    wine terminology, 494
  voice, 43–45
    active voice, 43–44
    passive voice, 44
  vowels
    long, 421
    short, 421
    sounds of, 419–421

W

we
  editorial **we**, 187
  royal **we**, 187
Webster, Noah, 384–385

well vs. **good**, 141–142
what
   used as interrogative pronoun, 196
   used as relative pronoun, 199
      implied antecedent of, 199, 216–217
when
   used as interrogative adverb, 143
   used as relative pronoun, 199
      as relative adverb, 345–346
where
   used as interrogative adverb, 143
   used as relative pronoun, 199
      as relative adverb, 345–346
which
   used as interrogative pronoun, 196
   used as relative pronoun, 198–199
      as real relative pronoun, 343
who/whom/whose
   used as interrogative pronouns, 195
   who/whom as real relative pro-
      nouns, 198, 344–345, 359–360
   whose
      as relative determiner, 346–347
      as replacement for **which**, 199
will vs. **shall**, 84–85
wine terminology, 494
word orders in sentences, 298–304
   in declarative sentences, 298–301
      canonical order, 298
      fronting, 299
      subject-verb inversions, 299
   in exclamatory sentences, 303–304
   in imperative sentences, 302–303
   in interrogative sentences, 301–302
      with interrogative adverbs, 301
      with interrogative pronouns, 301
      with subject–verb inversions, 301
would, as modal auxiliary verb, 86–89
why
   used as interrogative adverb, 143
   used as relative pronoun, 200
      as relative adverb, 346

Y

yes, 144
Yiddish
   words and phrases used in English,
      478–481

you
   number of verb used with, 186
   understood, 302–303
      diagrammed, 303

Z

zero relative pronouns, 348–349
zero **that**, 363